THE MEGAHIT MOVIES

Richard Michaels Stefanik

Copyright © 2004 by Richard Michaels Stefanik
All Rights Reserved.

Published by
RMS Productions Company
9299 Tower Side Drive #435
Fairfax, VA 20031

All Rights Reserved.
No part of this publication may be reproduced, stored in a retrieval system, or transmitted, in any form or by any means, electronic, mechanical, photocopying, recording or otherwise, without the prior written permission of
RMS Productions Company.

Library of Congress Catalog Card Number:
Available from the Publisher.

ISBN 1-882373-04-9

Printed in the United States of America

DEDICATED

to

K. C. CRAIG

whose

unconditional love

enabled me to write

The Megahit Movies

ACKNOWLEDGMENTS

The analysis of the films in *The Megahit Movies* book is based on the versions of the movies distributed on videocassettes and DVDs. The primary purpose of this book is to serve as an educational research resource for students of popular films, for teaching, and scholarship. These commentaries are published in compliance with the "fair use" doctrine, Section 107, of the U.S. Copyright Law.

BATMAN: Copyright 1989 Warner Brothers, Inc.
BRUCE ALMIGHTY: Copyright 2003 Universal Studios.
EMPIRE STRIKES BACK: Copyright 1980 and 1995 Lucasfilm, Ltd.
E.T. THE EXTRA-TERRESTRIAL: Copyright 1982 Universal City Studios.
FINDING NEMO: Copyright 2003 Disney/Pixar.
FORREST GUMP: Copyright 1995 Paramount Pictures.
GHOSTBUSTERS: Copyright 1984 Columbia Pictures Industries, Inc.
HARRY POTTER: THE SORCERER'S STONE: Copyright 2001 Warner Bros.
HARRY POTTER: CHAMBER OF SECRETS: Copyright 2002 Warner Bros.
HOME ALONE: Copyright 1990 Twentieth-Century Fox.
INDEPENDENCE DAY: Copyright 1996 Twentieth-Century Fox.
JAWS: Copyright 1997 Universal Home Video.
JURASSIC PARK: Copyright 1994 MCA Home Video.
LION KING: Copyright The Walt Disney Company.
LORD OF THE RINGS: RETURN OF THE KING: Copyright 2004 New Line.
LORD OF THE RINGS: THE TWO TOWERS: Copyright 2003 New Line.
LORD OF THE RINGS: FELLOWSHIP OF THE RING: Copyright 2001 New Line.
MEN IN BLACK: Copyright 1997 Columbia Pictures Industries, Inc.
MONSTERS, INC.: Copyright 2001 Disney/Pixar.
PIRATES OF THE CARIBBEAN: Copyright 2003 Disney.
RAIDERS OF THE LOST ARK: Copyright 1981 Lucasfilm, Ltd.
SHREK: Copyright 2001 Dreamworks LLC.
SHREK 2: Copyright 2004 Dreamworks LLC.
SPIDER-MAN: Copyright 2002 Columbia Pictures Industries, Inc.
SPIDER-MAN 2: Copyright 2004 Columbia Pictures Industries, Inc.
STAR WARS: Copyright 1977 Twentieth-Century Fox, 1995 Lucasfilm, Ltd.
STAR WARS: ATTACK OF THE CLONES: Copyright 2002 Lucasfilm, Ltd.
STAR WARS: RETURN OF JEDI: Copyright 1995 Lucasfilm, Ltd.
THE GRINCH: Copyright 2000 by Universal Studios.
THE MATRIX RELOADED: Copyright 2003 Warner Home Video
THE PASSION OF THE CHRIST: Copyright 2004 Icon Pictures.
THE PHANTOM MENACE: Copyright 1999 Lucasfilm, Ltd.
THE SIXTH SENSE: Copyright 2000 Spyglass Entertainment Group.
THE WIZARD OF OZ: Copyright 1939 Lowe's, Inc., Renewed 1966 MGM, Inc.
TITANIC: Copyright 1998 Paramount Pictures.

TABLE OF CONTENTS

Foreword by Chris Lockhart
  Executive Story Editor, International Creative Artists (ICM)   11

Introduction   15
  The Fundamental Question   17
  Story Design for Creating Popular Hollywood Movies   17

Popular Hollywood Movies   23
  The Megahit Movies   25
  U.S. Domestic Box-Office Grosses   25
  Worldwide Box-Office Grosses   26
  WGA Screenwriting Awards   27
  Film Critics Best Movies   28
  Sundance Film Festival   29
  The Academy Awards   30
  Megahit Movies Redux   31

Writing for an Audience   41
  Genres segment the mass market audience   43

High Concepts & Loglines   47
  How to hook the reader with one sentence   49

The Unique Object & The Main Characters   55
  The Unique Object   57
  The Protagonist   58
  The Antagonist   61
  The Love Interest   64

The Climax Scene of the Movie   67
  The final battle between the Protagonist and the Antagonist   69
  for possession of both the Unique Object and the Love Interest

Plotting for Audience Emotional Responses   75
  The psychology of the audience   77
  Understanding audience empathy and enmity   77

Character Development: Maintaining Audience Involvement
Personal Objectives 87
Character Motivation 91
Decisions: Hard Choices 95
Relationships: Lovers & Friends 99
Codes of Behavior 104
Transformations 109
Personalities 113
Supporting Characters 117

Subgoals & Plot Twists: Creating Unpredictability 123
The Story Objective 125
Concrete Objects 128
Personal Values 130
Subgoals & Subtasks 132
Strategies & Plans 134

Conflicts: Creating Excitement 137
Obstacles 139
Jeopardy 141
Self-Conflicts 145
Enemies 148
Relatives 151
Friends 154
Lovers 157
Physical Objects 160
Natural World 163
Supernatural World 166

Plots: Designing the Emotional Roller Coaster Ride 169
Plot & Story 171
Events & Actions 173
The Inciting Event 175
Subplots 178
Plot Arena 180
Plot Twists 183
Plot Organization 187
Plot Outline Worksheet 190
Emotional Plotting 192
Emotional Plotting Graph 194

Story: What's It All About? — 195
Human Values — 197
Virtues & Vices — 198
Community Ideals — 200
Basic Story Design — 201
A-Story & B-Story — 204
Story Climax & Plot Climax — 206

Scenes: Creating Those Special Moments — 211
Scene Actions — 216
Point of Attack — 217
Crisis, Confrontation, Climax, and Resolution — 217
A Model Scene — 218
Establishing Scenes — 219
Transition Scenes — 222
Opening Scenes — 225
Introduction of the Protagonist — 229
Introduction of the Antagonist — 233
Climax Scenes — 236
Resolution Scenes — 237
The Essential Scene Elements — 241

Emotions: Making the Audience Feel — 243
Emotion & Story — 245
Emotion Words — 247
Theories of Emotion — 251
The Cognitive Theory — 252
Intensity of Emotions — 253
Reactions to Events — 253
Reactions to Actions — 255
Reactions to Objects — 257
Dialogue & Emotion — 258

Humor: Release the Tension and Make Them Laugh — 261
Emotion & Humor — 263
Theories of Humor — 265
Humorous Dialogue — 275
Humorous Situations — 278
Humorous Characters — 280
Humor in the Megahit Movies — 287

Sequences: Designing a Series of Scenes	307
Entertaining the Audience	309
Visual Material	310
Excitement	314
Surprise	315
Suspense	316
The Chase	317
Ticking Clocks	320
Using Props	322
Exposition	325
Themes: Creating Universal Appeal	329
Mythic Structures	331
Megahit Movie Themes	332
Scene-by-Scene Analysis of a Popular Movie	
The Wizard of Oz	339
Story Structures in Megahit Movies	
Chicago	371
Shrek & Shrek 2	375
Spider-Man & Spider-Man 2	388
Pirates of the Caribbean	416
Finding Nemo	425
Monsters, Inc.	428
Bruce Almighty	434
The Matrix Trilogy	441
The Passion of the Christ	447
Harry Potter and The Sorcerer's Stone	448
Harry Potter and The Prisoner of Azkaban	456
The Lord of the Rings Trilogy	458
Screenwriting & Movie Magazines	489
Recommended Screenwriting Books	490
***The Megahit Movies Hollywood Story Design Workshop*™**	493
The Megahit Movies Website	502

Richard Michaels Stefanik
The Megahit Movies Hollywood Story Design Workshop™

The Megahit Movies book is a revised and updated version of a previous work on story structure, **Structures of Fantasy**, which analyzed dramatic and comic elements found in commercially successful movies.

Structures of Fantasy has been selected by the Writers Guild of America (WGA) Mentors Program for the Recommended Screenwriting Books list (www.wga.org/mentors/mentorbooks.html), and it is described as "one of the best books on story structure."

Richard Michaels Stefanik is the Writer-Director-Producer of the movie, **Henry Dodd**, which was released by **RMS Productions Company** in 2004. He consults with new writers to develop their original stories into high concept screenplays. He was a Screenwriting Fellow at the **American Film Institute**, where he wrote, directed, and produced a dramatic movie, "Michael & Christina." Richard then worked at several Hollywood studios, including **Paramount Pictures** and **Walt Disney Productions**. He received M.A. degrees in Philosophy from the University of California, Berkeley and Georgetown University, then studied Philosophy and Mathematics at **Oxford University**.

Richard has taught **Story Design and Screenwriting Seminars** in cities throughout the world, including London, Copenhagen, Los Angeles, San Francisco, Orlando, Las Vegas, New York, and Hollywood. He is a Honorary Board Member of **WriteMovies.com**. He taught a class, "Making Megahit Movies," at **UCLA Extension** in 2001. He conducted classes on "Story Structures in Megahit Movies" at the **Las Vegas Screenwriters Conference** in 2001, 2002, and 2003. Richard also conducted screenwriting seminars in Los Angeles at the 2002, 2003, and 2004 **Screenwriting Expos** sponsored by **Creative Screenwriting** magazine. He has taught online classes for **Scr(i)pt Magazine**.

In 2003, he lectured on comedy and story design to the **British Society of Comedy Writers** in London. The French translation of **The Megahit Movies** book was published by Editions Dixit in Paris in 2003, retitled as **"Les Clés Des Plus Grands Succès Cinématographiques"**

Richard conducts monthly online chats about popular movie story structures at **www.WritersChannel.net**. During 2004 he gave Story Design seminars at the **Script Magazine PitchXchange** in New York, and at the **Sherwood Oaks Experimental College** in Hollywood.

FOREWORD

Christopher Lockhart
Executive Story Editor
International Creative Management (ICM)
Beverly Hills, California

FOREWORD

As the Executive Story Editor at International Creative Management (ICM), I have read tens of thousands of scripts and have learned many things about the craft and business of screenwriting. However, the one lesson that I am reminded of on a daily basis is that writing a great screenplay is very difficult. Many scripts that I encounter are written by professional screenwriters but some are written by struggling scribes hoping to breakthrough. Regardless of the writer's credentials, the basic fact does not change: writing a great screenplay is very difficult. There can be many definitions of what "great" is, but primarily, **a great screenplay is one that creates an emotional experience for its audience.** By the time the read is finished, the audience (story analyst, agent, manager, producer, actor, director, costume designer) has been moved into feeling a certain way as intended by the writer.

It should be noted that screenplays are not movies. Screenplays are simply blueprints for movies. A movie has many additional elements to "move" the audience: a winning performance by a favorite actor, smart editing, a swelling musical score, for instance. By the very nature of its medium, a screenplay is more limited and can only use the influence of its story, characters and structure to move its audience, but when it is done with greatness, the results are undeniably powerful. Despite all the high tech trimmings of a Hollywood movie, the emotional core is its screenplay.

When a reader starts a screenplay, he begins with a certain amount of equanimity, but the screenplay should move the reader, for example, to happiness or anger or horror or sadness or anxiousness. If the reader is unmoved by the end of the screenplay, the writer has failed. Most reading experiences result in apathy. Writers will often complain that the reader didn't "get it." But it is not the reader's job to "get it." It is the writer's job to "give it." Often, what moves the writer simply doesn't move anyone else. It is similar to telling a joke that no one – but the teller – finds funny. The joke, however, is a quick venture, and its failure is often humorous in of itself and forgotten moments later. But a screenplay takes months of hard work to complete and, perhaps, months of effort to query the marketplace in the hopes of a read. And when (or if) that is achieved, someone gives two hours of his day to sit down and read the script. With this kind of investment, a writer must strive for a story with broad appeal. He cannot be as cavalier as that jokester. Unfortunately, if the screenplay fails to move the reader, the hard work will be easily dismissed and forgotten.

Richard Michaels Stefanik has studied movies that have achieved great success at the box-office. He calls them **MEGAHIT MOVIES**. In this book, he explores the commonalities of these screenplays. He examines the dramatic elements that move an audience, seducing them to return again and again to see the film – which is how a movie gains its megahit status. Writers often scoff at megahit movies. Backlash against *Titanic*, for instance, is common. "Where is the artistic integrity in that screenplay?" asks the indignant scribe. The art of screenwriting is in the ability to move the audience. Since Hollywood movies are huge investments, stories need to move the biggest audience possible. The talent lies in crafting a screenplay that can move millions of people by finding the universalities within a unique story. There are identifiable narrative elements within the screenplay for *Titanic* that brought audiences back to see it again and again. Some screenplays have the power to move reader after reader – straight on up to the executive with the clout to greenlight it. Other screenplays can hardly budge a part-time story analyst. These two examples are the difference between writing a screenplay and keeping a diary. This is not to suggest that the story that fails to move the Hollywood reader isn't worthy to be told. On the contrary, it may be a very worthy story. However, it may need to be told in another medium all together, like a novel. When a movie has the ability to attract crowds over and over – to the tune of a billion dollars worldwide – the story works.

Many new writers fall in love with the movies and sit down to write a screenplay without realizing there is craft involved. For instance, an audience cries at a particular scene because careful mechanics have been layered throughout the story to elicit that response at the appropriate time. It doesn't just simply happen. Why does an audience root for the hero? How does a writer weave a story in a way that creates tension, forcing the reader to stay with it through the end? And, most importantly, how does the writer create a story that audiences really care about? Writers must understand the dramatic craft and **THE MEGAHIT MOVIES,** which, in turn, could help them create a great screenplay that ensures the reader an emotional experience. It is a long, arduous journey from the first draft of a screenplay to opening weekend at the local multiplex. As a creative executive, I read each new script with the hope of finding a story that will move me and instill me with a sense of passion I clearly didn't possess at the beginning. It is a difficult challenge for the writer, but within these pages are the tools to empower the scribe on this journey to writing a great screenplay.

May all your screenplays be megahit movies.

Christopher Lockhart, Executive Story Editor
International Creative Management (ICM)
Beverly Hills, California
July 15, 2003

INTRODUCTION

The Fundamental Question

Story Design
for
Creating Popular Hollywood Movies

THE FUNDAMENTAL QUESTION

Hollywood has produced thousands of feature films, but only a few have received megahit status and generated more than $250 million in North American box office receipts. What is it about these films that made them so successful?

Story Design for Creating Popular Hollywood Movies

This book is designed to show a screenwriter how to create an original script that has the potential of becoming a popular Hollywood movie. Screenwriters reading this book should want to create commercially successful movies.

We start our story development process with a discussion with what it means to be a ***Popular Hollywood Movie.*** Popularity is defined by different measures: U.S. Domestic Box-Office Grosses, Worldwide Box-Office Grosses, Academy Awards, and WGA Screenwriting Awards. Every film critic also has his own choice for "The Best Movie of the Year," as do the filmmakers who attend the Sundance Film Festival and the IFP Independent Spirit Awards.

A writer should be certain about which type of popularity he wants to achieve. From the start of the screenwriting process, the writer should understand that he is writing for a specific audience. This is made clear when we discuss genres and the standard categories of scripts as classified by Hollywood producers and agents. Genres segment the audience into groups of people who enjoy different types of stories. The total potential audience is partitioned into market segments.

Some of the questions that a screenwriter should answer are:
Why do I want to write a screenplay?
Do I want to create a financially successful
or a critically acclaimed screenplay?
Who is my intended audience?

The first thing that a writer should create is the concept of the story. Will it be a high concept story? Next, he should create a logline for the movie: a single sentence description of the main character and the goal that the character is trying to achieve. Examples of high concepts and loglines will illustrate these notions.

Most popular movies are designed around three main characters: the protagonist, the love interest, and the antagonist, as well as a unique object that they are trying to possess. Since only one character can eventually obtain the unique object, this structure guarantees conflict throughout the story. The climax scene is a life-and-death struggle between the protagonist and the antagonist for the unique object.

A writer should try to imagine **the movie poster** that will be used to market the film to a global audience. Study the poster designs of the current popular movies. Within these images are the core elements of the story: protagonist, antagonist, love interest, and an image which defines the genre of the movie. A movie that hopes to become popular will need to have such a poster.

Given these core elements, we then go on to discuss the psychology of the audience. The writer must understand the importance of creating empathy in the audience for the protagonist and love interest, while simultaneously generating enmity (fear and hatred) for the antagonist. This is essential for creating mass-market popular Hollywood movies. The classic Hollywood Three-Act Structure is used to this effect. We explicate this structure in terms of the plotting of the story that will create an emotionally satisfying experience for the audience. **The key to creating popular and commercially successful Hollywood movies is to learn how to elicit specific emotional reactions from the audience.**

The writer should create an **empathy scene** for the protagonist and love interest and an **enmity scene** for the antagonist. The writer should also cast the three primary characters (protagonist, antagonist, and love interest) with currently popular Hollywood actors. This will make the characters easier to write and also will eventually help in marketing the finished screenplay to Hollywood producers.

We next focus on creating three-dimensional characters by analyzing character personality types, motivation, personal objectives, emotional decisions, character relationships, ethical values and codes of behavior, character arcs and transformations, and supporting characters. The screenwriter should write a description for the **protagonist supporter**, who should be humorous and likeable and the **antagonist supporter**, who should be vicious and hateful. They should also describe the **motivation, personal objective,** and **transformation** for each of the five primary characters of their story: protagonist, antagonist, love interest, protagonist supporter, and antagonist supporter.

Hollywood recognizes the importance of supporting roles by giving Academy Awards each year to the Best Supporting Actor and Actress.

Now that we have created the basic elements of our story, a unique object that is desired by the protagonist and antagonist and the key supporting characters, we will then show how to make the story **unpredictable**. This is done by creating **subgoals** to the protagonist's primary objective which conclude as plot twists. **Plot twists** result when the expected consequence of completing a subgoal does not happen once that subgoal is achieved. An example of this can be found in the *Wizard of Oz*. Dorothy believes that the Wizard will get her back home (her primary objective). Her first major subgoal is to get to the Emerald City to see the Wizard. She overcomes many obstacles to achieve this subgoal. When she meets the Wizard, he does not help her go home, but instead assigns her the task of getting him the broomstick of the Wicked Witch of the West. This is a plot twist. Examples of many other plot twists from popular Hollywood movies will be discussed in this book. Creating expectations in the audience with the intention of having these expectations not fulfilled is the key to creating surprise and unpredictability.

Essential to creating **excitement** is **conflict** that produces **jeopardy** for the protagonist and his supporters. These conflicts are generated by the **obstacles and problems** that the protagonist must solve in order to achieve the **subgoals** and **primary objective**. Jeopardy producing obstacles can be the result of self-conflicts, enemies, relatives, friends, lovers, physical objects, the natural world, and the supernatural world. We review many examples of each type of obstacle found in popular movies. The writer will also come to understand that in each scene of the script, there should be an obstacle or problem that the characters in the story must overcome. This ensures that there will be conflict and excitement in each scene.

We next discuss the difference between a **plot** and a **story**, events and actions, the inciting event, subplots, and different ways that a writer can organize a plot. At this stage, the writer will be prepared to design a **Prelude, Act 1, Act 2, Act 3,** and **Resolution** structure for their story. They should be able to write a **plot outline** that contains forty (40) major obstacles; one for each scene.

A story is different from a plot. While a **plot** is a series of events that constitute the movie, the **story** is the series of actions and decisions the protagonist makes in the movie. **Story** is the sphere in which human values, virtues, vices, and community ideals interact and come into the foreground of the movie. The screenwriter must choose virtues for their protagonist and vices for their antagonist. They should write scenes showing the protagonist exhibiting this virtue when confronting an obstacle and a scene showing the antagonist displaying a vice when dealing with a different obstacle or problem. An example of this is the way that Bruce Wayne and Jack Napier court Vickie Vale in *Batman*, or the way that Indiana Jones and the sadistic Nazi negotiate with Marion for the headpiece of the staff of Ra in *Raiders of the Lost Ark*.

We next discuss the design of scenes, concentrating on scene actions, point-of-attack, crisis, confrontation, climax, resolution, exposition scenes, transition scenes, opening scenes, protagonist introduction, antagonist introduction, climax scenes, and resolution scenes. The writer should create a 3x5 index card (40 cards) for each scene that includes the major **obstacle (or problem), crisis, confrontation, climax,** and the **emotional reactions of the characters** in the scene. These elements constitute the essential **moments** or **beats** of the scene. From these index cards the writer should create a **detailed plot outline.** A full length screenplay can have between 40 and 60 scenes, each between 3 to 2 minutes in length. We then discuss connecting scenes together into **sequences.** Each sequence should be designed to have a specific emotional effect on the audience. We will also analyze ways of entertaining the audience and conveying information during exposition scenes.

We will discuss how "Chase" sequences and "Ticking Clocks" sequences can generate **suspense**. These types of sequences are especially important in the third act of the story because they are used to drive the audience into an emotional frenzy before the final climax scene.

Since the key to creating a popular Hollywood movie is to create an **emotionally satisfying experience for the audience,** it is critical for a writer to understand how to create situations that will elicit specific emotions in the audience. We discuss the relationship of emotion to story design, the Cognitive Theory of Emotions, techniques to heighten the intensity of emotional reactions, and ways to elicit specific emotional reactions to events, actions, and objects. Emotions also form the subtext underlying powerful dialogue.

To **entertain** the audience is to make them laugh while vicariously experiencing situations of jeopardy. Eliciting emotions in the audience is very important when creating humorous scenes. We discuss the techniques used in creating humorous dialogue, humorous situations, and humorous characters.

Ultimately, the writer must be clear on the **theme** of the story. What is the movie really about? What does it have to say about the human condition? What will the members of the audience learn about life and human relationships? Does the story have universal appeal? Does the narration rely on mythic structures? How does the theme of this movie compare with the themes found in many of the megahit movies?

Included in the book is a scene-by-scene analysis of one of the most popular movies ever produced in Hollywood: *The Wizard of Oz.* Other recent megahit movies analyzed are: *Chicago, Shrek, Shrek 2, Spider-Man, Spider-Man 2, Monsters, Inc, Finding Nemo, Bruce Almighty, The Matrix Trilogy, Harry Potter and The Sorcerer's Stone, Pirates of the Caribbean,* and *The Lord of the Rings Trilogy.*

The Megahit Movies Hollywood Story Design Workshop™
Information about these workshops is included at the end of the book. They will be valuable to screenwriters who would like a class that will help them further develop their original stories into commercial scripts.

The Megahit Movies book is designed for screenwriters, directors, and producers who want to create commercially successful movies. We hope the reader finds this book to be a useful tool in achieving that objective.

POPULAR HOLLYWOOD MOVIES

The Megahit Movies

U.S. Domestic Box-Office Grosses

Worldwide Box-Office Grosses

WGA Screenwriting Awards

Film Critics Best Movie Awards

Sundance Film Festival

Academy Awards

The Megahit Movies Redux

THE MEGAHIT MOVIES

There are different ways to define what it means to be a "Popular Hollywood Movie." Popularity can be defined in terms of financial success, measured by box-office receipts. Below is a list of movies with **U.S. Domestic Box-Office Grosses** over $250 million as reported on September 30, 2004 at **www.BoxOfficeMojo.com**:

	U.S. Domestic	Worldwide
Titanic	$600,788,188	$1,835,400,000
Star Wars	460,998,007	797,900,000
Shrek 2	439,823,837	876,600,000
ET: The Extra-Terrestrial	435,110,554	775,913,554
The Phantom Menace	431,088,301	925,600,000
Spider-Man	403,706,375	818,100,000
Return of the King	377,027,325	1,116,356,159
Spider-Man 2	373,068,126	775,000,000
Passion of the Christ	370,274,604	591,557,850
Jurassic Park	357,067,947	920,100,000
The Two Towers	341,786,758	918,800,000
Finding Nemo	339,714,978	389,000,000
Forrest Gump	329,694,499	679,400,000
Lion King	328,541,776	767,700,000
Harry Potter: Sorcerer's Stone	317,575,550	968,600,000
Fellowship of the Rings	314,776,170	860,800,000
Attack of the Clones	310,676,740	644,300,000
Star Wars: Return of the Jedi	309,306,177	572,700,000
Independence Day	306,169,268	813,200,000
Pirates of the Caribbean	305,413,918	319,300,000
The Sixth Sense	293,506,292	672,800,800
The Empire Strikes Back	290,475,067	534,200,000
Home Alone	285,761,243	533,700,000
Matrix Reloaded	281,576,461	727,400,000
Shrek	267,665,011	481,900,000
Harry Potter: Chamber	261,988,482	827,000,000
The Grinch	260,044.825	340,400,000
Jaws	260,000,000	470,600,000
Monsters, Inc.	255,873,250	523,100,000
Batman	251,188,924	413,200,000
Men in Black	250,690,529	587,800,000

All the films in the above list have earned over a quarter of a billion dollars in the U.S. Domestic Market. These can be considered to be *The Megahit Movies*. They define popularity as measured by financial success and by the number of people who paid to watch these films. The mass audience is defined as all people who can purchase a ticket to see a movie. Below is a list of the films with over $500 Million in **Worldwide Box-Office Grosses**.

Titanic	$1,835,400,000
The Lord of the Rings: Return of the King	1,116,356,159
Harry Potter and the Sorcerer's Stone	968,600,000
Star Wars: Phantom Menace	925,600,000
Jurassic Park	920,100,000
Shrek 2	876,600,000
Lord of the Rings: The Fellowship of the Ring	860,800,000
Harry Potter and the Chamber of Secrets	827,000,000
Spider-Man	818,100,000
Independence Day	813,200,000
Star Wars	797,900,000
Harry Potter and the Prisoner of Azkaban	786,694,525
ET: The Extra-Terrestrial	775,913,554
Spider-Man 2	775,000,000
The Lion King	767,700,000
Lord of the Rings: The Two Towers	740,000,000
Matrix Reloaded	727,400,000
Forrest Gump	679,400,000
The Sixth Sense	672,800,000
Star Wars: Attack of the Clones	644,300,000
Lost World: Jurassic Park	614,300,000
The Passion of the Christ	609,493,825
Men in Black	587,800,000
Return of the Jedi	572,700,000
Mission Impossible 2	565,400,000
Armageddon	554,600,000
The Empire Strikes Back	534,200,000
Home Alone	533,700,000
Monsters, Inc.	523,100,000
Ghost	517,600,000
Terminator 2: Judgement Day	516,800,000
Aladdin	501,900,000

A different way of measuring popularity is by the **Academy Awards for Best Picture of the Year.**

2003	The Lord of the Rings: Return of the King	$376,958,965
2002	Chicago	170,684,505
2001	A Beautiful Mind	170,708,996
2000	Gladiator	187,670,866
1999	American Beauty	130,058,047
1998	Shakespeare in Love	100,317,794
1997	Titanic	600,788,188
1996	The English Patient	78,716,374
1995	Braveheart	75,545,647
1994	Forrest Gump	329,693,974
1993	Schindler's List	96,067,179
1992	Unforgiven	101,157,447
1991	Silence of the Lambs	130,726,716
1990	Driving Miss Daisy	106,593, 296

The Academy Awards list defines popularity as expressed by the votes of members of the Academy of Motion Picture Arts and Sciences. Movies on both lists are *Titanic* and *Forrest Gump,* so the lists are not exclusive. Box-office success does not exclude winning the Oscar for Best Picture of the Year but neither does it guarantee winning an Oscar.

A third way of defining popularity is by looking at the films that have won the **WGA Screenwriting Awards** for Best Original Screenplay and Best Adaptation. The list below for years 2003-1996 was obtained from the Writers Guild of America (www.wga.org).

2003	Lost in Translation (original)	$ 44,566,004
	American Splendor (adaptation)	$ 6,003,587
2002	Bowling for Columbine (original)	$ 21,363,913
	The Hours (adaptation)	$ 41,597,830
2001	Gosford Park (original)	$ 41,300,105
	A Beautiful Mind (adaptation)	$170,708,996
2000	You Can Count on Me (original)	$ 9,180,275
	Traffic (adaptation)	$124,107,476

1999	American Beauty (original)	$130,058,047
	Election (adaptation)	$ 14,943,582
1998	Shakespeare in Love (original)	$100,317,794
	Out of Sight (adaptation)	$ 37,562,568
1997	As Good As It Gets (original)	$147,666,088
	L.A. Confidential (adaptation)	$ 64,604,977
1996	Fargo (original)	$ 24,567,751
	Slingblade (adaptation)	$ 24,475,416

Four films, *A Beautiful Mind, American Beauty, Shakespeare in Love,* and *Braveheart* are on the WGA list and the Academy list, but none are on *The Megahit Movies* list. Also, not all the films on the WGA list are on the Academy list. Different people voted for their favorite films, and they used different criteria and standards for their selections.

None of the screenplays listed above have been acclaimed by all three groups. The point of these examples is that **there is no single criterion for a popular, good, or a successful film**. Films that are popular with one group of voters are not popular with another. **Different audiences like different kinds of movies.**

This can further be exemplified by looking at the different selections for "Best Picture of the Year for 2002" chosen by **Film Critics** in the January 10-12, 2003 issue of *The Hollywood Reporter* magazine:

"Y Tu Mama Tambien"	:	David Ansen, Newsweek
"Catch Me if you Can"	:	Jonathan Foreman, New York Post
"Far From Heaven"	:	Owen Gleiberman, EW
"Y Tu Mama Tambien"	:	Andrew Johnston, US Weekly
"Gangs of New York"	:	Leonard Maltin, Entertainment Tonight
"Time Out"	:	Peter Rainer, New York Magazine
"Talk to Her"	:	Richard Schickel, Time
"Adaptation"	:	Bob Strauss, Los Angeles Daily News
"Gangs of New York"	:	Peter Travis, Rolling Stone
"Bloody Sunday" (tie)	:	Kenneth Turan, Los Angeles Time
"Spirited Away" (tie)	:	Kenneth Turan, Los Angeles Time

Film Critics Societies voted to select the following films for the "Best Picture of the Year for 2002":

"The Pianist"	:	Boston Society of Film Critics
"Confessions of a Dangerous Mind":		Las Vegas Film Critics
"About Schmidt"	:	Los Angeles Film Critics
"The Hours"	:	National Board of Review
"Far From Heaven"	:	New York Film Critics Circle
"Far From Heaven"	:	San Diego Film Critics Society
"Adaptation"	:	Toronto Film Critics

2003 SUNDANCE Theatrical Box Office Chart
(Filmmaker Magazine Winter 2004)

FILM TITLE	BUDGET (in millions)	DISTRIBUTOR	BOX OFFICE (in millions)
All The Real Girls	2.5	Sony Classics	.550
American Splendor	2.5	HBO Films/Fine Line	6.10
Buffalo Soldiers	15.0	Miramax	.355
Ca	1.0	IFC Films	1.70
Capturing Friedmans	NA	Magnolia Pictures	3.10
City of Ghosts	17.5	United Artists	.358
Confidence	15	Lions Gate	12.2
The Cooler	3.8	Lions Gate	.675
Die Mommie Die	1.0	Sundance Film Series	.312
Dopamine	.75	Sundance Film Series	.070
Dysfunktional Family	3.0	Miramax	2.20
Girls will be Girls	NA	IFC Films	.147
An Injury to One	NA	First Run Features	.753
Laurel Canyon	7.0	Sony Classics	3.60
Levity	7.5	Sony Classics	.210
Masked & Anonymous	7.0	Sony Classics	.534
Northfork	1.9	Paramount Classics	1.40
Owning Mahowny	10.0	Sony Classics	1.00
Party Monster	2.0	Strand Releasing	.718
People I Know	20.0	Miramax	.127
Pieces of April	.30	MGM & United Artists	2.20
Raising Victor Vargas	1.0	Samuel Goldwyn	2.10
SPUN	3.5	NewMarket	.412
The Station Agent	.70	Miramax Films	3.90
The Shape of Things	4.0	Focus Features	.736
The Singing Detective	7.0	Paramount Classics	.322
Thirteen	1.8	Fox Searchlight	4.60

Movies selected for screening at the Sundance Film Festival are considered to be popular by the Independent Features audience, but as the numbers show, once they are distributed, they are not popular with the mass market audience, and do not generate much box office receipts.

The Independent Features Project (IFP.org) Independent Spirit Award for Best Feature and Best Screenplay of 2003 went to Sophia Coppola "Lost in Translation"

The **Academy of Motion Pictures Arts and Sciences** nominated the following five films for "**Best Picture of the Year for 2003**":

"The Lord of the Rings: Return of the King"	:	$376,958,965
"Seabiscuit"	:	$120,197,488
"Master and Commander"	:	$ 93,926,386
"Mystic River"	:	$ 90,135,191
"Lost in Translation"	:	$ 44,566,004

Sometimes the Oscar will go to the Top Box-Office Grossing film.

The Academy Award for Best Picture of the year in 2003 was "The Lord of the Rings: Return of the King"

The Top Box-Office Grossing film of 2003 was "The Lord of the Rings: Return of the King"

Winning an Academy Award for Best Picture usually adds at least $25 million or more to the box-office grosses of a movie. They become the movies that audiences believe that they should see. Films that are produced for critical acclaim can also become financially awarded.

A screenwriter who wants to create a popular movie must therefore decide which audience he wants to please. Do you want to create a popular story that can become a financially successful movie, or do you want to write a screenplay that may not be financially successful, but would win critical acclaim and awards from the smaller audiences of the Writers Guild of America, the Sundance Film Festival, Film Critics, or the Academy of Motion Picture Arts and Sciences? But sometimes, if you are both good and very popular, like "The Lord of the Rings: Return of the King," you can have it all.

THE MEGAHIT MOVIES REDUX

There are other films that have just missed the $250 million criteria, but which can certainly be considered megahit movies. Films in this group include *Harry Potter and the Prisoner of Azkaban* ($249 million), *Toy Story 2* ($245 million), *Raiders of the Lost Ark* ($242 million), *Bruce Almighty* ($242 million) , *My Big Fat Greek Wedding* ($241 million), *Twister* ($240 million), and *Ghostbusters* ($238 million). Scenes from these movies will also be discussed in this book if they exemplify a particularly important dramatic technique. For example, we will discuss the opening sequence to *Raiders of the Lost Ark*, which will illustrate the importance of using *obstacles* to create *jeopardy* for the *protagonist*. But for the most part, our analysis will be restricted to those films that have generated over a quarter of a billion dollars in box-office revenue.

Over 2000 years ago, Aristotle (384-322 BC), the famous Greek Philosopher, wrote *Poetics*, a book in which he presented a theory of dramatic structure. He developed this theory by analyzing the successful dramas of Greek culture: the stage plays of Aeschylus, Euripides, and Sophocles. Aristotle systematically studied the most popular works of drama that existed during his lifetime. From that research he then abstracted principles of dramatic structure that he presented in the *Poetics*.

Much has changed in the mediums of story presentation during the past two thousand years. The film, video or motion picture medium, which did not exist in Aristotle's lifetime, is now the dominant presentation mode for drama and comedy. In this book, *The Megahit Movies*, we shall continue within the research tradition established by Aristotle, and use empirical methods to develop a new theory of dramatic structure. We shall do this by studying the forms and constructs existing in the most successful and popular stories that currently exist in the motion picture medium.

A few of the megahits are sequels, such as *Return of the Jedi, Empire Strikes Back, The Phantom Menace, Harry Potter: Chamber of Secrets, The Matrix Reloaded, The Matrix Revolutions*. It can be argued that these films are successful because an audience already existed for the characters introduced in the originals. This can also be said for *Batman, Dr. Seuss' The Grinch, Harry Potter, Spider-Man* and *The Lord of the Rings* trilogy. Our main concern is with the megahit films for which a built-in audience did not already exist. What is it about the experience of viewing the original films that caused domestic theater patrons to pay over $250 million?

The enormous box-office gross of an original film with new characters is usually generated by "word-of-mouth" recommendations to view the movie and the repeat attendance by the initial audience. A film can only become a megahit if members of the audience tell their friends that they must see the film. They also must go back to see the movie not just a second time, but also a third, fourth, and fifth time.

Why do members of an audience want to see these movies again and again? When experiencing a movie, an audience sits in a dark room for about two hours. They begin by staring at a blank screen, then experience a series of images and sounds that have an emotional impact on them. How do these films create **a satisfying emotional experience** for the audience? To understand this is to understand **the psychology of the audience**. That is, how do members of the audience **emotionally react** to the characters and the situations that they see in the movie?

Is there something common to these films in terms of dramatic structure or the human values revealed by the characters under conflict? If so, what are the dramatic structures and human values that compel the audience to recommend these films to friends and to repeatedly watch these movies themselves?

Most of these movies are either fantasy films or action-adventure films with fantastic elements. I use the word "fantastic" to describe the exhibition of extremely imaginative images, or images extraordinarily unreal in conception, design or construction. But not all fantasy films achieve megahit status. Obviously, fantasy elements alone are not sufficient for large box-office grosses. So, what are the essential attributes of a megahit movie?

One final point should be emphasized about the megahit movies. It is notoriously difficult for critics to agree on which films are good or even to agree on acceptable criteria for application of the word "good" when analyzing films. Aesthetic debates have been taking place among critics and philosophers of art for hundreds of years and usually degenerate into questions of taste and subjective personal opinion. There are no universally accepted criteria that can be used to judge which movies are "good" and which are "bad." Every movie will find an audience, even if the audience is very small, and some members of that audience will believe the movie was "great"!

But there is an objective criterion for deciding which movies are **popular**: **box office revenues**. People vote for these films when they purchase their tickets. They often see these films more than once. These are the films that they want their family, friends, and lovers to experience. Popularity may not be accepted by critics as a legitimate criterion of what is "good," but popularity does clearly delimit a class of films worthy of analysis. They reflect the values and attitudes the movie-viewing public held during a specific historical period.

Some people have argued that if the box office receipts were adjusted for inflation, there would be an entirely different order to the list of popular films. But there is a problem with using "adjusted" data to construct a hierarchical order of popularity. "Popularity" is **not** a concept to which you can apply a mathematical function and compute a new ordering that maintains validity. This holds true for the movies. Movies and the stories that they tell that were popular in 1939 are often no longer popular today. The concept of *popularity* involves values and attitudes of a group of people that change over time. These values and attitudes change not only over generations but also several times within a generation.

To be specific, *Gone With The Wind* is listed as the movie with the greatest box-office revenues, after adjusted for inflation. But when *Gone With The Wind* was re-released, in the early 1990s, it generated only about $1 million in current box-office revenues. It failed as a movie because the story was **no longer popular**. Many producers have also tried to get financing to make a movie based on some Hollywood screenwriter's "new sequel" to *Gone With The Wind*. But they cannot get the project into production because the studio executives know that the story and the characters in the story would no longer be popular with the current mass market. Therefore, in our analysis of the megahit movies, we will **not** use an inflation-adjusted list of "biggest box-office hits of all time."

The fundamental question remains: what is it about the megahit movies that made them so popular? Stated differently, what does the audience feel and experience in a dark theater for about two hours that provides them with **an emotionally satisfying experience** that makes them enthusiastic about these movies?

When writing the first edition of **The Megahit Movies** book, I studied films that had U.S. Domestic Box-Office Grosses of $250 million or more, in order to determine if there existed story structures common to all these movies. Although there did appear to be a common paradigm for designing stories for popular Hollywood movies, not all of the megahits shared all of the same story structures. For example, many screenwriting gurus tell us that the essential structure of any story is that of a protagonist overcoming obstacles in order to achieve an objective. But not all of the megahits have a single protagonist. Some, like *Men In Black,* have dual protagonists, and others, like *Independence Day,* have multiple protagonists, who are all trying to achieve the same primary objective: save the human race from annihilation by aliens.

Yet most of these megahit movies have the same core story elements: a **unique object** desired by both a **protagonist** and an **antagonist**. For example, in *Raiders of the Lost Ark*, the Ark of the Covenant was the unique object desired by the hero, Indiana Jones, and the villain, Belloc. The protagonist was the character with whom the audience most identified and for whom the audience had empathy, while the antagonist was a villain hated by the viewers. The unique object, like the Ark, usually represented the ultimate power in the universe. Not only were the lives of the protagonist and antagonist at stake in the struggle for its possession, but in the middle of this conflict was another character, the **love interest** of the protagonist. Marion was this character in *Raiders*. The protagonist also had at least one primary supporter who helped him on his quest (the Egyptian Sallah for Jones) while the antagonist had one or more henchmen to do his dirty work (the sadistic Nazi and the German soldiers for Belloc).

In the first ten minutes of the movie, the story attempts to hook the audience. This is often done by first having a scene in which the antagonist is introduced: a faceless villain that produces terror and hatred in the hearts of the audience. A problem is introduced which needs a hero. The protagonist then comes into the story. He is shown in a situation guaranteed to generate empathy for him with the audience. He reveals his dreams, his motivation, and the primary objective that he hopes will satisfy his personal needs. Then something happens that throws the protagonist out of his complacent everyday world. This is the inciting event which causes him to take action to fulfill his dreams.

For example, in *Jurassic Park,* the Raptor in the metal cage devours a human being, then Dr. Grant is introduced as an expert on dinosaurs. The inciting event occurs when Dr. John Hammond requests that Dr. Grant come to Jurassic Park. The unique object in this movie will be "the control of Jurassic Park," with the humans as the protagonist and the raptors the antagonist. In *Jaws,* the great white shark devours a young woman swimming in the ocean, then the Police Captain Brody is introduced. The inciting event occurs with the discovery of the girl's mutilated body on the beach.

As shown above, in many movies Spielberg does use the classic opening structure. But in *Raiders of the Lost Ark*, Spielberg starts his movie with a prologue to establish the bitter relationship between Jones and Belloc. Jones gets possession of an idol in the South American jungle, only to have it taken away from him by Belloc. The real story of this movie does not start until Jones is teaching at the University. In *Raiders*, the military intelligence officers asking Jones to seek the Ark is the inciting event that takes Jones out of the college and starts him on his quest for treasure. The protagonist's primary objective becomes connected with the unique object that is also desired by the forces of the antagonist.

The first act of the movie shows the protagonist in pursuit of the first major subgoal he needs to accomplish to possess the unique object. For Jones, this is the headpiece of the staff of Ra. To achieve this subgoal he must overcome many obstacles and problems. The love interest is usually introduced in the first act, as a factor that creates more problems for the protagonist. Marion is not willing to give Jones the headpiece. The protagonist confronts the antagonist and prevents the antagonist from possessing both the primary objective and the love interest in the first act. The completion of the first subgoal results in the first plot twist and sends the protagonist off to accomplish subgoal 2. In *Raiders,* Jones fights with Belloc's henchman in order to save Marion and to get possession of the headpiece. Once that is achieved, Jones and Marion travel to Cairo in search of the Well of Souls.

The pursuit of subgoal 2 provides the structure for the second act. The hero still must overcome difficult obstacles. At the end of the second act, the antagonist defeats the protagonist and prevents the protagonist from possessing both the primary objective and the love interest.

In *Raiders*, this occurs when Jones and Sallah have found the Ark and lift it out of the Well of Souls, only to have Belloc take it from him. This is the surprise plot twist. The Germans then toss Marion into the Well of Souls. Jones and Marion appear to be doomed as the fires dim and snakes crawl toward them. This is the moment of hopelessness and despair for the hero, and the audience believes that he will never see his dream come true.

Jones and Marion escape from this desperate situation. Jones then pursues his quest for the Ark. There are many more subgoals and acts in this movie. Both the Ark and the Love Interest constantly change hands between the protagonist and the antagonist. The Germans plan to take the Ark back to Berlin for Hitler. Jones has to stop them by destroying the plane. They then put the Ark into a truck. Jones jumps on a horse and rides after the trucks. He succeeds in getting possession of the Ark and places it on a ship. Then the Germans board the ship and take possession of both the Ark and Marion. Jones has to board the submarine and ride it across the Mediterranean Sea. On the island Jones tracks down the Germans and threatens to destroy the Ark if Marion is not released. Belloc calls his bluff, and Jones is captured.

In popular megahit movies, the antagonist will have possession of both the unique object and the love interest during the climax scene. Classic story theory states that in the climax scene, the protagonist will fight with the antagonist for both. During the battle, the protagonist triumphs and the antagonist is destroyed. Yet Spielberg does not use this in *Raiders* or many of his other movies. In *Raiders,* Jones and Marion are tied to a post and are forced to watch as Belloc opens the Ark. Jones does not defeat Belloc and the Germans! It is the spirits unleashed from the Ark that destroy them. Jones and Marion survive only because they close their eyes and refuse to look at the spirits. In many megahit movies, the protagonist does not directly kill the antagonist, but the antagonist dies as a result of some action he initiated in his attempt to destroy the protagonist. This is the case in *Raiders.* In *Jurassic Park*, Dr. Grant, Elle, and the children do not defeat the raptors. The humans are about to be devoured when a T-REX enters and kills the raptors. The protagonist and love interest survive, but they are not the victors.

In classic Hollywood story structure, after the climax scene we have a resolution scene in which all loose ends are resolved. The protagonist either obtains the unique object, or it is destroyed in the climax scene. The protagonist and the love interest are reunited, and the community celebrates their victory. In *Raiders,* the government officials take possession of the Ark, while Marion gets possession of Jones. In *Jurassic Park,* Dr. Grant, Elle, and the children all fly away from the danger and leave Jurassic Park to the dinosaurs.

The summer of 2003 did have its share of megahit movies: *Finding Nemo* ($335 million), *Pirates of the Caribbean* ($295 million), *Matrix Reloaded* ($281 million), and two near misses with *Bruce Almighty* ($242 million) and *X2: X-Men United* ($214 million). Then, there were some potential contenders that did not make the cut: *Terminator 3: Rise of the Machines* ($150 million), *The Hulk* ($132 million), *The League of Extraordinary Gentlemen* ($66 million), and *Lara Croft Tomb Raider: The Cradle of Life* ($65 million).

Why did some of these films fail to become blockbusters? In order to become a megahit, the most important thing that a movie must do is give the audience an **emotionally satisfying experience. The audience must feel good when they leave the theaters**. They must also be

WRITING FOR AN AUDIENCE

Genres segment the mass market audience into different groups.

WRITING FOR AN AUDIENCE
Genres segment the mass market audience.

Besides the mass audience, the audience of all possible ticket buyers, there are different types of audiences. As discussed above, different groups of people will like different kinds of movies. Screenwriters who write within a genre understand this. A genre can be considered as a type of story that connects with only a particular segment of the mass audience. Robert McKee discusses twenty-five different genres in his screenwriting book, *Story*:

1. Love Story
2. Horror
3. Modern Epic
4. Western
5. War Genre
6. Maturation Plot
7. Redemption Plot
8. Punitive Plot
9. Testing Plot
10. Education Plot
11. Disillusionment Plot
12. Comedy
13. Crime
14. Social Drama
15. Action Adventure
16. Historical Drama
17. Biography
18. Docu-Drama
19. Mockudrama
20. Musical
21. Science Fiction
22. Sports Genre
23. Fantasy
24. Animation
25. Art

Different groups of the mass audience can be associated with each of these genres, and genres can be thought of as dividing the totality of all movie viewers into different segments. Each genre structures its stories in ways that meet its audience's expectations and interests. As Robert McKee says, "To anticipate the anticipations of the audience you must master your genre and its conventions."

A book that analyzes the audience expectations for different genres is *Alternative Screenwriting: Writing Beyond the Rules* by Ken Dancyger and Jeff Rush. The genres they analyze in detail are:

The Western
The Gangster Film
The Film Noir
The Screwball Comedy
The Melodrama
The Situation Comedy
The Horror Film
The Science Fiction Film
The War Film
The Adventure Film
The Epic Film
The Sports Film
The Biographical Film
The Satire Film

Genres are not only recognized by story gurus, but also by Hollywood agents and producers, who very often will only consider a screenplay within a specific genre. This is exemplified by online query services such as www.ScriptBlaster.com, which divides all screenplays into the a few genres that are common to the Hollywood Industry: Action-Adventure, Comedy, Drama, Family, Horror, Romantic Comedy, Romance, Sci-Fi, and Thriller (Crime, Mystery, and Suspense).

MovieLink.com, an internet broadband movie distribution company that enables consumers to download digital versions of popular films to watch on their home computers, divides the mass market audience into the following categories: Action, Classics, Comedy, Drama, Family, Romance, Sci-Fi, Thriller, and Western.

Some Story Consultants, like John Truby, recommend that some writers try to mix two genres together in order to increase their market segments and create a blockbuster movie. Some popular movies do this and become blockbuster films. But there is more to making a megahit movie than just mixing genres.

The Megahit Movies will focus on the design of stories that can be developed into mass audience commercially successful Hollywood movies: popular movies that can become megahit box-office successes. This is the audience for whom we intend to write our stories: the largest audience possible. The best way to hope to create such a story is to analyze *The Megahit Movies*; the most popular movies Hollywood has ever produced. We will not study specific genres, but instead, explicate the structure of the emotional subtext that is the foundation of these popular megahit movies.

Why do members of an audience want to see these movies again and again? When experiencing a movie, an audience sits in a dark room for about two hours. They begin by staring at a blank screen, then experience a series of images and sounds that have an emotional impact on them. The story takes the audience to a place that is very different from their ordinary everyday world. This new world could be a futuristic hi-tech society like that found in the *Star Wars* movies, the world of Middle-Earth as found in the *Lord of the Rings* movies, a magical place like the world of *Harry Potter* and *The Grinch*, or the world of the turn of the century as found in *Titanic*. Sometimes it is not the world that is different, but the point of view of the protagonist. In *Sixth Sense,* Cole Sears sees dead people; in *Forrest Gump,* Forrest lives his life completely absorbed with what he is doing each moment. There is some form of "magic" in almost all of these movies.

It is **repeat audience viewing** that makes a movie a **megahit**. Members of the audience have to want to go back to see the film again and again. This is accomplished by providing them with a new kind of experience, and one that makes them "feel good" when the movie ends.

But more than anything else, these films provide the audience with an **emotionally satisfying experience.**

HIGH CONCEPTS & LOGLINES
How to hook the reader with only one sentence!

HIGH CONCEPTS & LOGLINES
How to hook the reader with one sentence!

What is the difference between a **logline** and a **high concept**?

Both are one-sentence descriptions of the essence of a story.

A **logline** states who the main character of the story is, his primary objective, and what is stopping him from achieving that objective.

A **high concept** is an exciting *logline* whose purpose is to get an agent or producer to read the screenplay.

Robert Kosberg, in *How to Sell Your Idea to Hollywood,* states that "The essence of *high concept* is that it is both brief and provocative. It piques the imagination and promises that big things are going to happen out of an ordinary situation." A *high concept* is not limited to any specific genre, but can be used to promote a comedy, drama, action/adventure, horror, or fantasy project. It is meant to excite the audience, to tease them into wanting to see more. It is not so much a story design tool as a marketing and selling gimmick.

A *high concept* statement of your project is a one-line sentence intended to excite a producer. Your objective is to get him to read your script, or to buy your script, or to take your project up one level higher in the studio. How do you excite a producer or studio executive?

Studio executives are in the jobs they have because they want to produce movies that make money. When pitching a story idea, you must understand the motivation of the studio executive. You are asking them to put at least $50 million into your movie project plus another $25 million for prints and advertising. To justify that type of expenditure, they are going to have to make back at least two times their investment. This means that your project must gross at least $150 million. You have to persuade the execuuve that your story has that kind of box-office potential.

How do you do that? The easiest way is to tell him that it is very much like another picture that has recently grossed over $150 million but much better! Your project is just like yesterday's popular movie, but different in a way that will generate more money. Kosberg states, "remember, when you're pitching these ideas, executives are looking at both how commercial they are and how unique they are. An idea should be *like* something successful that's been done before and markedly different at the same time. Alike yet different."

Your project will not be commercially viable in the mind of the producer or studio executive unless there is an existing popular movie to which it can be compared. The screenwriter must understand that there are only a very few people in Hollywood that can actually give the "green light" to a studio feature film production. The rest of the development executives are there to listen to pitches and read scripts in the hope of finding a viable commercial project that they can take up to the next level. They will not pitch your project to their boss unless they think he will want to make it. You must excite him, and make him believe that your project has the potential of becoming the next megahit.

So how do you design a *high concept* for your story? Start by looking at a list of films that have grossed over $150 million in the last five to ten years. These lists are available from *Variety* and *The Hollywood Reporter* or on a web site like www.The-Numbers.com.

Why only the last five to ten years? Because what the mass audience likes changes. What was popular ten years ago may no longer be popular today. So it is best to look at only those blockbusters made in the last few years. Find a film that you personally enjoyed and that is in some respects similar to your story. It can't be identical, because then the studio executive will tell you that it has already been done. What you have to do is place the story into a different context. The point is to establish a reference film for the studio executives so that they can visualize your story and imagine its commercial potential.

Use only successful films! You defeat your objective if you tell the executive that your story is just like a movie that bombed and was pulled out of the theaters after the first weekend. Can you blame a producer for not wanting to put $50 million into that project? If you pitch *"Ishtar in Salt Lake City"* as the *high concept* for your movie, it will not get you a deal at a major studio.

Another way of creating a *high concept* project is that instead of taking one successful movie and placing it into a different context, link together the titles of two successful movies. Kosberg states, "by merging two contemporary movie titles that are immediately recognizable-X meets Y-you come up with a brand-new brainchild, a high-concept Z." For example, *"The Terminator meets The Men in Black"* would be a new *high concept*, as would *"Pretty Woman meets Apollo 13"* for some out-of-space fun. You could also try to pitch *"Forrest Gump meets Mission Impossible"* or *"Big Daddy meets Godsford Park"* for two "fish-out-of-water" stories.

Some *high concepts* use popular books in their statement instead of movies. For example, the movies *Batman, Spider-Man* and *MIB* were adaptations of popular comic characters. *Jurassic Park, Jaws,* and *Harry Potter* are inherently high concept projects because they were based on popular novels. This establishes a reference for the producer, and gives him confidence that there will be a market for the movie.

Kosberg believes that, "Science fiction and fantasy score well when combined with comic elements…the studios are looking to make films that have cross-over appeal or that will attract a wide audience margin." Looking at the list of megahit movies will verify this.

Audience identification with your protagonist is essential for commercial success. The members of the audience must become emotionally involved with the hero and the love interest in your story and hate the antagonist. This is often accomplished if you make the protagonist an ordinary person thrown into extraordinary circumstances. Put a normal person into a bizarre situation.

Ultimately, it is not "character studies" that are *high concept* movies. In our list of megahits, only *Forrest Gump* could be considered a character study. Kosberg believes that "when it is time for the studio to decide whether they want to buy your idea or not, its plot is going to be more important than character growth. But characters do not sell in the pitch meeting. Premises sell." It is a well-structured story that can be related to a commercially successful film that will close the deal.

The *DoneDeal* website (www.ScriptSales.com) lists the loglines of scripts that have recently been sold to Hollywood producers or production companies. *Creative Screenwriting* and *Script* magazines also list the projects that are presently being sold to Hollywood.

Below are high concepts and loglines for some spec screenplays developed by **RMS Productions Company**.

Entanglements by Richard Michaels Stefanik & Glen Underwood
"Sneakers meets Minority Report".
A Sci-Fi Thriller set in 2024 about a man who creates a Quantum Computer that can break any security code in the world, but then is framed for murder by the greedy CEO of his corporation. He tries to prove his innocence and get back his wife, but is relentlessly pursued by Federal Agents and a Crime Syndicate that wants the security code-breaking computer for their own use.

Borges in London by Richard Michaels Stefanik
"The Da Vinci Code meets a Digital Fortress"
A literary scholar who specializes in the work of Jorge Luis Borges, the magical realism writer, becomes involved in a murder and financial intrigue while researching the life of Borges in the City of London.

Elixir by Richard Michaels Stefanik
"Harry Potter meets Lord of the Rings"
A sword and sorcerer fantasy set in the time of Elizabethan England, where a group of witches, alchemists, and magicians pursue the "elixir of life," that potion which can transform a person into whatever they dream to become.

Mark Twain & The Mysterious Stranger
by Richard Michaels Stefanik. *"Mark Twain meets Satan"*
Mark Twain, when faced with bankruptcy and the death of his wife and two daughters in the last years of his life, turned to the problem of eternal evil, and wrote **The Mysterious Stranger**, the story of Angel # 44, a being of supreme intelligence who has no compassion for mankind.

Double or Nothing by Richard Michaels Stefanik & Michael Herst
"Get Shorty in Las Vegas"
A comedy about a loser who tries to run away from his life by buying a new identity, only to find that the Mob, the FBI, and a widow are now after him because he bought the identity of a mafia hit man that became an FBI informant.

Monte Carlo by Linda C. Wright
"Cinderella in Monte Carlo"
A young American woman discovers that she is the heir to a vast fortune in Monte Carlo, but then has to struggle with her evil step-sister who also claims the estate.

Once in a Blue Moon by Maria Iacuele
"You've Got Mail meets Ruthless People"
During the Christmas Season, a feisty young woman fights the effects of a "love potion" while trying to save her Toy Store from being taken over by a sinister competitor.

Running on Fumes by Magee Rowland
"Liar, Liar meets What Women Want"
A comedy about a sexually repressed woman who has a magical spell placed on her that forces her to tell men exactly what they really want to hear. She then uses this ability in hilarious situations to save the man she loves from an unscrupulous tycoon.

Writing Assignment: Write a one-sentence descriptive logline for your story. Express the high concept in terms of a single sentence or the comparison of two commercially successful movies.

THE UNIQUE OBJECT
&
THE MAIN CHARACTERS

The Unique Object

The Protagonist

The Antagonist

The Love Interest

THE UNIQUE OBJECT

The **unique object** guarantees conflict. It is that which both the protagonist and the antagonist want to possess. One example of this is "The Ark of the Covenant" in *Raiders of the Lost Ark*. The desire for the control of this unique object leads to the life-and-death struggle that concludes in the climax scene.

The Unique Objects in Megahit Movies

Titanic	The Heart of the Ocean Jewel
Star Wars	Plans to the Death Star
E.T.: The Extra-Terrestrial	E.T.
The Phantom Menace	Control of the Planet Naboo
Spider-Man	Control of the City
Return of the King	The One Ring
Jurassic Park	Control of Jurassic Park
Harry Potter and the Sorcerer's Stone	The Sorcerer's Stone
Fellowship of the Rings	The One Ring
Lion King	Control of the Pride Lands
The Two Towers	The One Ring
Finding Nemo	Nemo
Return of the Jedi	Control of the Universe
Independence Day	The Planet Earth
Star Wars: Attack of the Clones	Control of the Planet
The Sixth Sense	The Mind of Cole Sears
The Empire Strikes Back	Control of the Universe
Pirates of the Caribbean	The Aztec Gold Coin
Home Alone	Kevin's Home
The Matrix Reloaded	Zion
Shrek	Shrek's Home in the Swamp
How the Grinch Stole Christmas	Cheermeister of Whobilation
Jaws	Control of the Beach
Harry Potter-Chamber of Secrets	Control of Hogwarts
Monsters, Inc.	Boo, the Human Child
Batman	Control of Gotham City
Men in Black	Galaxy on Orion's Belt

Writing Assignment : Write a one-page description of the unique object for your story. Explain why it is so important that both the protagonist and antagonist are willing to die for its possession.

THE PROTAGONIST

The **protagonist** is the main character of the story. He/She/It is the character with whom the audience must bond and have the most empathy. The audience should identify with the point-of-view of the protagonist. It is his primary objective that becomes the story objective. Whether he can achieve this goal becomes the concern of the audience.

Perseverance and will power are the most important personality traits that a protagonist must possess. He must have an unshakable commitment to his primary objective. He also must be sincere and believe in the rightness of what he is doing. While he may have moments of self-doubt, he overcomes them and continues pursuing his objective.

He must have sufficient will to overcome all the obstacles that he will confront while pursuing his objective. He needs this strength to engage in the climactic battle with the antagonist. A character who gives up too easily would not be able to withstand attacks from the antagonist and his supporters. The protagonist must have the strength and stamina to carry the fight to its conclusion.

Not all of the protagonists are male. Some, like Rose in *Titanic,* are female, and some, like Nemo, Shrek, the Grinch, Sulley, E.T. and Simba, are non-human. The strength that the protagonist's needs is not always physical strength, as shown by the examples of Elliott, E.T., Frodo, Harry Potter, Cole Sears, and Kevin. What they have is the commitment to accomplish their goals. Their lives and the lives of the ones they love, if not the very existence of the world, often depend on them achieving their goals.

The protagonist is the character who makes most of the major decisions in the story. The choices and actions that he makes during conflicts reveal his values. These values will help him achieve his objective.

While most of the popular films have only one protagonist, some have a protagonist with dual personalities. Batman (Crime Fighter and Reclusive Millionaire), Indiana Jones (Adventurer and University Professor), Spider-Man (Crime Fighter and High School student), and Bruce Almighty (TV Reporter-God for a week) are examples of this. These protagonists are more intriguing for the audience and help them fantasize that they also could possibly live a secret adventurous life. This increases the audience's identification with and empathy for the protagonist.

In *E.T.,* both Elliott and E.T. share the role of the protagonist. This is essential for a story in which the feelings, emotions, and thoughts of two characters merge through telepathic communication. This technique helps to explain the success of the film, because merging the two characters into a double protagonist doubles the audience's empathy for the protagonist and increases the audience's concern for the story's outcome.

The films that have a protagonist without a dual personality usually also have protagonist supporters with whom the audience can have sympathy. This sympathy is then transferred to the protagonist. Examples of this can be found in *Star Wars* (Yoda, Han Solo, and Chewbacca), *Shrek* (Donkey), and in *Monsters, Inc.* (Mike).

Some films have more than one protagonist. This expands the scope of audience identification. J and K are the dual protagonists in *Men in Black,* Nemo and Marlin in *Finding Nemo. Pirates of the Caribbean* has three protagonists: Liz, Will Turner, and Jack Sparrow.

Independence Day has four characters who share the protagonist function: Captain Steve Hiller, David Levinson, President Tom Whitmore and Russell Casse.

Below are the protagonists in the Megahit Movies:

Titanic: Rose
Star Wars: Luke Skywalker
E.T. : Elliott and E.T. The Extra-Terrestrial
The Phantom Menace: Anakin Skywalker
Spider-Man: Peter Parker (Spider-Man)
Lord of the Rings- Return of the King : Frodo
Jurassic Park: Dr. Alan Grant
Forrest Gump: Forrest Gump
Harry Potter and the Sorcerer's Stone: Harry Potter
Lord of the Rings-The Fellowship of the Rings: Frodo
The Lion King: Simba

Lord of the Rings-The Two Towers: Frodo
Finding Nemo: Marlin and Nemo
Return of the Jedi: Luke Skywalker
Independence Day : Captain Steve Hiller, David Levinson, Tom Whitmore, Russell Casse
Star Wars-Attack of the Clones: Young Darth Vader
The Sixth Sense: Cole Sear
Star Wars-Empire Strikes Back: Luke Skywalker
Pirates of the Caribbean: Liz, Will, and Jack
Home Alone: Kevin
Matrix Reloaded: Neo
Shrek: Shrek
Harry Potter and the Chamber of Secrets: Harry Potter
Jaws: Police Captain Martin Brody
How the Grinch Stole Christmas: The Grinch
Monsters, Inc.: Sulley
Batman: Bruce Wayne (Batman)
Men In Black: J and K

Writing Assignment: Write a one-page description of the protagonist for your story. Cast this role with a contemporary bankable Hollywood actor or actress.

THE ANTAGONIST

The **antagonist** is the character who opposes the desires and primary objective of the protagonist. He is the villain who is always in conflict with the protagonist, either directly or through his surrogates. While both the protagonist and antagonist must persevere to bring the fight to the climax, the antagonist is the character who is ruthless and will stop at nothing to obtain his goal. He is the relentless force that the protagonist must finally defeat. He is also the character that generates the most dangerous obstacles for the protagonist.

Some antagonists are anti-human and reptilian in appearance, such as the Great White Shark (*Jaws*), Raptors (*Jurassic Park*), the Aliens (*ID4*), the Edgar-Bug (*MIB*), and Randall (*Monsters, Inc.*). These characters are naturally terrifying and repulsive to most people in the audience.

The antagonist usually wants power and control over the lives of the other characters. He or she will break all codes of human conduct to achieve this end. The antagonist often has a complete disregard for human life and will kill any character that opposes his objectives. He will kill even his most loyal friends, if it serves his purposes. Terror and betrayal are the standard modes of behavior for the antagonist, as best exemplified by the Joker in *Batman,* who kills his loyal bodyguard Bob. The audience learns that this is a character that they cannot trust.

The audience must understand the motivation of the antagonist, and these motivations must be believable. The more negative emotional involvement the audience has with the antagonist, the more engrossed they will become with the story. The audience should hate him so much that they will want to see the antagonist destroyed at the climax scene of the movie. For example in *Batman*, the Joker reveals his evil nature by disfiguring works of art in the Flugelheim Museum and scarring the face of his beautiful girlfriend, Alicia. He is a character that has no shred of humanity left with which the audience can identify.

At the beginning of the story, the antagonist is more powerful than the protagonist. This makes the protagonist's struggle to achieve his primary objective much more difficult. The antagonist is usually in control of the concrete object or the protagonist's love interest during the third act, before the climax scene. The protagonist must defeat the antagonist without destroying the love interest, while still attempting to achieve his primary objective. By this time in the story, the audience should have a great empathy for both the protagonist and his love interest, and therefore, the audience's emotional stake in the outcome of the climax will also be high. In the climax scene, the life-and-death battle, the antagonist wants to destroy the protagonist. In *Lord of the Rings,* the Dark Lord Sauron through his supporters wants to destroy Frodo and capture the One Ring; Voldemort wants to kill Harry Potter; Scar wants to destroy Simba in *The Lion King;* the Green Goblin wants to kill Spider-Man; and in *Monster's Inc.* Randall wants to destroy the human child, Boo.

The antagonist is the character that the filmmaker wants the audience to hate. But this does not have to be true in every scene of the movie. In *Batman,* the audience has some sympathy for the Joker because he is betrayed by Boss Grissom and horribly disfigured when dropped into the vat containing toxic chemicals. But most importantly, the Joker makes the audience laugh. The audience likes any character that has a sense of humor. Yet by the end of climax scene, the audience wants the mad Joker destroyed.

In order for the writer to ensure that the audience hates the villain, the writer will have the antagonist associated with characters that are evil, vicious and deserving of the audience's enmity. This is usually the function of the villain's henchmen. In *Star Wars,* the Commander of the Death Star destroys the planet Alderan even after Princess Leia has told him what he wants to know. He kills the whole population of a world just to test the destructive capacity of the Death Star. In *Spider-Man,* the Green Goblin attacks and terrorizes Peter Parker's Aunt May. In *Raiders of the Lost Ark*, this is accomplished by having one of Belloc's associates, the fiendish German, be the character that is hated for his sadistic acts. Hate by association is then transferred to Belloc. This technique allows Belloc to function as a realistic rival for the affections of Marion, the love interest of the story. The audience can have sympathy for Marion's emotional conflicts as she tries to choose between Jones and Belloc.

Deception is often used by the antagonist in his battle with the protagonist. Sometimes the true identity of the real villain is withheld from the protagonist and the audience until the climax. This device has been used in the Harry Potter movies, in which we finally discover that Voldemort is really controlling Quirrell in *Harry Potter and the Sorcerer's Stone,* and Voldemort is really Tom Riddle in *Harry Potter and the Chamber of Secrets.* Below are the antagonists in the megahit movies.

Titanic: Cal
Star Wars: Darth Vader
E.T. : "Keys" and the Government Agents
The Phantom Menace: Darth Sidious
Spider-Man: Green Goblin
Lord of the Rings-Return of the King: The Dark Lord Sauron
Jurassic Park: The Raptors
Forrest Gump: Being Normal
Harry Potter and the Sorcerer's Stone: Voldemort (Prof. Quirrell)
Lord of the Rings-The Fellowship of the Rings: Dark Lord Sauron
The Lion King: Scar
Lord of the Rings-The Two Towers: Dark Lord Sauron
Finding Nemo: The Dentist and Darla
Return of the Jedi: The Emperor
Independence Day : The Aliens
Star Wars- Attack of the Clones: Count Dooku
The Sixth Sense: Dead People
Empire Strikes Back: Darth Vader
Pirates of the Caribbean: Barbossa
Home Alone: The Two Burglars
Matrix Reloaded: The Matrix and Agent Smiths
Shrek: Lord Farquaad
Jaws: The Great White Shark
Harry Potter and the Chamber of Secrets : Voldemort (Tom Riddle)
How the Grinch Stole Christmas: Mayor August May Who
Monsters, Inc.: Randall
Batman : The Joker
Men In Black : The Edgar-Bug Alien

Writing Assignment: Write a one-page description of the antagonist for your story. Cast this role with a contemporary bankable Hollywood actor or actress.

THE LOVE INTEREST

Some story gurus call the **love interest** the "romance," but the character plays the same function under either name. In many films, the love interest, either male or female, is a character both the protagonist and antagonist desire. In other films, the love interest is the prize to be won after the climactic battle for power and dominance is resolved. While not all of the popular films include this character in their story structure, most of the megahit movies do.

Having a love interest in the climax scene intensifies the emotional drama for the audience. The protagonist is then faced with a moral dilemma: save the love interest and lose his primary objective (and the unique object), or focus totally on obtaining the unique object and risk having the love interest be killed. In *Raiders of the Lost Ark*, Indiana chose to first fulfill his mission to get the Ark of the Covenant and left Marion tied to the post in the tent. In *Spider-Man*, the Green Goblin forces Spider-Man to chose between saving the life of MJ or a tram filled with children. Jack decides to sacrifice his life in *Titanic* so that Rose may live, just as Russell Casse sacrifices his life to destroy the Alien warship in *Independence Day* so that his children and the human race can survive. In *The Matrix Reloaded*, Neo must decide between saving Trinity or Zion. Neo chooses to save Trinity. In *Monsters, Inc.*, Sulley must sacrifice his relationship with the human child, Boo, in order for her to safely return home.

Having another character besides the protagonist and antagonist caught in the middle of the life-and-death battle of the climax scene enhances the excitement and intensifies the audience's emotional involvement in the climax. The love interest complicates the situation for the hero and increases the emotional stakes. The antagonist usually uses the love interest as a hostage and is willing to kill her if the hero will not surrender. Somehow the protagonist must find a way to stop the villain, while also saving the life of the love interest.

If a movie has multiple protagonists of different genders, then some can be considered to be the love interests of others. For example, *Pirates of the Caribbean* has three protagonists: Liz, Will, and Jack. Liz could be considered to be the love interest of Will and Jack (plus Norrington) while Will is the love interest of Liz. Jack is definitely not the love interest of Liz, nor is Norrington. Sometimes "love quadrangles" can get complicated.

Titanic: Jack
Star Wars: Princess Leia
E.T. : E.T.
The Phantom Menace: Padme (Queen Amidala)
Spider-Man: MJ (Mary Jane)
Return of the King : Arwen for Aragorn (None for Frodo)
Jurassic Park: Ellie Sattler
Forrest Gump: Jenny
Harry Potter and the Sorcerer's Stone: Hermione
The Lion King: Nala
Finding Nemo: Nemo for Marlin
Return of the Jedi: Princess Leia
Independence Day: Jasmine (for Steve Hillier), Connie (for David Levinson), the First Lady (for President Tom Whitmore) and the children (for Russell Casse)
Star Wars-Attack of the Clones: Amidala
Empire Strikes Back: Princess Leia
Pirates of the Caribbean : Elizabeth Swan
Matrix Reloaded: Trinity
Shrek : Princess Fiona
How the Grinch Stole Christmas: Martha May Whovier
Jaws: Captain Brody's Wife and Son
Harry Potter and the Chamber of Secrets: Hermione
Monsters, Inc.: Boo, The Human Child
Batman: Vicky Vale
Men In Black: Dr. Laurel Weaver

Writing Assignment: Write a one-page description of the love interest for your story. Cast this role with a contemporary bankable Hollywood actor or actress.

THE CLIMAX SCENE OF THE MOVIE

The final battle between the Protagonist and the Antagonist for possession of both the Unique Object and the Love Interest.

THE CLIMAX SCENE OF THE MOVIE

Once a writer creates the **climax scene**, he will be able then to work forward from the opening scenes to design an **emotionally satisfying experience** for the audience.

The climax scene of the movie is always the most exciting and emotionally engrossing scene for the audience. This is the "obligatory scene" in which there is a battle between the protagonist and the antagonist. In popular movies, the survival of the love interest will also be achieved by the actions of the protagonist in this scene. The outcome of this battle will determine the fate of the unique object that is the primary objective of the story. Only one of the two main characters will survive the conflict that rages in this scene.

In the climax scene the following questions are resolved: What happens to the primary objective? Who obtains the unique object? What is the outcome of the battle between the protagonist and the antagonist?

Below are descriptions of the climax scenes found in the megahit movies. These scenes should all be studied by the writer in order to understand how to design a scene in which "the audience gets what they want, but in an unexpected way." This means that the audience gets an emotionally satisfying experience by watching the protagonist triumph over the antagonist, but in a surprising way.

Titanic
The climax occurs when Rose throws the jewel, "the heart of the ocean" back into the water above the sunken Titanic. She then rejoins Jack in her dreams (or after her death) on the top of the stairway beneath the clock in the Titanic.

Star Wars
The climax occurs when Luke Skywalker and Darth Vader fight with each other and the Death Star is finally destroyed.

E.T.
The climax occurs when E.T. and Elliott fly over the road blockade constructed by the agents of the U.S. Government.

Phantom Menace
The climax occurs when Anakin Skywalker destroys the control vessel making the warrior droids inoperative, thereby winning the battle for Naboo.

Spider-Man
Spider-Man battles the Green Goblin at the bridge over Roosevelt Island and must save both the love interest, MJ, and the children in the cable car. It is a fight for control of NYC.

Lord of the Rings-Return of the King
Frodo struggles with Gollum, and the Ring is destroyed in the lava river inside Mount Doom. The Eye of the Dark Lord Sauron collapses from the tower and is destroyed. The armies of Mordor flee and the people of Middle-Earth prevail.

Jurassic Park
The climax occurs when the T-REX destroys the raptors just as they are about to attack Dr. Grant, Ellie, and the children. The humans survive, but in an unexpected way.

Forrest Gump
Forrest meets his son and discovers that he has produced a normal child. Jenny tells him she is dying. Forrest offers to marry her and take care of her and the child. Jenny finally accepts his offer.

Harry Potter and the Sorcerer's Stone
Harry Potter fights with Prof. Quirell (and Voldemort) for possession of the sorcerer's stone.

Lord of the Rings-The Fellowship of the Ring
The Fellowship battle the Orcs in the mines of Moria. Gandalf falls into the depths while fighting with the fiery Balrog. Frodo survives, but loses his mentor.

The Lion King
The climax occurs when Simba defeats Scar in the battle for the Pride Lands.

Lord of the Rings-The Two Towers
The Fellowship confronts the forces gathered by the Dark Lord Sauron and the wizard Saruman in the battle of Helm's Deep. Gandalf and the Fellowship prevail.

Return of the Jedi
Luke Skywalker fights both Darth Vader and the Emperor. At the final moment when it appears that the Emperor will kill Luke, Darth switches sides, picks up the Emperor, and throws him to his death down the abyss in the center of the Death Star.

Independence Day
The climax occurs when the human pilots engage the aliens in an air battle, and the alien spacecraft is finally destroyed.

Star Wars-Attack of the Clones
Lord Dooku duels with Anakin and Obie-Wan Kenobi, and cuts off Anakin's arm. Lord Dooku then fights Jedi Master Yoda. He escapes because Yoda must protect Anakin and Obie-Wan Kenobi from the falling generator tower.

Sixth Sense
Cole Sears accepts that he can see dead people. He also understands that they do not want to terrorize him but need his help. The climax occurs when Dr. Malcolm Crowe realizes that he is dead, but since he helped Cole, he can now accept his death.

Empire Strikes Back
Luke Skywalker fights Darth Vader. Darth reveals that he is Luke's father, and pleads with Luke to join him, for together they could defeat the Emperor and put an end to the conflict. Luke refuses, and falls down into the abyss at the center of the spaceship.

Home Alone
The climax occurs when Kevin engages the two burglars in the battle for his home. Although the burglars capture Kevin at the end of the sequence, the old man saves Kevin by hitting the burglars with a shovel.

Shrek
Lord Farquaad needs to marry the Princess to become Lord of the Kingdom. Shrek confronts him at the wedding ceremony and fights for Princess Fiona.

Jaws
The climax occurs when Capt. Brody finally kills the great shark.

Harry Potter and the Chamber of Secrets:
Harry Potter fights with Tom Riddle (Voldemort) in the Chamber of Secrets.

Monsters, Inc.
Sulley and the human child Boo are chased by Randall. Sulley and Mike trick Mr. Waternoose to reveal his evil intent in the simulation room. tBoo is saved!

How the Grinch Stole Christmas
The climax occurs when the Grinch saves Cindy's life and holds the sleigh up over his head. Her love has transformed the Grinch and made him into a good person. The "evil" Grinch has been destroyed. The Grinch then returns the Christmas presents to Whoville and apologizes to the Whos. His apology is accepted, and he is integrated back into the Who community.

Batman
The climax occurs when Batman and the Joker fight on the top of the Cathedral. The weight of the gargoyle finally pulls the Joker off the helicopter rope-ladder and causes him to plunge to his death.

Men in Black
The climax occurs when the Edgar-Bug is destroyed by J, K, and Dr. Laurel Weaver. They gain possession of "the Galaxy on Orion's Belt" and save the earth from destruction.

Pirates of the Caribbean
The climax occurs when Liz, Will, and Jack together kill Barbossa. Liz forces Barbossa to point his gun at her, Jack shoots him, and Will drops his bloody coins into the Aztec chest. This makes Barbossa mortal again so that he can die from the gunshot wound.

Finding Nemo
The climax occurs when Nemo escapes from the Fish Tank and avoids being taken home by Darla.

Matrix Reloaded
The climax occurs when the Neo decides to save Trinity instead of saving Zion.

Writing Assignment: Write a climax scene for your story that includes a **unique object, protagonist, antagonist,** and **love interest.** The protagonist and the love interest survive the battle. The antagonist is destroyed but in an unexpected way.

PLOTTING FOR AUDIENCE EMOTIONAL RESPONSES

The psychology of the audience

Understanding audience empathy and enmity

THE PSYCHOLOGY OF THE AUDIENCE

The screenwriter who wants to create popular movies must get the audience to love the protagonist and hate the antagonist as soon as these characters are first shown on the screen. Audience empathy for the protagonist must be created as early in the story as possible. This is necessary so that the audience will care about the hero, his dreams, and his primary objective. The audience must also feel terror and hatred toward the villain because of the things they see this character do when he first appears on the screen.

The writer needs to understand **the psychology of the audience**. This means understanding **the emotional reactions** that members of the audience will have to the characters, actions, events, and situations that they see on the screen. The members of the audience have come to watch the characters on the screen in order to fulfill their own fantasies. They want the characters to do the things that they themselves have always dreamed of doing. The characters in popular films must both be bigger than life, yet, still emotionally accessible to the audience. This is accomplished by revealing the protagonist's dreams; dreams with which the audience can identify. But the writer must also show how far the character is from achieving these dreams. In the *Wizard of Oz,* Dorothy's dream of finding a place where there aren't any problems, "somewhere over the rainbow," is the most obvious example.

Each scene should be written in terms of **the emotional effect that the scene has on the audience**. The audience's emotional reactions to the characters in situations of jeopardy should be the prime consideration of the writer. The writer should always be aware of how a specific action will increase, decrease, or modify the audience's empathy or enmity for a character.

People in the audience will care about characters with which they can identify and with whom they share some human concern. One way to accomplish this is to show the protagonist when he is weak. Write a scene showing him in his moment of weakness, when all hope is gone, and he is his most vulnerable. It is easier to generate empathy for a character when he is helpless than when he is powerful. That is why the antagonist must be more powerful than the protagonist in the beginning of the story. This also explains why stories about underdogs who eventually prevail over their opposition are very popular.

A hero's humanity is best shown in his private moments, when he lets down his defenses and reveals himself. If the antagonist then invades this privacy and humiliates the protagonist, tremendous sympathy for the protagonist and hatred for the antagonist will be generated. A prime example of this technique is found in *The Wizard of Oz*. Dorothy has been captured by the Wicked Witch of the West. The sand is running through the hourglass, and time is running out. Dorothy, in her moment of total helplessness and desperation, cries out for help from her Auntie Em, whose image then appears in the crystal ball. This image transforms into the cackling, mocking face of the Wicked Witch of the West, who then mocks Dorothy and ridicules her desperation. At this moment, the audience becomes emotionally locked into empathy for Dorothy and hatred for the Witch. Another example can be found in *Raiders of the Lost Ark,* in the scene where Indiana Jones must run for his life while being pursued by natives intent on killing him. His enemy, Belloc, laughs with glee at Indiana's desperate situation.

One way to make the audience care about the protagonist is to show other characters unjustly mistreating him. Showing an injustice done to the protagonist by the antagonist is the surest way to establish the appropriate audience reactions. If the depicted injustice is accompanied by brutality, the scene will create sympathy for the victim and hatred for his antagonist. The first scene in which we see the antagonist of *Star Wars*, Darth Vader, shows him grabbing a rebel soldier by the neck, lifting him up off the floor, and choking him to death.

Abandonment or desertion also will generate audience empathy for a character, especially if the character is perceived to be small or weak and abandoned to a strange and hostile world. This technique is found in many popular films, including *E.T.* and *Wizard of Oz*.

A situation in which a character is trying to tell the world some important truth, and the audience knows that he is telling the truth, yet he is not believed by the other characters in the story, and perhaps even ridiculed by them, will create empathy for the character. Elliott is in this situation in the movie, *E.T.,* Molly in the movie *Ghost*, David Levinson in *Independence Day,* and Cole Sears in *Sixth Sense*.

The writer should make the people in the audience believe that what is happening to the characters in the story could happen to them. In crisis situations, show the characters having the emotions that the audience would have if the same thing were happening to them.

A protagonist displaying self-doubt will generate empathy in the audience. Make the protagonist fallible. Show the character reaching rock bottom, at his lowest point. Reveal his suffering and desperation. Show the character's vulnerability. All human beings tend to feel vulnerable at different times in their lives. Show what the protagonist fears most in the world. This fear makes the hero more human and easier for the audience to identify with. Use this fear in the story as the final obstacle that the protagonist must overcome before he can obtain his objective. This will help create more empathy for the protagonist in the audience.

In *Raiders of the Lost Ark*, Jones' fear of snakes is used in this way. In the opening sequence, he appears fearless as he overcomes every obstacle in his path and escapes certain death. It's only as the plane takes off that he reveals his humanity in his terror of snakes. The payoff to this setup comes later in the story when Jones has to overcome his fear of snakes as he descends into the Well of Souls to obtain his primary objective, the Lost Ark.

In *Titanic*, Rose must overcome her fear of disappointing her mother before she can be with Jack. In *Jaws*, Brody must overcome his fear of water before he can search for the great white shark.

The audience's emotions intensify to their highest pitch when the lives of the characters they most care about are endangered. Danger increases excitement in the audience that identifies with this character. It is in these situations that the audience becomes most involved with the protagonist and the story.

The audience also loves a character with a sense of humor. They will want to see more of a character that makes them laugh because his actions create joy and gives them pleasure. They will also become sad and angry if this character is harmed. The protagonist or the protagonist supporter should always have the best comic lines so that the audience will have greatest empathy for him. This is not true in *Batman*, where the antagonist, the Joker, was the source of most of the humor.

Besides creating empathy and enmity scenes for the protagonist and antagonist in the beginning of the story, many of the most successful films also have another major empathy scene. This is to ensure that the audience will emotionally bond with the protagonist and hate the antagonist before the final battle. The audience should hate the antagonist to such a great extent that they want to see him destroyed. Examples of this is the cackling witch mocking Dorothy in *The Wizard of Oz*; Bruce Wayne remembering the murder of his mother and father by the young Joker, before he engages with the Joker at the Gotham celebration, and the second humiliation of the Grinch by the Mayor who gives him an electric razor at the Whobilation Ceremony in the movie, *The Grinch*.

Underlying the classic Hollywood Three-Act Structure is a plotting structure that is used to take the audience on an emotional roller-coaster ride that ends with them having a **satisfying emotional experience**. Many popular movies begin by hooking the audience with scenes that terrorize them: a beautiful young woman on a moonlit ocean swim being eaten alive by a shark in *Jaws*; a powerful man being dragged into a metal cage and eaten alive by a raptor in *Jurassic Park*; a family being mugged in Gotham City in *Batman*; a librarian being terrorized by a ghost in *Ghostbusters;* and a little girl with her dog being pursued and terrorized by an unseen villain in *Wizard of Oz*. These situations "hook" the audience and emotionally engage them. They are also designed to elicit curiosity, since the source of evil behind these fearful moments is usually not revealed.

The emotional roller-coaster ride can be guaranteed by correctly structuring the relationship between the unique object, the protagonist, the antagonist, and the love interest throughout the three acts. At the end of Act One, the audience sees the protagonist prevail over the antagonist by preventing the antagonist from gaining possession of the unique object and the love interest. This is an emotional high point for the audience: they feel happiness in the belief that the protagonist, for whom they have empathy, will win and obtain his desires. At the end of the second act, the situation is reversed. The antagonist has possession of the love interest and the unique object, and the protagonist's situation appears to be hopeless. The audience now shares the protagonist's feelings of desperation and despair, for it appears to them that there is no way the hero will prevail. This is the emotional low point in the roller-coaster ride of the story. Then in the start of the third act, there is another major scene that elicits empathy for the protagonist, like the Wicked Witch in the crystal ball laughing at Dorothy, or Bruce Wayne realizing that the man who murdered his father and mother is Jack Napier, or when Peter Parker visits his Aunt May in the hospital and realizes that the Green Goblin knows he is Spider-Man. The audience shares the protagonist's pain and wants the antagonist to be destroyed.

The audience then cheers the protagonist in his battle with the villain in the climax scene, and they become ecstatic when he overcomes impossible odds and finally defeats the antagonist. **The hero triumphs but in an unexpected way**. The audience joins in with the members of the community in the movie as they celebrate the hero's victory and union with the love interest. The joy expressed by the people in the resolution scene of the movie is shared by the members of the audience. This is how to create an **emotionally satisfying experience** in the audience.

In conclusion, to create empathy in the audience for the protagonist, show situations where the protagonist suffers from jeopardy, terror, neglect, loneliness, unfairness, unkindness, injustice, desertion, abandonment, humiliation, frustration, insecurity, misunderstanding, desperation, or not being believed when he is telling the truth. Empathy scenes found in the megahit movies are described below.

Titanic: Jack Dawson is framed by Cal's bodyguard, who places the Heart of the Ocean jewel into Jack's pocket. Even though Jack proclaims his innocence, he is still taken away in handcuffs.

Star Wars: The small rebel spaceship is pursued by the gigantic Imperial battleship. Luke feels lonely and isolated because his uncle won't let him join his friends at college. Imperial Storm Troopers kill Luke's aunt and uncle, and destroy his home.

E.T.: E.T. is abandoned on the planet Earth. Elliott is not believed when he tells the truth about seeing a creature in the backyard. Elliott and his family were deserted by his father.

The Phantom Menace: Anakin Skywalker is a slave. He becomes upset when he has to leave his mother behind after he wins his freedom in the pod race.

Spider-Man: In the opening scene, we see Peter Parker being forced to run after the school bus while the students and driver in the bus laugh at him. Empathy is created for him when the Green Goblin attacks and terrorizes his aunt, and finally, when the Green Goblin forces Spider-Man to choose between saving the life of the woman he loves, MJ, or a tram filled with children.

The Lord of the Rings-The Return of the King: Gollum betrays Frodo and leads him into the cave of the spider, Shelob. Frodo fights Shelob but is poisoned by her stinger. She wraps him up in her webbing with the intention of eating him alive.

Jurassic Park: Dr. Alan Grant is a digger who hates computers. When he touches the screen of the computer, it malfunctions. He also despises children. He finds the children to be annoying. He terrorizes a little boy who called the raptors turkeys by describing how they stalk their prey. He has an attractive assistant who loves him. Later in the story he does everything he can to save the lives of the grandchildren of John Hammond, the creator of Jurassic Park.

Forrest Gump: Forrest, as a young boy is given braces that he must wear to straighten out his back. The teacher says that he is different. He is not normal and has to go to a special school.

Harry Potter and The Sorcerer's Stone: Harry is mistreated by his aunt, uncle, and cousin. He is forced to live in a room under the stairs.

Lord of the Rings-The Fellowship of the Ring: Frodo is pursued by the Dark Ringwraiths who want the ring.

The Lion King: Simba is made to believe that he is the cause of his father's death by his jealous uncle, Scar.

Lord of the Rings -The Two Towers: Frodo has a terrifying nightmare as he remembers the death of his mentor, Gandalf, by the fiery Balrog.

Return of the Jedi: Yoda tells Luke that he must confront and fight his father before he can finally become a Jedi Knight.

Independence Day: David Levinson is rejected by the wife he loves because of her interest in pursuing a political career. Russell Casse is ridiculed in the cafe by the men who joke about him being sexually abused by aliens. Captain Steve Hiller's dream of being a shuttle pilot is destroyed when he is rejected by NASA. President Tom Whitmore's wife dies from the wounds she has received from the aliens.

Star Wars-Attack of the Clones: Empathy is created for young Darth Vader when we watch his mother die in his arms.

The Sixth Sense: Dead people terrorize the young boy, Cole Sear. Dr. Malcom Crowe is shot by a disturbed former patient the night he and his wife celebrate receiving recognition from the city for his work as a child psychologist.

Empire Strikes Back: In the opening scene, Luke is attacked by a white snow creature. The creature pulls him into a cave and hangs him up by his feet. Luke is to be eaten by the snow creature.

Home Alone: Kevin is unfairly blamed for creating a mess at the family dinner. He is placed in isolation by his mother, then deserted by his family as they fly to Paris. Kevin, alone in his home, must defend it from the burglars.

Shrek: Empathy is created for Shrek when we watch him lose the love of his life because of a misunderstanding: he believes that Princess Fiona thinks that he is too ugly to love.

The Grinch: The Grinch as a young child is humiliated by his classmates in front of his love interest, Martha May Who, because he had cuts on his face from trying to shave off his facial hairs. At the ceremony for the Cheermeister of Whobilation, the Mayor presents him with an electric razor, just like the one that he used as a child. He relives the memories of his first humiliation.

Jaws: Capt. Martin Brody is slapped in the face by the mother of the boy who is killed by the shark. She tells him in front of a crowd that he knew the shark was in the water, that it had killed a girl, but Brody had refused to close the beach. This is unfair because Brody did try to close the beach, but the Mayor refused to allow this to occur.

Harry Potter and The Chamber of Secrets: His Guardians isolate Harry from his friends and will not allow him to return to Hogwarts.

Monsters, Inc.: Sulley must return the human child Boo to her home and believes that he will never see her again.

Batman: Bruce Wayne (Batman) is an orphan, who as a young child, witnessed the murder of his parents by Jack Napier (The Joker).

Men In Black: J finds K monitoring his lost love. J says to K "it is better to have loved and lost, than never to have loved at all." K tells J to "Try it!" K then shuts down his computer and walks away. Agent J shows concern for the farmer's wife and forces K to give her better new memories. J also shows concern for Dr. Laurel Weaver who has had her memories erased many times.

Pirates of the Caribbean: Captain Jack Sparrow sails into the harbor in a sinking boat. Will Turner loves Elizabeth Swan, but cannot show his love because he is not of the noble class. Liz's father wants her to marry Norrington, a man that she does not love.

Finding Nemo: Marlin's wife, Coral, and her eggs are destroyed by a barracuda. Only one egg survives, Nemo, who has a deformed fin.

Matrix Reloaded: Neo has nightmares watching the death of Trinity. This makes him vulnerable and sympathetic for the audience.

Writing Assignment: Study the scenes from the megahit movies listed above. Write a separate empathy scene for your protagonist and love interest. Then write an enmity scene for the antagonist in your story.

CHARACTER DEVELOPMENT
MAINTAINING AUDIENCE INVOLVEMENT

Personal Objectives

Character Motivation

Decisions: Hard Choices

Relationships: Lovers & Friends

Codes of Behavior

Transformations

Personalities

Supporting Characters

PERSONAL OBJECTIVES

The audience needs to know the dreams and goals of the major characters in order to take interest in what happens to them. Their dreams and the object that could satisfy these hopes determine each character's **primary objective**. The audience wants the characters to have dreams like their own: dreams of love, fulfillment, success, beauty, freedom, and power.

In order to achieve their primary objective, the characters in the story must also achieve subgoals. Each of these *subgoals* has an **object** or **objective** that must be obtained. These subgoal objectives are often needed to obtain the primary object: the subtasks that must first be completed. *Raiders of the Lost Ark* uses this structure. Jones' primary objective is to find the Ark of the Covenant, a concrete object. To accomplish this, he has the subgoal of finding the Headpiece to the Staff of Ra. Once he finds this, he must use the Headpiece to accomplish another subgoal, to locate the Well of Souls. Once that is found, he must next retrieve the Ark of the Covenant and get it to Cairo before the Nazis can possess it. These are all connected to the unique primary objective: the Ark of the Covenant.

In many of the popular films, the protagonist's primary objective becomes an attempt to either return home (*The Wizard of Oz, E.T., Finding Nemo, Monsters Inc.*) or to safeguard the home from destruction (*Shrek, Star Wars, Independence Day, The Phantom Menace, Jaws, The Lion King, Batman, Men In Black*). Both these objectives exist in *Home Alone:* Kevin's mother's objective is to return home, while Kevin's objective is to safeguard his home from destruction. Explicated in terms of character psychological motivation, "Home" is that place where the characters feel safe and secure with those who love them. This is an objective with which many people in the audience can identify.

Titanic
The primary objective of both Jack and Rose is to ride the Titanic to America, the land of Freedom. Later in the movie, Jack wants to save Rose's life: prevent her from jumping overboard, prevent her from marrying Cal, and prevent her from drowning after the Titanic sinks.

Star Wars
Luke's primary objective is to be at college with his friends. Later, he achieves the friendship and recognition of the rebels. Darth Vader wants the plans to the Death Star. Princess Leia wants Obi-Wan Kenobe to help her destroy the Death Star. The Rebel Forces want to protect their home planet from destruction.

The Phantom Menace
Queen Amidala wants to get to the Senate to appeal to them to save her home planet from invasion. Anakin Skywalker's primary objective is to obtain freedom for himself and his mother. He wants to win the pod race. The Jedi Knights want to protect Queen Amidala.

E.T.
E.T. wants to get back home. Elliott wants E.T. to stay with him and be his friend. Elliott's mother wants to protect her home from the government intruders.

The Lion King
Simba wants to become a great and powerful king like his father, Mufasa. Scar wants to be the ruler of the Pride Lands.

Return of the Jedi
Luke wants to return to Dagobah to continue his training with Yoda to become a Jedi Knight.

Batman
Batman wants to save his home, Gotham City, from the criminals. The Joker wants to control Gotham and poison the citizens.

Jurassic Park
John Hammond, the creator of Jurassic Park, wants to create a great tourist attraction. Dr. Grant is a scientist who wants to obtain new knowledge about dinosaurs. They later both want to survive the attack of the dinosaurs and get out of Jurassic Park alive.

Independence Day
The protagonists want to save their world and the human race from annihilation from the aliens.

Home Alone
The burglars want to rob Kevin's house, and Kevin wants to protect his home from the thieves.

Jaws
Capt. Brody wants to kill the Great White Shark because it is destroying his home, the village, and beaches of Amity.

Empire Strikes Back
Luke Skywalker wants to become a Jedi Knight.

Forrest Gump
Forrest Gump's primary objective is to stay completely focused in the moment. Then, like the feather that symbolizes him, he floats from situation to situation. His behavior in these different situations is the core of the story. His "home" is always with him because he is always totally engrossed in the present moment.

Men In Black
J and K want to save the earth from destruction. They must stop the Edgar-Bug from leaving earth with the Galaxy around Orion's Belt. If they fail, the earth will be destroyed.

Sixth Sense
Dr. Malcolm's primary objective is to save Cole Sears. He wants to help the child overcome the terror he experiences from seeing dead people. Cole wants to stop seeing dead people.

The Grinch
The Grinch wants revenge on the people of Whoville. He wants to destroy Christmas and the happiness that it brings them because they humiliated him as a small child and destroyed his chance of happiness with Martha May Whovier.

The Wizard of Oz
Dorothy's objective in the beginning of the movie is to find a place where there are no problems. Once in Oz, her goal is to return home to Kansas. The Tin Man wants a heart, the Scarecrow brains, and the Lion courage. Elmira Gulch wants Toto destroyed. The Wicked Witch wants the ruby slippers, which will make her the most powerful being in Oz.

Shrek
Shrek wants the privacy of his home (the swamp). He wants all the fairy tale creatures to leave.

Spider-Man
Peter wants MJ.

Finding Nemo
Marlin wants to find Nemo. Nemo wants to escape from the fish tank and get back home.

Monsters, Inc.
Sulley wants to generate more energy because of the power shortage.

Bruce Almighty
Bruce wants to be the TV News Anchorman.

Matrix Trilogy
Neo wants to know what the Matrix is in the first movie. Then Neo wants to save Trinity's life in the second movie. Neo wants to save the humans in Zion from destruction by the Machines in the final movie.

Pirates of the Caribbean
Captain Jack Sparrow wants his ship, the Black Pearl.
Barbossa wants the Aztec Gold coin.
Will Turner wants to save Elizabeth from the pirates.
Elizabeth wants to marry Will Turner.

Harry Potter: The Sorcerer's Stone
Harry wants to understand the mystery of his life.
Voldemort wants the Sorcerer's stone.

Lord of the Rings Trilogy
Sauron wants the Ring. Frodo wants to destroy the Ring.

CHARACTER MOTIVATION

"To give a motivational explanation of an action is to explain it as in some way due to a 'want' or a 'desire'."
—William Alston, *Motives and Motivation*

"...emotions are important determiners of motives...our theory ought to be capable of accounting for certain classes of behaviors in terms of certain emotions."
—Andrew Ortony, *Cognitive Theory of Emotions*

In order to maintain audience interest, it is necessary that **the audience becomes emotionally involved** with the characters. For this to happen, the actions of the characters must be believable. This means that the members of the audience would **feel** the same way and act the same way, if they were in the same situation as the characters in the movie. Once the audience understands the **motive** a character has for pursuing his primary objective, and the audience accepts this as a reasonable motive, the character then becomes believable, and the audience will care about him.

Some primary motives consist of organic processes, like *sex, hunger, thirst, the elimination of bodily waste, sleep*, and *exercise*. The others are associated with fundamental emotions: *anger-pugnacity, fear-escape, tenderness-protection, zest-mastery, sympathy, wonder-curiosity* and *creativity*.

The Humanist tradition in psychology focuses on the need for *competence and control* as basic motivations. Abraham Maslow, in *The Psychology of Being,* developed a motivational theory that focuses on the person striving to reach their full potential. He acknowledges **a hierarchy of needs**, where needs lower on the hierarchy are stronger and must be satisfied before needs higher on the hierarchy are activated. After the basic physiological needs of hunger, thirst, and sex, humans have a need to feel safe. The desire for security is one of the primary motivations of characters in popular films.

Next on the hierarchy is the need for love and the feeling of belonging to a person or group. An example of this is Elliott's need to be accepted by Michael's friends in *E.T.* Once this is satisfied, the esteem needs motivate the individual: the need for self-esteem and esteem from others.

Popular movies are stories about characters who have **needs,** not characters who do not know what they want or who want something only half-heartedly. Characters must have the fortitude to overcome all the obstacles that will be thrown in their path. If they are weak-willed, the audience will lose interest in them. This is why revenge is used as the protagonist's motivation in many films. It is a powerful emotional force that drives characters toward a clear goal. The opening scene in these films usually shows the hero experiencing a major injustice, which generates audience empathy for him. This incident, along with the protagonist's attempts to bring the perpetrators to justice, forms the foundation of his motivation.

As Eugene Vale states in *The Technique of Screen and Television Writing*, "A human being will act to remove pain...The lack of something wanted as well as the presence of something unwanted is reflected in pain. The human being acts to acquire something which it wants or to eliminate something which it does not want."

Titanic: Rose wants to be an artist, a free creative spirit like Jack.

Star Wars: Luke's search for self-esteem and a father figure that will provide him with a sense of security motivates much of his behavior.

The Phantom Menace: Anakin Skywalker wants to become a Jedi Knight so that he then could return and free his mother and the other slaves on Tatooine.

E.T.: Elliott is a lonely child, abandoned by his father and excluded by his brother's friends. He needs to feel that he belongs. His need for a friend motivates his relationship with E.T.

Jurassic Park: Dr. Alan Grant first wants to dig up the bones of dinosaurs, but then he wants to save the lives of the children. Dr. John Hammond wants to create a fantastic amusement park, more real than his first flea circus. He feels a need to create something special.

The Lion King: Simba runs away because he feels he caused his father's death.

Return of the Jedi: Luke wants to complete his training with Yoda and become a Jedi Knight so that he will be able to use the power of the force to defeat the Empire.

Independence Day: The four protagonists all want to save the world from being destroyed by the aliens: President Tom Whitmore because it is his duty as President; Russell Casse for payback because he was sexually abused when abducted by aliens; Captain Steve Hillier because they killed his best friend and it is his duty as an Air Force pilot; and David Levinson because he always wanted to save the world.

Batman: Bruce Wayne needs to overcome the feelings of helplessness that he experienced as he watched his parents being murdered when he was a young child. He has a need to feel safe, as does the community of Gotham City. The Joker wants esteem from others: he wants his "face on the one-dollar bill."

Home Alone: Kevin needs to feel that his family loves him. He also needs self-esteem because of his inability to take care of himself. Finally, he needs to safeguard his home against the burglars.

Jaw: Police Capt. Martin Brody wants to save the people of Amity from the shark that has already killed three people and almost killed his son. He feels guilty about the death of the child. The child's mother blames him unjustly, and he wants his reputation back.

Men in Black: J and K want to save the world. J feels a need to be back with the woman he loves and lost long ago. This is the need to love and be loved. He finally leaves the MIB to return to her at the end of the story.

The Grinch: The Grinch feels hatred for the Whos because as a child he was humiliated by the Who children in school. He feels a need for revenge and desires the esteem of others and public recognition of his importance.

Sixth Sense: Dr. Malcolm has a need for redemption. He feels that he failed the patient who committed suicide in his bathroom. The young boy, Cole Sears, appears to have similar emotional problems. Dr. Malcolm feels a need to save this boy and, thereby, remove his feelings of failure and inadequacy. This will enhance his self-esteem.

Empire Strikes Back: Luke is first motivated to become a Jedi Knight when he has a vision of Obie Wan Kenobe during the snowstorm that tells him to study under Yoda. While studying with Yoda, Luke has a vision of his friends, Han and Princess Leia, in trouble. He leaves Yoda to save them.

Forrest Gump: Forrest loves Jenny, even though for most of the film, she will not accept his love.

The Wizard of Oz: Dorothy's feelings of insecurity create her motivation to find a place where there are no problems. Once she discovers that Oz is filled with dangers, she is motivated to return to the safety of her home.

Harry Potter and the Sorcerer's Stone: Harry wants to learn the secret of his life.

Spider-Man: Peter Parker wants the love of MJ.

Bruce Almighty: Bruce first wants to be the famous TV Anchorman, then he wants to have the power of God.

Harry Potter and the Chamber of Secret: Harry wants to be with his friends back in Hogwarts.

Matrix Reloaded: Neo wants to keep Trinity alive. He needs her love.

Shrek: Shrek wants to be left alone in his swamp home.

Finding Nemo: Marlin wants to keep Nemo safe, then find him and bring him home. Nemo wants to have the respect of his peers and to overcome his bad fin.

Pirates of the Caribbean: Captain Jack Sparrow wants his ship, the Black Pearl. Will Turner wants to save Liz's life. Liz wants to marry Will Turner.

The Lord of the Rings Trilogy: Frodo wants to destroy the Ring in the fires of Mount Doom, but in the final scene, he wants to keep the Ring for himself.

DECISIONS: HARD CHOICES

"A *decision*, whether individual or group, involves a *choice* between two or more options or *acts*, each of which will produce one of several *outcomes*."
—Michael Resnik, *Choices*

The protagonist is the character who makes most of the major decisions, and who must respond to the decisions and actions of the antagonist.

To achieve their goals, characters must make **decisions**. They must devise strategies and plans of action. They must make choices between alternative tactics. When faced with obstacles, they must decide how best to overcome them. They also must decide whether they will cast aside their basic code of ethics to achieve these goals. Whether "the end will always justify the means."

Self-conflict is generated by characters making difficult decisions while pursuing their primary objectives. Often, they reject objects or people they value in order to reach their goals. These difficult decisions captivate members of the audience, who vicariously place themselves in the same situation. Characters who make the tough decisions, who choose to "do the right thing" under difficult circumstances, gain the audience's empathy. The writer should focus on the "hard choices" a character makes.

The audience doesn't want just to hear about these decisions. They want to watch the characters go through the decision making process. They also want to see the characters in torment as they make difficult choices. Viewing a human being going through the process of trying to make an emotionally stressful decision is always more dramatic than watching just the result of that decision. If the audience does not see this transformation, they will lose emotional involvement and empathy for the character. The character will no longer be "human" for them.

A decision made by one character sets in motion a decision by his adversary. For example, the protagonist must decide how to obtain his primary objective before the antagonist gets it. These chains of decisions, one resulting from the other, generate the conflicts that propels the story forward to its climax.

The audience is more concerned with the results of a character's decisions than the accidents that happen to him. If there is an accident, the audience is primarily interested in how the character responds to this accident, not whether this accident will resolve his conflict for him.

The most difficult choices are the emotional ones: those that involve a choice between the primary objective and the character's close relationships with lovers, a spouse, parents, children, siblings, or friends. The members of the audience can easily relate to these conflicts for they also often have to make these types of choices.

The scenes that have the most emotional impact are those in which the protagonist chooses his primary objective over a relationship in order to guarantee the survival of the community. This is a self-sacrificing "moral choice" in which he chooses to act for the benefit of the community rather than achieve his own selfish objective.

Once a character chooses his primary objective, he can alter his choice of subgoals, plans, procedures, tactics, and methods, but he cannot change his commitment to this primary objective. If he abandons his primary objective, the story is over. It ends with the character's failure to achieve his primary goal. This is different from the situation in which the protagonist must achieve important subgoals that change in order to accomplish his primary objective. For once the protagonist makes the decision to pursue a primary objective, the story ends when he either achieves this objective or fails. Below are listed some of the important decisions made by the characters in the megahit movies.

Titanic
Rose leaves the lifeboat and returns to the Titanic to be with Jack.

Star Wars
Luke decides to go with Ben to Alderan in order to fight with the rebels. Han Solo decides not to stay and fight with the rebels.

The Phantom Menace
The Jedi Qui-Gon decides to gamble with Watto for the supplies he needs and for Anakin's freedom. Queen Amidala decides to get down on her knees and beg the Gungan King, Boss Nass, to help fight the invasion.

E.T.
Elliott decides to help E.T get back home to his planet.

The Lion King
Simba decides to return to the Pride Lands and fight Scar.

Batman
Bruce Wayne decides to accept the Joker's challenge to meet him in a one-on-one fight during the Gotham City celebration.

Return of the Jedi
Luke decides to return to study with Yoda after freeing his friends from Jabba the Hut. Luke decides not to join the dark side of the force.

Independence Day
Captain Steve Hiller decides to end his July 4th holiday with Jasmine and return to El Toro. He also decides to "borrow" the helicopter in order to search for her. President Tom Whitmore decides to launch a nuclear attack against the alien spaceships. David Levinson decides to fly with Steve Hillier to give the alien mother ship a computer virus. Russell Casse sacrifices himself by flying his fighter into the alien's prime weapon.

Jurassic Park
Dr. Grant decides to light a flare to distract the dinosaur that is trying to break into the tourist car to eat John's two grandchildren. He places himself in jeopardy to save the life of the children.

Home Alone
Kevin decides to protect his home from the burglars. Kevin's mother decides to leave Paris and return home to Kevin.

Forrest Gump
Forrest doesn't have difficulty making decisions, but instead does pretty much whatever people ask him to do, like joining the football team and the army. Like the feather, he goes with the flow.

Jaws
The mayor decides not to close the beach for the July 4th holiday. Capt. Brody decides to hire Quint to kill the shark. Capt. Brody forces the mayor to decide to sign the voucher to hire Quint.

Men In Black
J decides to join the MIB. K decides to quit the MIB and return to the woman he loves.

Empire Strikes Back
Luke decides to leave the retreating rebel ships and search for Yoda so that he can be trained to become a Jedi Knight. Luke decides to leave Yoda in order to save his friends, Han and Princess Leia. Luke decides to fall into the abyss of the spaceship instead of joining the dark side of the force and his father, Darth Vader.

Sixth Sense
Cole Sears decides to tell Dr. Malcolm his secret: he sees dead people.

The Wizard of Oz
Dorothy decides to run away from home, to journey to the Wizard of Oz, and to get the broomstick from the Wicked Witch of the West. The Wicked Witch decides to take the ruby slippers from Dorothy. The Scarecrow decides to go with Dorothy to Oz in order to obtain brains. The Tin Man decides to go to Oz in order to obtain a heart. The Lion decides to go to Oz in order to obtain courage. Dorothy decides that she wants to return home to Kansas.

The Grinch
The Grinch decides to accept the invitation of Cindy Lou Who to become the Who's Cheermeister of the Whobilation.

Shrek
Shrek decides to stop Fiona from marrying Lord Farquaard.

Spider-Man
Peter decides not to tell MJ that he loves her.

Finding Nemo
Nemo decides to swim up the funnel in order to clog the fish tank.

Monsters Inc
Sulley decides to take Boo back home.

Bruce Almighty
Bruce decides to ask God to find someone who will make Grace happy.

Matrix Trilogy
Neo decides to save Trinity instead of Zion.

Pirates of the Caribbean
Elizabeth decides to marry Norrington to get him to save Will.

Harry Potter: The Sorcerer's Stone
Harry decides to fight Prof. Quirell/Voldemort for the Sorcerer's Stone.

Lord of the Rings Trilogy
Frodo decides not to destroy the Ring. Aragorn decides to lead the remaining soldiers of Gondor against Mordor so that Frodo will have a chance to destroy the Ring.

RELATIONSHIPS: LOVERS & FRIENDS

"Characters rarely exist alone—they exist in relationships...the dynamic between the characters can be as important as any individual character quality."
—Linda Seger, *Creating Unforgettable Characters*

"...people's self-esteem and their self-concept changed in sheer reaction to the kinds of people they found themselves among, and changed even more in response to the positive or negative remarks that people made to them."
—Jerome Bruner, *Acts of Meaning*

The most difficult choices that the protagonist must make are the emotional ones, those that involve a choice between his primary objective and his primary relationships: lover, spouse, mother, father, daughter or son, sister or brother, and friends. Decisions that the character makes which place any of these relationships in jeopardy or danger produce scenes that generate the most tension and are the most emotionally riveting for the audience.

The audience should clearly understand the protagonist's feelings about these relationships. Does he love the other characters, hate them, or is he indifferent? The protagonist gains the most audience empathy when he is forced to place another character that he loves in jeopardy in order to achieve a "higher good." He suffers a personal sacrifice for the good of the community.

These are also the decisions and choices that generate the most emotional conflicts in scenes. Characters are made known to us through conflict, and every action and every situation reveal something about their beliefs and personality. Characters are revealed by showing them relating to others who are in conflict with them over their objectives.

There are as many ways for one character to love as there are different types of people in the world. One conception of love is the active concern for the life and growth of the other that we love. When the satisfaction and security of another person becomes as important to us as our own, then love exists.

Loyalty to friends who are on the quest with the protagonist is a common theme in these popular films. Friends function as a surrogate family that helps the protagonist to achieve his goals when the "natural family" fails. Most of the protagonists in these popular films are either abandoned by their families (E.T., the Grinch, and Kevin in *Home Alone*), or separated from their families (Harry Potter in *Sorcerer's Stone*, Peter Parker in *Spider-Man*, Bruce Wayne in *Batman*, Luke and Princess Leia in *Star Wars*, Anakin Skywalker in *The Phantom Menace,* and Nemo in *Finding Nemo)*.

A character is revealed not only through how he resolves the conflicts with his friends and relatives, but also how he relates to other characters that oppose his attempts to achieve his objectives. These other characters can be classified in terms of those that help him obtain his objective, and those that oppose him. The writer must clearly show the audience how the main character emotionally interacts with these characters. What does he want from them and what do they want from him? How do they resolve their conflicts? What methods and codes of behavior do they use when dealing with each other?

A standard trait that the antagonist has is the tendency to betray his companions when it suits him and to ruthlessly destroy his supporters if they fail him. The antagonist is also usually consumed with hatred for the protagonist.

The issue of trust and betrayal is central to many of the popular films. A character that betrays another earns the enmity of the audience and is felt to be deserving of destruction. The audience will feel no remorse for any character that is killed if he is shown to have betrayed the trust and caused harm to the protagonist for whom the audience has empathy.

Titanic
Rose is in conflict with her mother and the aristocratic society into which she will marry. She has an appreciation for art and would like to be a free spirit. Jack is an artistic free spirit who leads a "rootless life" as characterized by Rose's mother.

Star Wars
Luke is an orphan and lives with his aunt and uncle who are killed by the Imperial Storm Troopers. Luke develops loyalty to his friends in the rebellion. Darth Vader has no friends among the Imperial soldiers, with whom he is ruthless whenever the situation demands. Obie Won Kenobe sacrifices his life for Luke and the Rebel cause. Princess Leia appears willing to sacrifice the rebellion to save the lives of the innocent people of Alderan. But she gives the Commander of the Death Star old information that would not threaten the rebellion. Initially, she exhibits an intense dislike for Han Solo. Han seems to care for no one but himself, yet he returns to help his friend Luke in the final battle sequence.

The Phantom Menace
Anakin Skywalker has a good relationship with his mother, who is very supportive.

E.T.
Elliott is loyal and committed to E.T., who is abandoned by the alien spaceship. E.T. then makes friends with the children. Elliott was abandoned by his father. Michael and his friends are loyal to Elliott once they have sworn that Elliott "has the power."

Jurassic Park
Dr. John Hammond loves his two grandchildren who also love him. Ellie Sattler loves Dr. Alan Grant, and he loves her.

The Lion King
Scar schemes with Jackals to get control of the Pride Lands. Simba has as friends Timon and Pumba, when he lives a carefree life in the jungle. Rafiki, the wise baboon, functions as his spiritual guide.

Return of the Jedi
Luke Skywalker discovers that his love interest, Princess Leia, is really his sister, and that they are both the children of Darth Vader. Luke has to fight Darth Vader to defeat the Empire.

Independence Day
Captain Steve Hiller has a relationship with his girlfriend Jasmine and her little son. He also has a good friendship with the other pilot who is killed in the first battle with the aliens. David Levinson has a relationship with his father and his ex-wife. President Whitmore has a good relationship with his wife and child. Russell Casse has a combative relationship with his children.

Batman
Bruce Wayne is a rich orphan who lives alone in a mansion. His only friend is the family butler. The Joker disfigures his girlfriend Alicia. The Joker shoots his loyal henchman Bob because Bob didn't tell him that Batman had a plane.

Home Alone
Kevin's family is angry with him for making a mess while they are eating. His siblings have contempt for Kevin. Kevin is loved by his mother. Kevin befriends the old man who lives next door, even though his brother says he is a murderer. The old man later saves Kevin from the burglars.

Forrest Gump
Forrest has a strong supportive relationship with his mother. His father had abandoned the family. His best friend since childhood is Jenny.

Jaws
Capt. Brody has a good supportive relationship with his wife and son. He becomes very upset when his son is almost killed by the shark.

Men In Black
Both J and K must sever all emotional relations from people not officially connected to MIB, yet, K misses the woman he left behind.

Sixth Sense
Dr. Malcolm was happily married to his wife in the beginning of the movie, but then they grew "distant" and could not communicate with one another (because he was killed in the opening scene and became a ghost that she could not see). Cole Sears is picked on by the other children and has a terrible secret that he cannot share with his mother and other people: he sees dead people.

Empire Strikes Back
Luke discovers that Darth Vader is his father. He screams with anguish and despair and allows himself to fall into the deep shaft of the spaceship.

The Grinch
The Grinch is abandoned at birth and found on the doorstep of the sisters, Clarinella and Rose Whobiddie. He is humiliated at the school party and then isolates himself in a cave above Whoville. He hates all the Whos and only relates to his dog.

The Wizard of Oz
Dorothy loves her aunt and uncle but runs away when they allow Elmira Gulch to take possession of Toto. She tries to return to her Aunt Em when she believes her aunt is sick. Dorothy also cares for the needs of her companions while on the journey to Oz. The Wicked Witch's only companions are the winged monkeys. She is ruthless and terrorizes any creature that gets in her way. She hates Dorothy. The Scarecrow, Tin Man and Lion are all loyal to Dorothy, and they are committed to rescuing her from the Wicked Witch.

Shrek
Shrek lives alone and likes it that way.
Donkey wants to be Shrek's friend.

Spider-Man
Peter is an orphan living with his aunt and uncle.
Peter does not like his uncle trying to act like his father.

Finding Nemo
Nemo's mother and siblings are eaten by a Barracuda.
Marlin is over-protective of Nemo.

Monsters, Inc.
Sulley has Mike as his best friend.

Bruce Almighty
Bruce has his girlfriend Grace who loves him, but Bruce is obsessed with success.

Matrix Trilogy
Neo is loyal to Morpheus and Trinity.

Pirates of the Caribbean
Captain Jack Sparrow betrays everyone when it is to his advantage, yet he joins forces with Will and Liz to defeat Barbossa.

Harry Potter: The Sorcerer's Stone
Harry is an orphan that lives with abusive guardians.
Harry makes friends with Ron and Hermione at Hogwarts.

Lord of the Rings Trilogy
The Fellowship of the Ring supports each other on the Quest.

CODES OF BEHAVIOR

"Character is that which reveals moral purpose, showing what kinds of things a man chooses or avoids." —Aristotle, *Poetics*

"A character in a story makes choices, and when these choices involve the lives and interests of other characters, they are moral choices. For if some judgment has overriding social importance, prescribes a course of action, is universalizable, and pertains to the general welfare of a social group, we can be reasonably assured that the judgment is a moral one..."
—Tom Beauchamp, *Philosophical Ethics*

"...the hero shows us what matters, what has value, what has meaning among the random and meaningless events of life."
—Orson Scott Card, *Characters and Viewpoint*

"Many films deal with characters at a time when they must make moral choices, confronting their values and choosing those that they will live by." —Linda Seger, *Creating Unforgettable Characters*

A character's **code of behavior (ethics)** guides his interpersonal actions. His ethics determine the way he treats the other characters. Only under intense conflict will his true code of behavior be revealed, for the audience will see whether he maintains his principles while pursuing his objective, or whether he discards them whenever it is convenient.

The protagonist's principles usually differ from those of the antagonist, but this is not always the case. The protagonist and antagonist can hold very similar codes of behavior. Many modern protagonists lack the values and virtues of the traditional hero. But they do reveal personal codes of behavior. Their value systems may not be the same as the prevailing culture, but they have a private code that is humane and perhaps even superior to the official code. The audience respects the tenacity of the anti-hero that maintains his code and breaks all society's rules while retaining his integrity.

Conflict is guaranteed by having both the protagonist and antagonist pursue the same unique objective, which only one of them can possibly attain, but with incompatible codes of behavior. The story then becomes an examination of which principles will help the characters obtain the objective, and what the cost will be to both the characters and the community. The character's codes are revealed in the decisions he makes in order to overcome obstacles while in pursuit of his objective.

Conflict is also created when a character's code of behavior becomes an obstacle to his efforts to attain his primary objective. These are self-conflicts. The character must decide between changing his objective or his code. If he changes his code, then his character is transformed.

Titanic
The wealthy people on the Titanic all exhibit aristocratic codes of behavior and promote the class distinctions that separate them from the working class people on the decks below.

Star Wars
Luke places his own life in jeopardy in order to help the Rebels destroy the Death Star. Darth Vader ruthlessly tortures Princess Leia in order to get the plans. Obie Won Kenobe sacrifices his physical existence so that Luke and the others can escape. Princess Leia, to save the innocent people of Alderan, reveals the location of the Rebel base. The Imperial commander destroys Alderan even though Princess Leia told him what he wanted to know. Han Solo is a mercenary who appears to desert the rebellion in order to save his own skin but returns to help Luke in the final battle.

The Phantom Menace
The Jedi Knights have a code of behavior binding their actions. They can only defend the life of Queen Amidala but not wage war against the Trade Federation without the permission of the Senate.

E.T.
Elliott deceives the government in order to free E.T. The government agents monitor Elliott's conversations and search his home while he is away.

Jurassic Park
The lawyer runs out of the car and leaves Dr. Hammond's two grandchildren to face the T-Rex alone. The lawyer is later eaten by the T-Rex while trying to hide in an outhouse. Both Dr. Grant and Ian, the Chaos Scientist put their own lives at stake to protect the children.

The Lion King
Because of the shame he feels in causing the death of his father, Simba accepts exile from his kingdom. Simba later accepts the responsibility of fighting Scar and the Jackals for the control of the Pride Lands.

Return of the Jedi
Luke refuses to join the dark side and use his powers for evil.

Men In Black
J and K must work anonymously and sever contact with people outside MIB.

Independence Day
Captain Steve Hiller loves Jasmine even if she is an exotic dancer. He will not sacrifice her for his career in the Air Force. David Levinson still loves his ex-wife, even though she has divorced him. President Whitmore believes he must use nuclear weapons to save mankind, even if it may cause environmental damage to the planet. Russell Casse believes he must sacrifice his own life to help save mankind.

Batman
Bruce Wayne places his life in jeopardy in order to safeguard the community. The Joker insanely attempts to poison the community in order to control Gotham.

Jurassic Park
It is the greed of Dennis, the computer technician, who places the characters in jeopardy by shutting down the computer power to the security system. Dennis only cares about getting more money.

Home Alone
Kevin protects his home from being robbed. His mother gives up her Paris vacation to get back home to Kevin.

Forrest Gump
Forrest has a simple moral code of loyalty and love for his mother and Jenny. He is always doing what he believes is the right thing. Forrest keeps his promise to be a business partner with Bubba even after Bubba was killed. He gives fifty percent of the profits to Bubba's family. Forrest always keeps his word.

Jaws
Police Capt. Brody feels he has the duty and responsibility to protect the people of Amity.

Sixth Sense
Dr. Malcolm is a kind man who sincerely wants to help children who have emotional problems.

Empire Strikes Back
Luke Skywalker decides not to join the dark side of the force and be with his father, Darth Vader.

The Grinch
The Grinch is a mean and vicious character determined to revenge himself on the people of Whoville because of the humiliations that he experienced as a child.

The Wizard of Oz
Dorothy tries to save the life of Toto by giving the Wicked Witch the Ruby Slippers. This makes her vulnerable and places her at the mercy of the Witch. When this attempt fails, the Witch ruthlessly plans to kill Dorothy for the slippers. The Scarecrow, Tin Man, and Lion all decide to risk their own lives to save Dorothy.

Shrek
Donkey feels that he must keep his promise and not tell Shrek that Fiona becomes ugly at night.

Spider-Man
Peter believes that with great power comes great responsibilities that often force personal sacrifice.

Finding Nemo
Gill feels guilty about putting Nemo's life in danger. Therefore, he places himself in jeopardy to save Nemo from Darla.

Monsters Inc
Sulley knows that the right thing to do is return Boo home and shred her door, even though that means he will never see her again.

Bruce Almighty
Bruce is willing to lose Grace if that's what it takes to make her happy.

Matrix Trilogy
Neo sacrifices his life to save the humans in Zion from destruction by the Machines.

Pirates of the Caribbean
Liz returns to the cave to save Jack. Will risks his life to stop Jack from being hanged. Barbossa makes Liz and Jack walk the plank.

Harry Potter-The Sorcerer's Stone
Ron sacrifices himself on the chessboard so that Harry can get the Sorcerer's Stone.

Lord of the Rings Trilogy
Frodo accepts the mission to carry the Ring to Mount Doom. King Theoden decides to ride to the aid of Gondor. Aragorn decides to attack the Black Gates of Mordor to help Frodo.

TRANSFORMATIONS

"Recognition, as the name indicates, is a change from ignorance to knowledge... the recognition which is most intimately connected with the plot and action is, as we have said, the recognition of persons. This recognition, combined with Reversal, will produce either pity or fear, and actions producing these effects are those which, by our definition, Tragedy represents."
—Aristotle, *Poetics*

A character goes through a **transformation** and changes when the obstacles he encounters while in pursuit of his objective force him to alter his values. He changes his code of behavior, or he keeps his code and fails to obtain his primary objective. In the craft of screenwriting, this is often called "the character arc" or the "arc of the story."

Powerful scenes are constructed whenever a character changes his fundamental values: he can no longer believe something he held to be true. This will be a significant change for the characters. In order to maintain audience empathy, this change must be believable. If not, the audience will no longer identify with the protagonist.

The protagonist and other major characters should be transformed by their experiences. They should not be the same after the climax. Irrevocable changes occur in them because of the decisions they make and the actions they take in their efforts to overcome obstacles that blocked the attainment of their goals. Growth comes from inner conflicts generated by obstacles, because a character will reflect on his code of behavior and change it.

Besides self-transformation, the primal relationships of the protagonist usually change. The transitions should be gradual and not abrupt. To avoid melodrama, the character must be shown going through a series of small changes. This ensures that the audience will believe the transformation. As Lajos Egri states in *The Art of Dramatic Writing*, "real characters must be given the chance to reveal themselves, and we must be given a chance to observe the significant changes which take place in them."

Often the relationship of the lovers goes from hatred to love, as shown in *Star Wars* by Princess Leia and Han Solo. Each relationship will change in some way, even if not to this extreme. Often, it may just be that a character has a better understanding of himselves and others.

The protagonist often makes a major discovery about himself at the end of the story. In the climax his conflict is resolved, a basic truth of human existence is revealed, and the protagonist comes to a new understanding of himself and the world. Traditionally, the protagonist gains wisdom, conquers some weakness, and emerges stronger. The antagonist usually refuses to change his code, which leads to a destruction of himself and his supporters, while the protagonist's transformations usually result in a better code that benefits both himself and the community.

Titanic
Rose decides to give up the ideals of the aristocratic life and to live an artistic life with Jack.

Star Wars
Luke, Princess Leia, and Han Solo reveal that characters with skill, courage, and perseverance can triumph over impossible odds and defeat the Empire.

The Phantom Menace
Jar Jar is made a General by Boss Nass because he helped to unify the Gungan and the Naboo, and thereby gains the respect of the world.

E.T.
Elliott and E.T discover that friendship and love can cause pain, and that even if they can't be together forever, their love for each other will survive.

The Lion King
Simba realizes that he can't abandon his destiny, and if the world is to thrive, he must assume his proper role in the circle of life.

Forrest Gump
Forrest goes from being an outcast to becoming the pride of his community (football player, ping pong player, and war hero) because he completely focuses on what he does at the moment. He changes by achieving public esteem and finally the love of Jenny, but his core never changes.

Return of the Jedi
Luke gains strength and knowledge from the force, and ultimately, with the help of his father, is able to defeat the Empire.

Men In Black
K finally decides to leave MIB and return to the woman he left behind. J replaces K and takes Dr. Laurel Weaver as his partner.

Independence Day
Captain Steve Hiller does not have to sacrifice Jasmine to become an astronaut. David Levinson wins back the love of his ex-wife. President Whitmore leads the fighters into battle and helps to save the world. Russell Casse regains his self-respect and public-esteem by helping to destroy the alien spacecraft.

Batman
Bruce Wayne transforms from a helpless child who watches his parents murdered to an effective crime fighter. He also changes from a man who will not reveal the truth about his secret life, to sharing this knowledge with the woman he loves, Vicki Vale. The Joker changes from a suave gangster into an insane mass murderer in pursuit of power.

Jurassic Park
Dr. Grant develops paternal instincts and an appreciation for children as he protects the lives of Dr. Hammond's grandchildren from the dinosaurs.

Home Alone
Kevin gains self-esteem and the respect of his siblings after he defends his home from the burglars.

Jaws
Capt. Brody becomes more assertive and aggressive with the mayor after his son is almost killed by the shark. He forces the mayor to sign the voucher to hire Quint to kill the shark.

Sixth Sense
Dr. Malcolm finally realizes that he is dead; that he died from the wound he received when shot by his distraught former patient. Cole Sears understands that he has special abilities that enable him to see dead people, but he also understands that this is a gift that he should use to help these lost souls.

Empire Strikes Back
Luke transforms by learning the ways of the force with the help of Yoda. His supernatural powers increase. He also becomes more mature after the discovery that his real father is Darth Vader.

The Grinch
The Grinch saves the life of Cindy Lou Who then returns the Christmas Gifts to Whoville. He apologizes to the Whos, and then is accepted back into their community.

The Wizard of Oz
Dorothy realizes that you can't run away from problems, and that there is no perfect world "over the rainbow." If you can't find the courage, intelligence, and compassion to solve your problems at home surrounded by those who love you, you won't be able to do it anywhere. You have the power within you; you just have to believe in yourself. The Wicked Witch doesn't grow or change and is destroyed by her pursuit of power. The Scarecrow, Tin Man, and Lion all come to realize that they already had the virtues that they sought, but a journey filled with conflicts and obstacles was necessary for them to understand this.

Shrek
Shrek goes from being a loner to marrying Princess Fiona and accepting Donkey as his friend.

Spider-Man
Peter learns that with great power comes great responsibility. He sacrifices his love for MJ to fulfill his responsibilities as a crime fighter.

Finding Nemo
Marlin goes from being over protective, to allowing Nemo the freedom to learn. Nemo gains confidence after escaping from the fish tank.

Monsters, Inc.
Sulley goes from scaring children to making them laugh.

Bruce Almighty
Bruce goes from wanting to be God to not wanting to be God.

Matrix Trilogy
Neo goes from not believing that he is the ONE (Matrix 1), to not caring or wanting to be the ONE (Matrix 2), to accepting that he is the ONE and saving Zion from destruction (Matrix 3).

Pirates of the Caribbean
Will Turner accepts that he is the son of a pirate and becomes a pirate.

Harry Potter: The Sorcerer's Stone
Harry goes from being despised by his guardians to winning the esteem and love of his new family at Hogwarts.

Lord of the Rings Trilogy
Frodo decides that he does not want to destroy the Ring, but instead he wants to keep it for himself.

PERSONALITIES

Characters also have **personalities**, which are specific idiosyncrasies, mannerisms, and unique physical traits that make them memorable. These idiosyncrasies usually reveal a character's feelings about himself and his primary relationships. They also are often directly connected to his motivation by revealing some weakness or need he desires to fulfill.

These traits either help the character achieve his goals or create obstacles that he must overcome to reach his goal. They play a stronger role in the story if they function as obstacles, for then the character must change and transform in order to achieve his primary objective.

If a character trait does not play a direct role in the story, it should not be emphasized. Physical, psychological, and sociological traits are irrelevant unless they somehow create obstacles for the characters. Drama is about individuals changing themselves and their values while under conflict as they attempt to achieve their goals. Much drama deals with characters overcoming environmental and socially conditioned belief systems in order to obtain a better understanding about themselves and life.

A character's physical traits will include his or her gender, race, age, sex, height, weight, appearance, and defects or diseases. Sociological traits can include economic class, occupation, education, religion, and political attitudes. These usually reflect each character's attitudes, likes, prejudices, hatreds, and values.

Character traits are usually intensified and exaggerated. One method of creating uniqueness in a character is to present him as the opposite of stereotype. Whatever his occupation may be, take this profession's stereotype and reverse the standard traits: the judge who is dishonest, the priest who has lost his faith, or the salesman who is socially inept.

The idiosyncrasy must be visual and cinematic. Illustrate each character trait with a specific visual action. Small actions and small gestures help to round out a character. Instead of making declarative statements about a character's actions or feelings, show these states through the character's bodily reactions to other characters and objects that have significance. Don't try to write a character's response by just showing the expressions on their face. Write about his body movements and his actions as he interacts with the other characters in the scene.

One effective technique is to establish an emotional relationship between the character and a specific object. Display this during a moment of privacy, when the character is alone on the screen. It becomes a secret moment shared by the audience. This will increase the audience's empathy for the character and establish an intimate bond between them that is not shared by other characters in the story. Then at another time, this object can be used to evoke an emotional response from the audience.

E.T's relationship with the potted flower, which becomes healthy or sickly depending on E.T.'s own state of health, is a prime example of this technique. The audience understands the significance of the flower and shares this secret relationship with E.T., Elliott, and the other children, as opposed to the adult characters who are unaware of its significance.

Titanic
Rose wears the clothing of an aristocratic lady living in the beginning of the twentieth century. Molly Brown is the loud and down-to-earth "new rich" member of the aristocracy.

Star Wars
Luke has a boyish innocence. Darth Vader is faceless, has heavy breathing, and an artificially amplified voice. Obi-Wan Kenobe wears monkish clothing and speaks like a mystic. Princess Leia is domineering and combative in her relationships. Han Solo has the mannerisms of a western gunslinger.

The Phantom Menace
Queen Amidala wears exotic costumes when not disguising herself as the handmaiden Padme.

E.T.
Elliott is a wholesome, yet lonely child. ET has alien features, is childlike in size and mannerisms, yet appears to be old and wise. The government agents are ubiquitous, yet faceless.

The Lion King
Simba is the young lion cub that leads a carefree life in the jungle.

Return of the Jedi
Luke has an artificial right hand received after his hand was cut off in a fight with his father, Darth Vader.

Independence Day
Captain Steve Hillier is a wise cracking, "street smart" airman. Russell Casse is a broken down drunk. David Levinson is a MIT graduate who decides to work as a Cable TV repairman. David is upset over the

divorce from his wife. David still wears their wedding ring. President Tom Whitmore is a devoted father and husband.

Batman
Bruce Wayne leads a dual life and has a fetish for bat paraphernalia. The Joker has insane mannerisms, a terrible color coordinated wardrobe, and a murderous sense of humor.

Jurassic Park
Dr. Grant does not care for children, an attitude that will change during the story.

Home Alone
Kevin is a scrawny inept young man who can't do anything right. The two burglars are complete reprobates, whose ineptness makes them humorous.

Forrest Gump
Forrest became handicapped as a young boy. He then developed the ability to run fast as a reaction to the boys who would chase him when he was a child.

Men In Black
K is a cold and emotionally unresponsive agent, who is extremely effective in his work. J is a wisecracking street smart former NYPD cop.

Jaws
Capt. Brody is afraid of the water and doesn't like to ride on boats. Quint has his living quarters filled with the mounted jaws of the sharks he has killed.

Sixth Sense
Cole Sears is a small vulnerable boy who is picked on by the other boys in his class. Dr. Malcolm is a mild mannered, kind middle-aged man who wants to help sick children.

Empire Strikes Back
Luke receives cuts and scars on his face from the white snow creature. Luke has his hand cut off in the fight with Darth Vader and has it replaced with a mechanical hand.

The Grinch
The Grinch is a green hairy beast with a potbelly and long hairs on his fingers. It is the hair on his face that he tried to remove in school that lead to him cutting his face and being humiliated by the other children.

The Wizard of Oz
Dorothy is weak and worrisome, always hugging Toto for security. The Wicked Witch of the West is ugly, has a greenish face, and a cackling voice. The Scarecrow has clumsy movements because he is made of straw. The Tin Man has stiff, rigid movements since he is made of metal. The Lion is fearful. He constantly rubs his hands and twists his tail.

Shrek
Shrek is a huge, green, ugly ogre. Donkey is a donkey that talks.

Spider-Man
Peter is a lonely young nerd who accidentally gains superpowers.

Finding Nemo
Nemo is a small clown fish with a damaged fin. Marlin is a nervous overprotective father. Dory is a blue fish with short-term memory problems.

Monsters, Inc.
Sulley is a big furry turquoise bear-like beast. Mikey is a short, green, one-eyed monster.

Bruce Almighty
Wacky Bruce is a news reporter who gets no respect.

Matrix Trilogy
Neo is a monk-like psycho-computer-tech martial arts messiah.

Pirates of the Caribbean
Captain Jack Sparrow is either "the worst pirate" or "the best pirate" that the British Sailors have ever seen. His ineptness enables him to excel beyond all reasonable expectations. To show his respect, Barbossa names his monkey "Jack."

Harry Potter: The Sorcerer's Stone
Harry is a mild mannered young Brit destined to become a great wizard.

Lord of the Rings Trilogy
Frodo, the small Hobbit with hairy feet, ends up saving Middle Earth from the evil Lord Sauron, in spite of his desire to keep the Ring for himself.

SUPPORTING CHARACTERS

Supporting characters interact with the primary characters and help to define them. Some are supportive of either the protagonist or the antagonist. The main characters gather around them the key minor characters that they need to accomplish their goals. These minor characters force the protagonist to reveal their true nature and values. They also usually have qualities that are radically different from the protagonist and the antagonist.

The minor character is often used as someone with whom the protagonist or antagonist can talk in confidence, thereby, expressing his plans to the audience. This also allows him to convey his feelings about situations to the audience.

A solely one-on-one conflict between the protagonist and the antagonist is usually too limiting for the audience and can quickly become boring. Most of the popular films involve several minor characters: supporters that hinder their opponents by creating obstacles and minor villains that support the antagonist. The villain's supporters are usually more nasty and vicious than the antagonist.

The minimal number of characters usually found in these films is five: the protagonist, the antagonist, the love interest, a minor character that supports the protagonist, and a minor character who supports the antagonist. The **protagonist supporter** may have objectives that are different from the protagonist, but they work together to achieve the protagonist's primary objective, which is also the primary objective of the story. For example, in *The Wizard of Oz*, the Scarecrow's objective is to get a brain, the Tin Man a heart, and the Lion courage, but they all work together to get to Oz and to help Dorothy obtain her primary objective, to get back home. The **antagonist supporter** usually does the vicious and dirty work for the antagonist.

Although their parts are small, minor characters still should be three-dimensional so that the story won't lose credibility for the audience. This is accomplished by having these minor characters go through changes as they attempt to resolve personal conflicts. One common way of introducing minor characters is to show them at work. In this way, the audience immediately learns their profession. You could introduce them while they are having a conflict with a co-worker or with another character with whom they have a personal relationship. Another technique used to create memorable characters is to exaggerate them as obsessive or eccentric. The easiest way to do this is to make them atypical to their profession's stereotype. As the minor characters become more involved in the scene, their personality will set a mood or make the situation more emotionally engrossing. The protagonist supporter, with a good sense of humor, will make the audience laugh and **emotionally feel good** about him and **the protagonist**. The antagonist supporter will be mean and vicious, do something terrible to another character in the story, and cause the audience to **emotionally feel anger and hatred** toward **the antagonist** and his supporters.

Spielberg often uses minor characters to manipulate the audience's emotional reactions to either the scene or the main character. The emotions that the minor character expresses are those that Spielberg wants the audience to feel. Every crowd has a personality. He often displays the emotional reactions of one or two specific members of the crowd to the characters in the scene. Crowds are often used during celebration scenes in movies, with the hope that the joy and happiness these crowds express for the protagonist will also become the audience's feelings.

Titanic
Molly Brown is supportive of Jack and Rose. The ship's captain and Mr. Andrews, the designer of the Titanic, are also supporting characters. A crowd waves goodbye as the Titanic embarks on its sea voyage. They are happy about the departure of the Titanic and express their joy. Crowds of people mob the lifeboats as the Titanic sinks. In this scene, the feeling of the crowd is that of terror.

Star Wars
The Death Star Commander, Imperial Storm Troopers, Obie Won Kenobe, Princess Leia, Han Solo, Chewbacca, R2-D2, and C-3P0 are all minor characters in this movie. Crowds of rebels celebrate the victory of Luke Skywalker and his supporters in the final scene of the movie.

The Phantom Menace
There are many interesting minor characters in this story, such as Jar Jar Binks and Boss Nass of the Gungans, Sebula of the Podrace, and Watto, the owner of the junk shop. During the battle scenes, there are crowds of Gungan Warriors and Battle Droids. A crowd celebrates the victory at the end of the movie.

E.T.
Michael and his friends, the faceless government agents, and the schoolteacher are all minor characters.

The Lion King
Timon and Pumbaa romp through the jungle and show Simba the ways of a carefree life. Rafiki, the mystic baboon, shows Simba his true nature and destiny.

Return of the Jedi
The spirit of Obi-Wan Kenobe gives advice to Luke. Yoda mentors Luke in the ways of the force before he dies. Lando Cairissian helps the rebels defeat the Empire. Imperial Storm Troopers, Han Solo, Chewbacca, R2-D2, C-3P0, and the Ewoks are all minor characters in this movie.

Men In Black
Agent Zed, who supervises K and J, is an important minor character. The friendly aliens who are living on Earth are also minor characters.

Independence Day
The owner of the Cable TV station at which David Levinson works, the Secretary of Defense, the General, and other military personnel are all supporting characters. The panicked people on the streets of New York City are important characters.

Batman
The Butler, Alexander Knox (the newspaper reporter), Bob (the Joker's goon), and the Police Commissioner are all minor characters.

Jurassic Park
Dennis, the fat computer technician who steals the dinosaur embryos from Jurassic Park and later gets devoured by a dinosaur is an important minor character. The lawyer who gets eaten by a dinosaur while sitting on a toilet is another character. Both exhibit values of greed that lead to their destruction. John's two grandchildren are the love interests that he wants to survive. Ian, the chaos theory scientist, is supportive of the protagonist.

Home Alone
Store clerks, police officers, the pizza delivery boy, and airport ticket agents are all minor characters.

Forrest Gump
Bubba and Lt. Dan are supporting characters as is Forrest's mother.

Jaws
The beaches of Amity are filled with swimmers on holiday. It is their terror of the shark that is transferred to the members of the audience.

Sixth Sense
All the dead people that Cole sees are important minor characters. At first he feels terrorized by the dead. They are obstacles and problems from which he attempts to escape. But later, with the help of Dr. Malcolm, he realizes that these dead people come to him for help. They have problems they believe Cole can help them solve.

Empire Strikes Back
The spirit of Obi-Wan Kenobe tells Luke to seek Yoda. He also gives advice to Luke throughout this story. Yoda mentors Luke in the ways of the force. Lando Cairissian helps the rebels fight the Empire.

The Grinch
All the people in Whoville are the minor characters that the Grinch hates. He hates them because they are happy and content with their lives. The crowd at the Whobilation expresses joy with the Grinch being chosen as the Cheermeister, then disappointment and anger with him when he goes on a rage and destroys their Christmas Tree.

The Wizard of Oz
The Winged Monkeys, Castle Guards, Scarecrow, Tin Man, Lion, Glinda, and Munchkins are all important minor characters. The crowds of Munchkins express happiness with Dorothy and characterize her as their liberator. The crowds of people in Oz express terror of the Wicked Witch of the West as she writes on the sky that they should surrender Dorothy.

Shrek
Donkey wants to get Shrek and Fiona back together again. Donkey helps Shrek to stop the marriage.

Spider-Man
Harry Osborn, the son of the Green Goblin (Norman Osborn), dates Peter's love, MJ, and vows to kill Spider-Man.

Finding Nemo
Dory helps Marlin find Nemo. Gill helps Nemo escape from the fish tank.

Monsters, Inc.
Randall's assistant manipulates the "scream extraction" machine of Mikey. Mike helps Sulley to get Boo back home.

Bruce Almighty
The Janitor and Homeless Man (God) help Bruce.

Matrix Trilogy
Morpheus, Trinity, and the Oracle help Neo.
The Agent Smiths try to destroy Neo.

Pirates of the Caribbean
The good pirates (like Gibbs) help Will, Liz, and Jack, while the cursed pirates help Barbossa.

Harry Potter: The Sorcerer's Stone
Ron and Hermione help Harry.

Lord of the Rings Trilogy
Gandalf, Sam, Aragorn, Elrond, Theoden, Legolas, Gimli, Pippin, Merry and the good people of Middle Earth help Frodo, while Saruman, Orcs, Uruk-hai, the Witch-King, Ringwraiths, and Fell-Beasts help the Dark Lord Sauron.

SUBGOALS AND PLOT TWISTS CREATING UNPREDICTABILITY

The Story Objective

Concrete Objects

Personal Values

Subgoals & Subtasks

Strategies & Plans

THE STORY OBJECTIVE

"In order to cause any kind of forward movement, a goal must be set. The setting of a goal is the preliminary condition for the forward movement. As soon as the goal is set, the spectator anticipates the possibility of its attainment. This anticipation expresses itself as a desire to arrive at the goal. And this desire causes the forward movement in the mind of the spectator."
—Eugene Vale, *The Technique of Screen and Television Writing*

The concepts of **story objective**, **concrete object**, **abstract value** and **subgoal** can be separated in analysis, but are closely connected in any story. These concepts essentially contribute to the theme of the story. The **primary objective of the protagonist** is identical to the **story objective**.

Each character has a **primary objective**, something that he desperately desires that is the focus of most of his actions. The **dramatic objective of the story** is the primary objective that is sought by both the protagonist and the antagonist. In the megahit movies, this is very often a **unique concrete object** which only one of the characters can possess. It is "concrete" in the sense that it can be physically held by the characters, and can be visually seen on the screen by members of the audience. Obtaining this unique object is of extreme importance and urgency to all the characters involved. It becomes an issue of life or death not only for the protagonist and the antagonist, but very often for the community as well. We will list examples of concrete objects found in the megahit movies in the next section.

Titanic
The primary objective of both Jack and Rose is to live a creative artistic life, while the primary objective of the treasure hunters is the jewel, the "heart of the ocean."

Star Wars
Luke and the rebels' primary objective is to be free from fear of destruction by the Empire.

The Phantom Menace
The primary objective of Anakin Skywalker and Queen Amidala is to be free from enslavement. Anakin wants to be free from Watto, the owner of the junk store, and Amidala wants freedom from the Trade Federation.

E.T.
E.T. wants to get back home where he will be safe with his own people.

Jurassic Park
Dr. Grant is a scientist who wants to gain knowledge about dinosaurs. Later, his primary objective is to save the children from the dinosaurs.

The Lion King
Simba wants to become a great and powerful king like his father and the ruler of the Pride Lands.

Return of the Jedi
Luke Skywalker wants to fully develop his powers, learn the ways of the force, become a Jedi Knight, and fight with the rebellion against the Empire. Both Darth Vader and the Emperor want to persuade Luke to use his Jedi powers for the Empire.

Independence Day
All of the four protagonists, Captain Steve Hiller, David Levinson, President Whitmore, Russell Casse want to save the human race from destruction by the aliens.

Batman
Batman wants to save his home, Gotham City, from the criminals.

Home Alone
Kevin wants to feel safe in his home and to protect it from the thieves.

Forrest Gump
Forrest Gump's objective is to stay completely focused in the moment, where he feels safe and secure.

Jaws
Capt. Brody wants to kill the Great White Shark because it is terrorizing his home: the village and beaches of Amity.

Men In Black
J and K want to save their home, the planet Earth, from destruction.

Sixth Sense
Cole Sears wants to stop seeing dead people. Dr. Malcolm Crowe's primary objective is to help Cole Sears feel safe and not feel terrorized by the dead people. He wants to help the child to feel "at home with himself."

Empire Strikes Back
Luke Skywalker's primary objective is to become a Jedi Knight and save the rebels from the Empire.

The Grinch
The Grinch's primary objective is to have revenge on the people of Whoville because they made him feel different and not acceptable to their community. He, too, wanted to feel at home in Whoville, but since he believed that was not possible, he sought to destroy the Whos.

The Wizard of Oz
Dorothy's primary objective in the beginning of the movie is to find a place where there are no problems. Since she learns that such a place does not exist once she arrives in Oz, her primary objective is to return to the safety of her home.

Shrek
Shrek wants the privacy of his home (the swamp).

Spider-Man
Peter wants Mary Jane to love him.

Finding Nemo
Marlin wants to find Nemo and bring him back home.

Monsters, Inc.
Sulley wants to generate as much energy as possible for Monsters, Inc.

Bruce Almighty
Bruce wants to be famous and respected.

Matrix Trilogy
Neo wants to save the human race from destruction by the Machines.

Pirates of the Caribbean
Captain Jack Sparrow wants his ship, the Black Pearl.
Will Turner wants to save Elizabeth from the pirates.
Elizabeth wants to marry Will Turner.

Harry Potter: The Sorcerer's Stone
Harry wants to understand the mystery of his life.

Lord of the Rings Trilogy
Sauron wants the Ring, and Frodo wants to destroy the Ring.

CONCRETE OBJECTS

Concrete objects are the tangible things that the characters pursue in the hope of obtaining their primary objectives. Because film is a visual medium, the audience must see those things for which the characters are fighting; they must be tangible, visible, and objects that the audience believes are valuable. Some objectives, like status and control, are more symbolic, but they do bring power to those who possess them.

Titanic: The Heart of the Ocean

Star Wars: The Plans to the Death Star

The Phantom Menace: Control of the Planet Naboo

E.T.: A Communication Device for calling home

Jurassic Park: The Computer Code to turn on the Security Systems

Home Alone: An AirplaneTicket Home, A Home safe from burglars

Forrest Gump: To be normal and accepted by people in the community

The Lion King: Control of the Pride Lands

Return of the Jedi: Luke's Light Saber

Independence Day: A weapon that will destroy the aliens

Men in Black: The Galaxy on Orion's Belt

Jaws: A Dead Great White Shark

Batman: Formula for the antidote to the Joker's Smylex poisons

Sixth Sense: Dead People

Empire Strikes Back: Luke's spaceship in the swamp

The Grinch: Being elected the Cheermeister of Whobilation

The Wizard of Oz: The Ruby Slippers

Harry Potter and the Sorcerer's Stone: The Sorcerer's Stone

Finding Nemo: Diver's Mask

Pirates of the Caribbean: The Aztec Gold Coin

The Matrix Reloaded: Human City of Zion

Spider-Man: Control of the City

Shrek: Shrek's Swamp Home

Monsters, Inc.:   Boo, the Human Child

Lord of the Rings Trilogy: The One Ring

PERSONAL VALUES

The primary objective usually involves a concrete object that also often represents a **personal value** or some code of interpersonal behavior that the characters reveal while in pursuit of the objective. This is directly connected to the character's **motivation**. The character believes that possessing this object will satisfy an **emotional need**. These stories examine the question of whether the ends (primary objective) justify the means (interpersonal values) and the personal sacrifice the conflicts entail for the characters.

It is important to restate that drama is not concerned with the accidental events that happen in the lives of individuals. It is about characters making decisions under conflict while in pursuit of objectives that represent fundamental human values and that satisfy core emotional needs. Personal growth often is achieved once these characters understand the real significance of what is at stake and "do the right thing," even if it results in self-sacrifice.

Titanic: The Heart of the Ocean (Eternal love)

Star Wars: The Plans to the Death Star (Freedom from destruction)

The Phantom Menace: A new hyper drive generator (Freedom to travel in order to get to safety)

E.T.: A Communication Device for calling home (Freedom to communicate to get to safety)

Jurassic Park: The Computer Code to turn on the Security System (The safety of the community)

Home Alone: An Airplane Ticket Home (To save her son, Kevin, from being alone)

Forrest Gump: Forrest "goes with the flow" (To be accepted by the other characters)

The Lion King: Control of the Pride Lands (The well-being of the Animal Kingdom)

Return of the Jedi: Using the power of the force for good or evil (The well-being of the Universe)

Independence Day: A weapon that will destroy the aliens (To save the world from destruction and maintain the independence of the human race)

Men in Black: The Galaxy on Orion's Belt (The preservation of the home planet, Earth)

Jaws: A Dead Great White Shark (The safety of the community)

Batman: Formula for the antidote to the Joker's Smylex poisons (To save the community from destruction)

Sixth Sense: To stop seeing Dead People (To save Cole)

Empire Strikes Back: Luke wants to develop his powers so that he can become a Jedi Knight and help the rebellion defeat the Empire. (To save the save from the empire)

The Grinch: Being Elected the Cheermeister of Whobilation (To be accepted by the community)

The Wizard of Oz: The Ruby Slippers (To have confidence in one's own abilities to solve problems)

Shrek: The swamp (The privacy of a home)

Spider-Man: Crime fighter (Saving the community from crime)

Finding Nemo: Nemo (To save the last member of his family)

Monsters Inc: Boo (To return the human child Boo to her home)

Bruce Almighty: God (To be powerful and loved by the community. To be loved by others Bruce must love others)

Matrix Trilogy: Zion (To save the humans in Zion from destruction)

Pirates of the Caribbean: Aztec Coin (To be saved from being a ghost) To show that Pirates can also be good men

Harry Potter-The Sorcerer's Stone: Family (To find a home, Hogwarts, and a family that loves him)

Lord of the Rings Trilogy: Ring (To save the people of Middle-Earth from destruction)

SUBGOALS & SUBTASKS

"It is a fundamental principle that it is the anticipation of an auxiliary goal which causes the forward movement, and not the briskness of the dialogue or the swift action of a scene."
—Eugene Vale, *The Technique of Screen and Television Writing*

Subgoals (or **subtasks**) are minor objectives that a character must achieve in order to obtain his primary objective. The concepts of *subgoals* and *plot twists* are closely related. The audience is made aware of the relationship of subgoals to primary objectives when the characters discuss their plans and strategies. **Plot twists** occur when the accomplishment of a subgoal does not cause the expected result of helping a character achieve his primary objective. This technique creates **surprise** and **unpredictability** in the story, and is found in many of the popular films.

Wizard of Oz: Dorothy's primary objective is to find a place where she will never have any problems. In order to achieve this, she attempts to accomplish several subgoals. Dorothy runs away from home in order to save Toto from Elmira Gulch. Dorothy returns home to help her "sick" Aunt Em, but a tornado takes her to Oz. This is a plot twist. Dorothy goes to Oz to get help from the Wizard to get her back to Kansas. This is her first major subgoal in the Land of Oz. The Wizard will not help her until she gets the broom of the Wicked Witch. This unexpected result produces a plot twist. Dorothy gets the broom, but still the Wizard fails to help her get home. This is another plot twist that is generated from an unexpected consequence of successfully accomplishing a subgoal. Dorothy's next subgoal is to fly back to Kansas in the balloon with the Wizard. But this fails because the balloon takes off without her. This is another plot twist. The final subgoal is to click the heels of the ruby slippers and to wish she is back home. She does this and finds herself back in the bed on her Kansas farm.

The Phantom Menace: The Jedi's primary objective is to safeguard Queen Amidala and get her to Coruscant so that she can plead for her people before the Senate. In order to achieve this, they attempt to accomplish several subgoals. They all escape from Naboo, but the ship is damaged. They need a new hyper-drive. To get the hyper-drive, they must negotiate with Watto. Anakin Skywalker must win the Pod race so that the Jedi can get the hyperdrive. Anakin wins the Pod race and his freedom. When they get to Coruscant and Queen Amidala appeals for help, her appeals are rejected. This is a plot twist.

She forces new elections but decides to return to help her people. The Queen's primary objective fails. Her new subgoal is to lead a battle against the Trade Federation on Naboo. This finally succeeds.

Antagonists also have subgoals. This can clearly be seen in *Star Wars*. The villains want to make the Death Star operational, secure the Death Star by retrieving the plans stolen by the rebels, and destroy the rebellion military base.

Empire Strikes Back: Luke Skywalker has the subgoal of finding Yoda so that he can study under him and achieve his primary objective: become a Jedi Knight.

Return of the Jedi: Han and Princess Leia must destroy the power station on the Ewok planet that provides a shield for the Death Star.

Independence Day: The series of subgoals revolve around finding weapons that will destroy the alien space ships. They first try to use fighter planes and standard missiles, but this fails. They next try to use nuclear weapons, but this fails. They then must find a way to disable the protective energy force surrounding the alien spaceships. David Levinson demonstrates the effectiveness of a computer virus on the alien spaceship in Area 51. They then must find a way to fly this spaceship up to the mother ship, and infect that ship with the virus. Then David and Steve must find a way to escape from the mother ship and get back to Earth.

Men In Black: J and K have the primary objective to save the planet Earth from destruction. To do this they have the subgoal of finding the "galaxy on Orion's belt". They must retrieve this Galaxy from Edgar-Bug and stop the Edgar-Bug from leaving the planet with the Galaxy.

Shrek: Shrek wants to be home alone in his swamp. To do this he must get rid of the fairy tale creatures. He goes to Lord Farquaard to persuade him to give them their land back. Before he will do this, Farquaard tells Shrek he must rescue Princess Fiona for him. (Plot Twist)

Spider-Man: Peter wants MJ. To win her, he wants to have a fancy car. This means he must get money. He decides to enter the wrestling contest to win $3,000. He has to design a costume. He wins the wrestling contest. He is only paid $100. (Plot Twist)

STRATEGIES & PLANS

A **plan** or **strategy** is **a series of actions** that a character intends to take in order to achieve his objective. He anticipates certain and possible obstacles then devises tactics to overcome these obstacles. These plans are usually communicated to an audience in an exposition scene. The strategy and tactics are discussed by the characters with his supporters. This exposition of **a plan creates expectations about future events for the audience.**

Both protagonists and antagonists make plans. In *Batman*, an example of an antagonist making plans can be found in the scene when Boss Grissom plans to break into Axis Chemicals to get documents that could incriminate his gang. But what he is really planning is the setup of Jack Napier (The Joker) to be killed by the police detective.

A story becomes **unpredictable** when things do not occur as planned. This happens when new, unexpected obstacles occur, or the planned tactics fail to overcome an expected obstacle. **Excitement** is created if the characters become endangered by these unexpected developments. It is only through the exposition of plans and strategies that **expectations** about the future can be generated in the mind of the audience.

Titanic
The Treasure Hunters plan to recover the jewel, the "Heart of the Ocean," from the Titanic.

Star Wars
The Rebel strategists plan to attack and destroy the Death Star.

The Phantom Menace
The Jedi, Queen Amidala, and Boss Nass design their battle plan against the Trade Federation.

E.T.
Elliot and Michael devise a plan to help E.T. send a message home.

The Lion King
Scar plans with the Jackals to destroy Mufasa to control the Pride Lands.

Forrest Gump
Forrest does not plan or design strategies. He does what he is told to do. This goes against the audience expectations of what is normal.

Return of the Jedi
The Rebel Commanders plan the attack on the Death Star, with General Solo tasked to destroy the power station on the Ewok's planet, and General Calrissian to lead the fighters to attack the Death Star.

Batman
Grissom and Jack plan to destroy evidence at the Axis Chemical factory.

Jurassic Park
Dennis, the fat computer technician, plans to steal dinosaur embryos for a competing firm.

Home Alone
The two burglars plan to rob Kevin's home.

Independence Day
The President and his military advisors plan to destroy the alien's ship using nuclear weapons. They then plan to coordinate a worldwide attack once the mother ship has been infected, and the protective energy shields around the alien spaceships have been disabled.

Jaws
Quint devises a plan to hunt and kill the great white shark.

Men in Black
K plans to get the "Galaxy on Orion's Belt" from the Edgar-Bug.

Sixth Sense
Dr. Malcolm Crowe plans to save Cole from seeing dead people.

Empire Strikes Back
Han Solo plans to land on the floating space station in order to fix the hyper-drive of the Millennium Falcon.

The Grinch
The Grinch plans to destroy Christmas in Whoville. He talks about this plan with his dog.

The Wizard of Oz
Dorothy plans to go to Oz to ask the Wizard to return her to Kansas. The Scarecrow, Tin Man, and Lion plan to get into the Witch's castle in order to save Dorothy.

Shrek
Once in the castle, Shrek plans to save the Princess while Donkey finds the dragon.

Spider-Man
Peter plans to get money by entering the wrestling contest.
Norman Osborn plans his revenge on the Board members.

Finding Nemo
Gill plans the escape from the fish tank.

Monsters, Inc.
Sulley and Mike plan to take Boo back home.

Bruce Almighty
Bruce plans to use his God powers to get the TV Anchorman job.

Matrix Trilogy
Neo plans to save the human race by working with the Machines to destroy the Agent Smiths.

Pirates of the Caribbean
Jack plans with Will to get a British ship.
Jack plans with Norrington to capture the pirates.
Jack plans with Barbossa to defeat the British and get two ships.

Harry Potter-The Sorcerer's Stone
Harry, Ron, and Hermione plan to discover what is hidden under the trap door guarded by Fluffy.

Lord of the Rings Trilogy
The Fellowship plans to take the Ring to Mount Doom to be destroyed.

CONFLICTS CREATING EXCITEMENT

Obstacles

Jeopardy

Self-Conflicts

Enemies

Relatives

Friends

Lovers

Physical Objects

Natural World

Supernatural World

OBSTACLES

Raymond Hull, in *How To Write a Play*, identifies five kinds of conflict that can generate obstacles for a character: man against nature, man against man, man against society, man against himself, and man against fate. "Fatalism is not the dominant doctrine of our society and time. Many religious, philosophical, and artistic theorists prefer the idea that each person is largely responsible for his or her own life. They believe that we can learn from our past, make choices by the exercise of free will, and thus shape our own futures."

The essence of story construction consists of creating **obstacles** that prevent the hero from obtaining his objectives. These can be both "internal" and "external" obstacles. Unexpected obstacles defeat the best devised plans and create surprise and excitement in the audience.

Internal obstacles fall under the category of *self-conflicts*. They can consist of ignorance, loss of memory, fear, lack of courage, lack of skills, or false belief. They are the result of a character's personality. These obstacles test whether the character really holds a certain code of beliefs while pursuing his objectives.

External obstacles can consist of the actions of the antagonist and his allies, objects in the environment, and natural or supernatural events.

From the perspective of story construction, to create obstacles, the writer should think of all the things that could possibly go wrong in a situation: how can the protagonist be blocked from achieving his goals? Then invent ways for him to imaginatively overcome these obstacles. The more dangerous obstacles in a story, the more exciting the story becomes. The antagonist and his supporters also have obstacles that they must overcome to obtain their objectives.

Granted there are many choices for any given situation, the writer should choose only those which will create the most obstacles for the characters to overcome. Try to construct conflicts that will involve the protagonist's primal relationships and that force him to choose between his moral code and his desired objective. Complicate his life, for "complications," in the traditional dramatic sense, are the result of conflicts and competition between characters. All chase scenes can be considered to involve obstacles that attempt to prevent the characters from obtaining their objectives, and such scenes keep the audience in suspense.

When constructing a series of obstacles, each one must be of greater intensity and danger to the protagonist than the previous one. Whenever he overcomes an obstacle, he is confronted by another one more perilous. If the audience becomes bored, this usually indicates a lack of tension, danger, and conflict in the story. To remedy this, create new obstacles for the protagonist that will further test his ingenuity and values.

It is not necessary to keep the obstacles within a realistic perspective. Actually, in many of the most successful films, the opposite is the case. In many films **impossible situations** prevent the protagonist from obtaining his objective. As long as the film is emotionally absorbing, the audience "suspends its beliefs" as they become emotionally engrossed in the story. In these films, the protagonist must discover ingenuous and unexpected ways to overcome the obstacles in order to achieve the objectives.

JEOPARDY

Jeopardy "is anticipated pain or loss. When a character is threatened with something bad, the audience automatically focuses its attention on him. The more helpless the character, and the more terrible the danger, the more importance the audience will attach to the character. That is why children in danger are such powerful characters."
—Orson Scott Card, *Character and Viewpoint*

"The stronger the tension is, the more the reader concentrates on finding out what happens next, the more attention he pays, the more intensely he feels all the emotions of the tale."
—Orson Scott Card, *Character and Viewpoint*

When constructing conflict in a scene, using just any obstacle is not sufficient to create excitement. It must be an obstacle that creates **jeopardy** for the character in the scene. A character is in jeopardy when he is placed in danger. There must be a high probability he will be physically or emotionally harmed by the obstacle or, that in some way, the obstacle will cause him pain or loss.

The opening sequence of *Raiders of the Lost Ark* demonstrates the relationship between obstacles, jeopardy and excitement. Below is a list of the jeopardy producing situations in the opening sequence:

1. The protagonist, Indiana Jones, with his back to the camera, stares at a large mountain in front of him. This appears to be an obstacle that he must overcome.

2. The sound of wild animals creates the threat of attack by jungle beasts.

3. The jungle itself is a dense environment that creates obstacles for Jones. He must assert a great amount of energy to make his way through the underbrush.

4. A native guide screams in terror when he unexpectedly uncovers a terrifying headstone.

5. Jones' party must cross a stream without the use of a bridge, a dangerous situation because someone could slip and fall against the rocks.

6. Jones finds a poison arrow in a tree. His guides state that they are being pursued by natives who will kill them if given the chance.

7. The party has to climb over large tree trunks in order to make their way forward.

8. While Jones is trying to decipher a map, one of the guides pulls out a gun with the intent to kill Jones.

9. Jones uses a bullwhip to disarm the killer. The gun falls to the ground and discharges.

10. Jones climbs up a steep, rocky hill from which he could fall.

11. Jones walks through hanging vines as he makes his way to a dark cave.

12. At the cave entrance, Jones states that Forrestal died there and "he was good." The guide says that no one has come out of the cave alive.

13. Jones and the guide walk into a dark cave that may contain unknown dangers.

14. Jones cuts an entrance through a giant spider web.

15. Poisonous spiders crawl onto the backs of Jones and the guide.

16. Forrestal's skeleton comes out from the wall when Jones passes his hand through the light entrance. This demonstrates that death is a real possibility.

17. They must swing across a deep pit. Jones saves the life of his guide, who almost falls into the pit.

18. The tree limb is weak and gives way as they swing across. This sets up an obstacle for their exit.

19. The guide's belief that there is nothing left to worry about concerns Jones. Jones hits the rock slab with his torch. An arrow strikes the torch, almost killing Jones.

20. They realize that all the stone slabs are death traps.

21. Jones must figure out how to remove the idol without activating a security mechanism.

22. Jones retrieves the idol by replacing it with a bag of sand, but the platform sinks and activates the destructive mechanisms.

23. The walls of the cave collapse.

24. Falling rocks and boulders endanger Jones.

25. Arrows shoot out from the wall as Jones runs for safety.

26. The guide swings across the pit, then the whip falls off the branch.

27. The guide negotiates for the possession of the whip. He wants the idol. Time is lost.

28. A stonewall is slowly closing the escape exit.

29. Jones must choose between the idol and his life. Jones throws the idol to the guide.

30. The native betrays Jones and drops the whip.

31. Jones dives across the pit and clings on to the ledge.

32. Jones clutches a branch and tries to pull himself up. The branch slips, and Jones almost falls into the pit.

33. The stonewall continues to move downward to close the exit.

34. Jones finally pulls himself up, quickly rolls under the rock slab, and retrieves his hat just as the rock slams against the ground.

35. Jones bumps into the dead guide who had betrayed him, then retrieves the idol.

36. A giant boulder rolls down toward Jones.

37. Jones runs for his life. He trips, falls to one knee, then gets up to run again.

38. Jones runs through the spider webs with the giant boulder at his heels.

39. Jones dives through the entrance just as the boulder slams against the entrance walls, closing it forever.

40. Jones is surrounded by armed natives who threaten him with spears.

41. The first guide, who tried to shoot Jones, falls face forward to the ground with arrows in his back. Jones knows the natives will also kill him.

42. Belloc takes the idol from Jones.

43. Jones hands his gun to Belloc. He is now disarmed in a dangerous situation.

44. Jones can't speak to the natives. This is an obstacle that prevents him from warning them about Belloc.

45. As Belloc raises the idol, the natives fall to their knees. Jones runs for his life.

46. Belloc signals the natives to cut Jones' throat. Belloc laughs at Jones' desperation.

47. Jones runs through a dense forest. The natives run after him. The odds against his surviving are overwhelming.

48. Jones must run across a large open field to escape the chasing natives.

49. Jones must swim across a river to reach the plane.

50. Jones grabs a vine and swings out into the river.

51. As Jones swims, the natives throw spears and blow darts at him.

52. Jones climbs onto the plane as it takes off.

53. A snake climbs into Jones' lap.

54. Jones screams in terror and says that he hates snakes.

55. Jock, the pilot, mocks Jones and tells him to "have a little backbone."

The humor at the end of the scene helps the audience to release the tension generated by all the obstacles and jeopardy in the opening sequence. The humor is generated by Jock's statement. It is inappropriate and a complete misrepresentation of Jones' character as experienced by the audience. Because of this, the audience laughs.

SELF-CONFLICTS

Self-conflicts generate obstacles whenever beliefs or values that the protagonist holds interfere with his ability to obtain his goal or interact with other characters. He then must decide whether to hold onto these values and lose his objective, to give up his principles, or in some way, obtain his goal while still keeping his values. Self-conflict can also arise when a character is forced to choose between two incompatible objectives, both of which are important to him. They can also be a result of the character losing confidence in himself or his abilities.

Titanic
Rose denies that she does not love Cal when questioned by Jack. She does not want to admit to herself that she intends to marry a man that she does not love.

Star Wars
Luke lacks confidence in the "force" and his ability to be a Jedi Knight.

Phantom Menace
Anakin must decide to either stay with his mother or leave to become a Jedi Knight.

E.T.
E.T. must overcome his inability to communicate with his new friend, Elliott.

Jurassic Park
None of the characters in this movie appear to have a self-conflict.

Lion King
Simba loses confidence in his ability to be king because he believes he caused his father's death. He must overcome his false sense of guilt.

Return of the Jedi
Luke must decide whether to use the force for good or join his father and the dark side of the force.

Batman
Bruce Wayne must overcome his fear of telling Vicki Vale the truth about being Batman. Without this, he will never have the complete intimacy that he desires.

Home Alone
Kevin must overcome his self-doubts about being able to survive alone.

Forrest Gump
Forrest doesn't have any self-conflicts. Like the feather, he goes with the flow of life, while maintaining a simple decency and a simple moral point of view.

Jaws
Capt. Brody must overcome his fear of water and boats in order to join Quint to hunt the shark.

Independence Day
Russell Casse is in torment because, whenever he tells people that he was abducted and sexually abused by aliens, they laugh at him. So he becomes an alcoholic.

Men in Black
K is in torment over whether he should continue to be a MIB, or whether he should erase his memories and return to the woman he loved so long ago.

Sixth Sense
Cole Sears doesn't want to tell Dr. Malcolm Crowe that he sees dead people because he does not think he will be believed.

Empire Strikes Back
Luke has the self-conflict of not believing that he has the ability to use the force to lift his spaceship from the swamp.

The Grinch
The Grinch argues with himself over whether he should accept the invitation from Cindy Lou Who to become the Cheermeister or whether to continue hating the Whos.

The Wizard of Oz
Dorothy lacks the confidence that she can solve her own problems.

Shrek
Donkey feels that he cannot tell Shrek the truth about Fiona. Shrek feels that he cannot tell Fiona he loves her because she will reject him as being too ugly. Fiona feels she cannot tell Shrek that she gets ugly at night because he will reject her.

Spider-Man
Peter feels that he cannot tell MJ he loves her because it will place her life in danger.

Finding Nemo
Marlin is afraid to let Nemo roam free.

Monsters Inc
Sully is torn between keeping Boo and returning her to her home.

Bruce Almighty
Bruce will not admit that his obsession with success is the cause of his problems.

Matrix Trilogy
Neo does not believe that he is the ONE.

Pirates of the Caribbean
Will cannot accept that his father was a pirate. He believes he cannot love Liz since he is only a blacksmith.

Harry Potter-The Sorcerer's Stone
Harry must decide between having his parents brought back to life or preventing Voldmort from having the sorcerer's stone.

Lord of the Rings Trilogy
Frodo will not destroy the Ring.

ENEMIES

Enemies are created when two characters both desire an objective (or object) that is unique and can be attained by only one of them. If they are unwilling to share and compromise, conflict is generated as they fight for sole possession of the objective (or object). This is the situation that faces the protagonist and the antagonist in the megahit movies.

Physical violence is characteristic of this relationship, since neither the protagonist nor the antagonist cares for the other and sees the other as nothing more than a physical obstacle to the primary objective. Usually this conflict ends with the death and destruction of the antagonist unless he is saved for the sequel (i.e., Darth Vader in *Star Wars*).

Titanic
Cal becomes the enemy of both Rose and Jack. He tries to shoot them as the Titanic sinks.

Star Wars
The Rebels and the Empire fight for possession of the plans for the Death Star, the ultimate power in the universe. Luke and Han Solo fight Darth Vader for possession of Princess Leia.

Phantom Menace
Darth Sidious, Darth Maul and members of the Trade Federation are the enemies of the other characters in this movie. They want control of the planet, Naboo.

Forrest Gump
When he is young, Forrest must run from the boys who chase him. He must also run from the enemy in Vietnam.

E.T.
Elliott and his friends battle the faceless government agents in order to help E.T. return home.

Jurassic Park
The Raptors are the enemies of the humans in Jurassic Park.

The Lion King
Simba and Scar fight for control of the Pride Lands.

Return of the Jedi
Luke must fight the Emperor who wants to control his powers and use him for the Empire.

Batman
Batman fights the Joker for control of Gotham. The Joker covets the social status and recognition that the community of Gotham is giving to Batman. If he can't have their love, then the Joker will have their fear and respect. Batman and the Joker fight for possession of Vicki Vale.

Home Alone
Kevin fights the burglars to prevent them from robbing his home.

Jaws
The Great White Shark is the enemy of all the humans in the story.

Independence Day
The Aliens are determined to exterminate the human race. They are the enemies of all the protagonists.

Men in Black
Aliens are determined to destroy the planet Earth unless they are given "the Galaxy on Orion's Belt." The Edgar-Bug wants the power from "the Galaxy on Orion's Belt" and will kill anyone who gets in his way.

Sixth Sense
Dr. Malcolm Crowe believes that Cole Sears will have to be institutionalized unless he can help him stop seeing dead people. Dead people are the "enemies" who terrorize Cole Sears.

Empire Strikes Back
Luke and the rebels fight the Imperial Forces on the ice planet, Hoth.

The Grinch
The Grinch is the enemy of the Whos, and the Mayor is the enemy of the Grinch. Both the Mayor and the Grinch want to be the Cheermeister and win the love of Martha May Whovier.

The Wizard of Oz
Dorothy and Elmira Gulch fight for possession of Toto. Dorothy and the Wicked Witch of the West fight for possession of the Ruby Slippers. The Ruby Slippers represents the ultimate source of power in Oz.

Shrek
Lord Farquaard wants to marry Fiona, the woman Shrek loves.

Spider-Man
The Green-Goblin wants to terrorize and rule the city.

Finding Nemo
The Dentist and Darla are the enemies of Marlin and Nemo.

Monsters, Inc.
Randall is the enemy of Sulley and Mike.

Bruce Almighty
Evan is Bruce's rival for the TV Anchorman position.

Matrix Trilogy
The Agent Smiths and the Machines are Neo's enemies.

Pirates of the Caribbean
Barbossa is the enemy of all.

Harry Potter-The Sorcerer's Stone
Voldemort and the Slytherin's are Harry's enemies.

Lord of the Rings Trilogy
The Dark Lord Sauron and his minions are the enemies of the Fellowship and the people of Middle Earth.

RELATIVES

"...when the tragic incident occurs between those who are near or dear to one another—if, for example, a brother intends to kill a brother, a son his father, a mother her son, a son his mother, or any other deed of this kind is done—these are the situations to be looked for by the poet."
—Aristotle: *Poetics*

Emotionally gripping conflict often occurs between the protagonist and a member of his family: his father, mother, brother, sister, spouse, or child. If one of these characters produces obstacles for the protagonist, then the conflict becomes emotionally intense for the audience. This is because these primal relationships are expected to be loving and supportive, not conflict generating.

Titanic
Rose's mother wants her to stop seeing Jack because she needs Cal's money for the family to survive.

Star Wars
Luke fights with his aunt and uncle over his desire to leave the farm and join his friends at college.

Phantom Menace
Anakin's mother is supportive of him going with the Jedi Knights. There are no conflicts among relatives in this movie, unless you consider the Jedi Knights a family. Then, there is a conflict between Yoda and Qui-Gon over the training of Anakin Skywalker.

E.T.
Elliott has conflicts with his brother and mother; they don't believe him when he tells them he saw a creature in the back yard. He is also unhappy about his father deserting the family.

Jurassic Park
Dr. Hammond has placed the lives of his grandchildren in danger, although he didn't intend to do this.

The Lion King
Simba must fight his uncle, Scar, for control of the kingdom.

Forrest Gump
Forrest has the complete support of his mother but lacks a father.

Return of the Jedi
Luke must fight with his father, Darth Vader, who wants Luke to join the dark side of the force.

Batman
Bruce Wayne has problems establishing any intimate relationships since he witnessed his parents murdered as a child.

Home Alone
Kevin's family rejects him because of the mess that he made while they were eating. He is unhappy with them because they treat him like an inept child.

Jaws
Capt. Brody has the support of his wife throughout the story. His son places himself in jeopardy by going out on a boat on July 4th. This causes a lot of stress for Capt. Brody.

Independence Day
Russell Casse has conflicts with his children because they consider him to be a crazy drunk. David Levinson is constantly bickering with his father who believes he should be much more than just an engineer at a Cable TV station. President Tom Whitmore has a conflict with his wife because he wants her to vacate Los Angeles immediately. She refuses and wants to stay until the end of the press conference, a delay that causes her death.

Men in Black
J and K do not have families. To join MIB, they had to dissociate themselves completely from their previous life.

Sixth Sense
Cole Sears feels he cannot tell his mother that he sees dead people.

Empire Strikes Back
Luke Skywalker has to fight with his father, Darth Vader.

The Grinch
The Grinch does not have a family. His only companion is his dog. Cindy Lou Who's parents support her and all her actions.

The Wizard of Oz
Dorothy fights with her aunt and uncle in order to save Toto from Elmira Gulch. When she loses, she runs away from home.

Shrek
Shrek and Donkey do not have relatives, but Fiona was placed in the catle by her parents.

Spider-Man
Peter argues with his uncle Ben, then feels responsible when Ben is killed. Peter loves Aunt May, but his actions as Spider-Man place her in jeopardy.

Finding Nemo
Marlin is over-protective of Nemo but loves him dearly. Nemo wants his father to let him play with his friends.

Monsters, Inc.
There are no relatives in this movie.

Bruce Almighty
Grace's sister Debbie thinks that Bruce is wasting Grace's life.

Matrix Trilogy
Neo does not have relatives.

Pirates of the Caribbean
Will cannot accept that his father was a pirate. Liz fights with her father who wants her to marry Norrington instead of Will.

Harry Potter-The Sorcerer's Stone
Harry lives with abusive relatives.

Lord of the Rings Trilogy
Frodo enjoys the company of Bilbo, who bequeaths Frodo the Ring.

FRIENDS

Friends are the people we choose to spend time with as opposed to relatives with whom we have a biological relationship and years of shared experiences while growing up together. Friendships are also usually the results of shared values and goals. Conflict is generated between friends when either the common objectives change or the shared values change.

When characters that are friends fight over an object, there is more at stake emotionally than when people who are strangers engage in conflict. In these situations, questions of loyalty versus personal gain come into play that create emotional torment within both the characters and the audience. Betrayal by a friend is a powerful emotional situation in a story.

Titanic
There are no conflicts among friends in this movie, unless you consider the sailors blocking the efforts of men and the lower classes to board the lifeboats.

Star Wars
There is conflict between Han and Leia concerning tactics. Luke and Han argue about Han's mercenary attitude, and C-3P0 is always bickering with R2D2.

Phantom Menace
There is a conflict between Yoda and Qui-Gon over the training of Anakin Skywalker to become a Jedi Knight.

E.T.
Elliott has conflicts with his brother's friends, but in the end, they help Elliott and E.T. escape.

Jurassic Park
Dr. Hammond has a conflict with Dennis, the computer expert, who demands more money to run the Jurassic Park computer systems.
Dr. Hammond also has a conflict with Ian, the Chaos Scientist, and both Dr. Grant and Ellie about the dangers involved in operating Jurassic Park.

The Lion King
Scar's friends, the hyenas, destroy him at the end of the story. Timon and Pumba fight with Simba against Scar.

Return of the Jedi
Han and Princess Leia first fight with the Ewoks, who later become their allies in the battle against the Empire.

Batman
Bruce Wayne has only one close friend, his butler Alfred, who is supportive of his crime fighting activities.

Home Alone
Kevin doesn't have any friends except the old man who saves him at the end of the movie.

Forrest Gump
Lt. Dan hates Forrest, his "friend," for saving his life when he believes he should have died with his men in Vietnam.

Jaws
Capt. Brody has a conflict with his friend, the Mayor, about closing the beach because of the shark.

Independence Day
There are only minor conflicts among friends in this film, like the scene in which Steve "borrows" the helicopter to search for his girlfriend. Steve also has a conflict with his pilot friend who advises him to break off his relationship with Jasmine if he wants to advance his career. President Tom Whitmore has a conflict with the Secretary of Defense whom he removes from office.

Men in Black
There is no conflict among friends. Any possible conflict is dealt with by erasing the person's memory.

Sixth Sense
Cole Sears' schoolmates abuse him. He has no friends and is tormented by dead people.

Empire Strikes Back
Leia and Han are constantly bickering throughout the movie.

The Grinch
The Grinch doesn't have any friends, except for his companion dog. There is much conflict among the Whos, generated by the Mayor, on the issue of the Grinch being selected as the Cheermeister.

The Wizard of Oz
Conflict among friends only exists in the prelude, when all the farmhands are too busy to listen to Dorothy's problems. Once she gets over the rainbow, all her new friends are always supportive.

Shrek
Donkey wants to be friends with Shrek, who rejects him.

Spider-Man
Peter's best friend, Harry Osborn, starts dating MJ, the girl Peter loves.

Finding Nemo
Marlin argues with Dory.

Monsters, Inc.
Sulley and Mike constantly bicker and break up when in Nepal.

Bruce Almighty
Bruce fights with the Station Manager.

Matrix Trilogy
Neo has the support of Morpheus but is betrayed by Cypher.

Pirates of the Caribbean
Jack cheats and betrays everyone because he is a pirate.

Harry Potter-The Sorcerer's Stone
Harry and his friends, Ron and Hermione, support each other.

Lord of the Rings Trilogy
Gandalf is betrayed by Saruman. Members of The Fellowship support each other while on the quest.

LOVERS

The most emotionally intense relationship, of course, is between **lovers**. If the protagonist decides to place a lover in jeopardy for an objective, the objective must be extremely important, or he will lose the empathy of the audience. This type of sacrifice is usually only acceptable when the survival of the community is at stake, and only when the protagonist makes his choice after much anguish and sorrow.

Titanic
Cal argues with Rose and insists that she stops seeing Jack.

Star Wars
A constant bickering exists between Han and Leia who are potential lovers.

Phantom Menace
There is no conflict between the lovers in this film.

E.T.
There is no love interest in this film. Elliott wants possession of E.T., but only as a friend.

Jurassic Park
Dr. Grant and Ellie have disagreements over his attitude towards children.

The Lion King
Simba and Nala quarrel over Simba's refusal to return and accept his rightful place as king.

Return of the Jedi
There is not a conflict between lovers in this film.

Batman
Bruce Wayne loves Vicki Vale but has problems telling her the truth about his secret life.

Home Alone
There is no conflict between lovers in this film.

Forrest Gump
Forrest loves Jenny, who doesn't want him as a lover, just a friend.

Jaws
Capt. Brody has the support of his wife.

Independence Day
There are only minor conflicts between Jasmine and Steve when he decides to return to El Toro military base. Connie and David Levinson got divorced, yet he continues to love her.

Men in Black
K still loves the woman that he had to leave behind years ago when he joined the MIB. He watches over her, but he cannot make contact with her until he leaves the MIB and has his memory erased.

Sixth Sense
Dr. Malcolm Crowe and his wife seem to have a problem of communication throughout the film, until at the end, the audience realizes that this is because Dr. Malcolm is dead.

Empire Strikes Back
Princess Leia and Han Solo are constantly arguing throughout the story.

The Grinch
Martha May Whovier is the lover that the Grinch desires, but he is blocked by the efforts of the Mayor.

The Wizard of Oz
There is not a conflict between lovers in this film.

Shrek
Shrek and Fiona separate because of a misunderstanding.

Spider-Man
Peter, MJ, and Harry have a love triangle.
Peter will not tell MJ that he loves her.

Finding Nemo
There are no lovers in this movie.

Monsters, Inc.
Mike and Celia argue about why he left her at the restaurant on her Birthday.

Bruce Almighty
Bruce and Grace argue, then separate.

Matrix Trilogy
Trinity is supportive of Neo.

Pirates of the Caribbean
Will does not tell Liz he loves her after they defeated Barbossa.

Harry Potter-The Sorcerer's Stone
There are no lovers in this story.

Lord of the Rings Trilogy
Aragorn loves Arwen, not Eowyn.

PHYSICAL OBJECTS

Physical objects are obstacles that can create conflict for the protagonist and excitement for the audience, especially when these objects create *jeopardy* for the protagonist. The audience feels happy whenever a character overcomes a dangerous obstacle.

Titanic
When the Titanic is sinking, the locked gates become an obstacle that prevents the lower class people from getting on deck.

Star Wars
Luke and his companions struggle to survive the snakelike beast in the garbage pit. Luke must get R2D2 to stabilize the fighter plane during the attack on the Death Star.

Phantom Menace
The Jedi Spaceship needs a new Hyper-drive. Anakin must avoid rock formations and the other pods during the Pod race.

E.T.
E.T. must integrate the children's toys in order to create a communications device. They must get over the police barricade during the climax scene.

Jurassic Park
Dr. Grant must climb up a tree to save Tim who is stuck in a car in the tree branches. The branches collapse, and Dr. Grant and Tim are almost crushed by the car as they race down the tree. The security fences block their escape.

The Lion King
Simba must survive the stampede of the wild beasts.

Forrest Gump
Forrest must learn to play ping pong.

Return of the Jedi
The Rebel fighters must maneuver through the Death Star to destroy the power source at its center.

Batman
Batman must devise a solution to the Smylex poison formula. Batman must climb the long stairway to the top of the cathedral.

Home Alone
Kevin must devise a way of using household objects to protect his home from the burglars. These household objects become physical obstacles for the burglars.

Jaws
The ocean and the water are the primary obstacles that the humans face when trying to escape from the shark.

Independence Day
Humans on the streets of New York City must escape from the fireball produced by the aliens if they hope to survive.

Men in Black
J must run through traffic in the opening scene in order to catch an alien.

Sixth Sense
Dr. Malcolm breaks a door window as he watches his wife being courted by another man. He tries to stop the man as he drives away from his house.

Empire Strikes Back
Han Solo must maneuver the Millennium Falcon through the asteroid field.

The Grinch
The Grinch must stop the heavy sleigh filled with presents from sliding over the cliff. Cindy Lou Who is sitting on top of the sleigh and will be killed if it falls.

The Wizard of Oz
Dorothy cannot open the door to the underground shelter during the tornado. Dorothy is hit on the head by her bedroom window. Dorothy's friends must break through the door in the witch's castle to save her.

Shrek
Shrek and Donkey must cross the old wooden bridge to get to the castle.

Spider-Man
Peter must run across rooftops to get to the thief that killed Uncle Ben.

Finding Nemo
Nemo must place the pebble into the fish tank filter.

Monsters, Inc.
Sulley must ride the conveyer belts to find Boo's door.

Bruce Almighty
Bruce tries to stop his pager from ringing.

Matrix Trilogy
Trinity must complete the phone call before she is crushed by the truck.

Pirates of the Caribbean
Jack Sparrow must find a way to get out of jail.

Harry Potter-The Sorcerer's Stone
Harry must get across the magical chessboard.

Lord of the Rings Trilogy
Frodo must escape from the Spider's webs before he is eaten by Shelob.

NATURAL WORLD

The **natural world** is also a major source of conflict in stories, both in the obstacles that it creates for the characters, and in not easily conforming to their will. *Time* plays a critical factor in many of these films. The fact that the objective must be obtained within a set period produces tension and excitement within the story. *Distance, the nature of the terrain*, and *weather conditions* also create obstacles. *Social structures, customs, laws* and *politics* can be used to create frustration for the characters.

Titanic
The iceberg and the frigid waters of the Atlantic Ocean are the major natural obstacles for the characters in this movie.

Star Wars
R2D2 and C-3P0 are stranded in a desert on an alien planet. Han must travel through light speed to escape from the Imperial Star Cruisers.

Phantom Menace
The Jedi Knights must escape from the underwater sea monsters.

E.T.
E.T. must overcome a vast distance of space to communicate with his home planet. E.T. and Elliott must ride a bicycle through a forest. E.T. must combat disease in order to survive.

Jurassic Park
Dennis must drive his jeep through the jungle roads during a rainstorm.

The Lion King
The young Simba and Nala must survive the dangers of the Elephant graveyard. Simba must survive his trek through the desert after he leaves the Pride Lands.

Return of the Jedi
Princess Leia and Luke Skywalker must maneuver through the forest trees on their air-motorbikes to capture the fleeing storm troopers.

Batman
The streets of Gotham City are the "natural" environments filled with obstacles for Batman.

Home Alone
Kevin must ride across the clothesline to escape from the burglars.

Forrest Gump
Forrest has to survive the tropical rains in Viet Nam.

Jaws
The ocean and the water are the primary obstacles that the humans face when trying to escape from the shark.

Independence Day
Humans running through the streets of New York overcoming the obstacles produced by cars and traffic while trying to survive the alien's fireball is the "natural environment" of this story. Captain Steve Hiller has to drag the body of a captured alien across a desert.

Men in Black
Driving through the congested traffic in the Holland Tunnel is an urban "natural environment" filled with obstacles for J and K.

Sixth Sense
The major "natural" obstacles in this story are the customs and beliefs of the community. Cole's culture believes that people who see dead people are crazy.

Empire Strikes Back
Luke must make his way through the swamp to find Yoda. He also must retrieve his spaceship from the swamp.

The Grinch
The Grinch has to steer the sleigh safely down the mountainside to deliver all of the presents to the people of Whoville.

The Wizard of Oz
Dorothy wants to get back to Kansas from the Land of Oz. Dorothy and her friends must run through a field of poisonous poppies to get to the Emerald City. The Scarecrow, Tin Man, and Lion must travel across mountains to get to the Witch's castle in order to save Dorothy.

Shrek
Shrek and Donkey must travel a long distance through the countryside to get to Fiona's castle.

Spider-Man
Spider-Man must climb up the side of a building to save MJ.

Finding Nemo
Marlin has to swim through the ocean to find Nemo.

Monsters, Inc.
Sulley must travel through a blizzard to get to the village in Nepal.

Bruce Almighty
Bruce must drive through traffic jams.

Matrix Trilogy
Morpheus must fight agents while traveling down a freeway.

Pirates of the Caribbean
The cursed pirates must walk under water to attack the British ships.

Harry Potter-The Sorcerer's Stone
Harry must survive the dark forest.

Lord of the Rings Trilogy
Frodo and Sam must survive the lava rivers of Mount Doom.

SUPERNATURAL WORLD

The **supernatural**, that which produces terror and is beyond our understanding and control, plays an essential role in many of these megahit movies. Most of these films have characters with powers that are beyond normal human capabilities and antagonists who terrorize the community with their supernatural powers.

Titanic
There are no "supernatural" obstacles in this film. Most of the obstacles result from the cold ocean water and the attitudes of the aristocracy. But there is an extraordinarily large iceberg that sinks the Titanic.

Star Wars
The Force, the mystical powers of Darth Vader and the telepathic powers of the disembodied Obi-Wan Kenobi are crucial to the story.

Phantom Menace
The Jedi Knights must battle the supernatural power of Darth Maul and the surviving Sith.

E.T.
The telepathic and psychokinetic powers of E.T., especially his ability to fly a bicycle across the moon, are important elements of the story.

Jurassic Park
The prehistoric dinosaurs are supernatural creatures that threaten the lives of the characters.

Home Alone
The ability of the young boy, Kevin, to outwit the two burglars and defend his home, if not "supernatural," is definitely extraordinary.

Forrest Gump
There are no supernatural obstacles that Forrest has to overcome. His greatest obstacle in life is being considered different, "inferior" and stupid because of his IQ.

The Lion King
Simba has the supernatural experience of seeing his father among the stars, who advises him to return to the Pride Lands.

Return of the Jedi
Luke must battle the Emperor's supernatural electrical powers.

Batman
The "supernatural-like powers" of Batman, especially his ability to float through space and withstand gunshots, frustrate the criminals.

Jaws
The twenty-five foot 3,000 pound great white shark is the "supernatural" beast that threatens the life of the people of Amity.

Independence Day
Aliens with extraordinary weapons proceed to exterminate the human race. Their defense systems are impenetrable by the most sophisticated weapons available to mankind. Humans must understand their technology and disable or destroy the alien weapons.

Men in Black
Aliens from different worlds seek refuge on Earth. The Edgar-Bug comes to Earth in search of the "Galaxy on Orion's Belt," and destroys any human that gets in his way.

Sixth Sense
Dead people terrorize Cole Sears.

Empire Strikes Back
Luke Skywalker must learn the "ways of the force" to use its power to become a Jedi Knight. Luke must also combat the supernatural powers of Darth Vader and the dark side of the force.

The Grinch
The Grinch is the strange green being who terrorizes Whoville.

The Wizard of Oz
The magical powers of the Wicked Witch, the Wizard of Oz, and the good Witch Glenda are all essential to this story.

Shrek
Fiona was placed under a magical spell. The Dragon becomes an ally of Shrek and Donkey.

Spider-Man
Peter is given the spider-like supernatural powers.

Finding Nemo
There are no supernatural powers or obstacles in this story.

Monsters, Inc.
Randall can become invisible.

Bruce Almighty
Bruce is given the powers of God and gets to walk on water.

Matrix Trilogy
Neo can alter the Matrix.
Agent Smiths can take control of anybody in the Matrix.

Pirates of the Caribbean
The ghost undead pirates of the Black Pearl are cursed by an Aztec magical spell.

Harry Potter-The Sorcerer's Stone
Magic is everywhere in Hogwarts.

Lord of the Rings Trilogy
The Ring makes Frodo invisible.
The Wizards all use supernatural powers.

PLOTS

Plot & Story

Events & Actions

The Inciting Event

Subplots

Plot Arena

Plot Twists

Plot Organization

Plot Outline Workshop

Emotional Plotting

PLOT & STORY

The words **plot** and **story** have many different meanings for screenwriters and academic film theorists. Aristotle, in his book, *Poetics*, states that "The *story*, which are all the events that are presented to us or which we can infer to have happened is different from the *plot*, which is the arrangement of those events in a certain order or structure."

In *Story and Discourse*, Seymour Chatman states "the events in a story are traditionally said to constitute an array called "plot." Aristotle defined plot (mythos) as the 'arrangement of incidents." Structuralist narrative theory argues that the arrangement is precisely the operation performed by discourse. The events in a story are tuned into a plot by its discourse, the modus of presentation. The discourse can be manifested in various media, but it has an internal structure qualitatively different from any one of its possible manifestations. That is plot, story-as-discoursed exists at a more general level than any particular objectification, any given movie, novel, or whatever. Its order of presentation may not be the same as that of the natural logic of the story. Its function is to emphasize or de-emphasize certain story-events, to interpret some and to leave others to inference, to show or to tell, to comment or to remain silent, and to focus on this or that aspect of any event or character. The author "can arrange incidents of a story in a great many ways."

Eugene Vale, in *The Technique of Screen and Television Writing*, offers another distinction. "...we must define the difference between the story and the dramatic construction. The story is the actual happening. The dramatic construction is the way that the happening is told. The story is varied and rich as the life and the world. The dramatic construction consists of a limited number of rules that are applied in order to get certain effects. The story springs from the imagination of the author; the dramatic construction from his technique. The story is the creation; the dramatic construction is the form into which this creation must be poured."

The problem of the same word ("story") being used differently within two traditions (screenwriting and academic film theory) is exacerbated when writing a book to be read by people working in both fields. The only solution possible is to make certain that the word is clearly defined within the context of this book.

We will use **three** distinct fundamental terms in **the conceptual framework for story construction**. The first is ***cinematic experience***, which refers to the immediately perceived unanalyzed phenomena of viewing a movie. The second is the term *plot*, which is equivalent to the traditional meaning of the term: "an ordering of the events" used to represent the cinematic experience. The third will be *story*, which is defined as "the series of actions that a character performs while pursuing his primary objective and its subgoals." The story is also a representation of the cinematic experience. Our use of the terms "story" and "plot" differ from Aristotle's terminology. This is justified since more than 2,250 years also separates our theories, along with the many different modes and mediums of dramatic presentation which did not exist during Aristotle's lifetime.

A *story* focuses on the **actions**, the transformations of a character's values, his emotional reactions, interpersonal relationships, and code of behavior, as he faces conflict while pursuing his primary objective and subgoals. The character's emotional reactions to events and the actions of other characters are essential elements in the story.

A *plot* is the series of events that occur from the beginning of the cinematic experience to its conclusion. It is a description of things that **happen** to the characters and is not concerned with the character's emotional reactions. To describe a plot is to list all the events that occur in a chronological order.

These distinctions will be further developed in the section on **events and actions.** They will help to explain why audiences have more appreciation for a "well-constructed story" than "a complex plot". While the later may be intellectually challenging, the former is more emotionally engrossing and produces a much higher degree of audience empathy for the characters. The audience finds "over plotted" films to be unsatisfactory because there is not enough change and development in the personal lives of the characters. These distinctions also will be fruitful in helping us to define the structures necessary for a film to be a **satisfying emotional experience.**

EVENTS & ACTIONS

There is much philosophical debate about the meanings of the words "event" and "action."

Seymour Chatman, in *Story and Discourse*, asks "but what is an event, in the narrative sense? Events are either actions (acts) or happenings. Both are a change of state. An action is a change of state brought about by an agent or one that affects a patient. If the action is plot-significant, the agent or patient is called a character."

How are we to understand the distinction between actions and happenings; between actions we perform and things that happen to us? Carlos J. Moya, in *Philosophy of Action*, offers the following considerations:

> One of the most fundamental distinctions in our worldview is the one we draw between what we do and what happens to us, between actions and mere happenings...We have a consciousness that at least some things—even if a few—are in our power, depend on us; we think we can somehow influence the course of events by acting, instead of suffering it; we think that we are agents, and not just passive things...

The distinction between **events** and **actions** is also essential for the application of the cognitive theory of emotions to the analysis of popular films. This theory analyzes emotional reactions to three fundamental entities: events, agents (and their actions), and objects. The value of this distinction will be born out by the theory's explanatory power in the analysis of popular films.

An **action** is something that a character does to himself, an object, or another character.

An **event** is something that happens to the character, something that impacts him, and over which he has little control.

Being hit by a car is an *event*, but the antagonist intentionally hitting another character is an *action*.

Drama is not about accidental *events* that happen to individuals. It is about **how the characters react to these *events***. It is also about characters making decisions under conflict and performing actions while in pursuit of an objective that represents fundamental human values.

Audiences tend to lose interest in stories where the character's problems are not solved through their own decisions and actions but by accidental events. These conceptual distinctions also start early in life. The psychologist, Jerome Bruner, in *Acts of Meaning,* states,

> Once young children come to grasp the basic idea of reference necessary for any language use—that is, once they can name, can note recurrence, and can register termination of existence—their principle linguistic interest centers on human action and its outcomes, particularly human interaction.
>
> Agent-and-action, action-and-object, agent-and-object, action-and-location, and possessor-and-possession make up the major part of the semantic relations that appear in the first stage of speech...the young child, moreover, is early and profoundly sensitive to "goals" and their achievement...

THE INCITING EVENT

Each movie has an important incident called the **inciting event**, in which something happens to the protagonist that radically changes his life. Often his home is destroyed, or his life, as he knew it, is radically altered. This is the point when the story begins as the protagonist tries to regain something that he has lost: usually a feeling of safety. In the megahit movies, he attempts either to find a new home or to preserve his home from further destruction.

The inciting event will eventually lead to the climax scene and can be considered to be the "root cause" of that scene. It is also the event that forces the protagonist to make a major decision: the decision of personal commitment to the primary objective of the story.

The inciting event is usually not the result of the intentional action of the protagonist, but is an external event that has an impact on his life. This becomes a point of no return from which the protagonist must move forward, overcoming obstacles in his efforts to achieve his primary goal.

Titanic
In this movie there are two inciting events. The first occurs when Jack wins tickets for a trip on the Titanic in a poker game. This event changes his life and the life of the protagonist, Rose. The second inciting event occurs when the Titanic runs into an iceberg and begins to sink. This happens immediately after Jack and Rose make love. The floating home of all the characters is destroyed, and they must find some way to survive.

Star Wars
Luke Skywalker's Aunt and Uncle are killed and his home burned by the Imperial Storm Troopers.

Phantom Menace
The Trade Federation creates a space blockade of Naboo.

E.T.
E.T. is abandoned by his space ship. He feels alone and unsafe in the alien world, planet Earth.

Jurassic Park
The unexpected rainstorm forces the boat to leave earlier than expected. Dennis shuts down the security systems but then gets killed while going through the jungle.

The Lion King
Scar causes the stampede that brings about the death of Mufasa and the exile of Simba. Simba is not safe in the Pride Lands and now must find a new home.

Forrest Gump
Forrest is fitted with leg braces.

Return of the Jedi
The inciting event occurred at the end of the prior film, *Empire Strikes Back,* when Han Solo was encased in the carbonic slab and sent to Jabba the Hut. Luke's objective is to free Han.

Batman
The personal inciting event for Bruce Wayne was his witnessing the murder of his parents when he was a child. This provides him with the motivation of a lifetime: the elimination of crime from the city. But in this movie, when Jack Napier falls into the green vat of chemicals, he is transformed into The Joker. Then through his actions, he transforms the world of Batman, Gotham City, and makes it a much more dangerous place for everyone.

Home Alone
A storm knocks out the power lines, causing the clocks to stop and the family to oversleep. Kevin is forgotten and abandoned by his family as they rush to catch a plane to Paris. Alone, he must learn to survive and also to protect his home from the burglars.

Jaws
The shark kills a woman swimming in the ocean at night. The next day the woman's body is found by the Police Capt. Brody. Brody must then protect his home and the community of Amity from being destroyed by the shark.

Men in Black
The Edgar-Bug crashes on earth and starts a rampage as it searches for "the Galaxy on Orion's Belt." J and K must find this "galaxy," before their home, the planet Earth, is destroyed by the other Aliens.

Independence Day
Alien spaceships fly into the Earth's atmosphere on the July 4th weekend and proceed to exterminate the human race.

Sixth Sense
A former child patient of Dr. Malcom Crowe sneaks into his house during a celebration party and shoots him.

Empire Strikes Back
Luke Skywalker has a vision of Obi-Wan Kenobi who tells him to go to Dagobah and study with Yoda to become a Jedi Knight.

The Grinch
Four young Who teenagers (two boys and two girls) climb to the top of Mt. Crumpit and knock on the Grinch's door.

The Wizard of Oz
The tornado destroys Dorothy's home and transports her to Oz.

Shrek
Fairy Tale creatures invade Shrek's swamp.

Spider-Man
Peter Parker is bitten by a genetically enhanced spider.

Finding Nemo
Nemo is captured by the fishermen.

Monsters, Inc.
Boo leaves her room and walks into the factory.

Bruce Almighty
Bruce loses the anchorman position, goes crazy, and is fired from his job.

Matrix Trilogy
Neo takes the red pill.

Pirates of the Caribbean
Liz falls into the ocean wearing the Aztec Gold coin. Once it hits the water, the ghost pirates know where to look for it.

Harry Potter-The Sorcerer's Stone
Harry is taken to Hogwarts on his eleventh birthday.

Lord of the Rings Trilogy
Bilbo leaves Frodo the Ring.

SUBPLOTS

"A strong subplot mirrors the main plot in some way. It presents a similar conflict from a different angle, from another character's perspective. It becomes a counter-theme of sorts, underscoring the message of the premise."
—T.L. Katahn, *Reading for a Living*

Subplots have been traditionally defined as "supportive" of the main plot and in some way related to it. Using subplots can also cause many problems. Linda Seger, in *Making a Good Script Great*, states:

> Subplots are responsible for many script problems. Some films have failed because of weak subplot integration. These problems seem to fall into several categories. First of all, many times subplots lack structure. They ramble, they're unfocused, and they disorient the audience so that the audience doesn't know what the story is really about or what's going on. Sometimes a film has problems because the subplot doesn't intersect the plot and it doesn't seem to have any bearing on the story. Although the subplot might be interesting, it seems to float, unconnected, apart from anything else happening in the story.

The concept of a ***subgoal*** is much more helpful for constructing stories. While there is only one primary objective to a story, there may be many subgoals that the characters pursue in their attempt to achieve this objective. Minor characters help to accomplish these subgoals, and each of the minor characters has their own set of values. The values of the minor characters are very often different from the values of the protagonist. This contrast helps the audience to focus on the codes of behavior that are being tested in these conflicts. The way a minor character's values impact the successful or unsuccessful obtainment of the subgoal constitutes a ***subplot***. In this way, the subplot can be connected to the primary objective of the story.

The effective use of subplots demonstrates alternative codes of behavior that often lead to failure. Eventually, all subplots should converge to the final story climax where the protagonist reveals his true values in the battle with the antagonist.

Most megahits use the subgoal structure instead of the subplot structure. This allows the action line to be more focused for the audience. The audience also does not have to dilute their emotional involvement among too many different characters. But some megahits do use subplots.

In *Batman*, for example, there is the subplot involving Alexander Knox, the newspaper reporter who seeks to expose Batman in order to win a Pulitzer Prize. This character is seeking the limelight and pursues the prize for his personal glory, even if it damages the fight against crime and leads to the destruction of the community. Bruce Wayne, on the other hand, performs his community-protection service effectively and anonymously. Both characters are also pursuing the love-interest, Vicki Vale, as is the antagonist, the Joker. At the end of the story, both Alexander and the Joker lose Vicki, who decides to join Bruce Wayne.

In *Independence Day*, there are four subplots that revolve around the four protagonists, each of whom share the ultimate objective of saving the human race from destruction by the aliens. But they each also have a specific primary objective. Russell Casse wants to regain his self-respect and the respect of his children and the community. He does this by warning the community of the destructive intentions of aliens and, finally, by flying his fighter into their ultimate weapon and destroying their ship. David Levinson wants to save the world and win back the love of his ex-wife. He accomplishes both. Steve Hillier wants to become an astronaut and marry Jasmine. He does both. President Tom Whitmore wants to preserve his family and fulfill his duties as President and help save the world. Although he loses his wife, he does preserve the life of his child and helps to destroy the aliens.

In *Pirates of the Caribbean*, there is the subplot of the love triangle between Norrington, Liz, and Will. The main story line involves the antagonist Barbossa's efforts to gain the Aztec Gold Coin from Liz, Will, and Jack in order to eliminate the curse. After Barbossa has been defeated, the problem of the love triangle with Norrington still has to be resolved.

In *Lord of the Rings*, the main story line is about Frodo and his efforts to destroy the Ring in Mount Doom. The major subplot concerns Aragorn becoming King of Gondor. This subplot also involves the stories of Theoden of Rohan, Steward Denethor of Gondor, Aragorn's love for Arwen, and Eowyn's love for Aragorn.

PLOT ARENA

The **plot arena** or **the setting of the story** is the historical time and place in which the events occur. This is the environment in which the characters struggle for their objectives and reveal the values and interpersonal codes of behavior by which they live. Some screenwriters also refer to this as the **frame of the story**.

The plot arena defines the limits of the actions and conflicts: what is and is not possible in that world. In this way it serves as a restrictive constraint, for there is no conflict in a world where people can do anything without loss. If scarcity did not exist, then there would be no conflict. This is why dramatically effective stories are designed around **one unique object** both the protagonist and the antagonist desire to possess.

The plot arena provides a 'symbol system' for the story. This system visually enriches the drama. But it must be emphasized that **the story** is more important than **the plot**, because the audience will only have empathy for the characters with which they can relate. The story must focus on the emotional reactions, universal concerns, and the values by which characters live and die. Ultimately, stories are about characters under conflict, and not about foreign places and different times. Megahit movies place their stories in extraordinary worlds different from the normal everyday world that the audience experiences.

Titanic
The plot arena is the attitudes and values of the aristocratic class on a transatlantic ocean voyage.

Star Wars
The plot arena is the distant high-tech future where an Imperial Army fights with rebels for control of the universe.

Phantom Menace
The plot arena is the distant high-tech future where Jedi Knights battle a Trade Federation and Sith Lords.

E.T.
The plot arena is contemporary suburban America where Elliott and the space alien E.T. struggle to preserve their freedom and return home to safety.

Jurassic Park
The plot arena is a jungle island where Dr. Hammond has created a prehistoric theme park containing live dinosaurs.

The Lion King
A jungle kingdom filled with animals that have human personalities and emotional conflicts is the plot arena of this story.

Return of the Jedi
The plot arena is the distant high-tech future where Rebels fight an Imperial Army for control of the universe.

Batman
The plot arena is a mythic urban Gotham City. Here, a classic battle between Good and Evil takes place for the control of the city.

Home Alone
The plot arena is a contemporary middle-America suburban neighborhood and home which allows for mass audience identification.

Forrest Gump
The plot arena is the history of American life in the 1960s and 1970s from the point of view of a simple moral man.

Jaws
The plot arena is the July 4th holiday on the beaches of Amity.

Independence Day
The plot arena is the contemporary United States and the World, invaded by aliens from another planet.

Men in Black
The plot arena is the contemporary New York City metropolitan area visited by aliens from another planet.

Sixth Sense
The plot arena is a contemporary middle-America suburban neighborhood and home in which lives a young boy who sees dead people.

Empire Strikes Back
The plot arena is the distant high-tech future where an Imperial Army fights with rebels for control of the universe.

The Grinch
The plot arena is the imaginary snow covered world of Whoville in which people with funny noses are terrorized by a large hairy green beast.

The Wizard of Oz
The plot arena is the magical Land of Oz where Witches and Wizards battle for power and one young girl desires to get back home to Kansas.

Shrek
The plot arena is a fairy tale kingdom.

Spider-Man
The plot arena is contemporary New York City where a young man wearing a red-blue spider costume swings between skyscrapers and climbs up the side of buildings.

Finding Nemo
The plot arena is the ocean and a fish tank, experienced from the point-of-view of the fish.

Monsters, Inc.
The plot arena is in a world where harmless monsters scare little children.

Bruce Almighty
The plot arena is a city where an average guy gets to play God.

Matrix Trilogy
The plot arena is the futuristic world of the Matrix.

Pirates of the Caribbean
The plot arena is the world of cursed pirates who are ghosts.

Harry Potter-The Sorcerer's Stone
The plot arena is the magical world of Hogwarts: a school for young magicians.

Lord of the Rings Trilogy
The plot arena is the magical world of warring Wizards, Hobbits, and Kings in Middle-earth.

PLOT TWISTS

"Reversal of the situation is a change by which the action veers round to its opposite, subject always to our rule of probability or necessity."
—Aristotle, *Poetics*

"Construct a course that keeps the reader off balance. The pleasure of reading is in experiencing the unexpected twist of character or plot that keeps us guessing. Precisely at the moment when the reader thinks he knows what is going to happen, something else happens that upsets his theory and forces him to come up with a new one."
—Ronald Tobias, *Theme and Strategy*

A **plot twist** usually occurs when a character successfully obtaining a subgoal does not achieve the expected result. This introduces the element of surprise and unpredictability to the story, especially when the audience had been made aware of the plans to achieve the subgoal.

Characters create **audience expectations** by **discussing plans** for future events and **designing strategies** so that a series of actions will result in the accomplishment of a subgoal. But when the event fails to occur, the audience is surprised. These plot twists force the characters to devise new strategies and plans that also will fail to result in the desired outcome. This new result will then "spin" the characters off into another course of action (i.e., in search for a new subgoal).

Other plot twists occur when something happens in the story that was not anticipated by either the characters or the audience. These plot twists were not a result of the subgoal not being obtained. But this new unexpected event forces the characters to completely change their plans, and to come up with a new set of subgoals to achieve their primary objective. A plot twist can also be a moment of sudden recognition, like when Luke Skywalker discovers that Princess Leia is his sister in *Return of the Jedi.* Syd Field, in *Screenplay,* calls these surprise events *plot points.*

A story can have many subgoals, provided that the one primary objective is retained throughout. The audience should always know the final objective, otherwise, they become confused and could lose interest in the story. Using the plot twist structure makes the story unpredictable, constantly surprises the audience, and helps to keep them engrossed in the story.

Plot Twists are based on a *setup and payoff* structure in which the audience is intentionally misled by the writer. But it is important that the characters within the story be sincere about their plans and objectives in order to maintain audience empathy. If a character becomes untrustworthy, the audience will usually lose empathy for him. If the expected result fails to occur because of actions from the opposing characters, then the audience is surprised. They also become intrigued and wonder what will happen next. If the failure is due to bad planning or the incompetent execution of the plans, then the audience will laugh. Incompetence is one of the standard comic techniques that will be discussed in greater detail in the sections on humor.

The more plot twists in a story, the more excitement the audience will feel. This is especially true in the climax scene which should never be predictable. Events should never conclude exactly the way the audience expects. The protagonist should accomplish his objective in this scene but never in the manner planned and expected. This is true in almost all of the megahit films.

Titanic
Cal places the jewel, "the heart of the ocean," into his coat pocket, intending to ensure that he will take it with him when the ship sinks. Instead, he gives the coat to Rose, who gets to keep the jewel.

Star Wars
This climax scene proceeds as planned. Luke is able to "lob" the torpedo into the shaft and destroys the Death Star. He accomplishes this not by using the "computerized technology," but instead "spiritually," by listening to the voice of Obi-Wan Kenobi, which was unexpected. It is not the intelligence or technology that destroys the Death Star. It is Luke working in conjunction with "the force." Han Solo's unexpected return at the last moment defeats Darth Vader's attempts to destroy Luke.

Phantom Menace
Padme is the real Queen Amidala.

E.T.
E.T.'s death is unexpected as is his return to life after "phoning home". E.T. and friends escape the police barricade by flying over it.

The Lion King
Scar is destroyed by the Jackals whom he had chosen as his allies.

Forrest Gump
Every major event in Forrest's life ends in a plot twist, since he becomes a great success by completely focusing on whatever it is he is doing.

Return of the Jedi
Luke Skywalker learns that Princess Leia is his sister.

Batman
The Joker is defeated by Batman and falls to his death but not in a manner expected by the audience.

Jurassic Park
An unexpected tropical storm forces the tour of the park to be cut short. It also causes problems for Dennis as he tries to get to the boat with the dinosaur embryos. Dr. Hammond shuts down the computer systems with the expectation that they will immediately come back up, but they do not. Dr. Hammond sends his grandchildren on what he believes will be an entertaining ride, but instead, places their lives in danger.

Jaws
Quint, the hunter of sharks, is hunted and eaten by the great white shark.

Home Alone
Kevin finally defeats the two burglars in the climax scene but only with the unexpected help of the old man.

Independence Day
Russell Casse, the incompetent alcoholic pilot who was sexually abused by aliens, destroys the alien spaceship.

Men in Black
The "Galaxy on Orion's belt" is inside a jewel on the collar around the neck of the cat, Orion.

Sixth Sense
Dr. Malcolm Crowe believes he can help Cole stop seeing dead people, but it turns out that he is one of the dead. He died the night he was shot by his former patient.

Empire Strikes Back
In the climax fight scene, Luke Skywalker learns that his enemy, Darth Vader, is really his father.

The Grinch
The Grinch is elected Cheermeister but then goes on a rampage and destroys the Whobilation Celebration. The Grinch later returns all the presents that he stole from the people of Whoville, apologizes, and ends up actually saving Christmas for them.

The Wizard of Oz
Dorothy gets the Witch's broomstick, but not as expected, for she never planned to throw water on the Witch. Dorothy gets back to Kansas, but not as expected, for the Wizard floats off in the balloon without her. It's the power in the ruby slippers that takes her back home.

Shrek
After the magical spell wears off in the climax scene, Fiona is still ugly.

Spider-Man
Peter does not tell MJ that he loves her in the final scene.

Finding Nemo
After the fish tank filter is clogged, the Dentist just replaces it without removing the fish from the tank.

Monsters, Inc.
Mr. Waternoose is in cahoots with Randall.

Bruce Almighty
Answering "yes" to everyone's prayers makes people unhappy and causes a riot.

Matrix Trilogy
Neo chooses to save the life of Trinity instead of the people of Zion.

Pirates of the Caribbean
Barbossa believes that Liz is the daughter of Bootstrap Turner. But when he cuts her, and her blood drops into the treasure, the curse does not end.

Harry Potter-The Sorcerer's Stone
Prof. Quirrell is the real villain of the story, not Snape.

Lord of the Rings Trilogy
Frodo decides not to destroy the Ring. As prophesied by Gandalf, Gollum does have an important role to play in the destiny of the Ring. But it is Gollum who destroys the Ring by falling into the lava of Mount Doom.

PLOT ORGANIZATION

A plot is an arrangement of events that organizes a cinematic experience. *Acts* are collections or sets of events ordered into a sequence. One way to organize a plot is to arrange it into a *three-act structure*. The acts are distinguished in terms of the specific types of events that occur at the end of each sequence.

Paul Lucey, in *Story Sense*, states that the following three-act story pattern applies to most movies:
The hero takes on the problem in the first act.
The hero seems defeated at the end of the second act.
The hero solves the problem in the third act.

The term *problem* as used in Lucey's story pattern definition can be considered to consist of the primary objective and the major obstacles (including the antagonist) that confront the protagonist as he attempts to achieve his objective.

Many plots in the megahit films are constructed along the following divisions that are **emotionally satisfying for the mass audience**:

Prelude
Introduces the protagonist, love interest, antagonist, story objective; generates empathy for the protagonist and love interest, enmity for the antagonist, and includes the inciting event which transforms the protagonist's world.

Act One
The protagonist's pursuit of the first major subgoal results in the first plot twist. The protagonist confronts the antagonist and prevents the antagonist from possessing both the primary objective and the love interest.

Act Two
The protagonist's pursuit of the second major subgoal results in the second plot twist. The antagonist defeats the protagonist and prevents the protagonist from possessing both the primary objective and the love interest. At the end of the second act the situation of the protagonist appears to be hopeless.

Act Three
The protagonist's pursuit of the third major subgoal results in the third plot twist. The antagonist will have possession of both the primary

objective and the love interest toward the end of this act. In the climax scene, the protagonist will fight with the antagonist for both of these objects. During the battle, the protagonist triumphs, and the antagonist is destroyed. The protagonist usually does **not** directly kill the antagonist, but the antagonist dies as a result of some action by which he attempted to kill the protagonist.

Resolution
The protagonist achieves the objective, saves the love interest, and is celebrated by the community.

E.T. clearly exhibits this structure. In the prelude, E.T. is introduced, the faceless antagonist "keys" pursues him, he is abandoned by his companions in the inciting event, and his primary objective to return home is established. At the end of the first act, Elliott possesses E.T. in his room, thereby preventing the antagonist from getting him. At the end of the second act, the antagonist invades Elliott's home and captures both him and E.T. In the third act, Elliott arranges for the escape of E.T. and defeats the antagonist. In the resolution, E.T. is rejoined with his companions and returns home as Elliott and his family watch E.T. fly away.

When screenwriters are designing their story, and before they write the first draft of their screenplay, they usually proceed by writing a plot outline, a synopsis, and then a treatment. Once the treatment is written and approved by a producer, then it should be very easy to write the screenplay.

In the motion picture industry, it is traditional to assume that one page of a screenplay equals one minute of screen time. Therefore, producers expect a screenplay to be about 120 pages for a two hour movie.

Since a feature film is about two hours long, or 120 minutes in duration, many screenwriters often attempt to divide the movie into forty (40) segments of three (3) minutes each. Each of these 40 three-minute segments is designed to be a scene. Essential to each scene is a major obstacle that the characters in the scene have to overcome. This is a model of an ideal screenplay. Not all of the produced screenplays will have this structure, but a model is a useful tool that helps the writer design the story. Some story gurus recommend sixty (60) scenes of two (2) pages each. This would quicken the pace of the action and the movie.

If the writer decides to use the structure discussed earlier in this chapter, then they may want to consider allotting the following number of pages to each section:

Prelude = 10 pages; Act 1 = 30 pages; Act 2 = 45 pages; Act 3 = 30 pages; and Resolution = 5 pages.

In the Prelude, the first ten pages of the screenplay, the writer must "hook" the audience by creating empathy for the protagonist and love interest, hatred for the antagonist, and show the primary objective of the story. This is the most important section of the screenplay. In Act One, the conflict between the protagonist and antagonist is further developed up to the first plot twist. In Act Two, the conflict is further "complicated" up through the second major plot twist. By this time, about 85 minutes of screen time will have passed. In Act Three, the climatic battle between the protagonist and antagonist will occur. The action will be extremely intense and very fast, ending with the victory of the hero over the villain. The Resolution scene of the story will be the shortest, showing that the protagonist has achieved his primary objective and showing his victory being celebrated by the community.

An *outline* of the plot consists of one sentence for each of the forty (40) scenes. Each describes the major obstacle of that scene and the character's actions in overcoming that obstacle.

A synopsis is a narration of the story developed from the plot outline. It focuses on presenting the objectives, subgoals, obstacles, events, actions, and plot in a simple easy to read format.

A *treatment* is a dramatization of the plot outline and synopsis. While including all the elements of the plot outline and the synopsis, it focuses on the emotional reactions of the characters in the story. It is designed to sell the story to a producer or studio executive. Therefore, understanding the psychology of the audience (in this case, the readers of the treatment) is necessary because, after reading it, they should have an emotionally satisfying experience. They should be so happy and excited after reading the treatment that they want to buy the story and have the writer develop it into a 120-page feature film screenplay.

On the next two pages is a Plot Outline Worksheet that a writer can use as a template for creating a script. Following that is a graph that represents the audience's emotional responses to plot points in a story. This is one way that a writer can design a story so that the emotional plotting will result in an emotionally satisfying experience for the audience and make the story a popular Hollywood megahit movie.

PLOT OUTLINE WORKSHEET

Unique Object:
Protagonist:
Antagonist:
Love Interest:
Protagonist-Supporter:
Antagonist-Supporter:

Prelude: (10 pages)
Introduces the antagonist: enmity scene (3 pages)

Introduce the protagonist: empathy scene (3 pages)

The protagonist's dream: motivation and the primary objective (2 pages)

The Inciting Event: changes the everyday world of the protagonist and causes him to begin his quest for the unique object (2 pages)

Act One: (30 pages) with at least 10 Obstacles
The protagonist pursues the first subgoal with some resistance, but for each two steps forward, he only takes one step back.

Obstacle 1 - Character overcomes this obstacle-problem
Obstacle 2 - Character overcomes this obstacle-problem
Obstacle 3 - Character overcomes this obstacle-problem
Etc....
Obstacle 10 - Character overcomes this obstacle-problem

The protagonist confronts the antagonist and prevents the antagonist from possessing both the primary objective and the love interest. The completion of the first subgoal results in the first plot twist and sends the protagonist off to accomplish subgoal 2.

Act Two: (45 pages) with at least 15 Obstacles
The protagonist pursues the second subgoal. The antagonist dominates this act. For each step forward, the hero takes two steps back.

Obstacle 1 - Character overcomes this obstacle-problem
Obstacle 2 - Character overcomes this obstacle-problem
Obstacle 3 - Character overcomes this obstacle-problem
Etc....
Obstacle 15 - Character overcomes this obstacle-problem

Protagonist's Desperation Scene

At the end of the second act, the antagonist defeats the protagonist and prevents the protagonist from possessing both the primary objective and the love interest. The protagonist's situation is hopeless and all appears lost. The completion of second subgoal results in the second plot twist.

Act Three: (30 pages) with at least 10 Obstacles

There is a major empathy scene for protagonist. Because of this scene the audience wants the protagonist to win the battle and defeat the antagonist. The protagonist pursues of the third major subgoal.

Obstacle 1 - Character overcomes this obstacle-problem
Obstacle 2 - Character overcomes this obstacle-problem
Obstacle 3 - Character overcomes this obstacle-problem
Etc....
Obstacle 10 - Character overcomes this obstacle-problem

Chase Scene with Ticking Clock
This creates maximum suspense and excitement for the audience.

Climax Scene
The protagonist's attempt to achieve the third major subgoal results in several plot twists. The antagonist will have possession of both the unique object and the love interest before the climax scene. In the climax scene, the protagonist will fight with the antagonist for both. During the battle, the protagonist triumphs and the antagonist is destroyed. The protagonist does not directly kill the antagonist, but the antagonist dies as a result of some action he initiated in his attempt to kill the protagonist.

Resolution (5 pages)
The protagonist either obtains the unique object, or it is destroyed in the climax scene. The protagonist saves the love interest. The community celebrates their victory.

THE EMOTION SCALE

An **Emotional Scale** ranging from +10 to -10 is used in the examples of **Emotional Plotting** and the graph developed in the following sections.
A rating of +10 represents joy, while a -10 represents terror.
A rating of +5 represents happiness, while a -5 represents fear or anxiety.
A rating of 0 represents emotional indifference.

EMOTIONAL PLOTTING
Plotting the Emotional Responses of the Audience
(Examples are from a variety of megahit movies)

Page	Plot Point	Description of Action	Emotion Scale
1	A	Introduce likeable characters. Audience is pleased. (Jaws: Young couple on beach. Naked girl swims in ocean.)	+9
3	B	Introduce the antagonist. Terrorize the audience. (Jaws: Shark eats girl. She screams in terror.)	-10
4	C	Introduce the likeable protagonist. Audience is pleased. (LOR: Frodo reads a book under a tree.)	+3
6-8	D	Protagonist Empathy Situation. Audience has anxiety. (Woz: Dorothy seeks help from aunt, uncle and farmhands)	-3
9	E	Protagonist expresses her motivation. (dreams, hopes, and needs) Audience empathizes and feels good about the protagonist (WIZ: Dorothy sings "Over the Rainbow" song)	+7
10	F	Inciting Event. Audience is anxious for the protagonist. (WIZ: Tornado takes Dorothy away from Kansas)	-7
11	G	Subgoal 1: Protagonist plans and starts towards her goal Audience feels better, but still concerned about protagonist (WIZ: Dorothy plans to go to Oz to see the Wizard)	-5
12-29		Protagonist overcomes obstacles to her subgoal. Emotions of the audience varies in each scene depending on the jeopardy involved and the triumph of the protagonist overcoming her problems. Two steps forward, one step back. (WIZ: Dorothy journeys to the Emerald City)	-5 to +5
30	H	Protagonist protects the unique object & love interest. from antagonist The audience feels good. They believe that the protagonist will prevail. (WIZ: Dorothy arrives at the Emerald City to meet Wizard)	+5
31	I	Plot twist. Need to create a new subgoal and plan. (WIZ: Wizard tells Dorothy to get the Witch's Broomstick)	-1
32-83		Complications: Antagonist attacks and wears down the protagonist. One step forward, two steps back.	+4 to -8

EMOTIONAL PLOTTING
Plotting the Emotional Responses of the Audience
(Examples are from a variety of megahit movies)

84-89	J	Protagonist Desperation: Antagonist has Love Interest and Unique Object. The audience feels that things are hopeless: the protagonist will not win. (WIZ: Dorothy is trapped in the Witch's Castle with Toto and Ruby Slippers.)	-9
90-92	K	Protagonist second major empathy scene. Audience feels bad for the protagonist, hates the antagonist and wants the protagonist to destroy the antagonist. (WIZ: Witch appears in the crystal ball. She mocks Dorothy's cries for help.)	-9
93-99	L, M	Chase &Ticking-Clock: Protagonist life-death fight The audience is driven to a frenzy; between hope and despair. (Woz: Sand slides down the hour clock to the time of Dorothy's death. Dorothy and her friends are chased around the castle by the Witch and Monkeys.)	-4 to +4
100-105	N, O	Climax: Protagonist battles antagonist and appears to be winning.	+6 to +10
106-111	P, Q, R	Climax: Antagonist turns the tables. Protagonist fights back. It appears that the antagonist will win.	-6 to +4
112	S	Climax: Protagonist hits back hard and appears to defeat antagonist. (Spider-Man: Peter knocks the Green Goblin into a brick wall.) Audience is elated by the anticipated victory of the hero.	+8
113-114	T	Climax: Antagonist strikes the death blow. The Protagonist will not survive. (Spider-Man: Green-Goblin launches his spike vehicle to impale Spider-Man) The audience is terrorized.	-10
115-119	U	Climax: Unexpected last minute surprise. The antagonist is destroyed. The audience is relieved and happy. (Spider-Man: Spider jumps out of the way. Goblin is impaled.) (Jurassic Park: T-Rex appears and kills the Raptors)	+9
120	V	Resolution: Protagonist and Love Interest prevail. Happy Ending. The audience is filled with joy. (WIZ: Dorothy and Toto are back home with family.) (Shrek: Wedding celebration scene in the swamp.)	+10

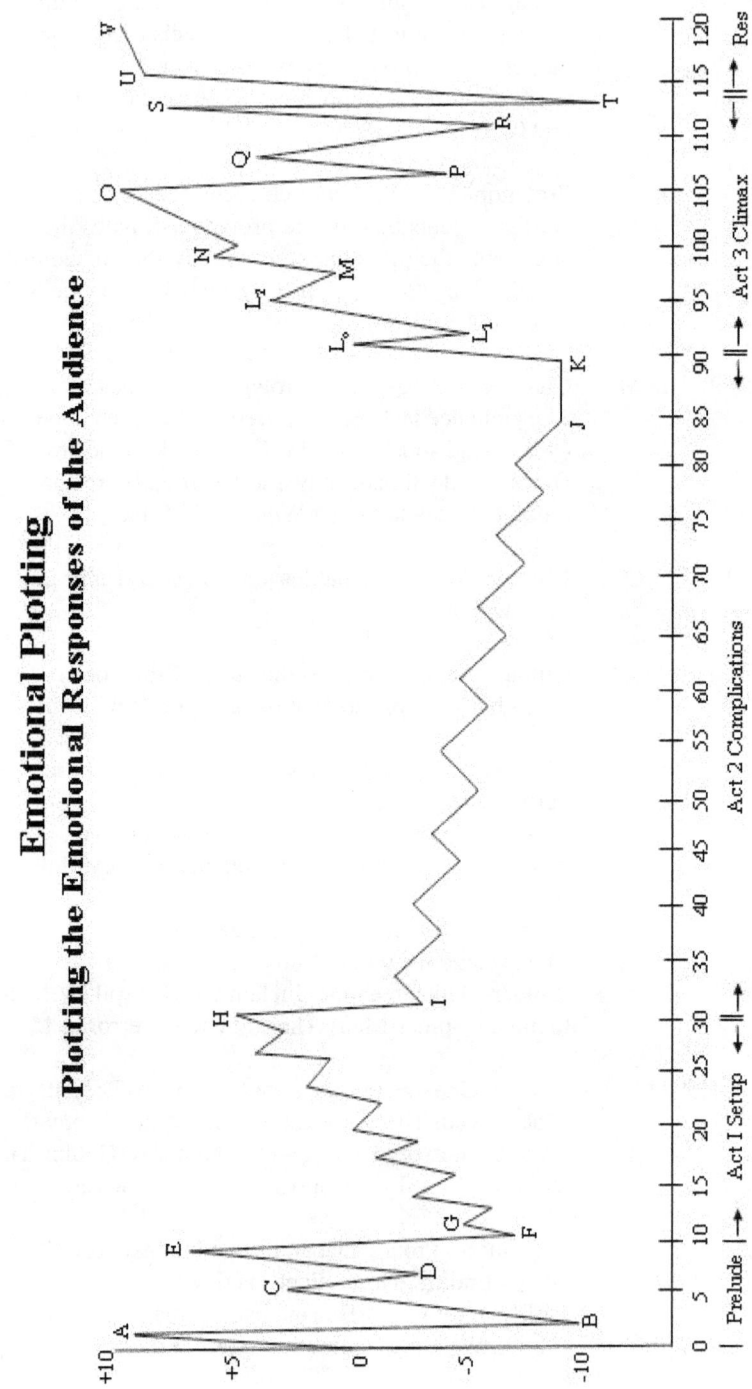

STORY
WHAT'S IT ALL ABOUT?

Human Values

Virtues & Vices

Community Ideals

Basic Story Design

A-Story & B-Story

Story Climax & Plot Climax

HUMAN VALUES

Throughout the history of civilization, human beings have desired and held almost everything conceivable to be valuable. Although values are often relative to a culture and historical period, most people living would agree that the following personal values are worthy of pursuit: life, security, love, freedom, health, wealth, education, and personal growth.

Aristotle, in *Nicomachean Ethics*, analyzed the relationship between the good, happiness, and the virtues. *Virtue* in a character is whatever makes him a good person and causes him to perform his functions well. *Moral virtue* is a mean between two vices, one that is an excess and the other a deficiency. Some of the virtues that Aristotle identified are intelligence, courage, self-control, generosity, ambition, gentleness, friendliness and truthfulness.

A distinction can be made between instrumental values (virtues and vices) and community ideals. *Instrumental values* can be conceived of as 'patterns of interpersonal behavior' that guides one's efforts to obtain an individual objective. The *community ideals* are those values that a culture or community promotes to maintain its well-being.

The values discussed below that can be considered to be virtues, vices and community ideals are explained in great detail in *The Nature of Human Values* by Milton Rokeach.

VIRTUES & VICES

Instrumental values can be conceived of as 'patterns of interpersonal behavior' that guides a character's efforts to obtain an objective. The positive values (**virtues**) are usually promoted by the protagonist and his supporters. The negative values (**vices**) are often found in the attitudes and behavior of the antagonist and his supporters.

PROTAGONIST VALUES (VIRTUES)

Ambitious (hard-working, aspiring)

Broadminded (open-minded)

Capable (competent, effective)

Cheerful (lighthearted, joyful)

Clean (neat, tidy)

Courageous (standing up for one's beliefs)

Forgiving (willing to pardon others)

Helpful (working for the welfare of others)

Honest (sincere, truthful)

Imaginative (daring, creative)

Independent (self-reliant, self-sufficient)

Intellectual (intelligent, reflective)

Logical (consistent, rational)

Loving (affectionate, tender)

Obedience (dutiful, respectful)

Responsible (dependable, reliable)

Self-controlled (restrained, self-disciplined)

ANTAGONIST VALUES (VICES)

Unambitious (lazy, sloth)

Intolerant (prejudiced, dogmatic)

Incompetent (unskilled, inept)

Gloomy (depressed, miserable)

Dirty (untidy, messy, disorderly)

Cowardly (timid, fearful)

Blaming (condemning, censure)

Worthless (destructive, harmful)

Dishonest (untruthful, deceptive)

Subservient (servile, controlled)

Illiterate (unlearned, lowbrow)

Illogical (irrational, unreasonable)

Hateful (hostile, frigid, mean, cruel)

Rebellious (stubborn, obstinate)

Rude (discourteous, impudent)

Irresponsible (untrustworthy)

Undisciplined (unstable, hotheaded)

In many movies, the protagonist is developed as an anti-hero, in that his character is a mixture of virtues and vices. Also, when a writer gives an antagonist some virtues, along with vices, he becomes more sympathetic for the audience. This makes the story more emotionally engrossing for the audience because they are not emotionally certain which is the most evil character. *Raiders of the Lost Ark* is structured this way with Indiana Jones and Belloc being "mirror images" of each other.

COMMUNITY IDEALS

Many of the megahit movies advocate freedom, true friendship, and family security as fundamental values, with the most common being the pursuit of the safety of a home (getting back home), or the preservation of the home from destruction (saving the world or the community). Other possible fundamental values expressed as community ideals are:

A comfortable life (a prosperous life)

An exciting life (a stimulating, active life)

A sense of accomplishment (lasting contribution)

A world at peace (free of war and conflict)

A world of beauty (beauty of nature or creativity in the arts)

Equality (brotherhood, equal opportunity for all)

Family security (taking care of loved ones)

Freedom (independence, free choice)

Happiness (contentment)

Inner harmony (freedom from inner conflict)

Mature love (sexual and spiritual harmony)

National security (protection from attack)

Pleasure (an enjoyable, leisurely life)

Salvation (saved, eternal life)

Self-respect (self-esteem)

Social recognition (respect, admiration)

True friendship (close companionship)

Wisdom (a mature understanding of life)

BASIC STORY DESIGN

A story can be designed by choosing a unique concrete object that both the protagonist and antagonist desire. The protagonist desires it because it represents a positive value (such as national security or world preservation). The antagonist should want the same concrete object because it represents for him the opposite value (in this case, the destruction of the world so that he can create a new order with himself in power). The antagonist and the protagonist values express opposing community ideals.

Assign a set of positive instrumental values to the protagonist (loyalty, compassion) and the opposite negative instrumental values to the antagonist (disloyalty, hatred). Next, create imaginative conflict scenes in which the protagonist and antagonist, along with their supporters, fight for the unique concrete object. In popular movies, the protagonist will eventually be the victor and obtain the objective, **but in a way unexpected by the audience**. Variations of this dramatic structure can be found in many of the megahit movies.

The *theme* of the story is revealed through the interplay of the instrumental virtues and vices. Which values help or hinder the protagonist in the pursuit of his objective becomes the explicit theme of the story. The *theme* of the movie can also be considered to be the *premise* of the story.

The Wizard of Oz most clearly exhibits the connections between the concrete objects that the characters desire and the values that these objects represent:
Elmira Gulch wants Toto to be killed in order to obtain revenge.
Dorothy desires a home as a safe haven from her problems.
The Scarecrow desires a brain in order to obtain intelligence.
The Tin Man desires a heart in order to have feelings and compassion.
The Lion desires courage in order to have freedom from fear.
The Wicked Witch of the West wants the ruby slippers to obtain absolute power in Oz.

Some of the themes exhibited in the megahit movies are listed below:

Titanic
True love means being willing to sacrifice your life for the person you love, as Jack does for Rose. (True Love)

StarWars, Empire Strikes Back, Return of the Jedi
Freedom from tyranny necessitates fighting for control of the absolute power of the universe. (World Security and Freedom)

Phantom Menace
Freedom from tyranny necessitates fighting for control of your home. (World Security and Freedom)

E.T.
Friendship sometimes means helping the person you love to achieve his desires, even if it means separation. (Loyalty and Freedom)

Batman
Preservation of the community from crime necessitates fighting and destroying the sources of evil. (World Security)

Home Alone
A person must use all his intelligence and resources in order to protect his home from destruction. (World Security and Self-Esteem)

Jurassic Park
To obtain family security, one must preserve the lives of the young and protect them from destruction. (Family Security)

Jaws
Preservation of the community from terror necessitates fighting and destroying the source of evil, the Great White Shark. (World Security)

Forrest Gump
To obtain happiness in life, one must "go with the flow," be flexible, but also be completely absorbed in the moment. (Happiness)

Independence Day
Preservation of the community from terror necessitates fighting and destroying the source of evil. (World Security)

Men in Black
Preservation of the world from destruction necessitates fighting and destroying the source of evil. (World Security)

Sixth Sense
To obtain freedom from terror means that one must confront and understand that which terrorizes them. (Happiness)

The Grinch
To become part of a community sometimes means having to apologize and change your behavior. (Social Recognition, Esteem)

The Wizard of Oz
Security, or freedom from fear, is found in the power of self-confidence used to confront life's problems. (Self-Esteem)

Shrek
To achieve happiness one must share their home with others. (Happiness)

Spider-Man
With great power comes great responsibility. Preservation of the community from crime necessitates fighting and destroying the sources of evil. (World Security)

Finding Nemo
To obtain family security, one must preserve the lives of the young and protect them from destruction. (Family Security)

Monsters, Inc.
Friendship sometimes means helping the person you love to achieve her desires, even if it means separation. (Loyalty and Freedom)

Matrix Trilogy
Preservation of the community from terror necessitates fighting and destroying the source of evil, even if it requires self-sacrifice. (World Security)

Pirates of the Caribbean
A person can both be a pirate and a good man.(Self-Esteem)

Harry Potter-The Sorcerer's Stone
Sometimes one needs to break all the rules to save the world. (World Security)

Bruce Almighty
Security, or freedom from fear, is found in the power of self-confidence used to confront life's problems. (Self-Esteem)

Lord of the Rings
Preservation of the community from terror necessitates fighting and destroying the source of evil. (World Security)

A-STORY & B-STORY

The **A-Story** in a movie tracks the efforts of the protagonist to obtain his primary objective. It is the sequence of choices that he makes to overcome the obstacles and problems that prevent him from achieving his goal.

The **B-Story** of the movie tracks the character's arc and tranformation of his values as he pursues his objective. It usually also involves the changes in his relationship with the love interest of the story. The main emotional thrust of the movie is to be found in the B-Story.

Titanic
The B-Story is the transformation of Rose from the obedient daughter who will marry the man her mother wants for her, to a free spirit and an artist.

Star Wars
The B-Story is the transformation of Luke into a Jedi Knight.

E.T.
The B-Story is about Elliott earning self-respect plus the esteem of Michael's friends and his family.

Jurassic Park
The B-Story concerns the change of Dr. Alan Grant from a man who hates to be around children to a protective parent.

The Lion King
The B-Story is about Simba overcoming his feelings of false guilt and fighting for his rightful position as ruler of the Pride Lands.

Batman
The B-Story is about Bruce Wayne finally being able to share his secret and tell Vicki Vale that he is really Batman.

Home Alone
The B-Story is about Kevin's transformation from being a helpless child to someone who can protect his home from burglars.

Sixth Sense
The B-Story is about Cole overcoming his fear of seeing dead people.

Jaws
B-Story is about Capt. Brody overcoming his fear of water in order to kill the shark.

Men In Black
The B-Story is about K leaving the MIB to go back to the woman he left behind.

The Grinch
The B-Story is about the Grinch finally forgiving the people of Whoville for his childhood humiliations.

The Wizard of Oz
The B-Story is about Dorothy finally learning that she has the ability to solve her problems by using intelligence, courage, and compassion.

Shrek
The B-Story is about Shrek accepting the friendship of donkey and expressing his love for Fiona.

Spider-Man
The B-Story is about Peter accepting that with great power comes great responsibility and shielding the people he loves from danger.

Finding Nemo
The B-Story is about Marlin finally stopping being over-protective of Nemo and to have faith in his son.

Bruce Almighty
The B-Story is about Bruce changing from being selfish to giving blood to the community.

Matrix Trilogy
The B-Story is about Neo being loyal to Morpheus and Trinity.

Pirates of the Caribbean
The B-Story is about Will Turner accepting that he can be both a pirate and a good man.

STORY CLIMAX & PLOT CLIMAX

The **plot climax** answers the following question: What happens to the primary objective? Who obtains the objective at the end of the film? What is the outcome of the battle between the protagonist and the antagonist?

The **story climax** answers a different set of questions: What is the final choice of the protagonist? What is the value expressed by this final choice? What code of behavior does this choice represent?

The **plot climax** focuses on the things that happen to the protagonist during his final battle: the events and obstacles that he has to overcome to obtain the final prize.

The **story climax** focuses on the final choice of values that the protagonist makes in his last battle with the antagonist. At this last moment before the completion of his "life and death" struggle with the antagonist, what interpersonal code of behavior does he ultimately choose?

In some stories, the primary objective itself is transformed when the protagonist decides that the "prize" is not worth the destruction of certain values that he holds dear. For the plot, it is the final events that are important. For the story, it is the final choice of the protagonist that is significant.

Titanic
The story climax occurs when Rose decides to rejoin Jack on the Titanic instead of staying on the lifeboat: she decides to stay with the man she loves. The plot climax occurs when Rose throws the jewel "the heart of the ocean" back into the ocean above the sunken Titanic, then rejoins Jack in her dreams (or after her death) on the staircase under the clock on the Titanic.

Star Wars
The story climax occurs when Luke decides to rely on "the spiritual force" instead of "computerized technology" to guide his final torpedo drop. The plot climax occurs when the Death Star is destroyed.

Phantom Menace
Queen Amidala decides to return to Naboo and wage war against the Trade Federation. The story climax occurs when she humbles herself and begs the Gungan Boss to help them defeat the Trade Federation. The plot climax occurs when Anakin destroys the control vessel, making the warrior droids inoperative, thereby, winning the battle for Naboo.

E.T.
The story climax is Elliott's decision to help E.T. escape, even if it means losing him. The plot climax occurs when E.T. and Elliott fly over the road blockade constructed by the U.S. Government Agents.

The Lion King
The story climax occurs when Simba decides to return to the Pride Lands. The plot climax occurs when Simba defeats Scar in battle.

Return of the Jedi
The story climax occurs when Luke Skywalker refuses to join the Emperor and the dark side of the force. The plot climax occurs when Darth Vader kills the Emperor by throwing him into the abyss at the center of the Death Star.

Batman
The story climax occurs when Batman realizes that the Joker is the man who murdered his parents. Batman then decides to fight him in the public arena. The plot climax occurs when the weight of the gargoyle pulls the Joker off the helicopter rope ladder and causes him to plunge to his death.

Jurassic Park
The story climax occurs early when Dr. Grant expresses a paternal concern for the survival of the children. He drops the raptor claw and shelters the children in his arms. The plot climax occurs when the T-Rex destroys the Raptors.

Home Alone
The story climax occurs when Kevin decides to defend his home against the burglars. The plot climax occurs when the old man saves Kevin by hitting the burglars with a shovel.

Forrest Gump
Since Forrest never makes a major decision, the real story climax comes from Jenny, when she decides to marry Forrest. The plot climax occurs when they get married.

Jaws
The story climax occurs when Capt. Brody decides to force the Mayor to sign the voucher to hire the shark killer, Quint. The plot climax occurs when Capt. Brody finally succeeds in killing the shark.

Independence Day
The story climax occurs when Russell Casse decides to sacrifice his life and steer his fighter plane up into the alien's ultimate weapon. The plot climax occurs when the alien spacecraft implodes and is completely destroyed before it destroys Area 51 base and the remaining human fighters.

Men in Black
The story climax occurs when K allows himself to be swallowed by the Edgar-Bug in order to get his weapon in the belly of the beast. This is an act of potential self-sacrifice for the good of the community. The plot climax occurs when the Edgar-Bug is destroyed by K and Dr. Laurel Weaver.

Sixth Sense
The story climax occurs when Cole Sears accepts that he can see dead people. He understands they do not want to terrorize him, but need his help. The plot climax occurs when Dr. Crowe realizes that he is dead.

Empire Strikes Back
The story climax occurs when Luke Skywalker decides not to join his father, Darth Vader, and become part of the dark side of the force. The plot climax occurs when he falls down the central tunnel of the space station and escapes being destroyed by Darth Vader.

The Grinch
The story climax occurs when the Grinch decides to save Cindy Lou Whos' life and to return the Christmas presents to Whoville. He then apologizes. The plot climax occurs when his apology is accepted and he is integrated back into the Who community.

The Wizard of Oz
The story climax occurs when Dorothy believes that she has the power to solve her own problems. The plot climax occurs when Dorothy is transported back to Kansas.

Shrek
The story climax occurs when Shrek tells Fiona he loves her.
The plot climax occurs when Farquaard is eaten by the Dragon, Shrek kisses Fiona, and the spell on Princess Fiona is broken.

Spider-Man
The story climax occurs when Peter does not tell MJ that he loves her. The plot climax occurs when the Green Goblin is impaled by his transport.

Finding Nemo
The story climax occurs when Marlin backs Nemo's instructions for all the fish to swim downwards. The plot climax occurs when Nemo is freed from the Dentist's fish tank and the clutches of Darla.

Monsters, Inc.
The story climax occurs when Sulley puts Boo in her bed and her door is shredded. The plot climax occurs when Mr. Waternoose is exposed in the Simulation Room and is taken away by Roz and the CDA.

Bruce Almighty
The story climax occurs when Bruce prays for Grace's happiness and not his own. The plot climax occurs when Bruce comes back to life and is reunited with Grace.

Matrix Trilogy
The story climax occurs when Neo accepts that he is the ONE and sacrifices himself to save the people of Zion. The plot climax occurs when the Machines stop destroying Zion.

Pirates of the Caribbean
The story climax occurs when Will accepts that he can be both a pirate and a good man. The plot climax occurs when Barbossa is killed by Liz, Will, and Jack, and the curse is ended.

Harry Potter-The Sorcerer's Stone
The story climax occurs when Harry decides to fight Prof. Quirrell (Voldemort) for the Sorcerer's Stone. The plot climax occurs when Harry triumphs over Prof. Quirrell (Voldemort).

Lord of the Rings Trilogy
The story climax occurs when Frodo decides not to destroy the Ring. This shows that the Ring is too powerful for any human or hobbit to possess. The plot climax occurs when Gollum falls into the lava river holding the ring which is then destroyed.

SCENES
CREATING THOSE SPECIAL MOMENTS

Scenes

Scene Actions

Point of Attack

Crisis

Confrontation

Climax

Resolution

A Model Scene

Establishing Scenes

Transition Scenes

The Opening Scene

Introduction of the Protagonist

Introduction of the Antagonist

Climax Scenes

Resolution Scenes

The Essential Scene Elements

SCENES

"Dramatic structure is actually made up of a connected series of ministories (scenes or sequences) which combine to make up larger blocks (acts or chapters) that combine to make up your work as a whole. A scene, the smallest dramatic unit, is really not different in its structure from a chapter or an act, and in turn, they are not different from your plot as a whole. Each has a beginning, a middle, and an end."
—Ronald Tobias, *Theme and Strategy*

Scenes are the basic units through which a story is told. In each scene the characters are in conflict over some "objective" that is necessary for the completion of either a subgoal or the primary objective of the story. By the end of the scene, one character will win the "objective" and the other will lose it. During the conflict over this scene objective, characters will make choices about their values, and character transformations will occur.

The *objective* of the scene may not be something physical. It could very well be a piece of information that one character is trying to get from another character, or it could be a change in attitude that one character is trying to bring about in another. But something vital to both characters is usually at stake.

Since film is a visual medium, its primary mode of communication is through actions and images, instead of dialogue. Dialogue is more essential to radio or stage plays.

There are four moments (or beats) in the *model* or *ideal* standard scenes: a scene crisis occurs when one of the characters receives information that forces him into action; a scene confrontation between two opposing characters; a scene climax in which the conflicting character's actions reach a peak; and the scene resolution that reveals which character obtains the objective and how they emotionally feel about the result.

The story is told through a series of scenes starting from the opening scene and ending with the final scene of the story. There are specific types of scenes that must be part of this structure: a scene that introduces the protagonist to the audience; a scene that introduces the antagonist; a climax scene in which these two characters battle for control of the primary objective; and a resolution scene in which one of the characters is established as the victor.

Some writers believe that there must be two other critical scenes in each story: *plot points* (or *plot twists*) that occur one-third and two-thirds of the way through the series. They believe that this is necessary to make the story unpredictable and, thereby, hold the audiences' attention.

A *plot twist* is a *subgoal* that leads to a dead end and that fails to help the protagonist achieve the primary goal as he expected that it would. He must, therefore, revise his plans and choose another subgoal. Two thirds of the way through the story, this new subgoal will also fail to bring about the desired objective. He is then forced to choose one more course of action that will lead directly to the climax scene in which the protagonist will fight with the antagonist.

The scenes should naturally flow into each other; the actions taken by characters in the earlier scenes must cause actions in the scenes that follow. The intensity of the conflict should increase with each scene. This can be accomplished by sequentially placing in danger objects that are of a higher personal value to the protagonist and the audience.

The protagonist will demonstrate the priority of the objects that he values through his actions, decisions, and the intensity of the anguish that he exhibits at the possibility of loss of these objects. For example, one preference ordering, from the lowest to the highest priority, might be as follows: material possessions, a job, money, status, honor, integrity, self-respect, respect of his family, his personal freedom, the survival of the community, his life, the life of his lover, and the life of his child.

The same preference ordering might also be shared by the audience. The conflict is intensified when objects that have a lower value are placed in jeopardy first at the beginning of the story, while objects with the highest value are placed in jeopardy during the climax scene.

This priority structure increases the audience's emotional involvement with the story since the protagonist's order of values reflects their own, or what the audience would like their values to be, under ideal or heroic conditions. This structure also solidifies the audience's empathy for the protagonist, and hatred for the antagonist who continues to place these objects of value in danger of being destroyed.

Each scene should emotionally advance the story forward. Once the internal structure of each scene is clearly understood, this can be easily accomplished. Each scene would consist of a unique decision and transformation of character that would not be repeated again in a later scene.

In each scene, either the protagonist and his supporters win, or the antagonist and his supporters win. Alternating the victors helps to keep the audience involved and makes the conflict less predictable. Alternating the scenes between interior and exterior locations also maintains the audience's interest because it induces a visual variation for the audience.

SCENE ACTIONS

Scene actions consist of the actions that the characters perform in order to obtain the "objective" at stake in the scene. Each action provokes a reaction from another character. The audience maintains interest in the conflict whenever unexpected tactics are used by the characters to obtain their goals. But if the actions are predictable, the audience will become bored.

Some actions may be morally objectionable to the audience. If the antagonist performs these immoral acts it will solidify the audience's enmity for him. If the protagonist commits what is usually accepted as an immoral act, then he must establish a justification for his behavior by appealing to extenuating circumstances in order to maintain the audience's empathy. The audience will decide whom to like and whom to hate based primarily on what characters do instead of just what they say.

In each scene, the characters are trying to accomplish some part of his or her plan (a subgoal) in order to ultimately achieve the primary objective. Either they achieve that subgoal, or they don't. If they achieve the subgoal, then they go on to the next part of the plan. If they fail, they must either try new tactics to obtain the same subgoal or change their plans.

Each scene will have a rhythm and a tempo. The rhythm is the number of actions within a scene during a fixed length of time. The tempo is the character's energy level or intensity that he brings to an action. Usually, the earlier scenes of the story have a fast rhythm and high tempo to gain the audience's attention. This means there will be a lot of action within a short period of time. The middle of the story usually has a slower rhythm and lower tempo. This changes to a faster rhythm and higher tempo as the scenes approach the climax. Different tempos and rhythms help to create variety between scenes and keep the story from becoming monotonous.

SCENE POINT-OF-ATTACK

Scenes usually start in the middle of the action, within the midst of the conflict. They should start at the beginning of the essential information, which is the *scene crisis*. The real-life time span is never used because this would bore the audience. Character entrances and exits are often not written into the scene. Instead the characters are shown in the midst of an emotion or action. This causes the audience to remain emotionally involved with the story.

SCENE CRISIS

This is the event in which the primary character receives information that forces him into confrontation with his opposition. It is a turning point for the character. During the crisis, the character decides to take action that will lead to confrontation and then to the climax.

SCENE CONFRONTATION

This is the section of the scene in which a character confronts another character with the information that he has received during the scene crisis. This generates the conflict that will peak in the climax.

The final confrontation in the series of scenes is between the protagonist and the antagonist, which leads to the fight to the death. This has traditionally been called the "obligatory scene."

SCENE CLIMAX

This is the moment of greatest tension, with the characters in the greatest jeopardy at the peak of the conflict. One character will lose, and the other will win whatever is at stake in the scene. If the outcome is not predictable, the audience will remain on the edge of their seats, completely engrossed in the scene.

SCENE RESOLUTION

The resolution presents the outcome of the climax fight. It reveals which character won the battle, and how each of the characters feels about this situation. The emotional reactions of the characters are important, for these reactions will propel them into the next scene and cause the next crisis. With the scene resolution, the scene quickly ends, and the story continues to the next scene of the series.

A MODEL SCENE

As an example of a standard structured scene, consider the scene from the *The Wizard of Oz,* within which Elmira Gulch comes for Toto.

POINT-OF-ATTACK
The scene does not start with Elmira entering the house and exchanging social pleasantries with Dorothy and Aunt Em. It begins in the midst of the argument, with Elmira demanding Toto.

SCENE CRISIS
Elmira tells Aunt Em that she is going to take Toto to the Sheriff, where Toto will be destroyed. Dorothy listens to this information then decides to save Toto, the "objective" of the scene.

SCENE CONFRONTATION
Dorothy confronts Elmira Gulch and says that she will not let her destroy Toto. Dorothy appeals both to her aunt and uncle to help her save Toto. The aunt and uncle are supportive until Elmira shows them an order from the Sheriff. Elmira threatens to take away their farm if they "go against the law."

SCENE CLIMAX
Dorothy physically struggles with Elmira as she tries to place Toto into the basket. Dorothy pleads for help from her aunt and uncle. Finally, Aunt Em tells Uncle Henry to put Toto into the basket, because "they can't go against the law."

SCENE RESOLUTION
Elmira wins the "objective": possession of Toto. Dorothy cries in despair and runs out of the room. Aunt Em wants to tell off Elmira but can't because she's "a Christian woman." Uncle Henry is amused by the situation, and Elmira indignantly leaves the house. As each character's emotional reactions are recorded for the audience, the scene quickly ends. The audience does not even see Elmira exiting through the door.

ESTABLISHING SCENES
(Establishing Shots)

Establishing scenes do not have the complete structure of a model standard scene that includes a crisis, confrontation, climax, and resolution. Instead, establishing scenes are used to show the time and location of the actions in the scenes that follow. These "scenes" are also often called *establishing shots*.

There is another type of scene, an *exposition scene*, which consists almost solely of dialogue. In these types of scenes information about past or future events and plans are conveyed to the audience. The function and structure of these types of "exposition scenes" are discussed in more detail in the *Exposition* section within the *Cinematic Structures* part of the book.

Titanic
The establishing shot of the Titanic in dock as passengers are boarding the ship.

Star Wars
The establishing shot of the spaceport before Luke and Obi-Wan Kenobe drive up in their space vehicle.

Phantom Menace
The establishing shot of the Trade Federation battleships in space above the planet Naboo.

E.T.
The establishing shot of the suburban community in which Elliott lives.

Jaws
The establishing shot of Amity beach filled with bathers on the July 4th holiday.

The Lion King
Establishing shots of the animals in the jungle.

Return of the Jedi
The image of the forest in the resolution scene establishes that the celebration of the victory over the Empire takes place on the Ewok's planet.

Batman
The opening shots of the streets of Gotham City.

Jurassic Park
The helicopter flight over the mountainous island that contains Jurassic Park.

Home Alone
The establishing shot of the middle class neighborhood in which Kevin lives.

Forrest Gump
The establishing shot of the Army base in Vietnam.

Independence Day
The establishing shot of the White House in Washington, D.C.

Men in Black
The establishing shot of the farmhouse yard and truck as the Edgar-Bug spacecraft crash lands.

Sixth Sense
The establishing shot of the streets in front of the house where Cole Sears lives.

Empire Strikes Back
Luke, Obie-Wan Kenobe, and Yoda argue with Luke Skywalker about his plans to leave his training to become a Jedi Knight and run off to save his friends.

The Grinch
The establishing shot of Whoville during the Christmas celebrations.

The Wizard of Oz
The establishing shot of the sign in the Witch's Forest before Dorothy and her companions enter.

Shrek
The establishing shot of Shrek's swamp.

Spider-Man
The establishing shot of the Science Museum.

Finding Nemo
The establishing shot of the Dentist Office.

Monsters, Inc.
The establishing shot of the factory floor of Monsters, Inc.

Bruce Almighty
The establishing shot of the warehouse where God is the janitor.

Matrix Trilogy
The establishing shot of the Rebel Ship.

Pirates of the Caribbean
The establishing shot of the Black Pearl.

Harry Potter-The Sorcerer's Stone
The establishing shot of Hogwarts.

Lord of the Rings Trilogy
The establishing shot of Minas Tirith.

TRANSITION SCENES

Transition scenes do not have the same structure of a model standard scene that includes a crisis, confrontation, climax, and resolution. Transition scenes are used to "transport" the characters across a distance of space or an interval of time. Sometimes a series or sequence of images are called *montages*, and they are used to express transitions of time, space, changes in status, or any transformation that would take too long to show in real time. These are changes that move the characters forward in the story toward the next major conflict or subgoal.

Titanic
The Titanic sails across the ocean.

Star Wars
Luke drives his space vehicle across the desert in the hope of saving his aunt and uncle. Whenever Han Solo accelerates into light speed, a visual montage occurs that represents him traveling great distances in a brief period of time.

Phantom Menace
Qui-Gon and Obi-Wan Kenobi with Jar Jar Binks escape underwater monsters as they travel to Theed on the planet, Naboo.

E.T.
Elliott and E.T. ride a bicycle into the forest so that E.T. can try to call home.

Jurassic Park
Dennis, the fat computer technician, drives his jeep through the jungle during a storm in order to get the dinosaur embryos to the dock before the ship departs. The survivors fly in a helicopter over the ocean away from the Jurassic Park.

Forrest Gump
Forrest and Bubba ride on a bus on their way to basic training.

Lion King
The opening sequence of animals running through the Jungle is a montage. Simba and his friends run through the jungle in order to get back to the Pride Lands.

Return of the Jedi
Luke flies his fighter plane to Dagobah to continue his studies with Yoda.

Independence Day
The caravan of human survivors drive across the desert to the Area 51 military base.

Sixth Sense
Cole Sears and his mother are riding down the street in his car when Cole tells her that Grandma says hello.

Empire Strikes Back
Han Solo, Princess Leia, and the Millenium Falcon race through space to escape the Imperial Battleships. The rebel pilots preparing for battle is a montage sequence.

Home Alone
Kevin's mother travels in the back of the truck as she tries to get home to Kevin.

Jaws
The boat carrying Quint and Capt. Brody sets out to sea to search for the great white shark.

The Grinch
The Grinch and Cindy Lou Who ride the sleigh filled with Christmas gifts down the mountainside to Whoville.

Batman
Batman drives Vicki Vale in his Bat mobile through the forest on the way to his cave.

Men in Black
J and K drive upside down in their car through the Holland Tunnel in order to prevent the Edgar-Bug from flying off the planet earth. The transformation of the Will Smith character into the MIB agent J is a montage sequence.

The Wizard of Oz
The tornado sequence takes Dorothy from Kansas into the Land of Oz. This is a transition through space, time, dimensions, or possibly just her imagination.

Shrek
Shrek and Donkey journey to Fiona's Castle.

Spider-Man
Spider-Man chases the car thief by running across rooftops.

Finding Nemo
Marlin rides on the current through the great coral reef.

Monsters, Inc.
Sulley and Mike ride on the door conveyor system.

Bruce Almighty
Bruce drives his new car to work.

Matrix Trilogy
Neo drives his spaceship into the center of the machine world.

Pirates of the Caribbean
Will and Jack sail the British ship in search of the Black Pearl.

Harry Potter-The Sorcerer's Stone
Harry and the other first year students sail with Hagrid to Hogwarts.

Lord of the Rings Trilogy
Frodo and Sam journey up the side of Mount Doom.

THE OPENING SCENE

Most popular filmmakers attempt to emotionally engage the audience in the story as soon as possible. One device is to place them into a "semi-hypnotic receptive state," even as the opening credits role onto the screen. This technique is evident in the beginning of *Batman*. Some films start with diffused imagery that forces the audience to concentrate their full attention in order to understand what is occurring on the screen. Other films engage the audience with a surprise event or a violent action.

A character is often shown to be in jeopardy in the first scenes, even though this character may not be the protagonist. While the protagonist is the first character that we see in *Wizard of Oz* and *E.T.*, this is not the case for *Star Wars*, *Batman,* or *Home Alone*. In these cases, it is the antagonist or his supporters that are introduced first, with the intention of creating audience enmity for them.

Usually, the world of the story is immediately revealed through a specification of the locale and the historical period. Most stories, like scenes, do not start at the beginning of a situation, but in the midst of the action. This forces the audience to concentrate their full attention on the action in order to understand the situation.

In these popular films, many of the characters can be considered **abandoned**, or, in some sense, left on their own in a dangerous situation. This is definitely the case for Dorothy in *Wizard of Oz*, E.T., and Kevin in *Home Alone*. This is an effective technique for creating strong audience empathy for the protagonists, for the feelings of insecurity and being rejected are universal and easily give rise to sympathy.

Titanic
The people hunting for "the heart of the ocean" jewel retrieve a safe from the sunken Titanic. When they open the safe, they discover that the jewel is not there.

Star Wars
Against the background of a desolate star-filled space scrolls text that presents the background story to the audience; a civil war is taking place between the Empire and Rebel forces. A small ship crosses the screen pursued by a gigantic battleship. The structure is similar to *Wizard of Oz*; a small object is being pursued and threatened by something larger and more powerful. Audience empathy is immediately generated for the "underdogs" in the smaller spaceship.

Phantom Menace
Two Jedi Knights, Qui-Gon and Obi-Wan fly through a Trade Federation Space Blockade of the planet Naboo as Ambassadors from the Supreme Chancellor negotiate an end to the conflict. Instead, Darth Sidious tells the leaders of the Trade Federation to kill the Jedi Knights.

E.T.
The first image is of a star-filled night and a dark forest, which is visually confusing and demands the audience's undivided attention. A spaceship with bright lights is barely seen through the forest trees. Smoke diffuses the atmosphere. Creatures seem to be moving about in the forest, but no image is clear or distinct. Strange long fingers move a branch. Exotic plants lie on the floor inside the spaceship. Outside a dog howls, causing the red hearts of the creatures to intensify their glow. A small tree sprout is dug up by alien fingers. In another shot, a small child-like creature is seen in the far distance as it walks among tall trees. The gigantic trees overwhelm the creature, who still cannot be seen clearly by the audience. This forces the audience to pay close attention because they want to see what the creature looks like. Sympathy is also generated for the child-like creature as it stands under the over-towering trees. The creature walks to the edge of the forest and looks at the city lights in the distance. Suddenly, a truck, with headlights glaring, drives up and suddenly stops at the edge of the forest. More trucks pull up and men with flashlights get out of the trucks. They are shadow figures covered in darkness. The audience cannot see their faces. The small creature runs away and is pursued by the men with flashlights. The alien spaceship departs. The creature squeals like a terrified small animal as he runs toward the departing ship in his efforts to escape from his faceless pursuers. Finally, the creature is abandoned in a strange land as the spaceship disappears into the night sky.

The Lion King
Simba, the future king of the Pride Lands, is presented to his animal subjects.

Jurassic Park
The Raptor, a vicious highly intelligent dinosaur, eats one of the workers.

Batman
A middle class couple, along with their young boy, are visiting Gotham City. They lose their way and wander into an alley where they are beaten and robbed by two muggers. One of the muggers points a gun at the small boy and threatens him. They then climb to the rooftop in order to rifle through the woman's purse. They are confronted by Batman. He

beats and terrorizes them in an act of retribution. Batman leaves them alive so that they can spread the word to the other criminals that "it is he who rules the night." The audience identifies with the vulnerable couple who are robbed and become angry when they are terrorized by the muggers. They appreciate Batman when he punishes the muggers for their crimes.

Home Alone
Images of a blue moon against a black sky, a blue house silhouetted against a black sky, then the house recedes into the background, getting smaller and smaller. An opening shot of an upper-middle class home with Christmas decorations. There are sounds of many people speaking at once. "Where's my suitcase?" asks a child. Inside the house a police officer, with his back to the camera, stands in the hallway. He tries to get someone to pay attention to him, but everyone ignores him. This is humorous because a "traffic cop" who is supposed to be a figure of authority is being ignored by the "traffic of children" running through the house. Two small girls walk down the staircase. A third girl walks up, while a fourth girl walks down. They pass the policeman as if he didn't exist. He stands with his hands on his hips as he expresses exasperation. Holding an authority figure up to ridicule creates laughter. In this scene, the antagonist is introduced, although not explicitly. He is presented as a trustworthy figure, only so that he can later betray the trust of the family. He is really a burglar who is staking out the house to determine when best to rob the trusting family of their possessions.

Forrest Gump
The feather, which represents Forrest, floats through the air and lands on Forrest. He picks it up and places it in his suitcase.

Jaws
The story opens with shots of a night beach party. A young man sees an attractive girl and approaches her. She runs away and he follows. She takes off her clothes as she runs for a nighttime swim in the ocean. She swims out to sea then is attacked and eaten by a shark.

The Wizard of Oz
A young girl and her dog are running down a deserted country road. She looks behind her to see if she is being followed. The girl picks up her dog and says, "She isn't coming yet, Toto. Did she hurt you? She tried, didn't she?" We immediately have a situation of a frightened young woman in jeopardy being pursued by an unseen villain, who has tried to hurt her little dog. Dorothy instantaneously captures the audience's empathy while the unseen antagonist earns the enmity of the viewers.

Shrek
Shrek reads from the fairy tale book while in the outhouse. He then takes his morning mud bath.

Spider-Man
Peter Parker has to run after his school bus.

Finding Nemo
Marlin and Coral look over their new home and batch of eggs when they are attacked by a barracuda.

Monsters, Inc.
A child in bed is scared by a monster that, in turn, is terrified by the child's screams. This is all taking place in a simulation room monitored by Mr. Waternoose.

Bruce Almighty
Bruce has to wear a hairnet while doing a news story about a bakery.

Matrix Trilogy
Neo is sleeping by his computer which sends him a message.

Pirates of the Caribbean
The young girl, Liz, is standing in front of a ship as it sails out of the fog. She is singing a song about pirates.

Harry Potter-The Sorcerer's Stone
Prof. Dumbledorf extinguishes all the lights on Privet Lane. Harry Potter is delivered by Hagrid and left on the doorstep of his guardian's house.

Lord of the Rings Trilogy
The back story of the creation of the one Ring, the death of Sauron, and the loss of the Ring is narrated.

INTRODUCTION OF THE PROTAGONIST

The protagonist is usually introduced in a way designed to immediately generate audience empathy for the character.

Dorothy and E.T. are sympathetic characters chased by unseen "faceless" assailants. By not showing the pursuers, the audience's empathy increases because they envision the pursuer to be the most horrible creature they can imagine. Dorothy, Luke Skywalker, and Kevin are both neglected by their families. Elliott has the additional problem that his mother does not believe him when he tells her he has seen a creature in the yard. This immediately generates empathy for him in the audience because they know he is telling the truth, yet he is not believed. Luke Skywalker also feels that he is not getting the support that he deserves from his aunt and uncle.

Each of the protagonists are initially presented in a manner designed to immediately create an empathetic bond between them and the audience.

Titanic
Rose is working with her pottery when she hears a news story on the television discussing the adventures of treasure hunters for the Titanic. The TV displays a picture of a naked woman wearing the jewel, "the Heart of the Ocean." It is Rose as a young woman.

Star Wars
Luke is unhappy living on the farm with his aunt and uncle. He is lonely and wants to join his friends at college.

Phantom Menace
Anakin Skywalker is working as a slave in a junk shop owned by Watto.

E.T.
The small child-like extra-terrestrial is chased by "faceless" creatures with flashlights. He is then abandoned by his spaceship.

The Lion King
Simba, the future King of the Pride Lands, is presented to his animal subjects.

Return of the Jedi
Luke Skywalker, dressed as a Jedi Knight, enters the domain of Jabba the Hutt and demands he release Han Solo, Chewbacca, and Princess Leia.

Jurassic Park
Dr. Alan Grant, a digger, who hates computers and children, is working on an excavation, digging up dinosaur fossils. He discusses the attack patterns of the Raptors.

Batman
Batman punishes two muggers who have terrorized and robbed a couple in front of their young son.

Home Alone
Kevin tries to get a member of his family to help him pack his suitcase, but they are all too busy and ridicule him for being incompetent.

Forrest Gump
The floating feather, which represents Forrest, flows through the air and lands on Forrest. He picks it up and places it in his suitcase.

Jaws
Cpt. Martin Brody gets out of bed in the morning. He receives a phone call telling him to go to the beach to search for a missing girl. When he arrives at the beach, he searches with the girl's boyfriend, and, together they find the girl's half-eaten body.

Independence Day
Each of the four protagonists of this movie is introduced in an empathy producing situation: Captain Steve Hiller with his girlfriend Jasmine; David Levinson playing chess with his father; President Whitmore on the phone with his wife and daughter at the White House; and Russell Casse drunk as he flies his crop dusting plane above the wrong field.

Men in Black
A van, filled with Mexican aliens, is stopped by a Border Patrol. The aliens all exit from the van. Suddenly D and K, two MIB agents drive up to the scene. K gets out and starts to speak to the aliens in Spanish until he identifies one who does not understand the language. K and D escort this alien down a slope and unveil him to be Mikey, a convict from another planet. When one of the Border Patrol men approaches, Mikey decides to run for it. K's partner D falls to the ground and is unable to stop Mikey. K takes out a gun and destroys Mikey. Since the alien was seen by the Border patrol, K erases their memories with a flash of the Neuralyzer. K must also erase the memory of his partner D, who has become too old for the chase. Now K must find a new partner. The story

then switches to the Will Smith character that will later become J in MIB, running down a city street chasing a criminal, who he will later discover is an alien. K and J will become the dual protagonists of this story.

Sixth Sense
Dr. Malcolm Crowe is first seen celebrating his award with his wife. He is then shot in his bedroom by a deranged former patient. This generates tremendous empathy for the character.

Empire Strikes Back
Luke is attacked by a white snow creature while on patrol on the ice planet Hoth. The creature intends to eat him and hangs him upside down in the ice cave. Luke is in jeopardy: a life and death situation. This is an empathy scene for him. Luke awakes and uses his powers to free himself from the ice and the creature.

The Grinch
We first see the Grinch when four teenagers from Whoville approach his cave on Mt. Crumpit. The Grinch scares them away.

The Wizard of Oz
Dorothy, in distress, is running down a deserted country road, pursued by an unseen assailant. Dorothy is shown being ignored by her aunt, uncle, and the farmhands when she appeals to them for help.

Shrek
Shrek reads from the fairy tale book while in the outhouse. He then takes his morning mud bath. He is likeable, but he is a sloppy Ogre.

Spider-Man
Peter Parker has to run after his school bus.

Finding Nemo
Marlin and Coral look over their new home and batch of eggs when they are attacked by a barracuda. Marlin tries to defend his home, but is knocked out.

Monsters, Inc.
Sulley is in bed sleeping when Mike wakes him up.

Bruce Almighty
Bruce has to wear a hairnet while doing a news story about a bakery.

Matrix Trilogy
Neo is sleeping by his computer which sends him a message.

Pirates of the Caribbean
The young girl, Liz, is standing in front of a ship as it sails out of the fog. She is singing a song about pirates.

Harry Potter-The Sorcerer's Stone
Harry Potter is delivered by Hagrid to Prof. Dumbledore and is left on the doorstep of his guardian's house. Harry has a scar on his forehead. Because he is in danger, it is best for him to live away from the world of magic until he is older.

Lord of the Rings Trilogy
Frodo sits under a tree in the Shire. He is reading a book when he sees Gandalf approach in a cart. Frodo and Gandalf are happy to see each other.

INTRODUCTION OF THE ANTAGONIST

Ruthlessness and betrayal are traits that will generate enmity for the antagonist. Especially betrayal! It is important that a relationship of trust is established in the mind and feelings of the audience between the antagonist and one of the sympathetic characters in the story. The audience should not suspect that the sympathetic character will be betrayed. Then, when the betrayal occurs and major harm is caused to the character with whom the audience has empathy, the audience will react with intense emotion, hate the antagonist, and feel that he is worthy of destruction. This is the type of emotional hatred that the writer wants the audience to feel because they must emotionally want the protagonist to destroy the antagonist.

To have the antagonist laugh with glee at the desperate state of a sympathetic character is another way to create enmity for the antagonist. If the antagonist terrorizes a vulnerable character, then enmity is generated for him and his supporters. Both Elmira Gulch (Wicked Witch) and Darth Vader are introduced pursuing young women whom they place in jeopardy (Dorothy and Princess Leia).

Titanic
Cal exits his car near the boarding plank to the Titanic. He displays aristocratic arrogance when talking to Rose and the Porter.

Star Wars
Darth Vader is introduced while leading an attack of the Imperial Soldiers against the Rebel spaceship. He captures Princess Leia and is characterized by her as a villain.

Phantom Menace
Darth Sidious advises the leaders of the Trade Federation to kill the two Jedi Knights, who have just arrived as ambassadors to negotiate a settlement to the blockade.

E.T.
Faceless men with flashlights chase the child-like E.T. through the forest underbrush.

The Lion King
Scar is reprimanded by Zasu and Mufasa for not attending the presentation of Simba. This reveals Scar's resentment at losing his position as first in line for the throne.

Return of the Jedi
Darth Vader lands his spaceship on the Death Star and informs the Commander that the Emperor will soon be arriving to inspect the work. He also says that the Emperor is not as forgiving as Vader.

Batman
Jack Napier (who later becomes the Joker) is introduced in his apartment with Alicia, boss Grissom's girlfriend, with whom he is having an affair. Napier is listening to a TV newscast announcing the City Hall's new war on crime. He expresses arrogance and contempt for the police, contempt for his boss by having an affair with his girlfriend, and contempt for Alicia.

Jurassic Park
The Raptor, a vicious highly intelligent dinosaur, devours one of the Jurassic Park workers.

Home Alone
The principal thief is introduced as a police officer. This betrayal of trust is later revealed when it is shown that this is the disguise he uses to scout out houses he intends to rob.

Jaws
The great white shark eats a girl swimming late at night in the ocean.

Forrest Gump
People who do not believe that Forrest is normal and should be respected as a human being are the antagonists of the story. The first instance of this are the men sitting outside the store who stare at Forrest because he wears braces. Next is the scene with the school principal, who wants Forrest to go to a special school because he is not normal. His IQ is 75.

Independence Day
The shadow alien spaceship moves across the moon surface and darkens the U.S. Flag. The alien spaceship then moves toward the planet earth.

Men in Black
The Bug crash lands his spacecraft near a farmhouse, destroying the farmer's truck in the process. He devours Edgar, the farmer, then uses Edgar's skin as a disguise and searches for "the Galaxy on Orion's belt."

Sixth Sense
A dead person terrorizes Cole Sears.

Empire Strikes Back
Darth Vader is searching for the Rebel base.

The Grinch
Mayor August May Who scolds the children for going near the Grinch's cave on Mt. Crumpit. He warns them about awakening the Grinch.

The Wizard of Oz
Elmira Gulch is introduced as the person who was pursuing Dorothy. She then takes away Toto. The Wicked Witch of the West is introduced as seeking revenge for the death of her sister, the Wicked Witch of the East.

Shrek
Lord Farquaard tortures the Ginger Bread Man. He has cut off his legs.

Spider-Man
Norman Osborn is driving his son, Harry, to school. He is later arguing with the military about the progress made in his research project.

Finding Nemo
Human divers capture Nemo and take him to their boat.

Monsters, Inc.
Mr. Waternoose reprimands a monster for not performing as he should in his efforts to scare children.

Bruce Almighty
God appears as a janitor. Bruce is his own worst antagonist.

Matrix Trilogy
Agent Smith interrogates Neo.

Pirates of the Caribbean
Barbossa confronts Liz who wants to parlay with him.

Harry Potter-The Sorcerer's Stone
Prof. Quirrell first meets Harry in a London pub. Voldemort comes after Harry in the forest by the dead unicorn.

Lord of the Rings Trilogy
Sauron slaughters men in the opening sequence, until the ring is finally cut off his finger.

CLIMAX SCENES

The **climax scene** of the movie is always the most exciting and emotionally engrossing scene for the audience. This is the "obligatory scene" in which there is a battle between the protagonist and the antagonist. The survival of the love interest will also be determined by the actions of the protagonist. The outcome of this battle will determine the fate of the unique concrete object and the primary objective. Only one of these characters will survive the conflict that rages in this scene.

The *story climax,* the final choice of values by the protagonist as discussed in another section of this book, may or may not be part of this scene. But the *plot climax* always is. In this scene, the following questions are resolved: What happens to the primary objective? Who obtains the unique concrete object at the end of the film? What is the outcome of the battle between the protagonist and the antagonist?

For examples of the *climax scenes*, and the difference between the *story climax* and the *plot climax*, read the relevant chapters in this book.

RESOLUTION SCENES
(The Final Scene of the Movie)

The final scene consists of the resolution of the story. The conflicts are resolved both for the protagonist and the community (including the audience). All open questions, complications, and loose ends are tied up. After this scene, there are no more crises and no more confrontations, for there no longer is any opposition that could generate conflict.

In the climax scene of the movie, the threat to the protagonist and the community has been destroyed, and the community returns to stability and equilibrium. There is usually a celebration for the defeat of the antagonist and his forces; a joyous event where the protagonist reunites with the community. This allows the audience to express joy and release all the final emotional tensions that has been built up in the climax scene.

Once the conflicts are resolved, the movie usually ends as quickly as possible. This resolution has traditionally been called the "denouement" of the story. In most popular films, there is a preference for clear endings that lack any moral ambiguity. The protagonist and his values have overcome the obstacles, and he has triumphed over the antagonist. The audience is left happy, feeling that once again, all is well with the world. To paraphrase Aristotle, their emotions have been purged through pity (for the protagonist) and fear (of the antagonist). The audience then leaves the theatre having had an **emotionally satisfying experience.**

Titanic
Rose walks into the Titanic stateroom and up the stairway to meet Jack by the clock. They kiss and Rose rejoins the community on the Titanic. The ghosts of those who drowned on the Titanic applaud.

Star Wars
Luke Skywalker returns to a joyous rebel base after destroying the Death Star. The community honors Luke and Han in a celebration in which they are awarded medals for saving the planet.

Phantom Menace
There is a grand parade in the central plaza of Theed, Naboo, celebrating the victory over the forces of the Trade Federation. Queen Amidala stands next to the Supreme Chancellor Palatine, Anakin, Obi-Wan, Sio Bibble, and the Jedi Council. In the parade are Boss Nass and Jar Jar. They stop by the Queen and walk up the steps to stand by her side. Boss Nass holds up the Globe of Peace. Everyone cheers. The parade moves on.

The Lion King
The same as the opening, but now it is Simba and Nala's cub that is raised up for the animals of the kingdom, completing the "circle of life."

E.T.
Elliott learns the lesson that sometimes the people you love must leave, and although this may be a painful experience, the friendship can still remain for a lifetime. Elliott and E.T. have triumphed over the forces that have sought to keep E.T. a captive. He has won his freedom. Their final parting is witnessed by Elliott's family and "Keys," the government agent. Friendship, along with freedom, are reconfirmed as values that the community should cherish.

Return of the Jedi
Luke Skywalker has a victory celebration with the Ewoks, Han Solo, Lando Calrissian, and Princess Leia. Luke then sees the smiling spirits of Obi-Wan Kenobi, Yoda, and his father, Darth Vader.

Batman
The Mayor and Police Commissioner stand in front of City Hall and address the community, acknowledging Batman's triumph in saving Gotham from destruction. They read a letter in which Batman promises to help them if crime returns. All they have to do is call him with the Bat Signal. Alfred calls to Vicki Vale, who enters the limousine and sips champagne as Alfred drives her home to wait for Bruce. Batman stands in silent vigilance from the dark rooftops above Gotham City.

Jurassic Park
Dr. Grant and Dr. Hammond both agree to close down Jurassic Park. In the helicopter, Dr. Grant displays a paternal concern for the two children that he holds in his arms as Ellie watches and smiles. They all fly away from Jurassic Park as he watches prehistoric-type birds also fly across the water away from the island.

Home Alone
Mother and family return home and are happy to be reunited with Kevin. Kevin earns the respect of his siblings.

Forrest Gump
Forrest tells his son that he loves him and will be waiting for him after school then watches as the child gets on the bus. Forrest continues to sit on the stump, and the audience knows that he will keep his promise, as the feather floats away in the breeze. And that's all I'll say about that.

Jaws
Capt. Brody finally kills the Great White Shark. He does this by shooting a metal container that has compressed oxygen that the shark has in its mouth. The container explodes and blows the shark in two. Matt Hooper, the oceanographer, then returns to the surface and joins Brody. Together, they swim towards shore.

Independence Day
Captain Steve Hiller and David Levinson return from space and are greeted by President Whitmore, Jasmine, her child, and Connie. The President congratulates them for destroying the main alien spaceship. Together, they all celebrate the 4th of July by watching the remains of the spaceship fall from the sky.

Men in Black
K goes back to the woman he loves, and J gets a new partner. The love interest, Dr. Laurel Weaver, joins the MIB team as J's partner.

Sixth Sense
Dr. Malcolm Crowe, now realizing that he died from the gunshot wounds, accepts his fate and says goodbye to his wife.

Empire Strikes Back
Chewbacca and Princess Leia return for Luke Skywalker and save him from falling off the space station.

The Grinch
The Grinch apologizes for all he has done and is accepted back into the Who community. He holds the hand of the love interest, Martha May Whovier, and joins in the community Christmas Celebration.

The Wizard of Oz
Dorothy wakes up in bed surrounded by her aunt, uncle, the farmhands, the traveling Wizard, and Toto, with an understanding and confirmation of the moral principle that "there is no place like home."

Spider-Man
The funeral of Norman Osborn in the cemetery. Harry Osborn tells Peter Parker that Spider-Man is the cause of his father's death, and he will never forgive him. MJ announces her love for Peter, and he does not tell her that he loves her but instead walks away. The last images are of Spider-Man swinging along the skyscrapers of New York City.

Shrek
The wedding party in Shrek's swamp.

Finding Nemo
Nemo goes to school with his buddies.

Monsters, Inc.
Sulley opens the closet door to Boo's room. She says, "Kitty!"

Bruce Almighty
Bruce donates his blood at the community blood drive.

Matrix Trilogy
Neo sacrifices his life so that the humans in Zion will not be destroyed.

Pirates of the Caribbean
Will and Liz will marry. Will accepts that he can be a pirate and a good man. Jack sails the Black Pearl toward the horizon.

Harry Potter-The Sorcerer's Stone
Hagrid gives Harry an animated photograph of him as a child with his mother and father.

Lord of the Rings Trilogy
Gandalf, Bilbo, and Frodo sail off to the west in the Elf ship. Sam enters his cottage with his wife and two children.

THE ESSENTIAL SCENE ELEMENTS

When constructing a standard scene, the following questions should be considered:

Who is the primary character in the scene? Is he the protagonist (or protag-supporter) or the antagonist (or antag-supporter)?

Which character is opposed to this character's desires in this scene? Is he the protagonist (or protag-supporter) or the antagonist (or antag-supporter)?

What is in jeopardy? What is at stake for the main character in this scene? How can he be harmed in this scene?

What is the object (or objective) of the conflict in this scene?

What are the obstacles that the characters must overcome in this scene?

Which character wins the objective of this scene?

Does the scene start in the midst of a conflict?

What is the scene crisis?

What is the scene confrontation?

What is the scene climax?

What is the scene resolution?

What is the protagonist's emotional reaction to the events that occur in this scene?

What is the antagonist's emotional reaction to the events that occur in this scene?

What virtues or vices are expressed by the protagonist (or protag-supporter) in this scene?

What virtues or vices are expressed by the antagonist (or antag-supporter) in this scene?

How does the protagonist change as a result of the conflict in this scene?

Is the scene cinematic? Does it consist primarily of characters' physical actions or is it only dialogue?

How do you think the audience will emotionally react to this scene? How will they feel about the protagonist? How will they feel about the antagonist?

EMOTIONS
MAKING THE AUDIENCE FEEL

Emotion & Story

Emotion Words

Theories of Emotion

The Cognitive Theory

Intensity of Emotions

Reactions to Events

Reactions to Actions

Reactions to Objects

Dialogue & Emotions

EMOTION & STORY

"Fear and pity may be aroused by spectacular means; but they may also result from the inner structure of the piece, which is the better way, and indicates a superior poet."
—Aristotle, *Poetics*

"... let us determine what are the circumstances which strike us as terrible or pitiful."
—Aristotle, *Poetics*

"Movies provide an opportunity to experience emotion. All filmmakers therefore, have a single goal: to elicit emotion in an audience."
—Michael Hauge, *Writing Screenplays That Sell*

"When you open the dramatic works of Shakespeare, you find a number of words on white paper. These words were arranged in a certain order about four centuries ago. Today, they still have the unbelievable power of making us cry in certain places and laugh in others. Because they were arranged in such manner as to contain emotional stimuli, they have the effect of making us feel sympathy or hatred, of filling us with pity or horror. If such a transmission over hundreds of years can take place, if generations and generations of audiences consisting of different kinds of people are able to experience the same emotions, surely there must be laws and rules which effectuate such an amazing feat."
—Eugene Vale, *The Technique of Screen and Television Writing*

The concept of a **situation** is essential to the analysis of emotions. Within the theory of story design, the concept of a situation can be associated with a scene. Ortony, Clore, and Collins, in *The Cognitive Structure of Emotions*, connect the concepts of emotion, situation, and story:

> It is apparent that writers can reliably produce in readers an awareness of a character's affective states by characterizing a situation whose construal is assumed to give rise to them. This suggests that writers use an implicit theory that individual emotions can be specified in terms of personal and interpersonal situational descriptions that are sufficient to produce them. Thus writers do not always have to state what emotions a character is experiencing because if the described situation contains the eliciting conditions for a particular emotion, the experience for that emotion can be inferred.

The most certain method of effectively communicating to a mass audience is through the emotions.

The theory of emotions, therefore, has a dual role to play in the theory of story construction:

(1) The analysis of the situations that produce different types of emotional reactions in characters within the story.

(2) The analysis of situations that produce emotional reactions in members of the audience, especially empathy for the protagonist and enmity for the antagonist.

The second, analyzing situations that produce emotional reactions in members of the audience, is the most important for designing stories which result in the audience having **a satisfying emotional experience**, which is critical for a film to become a megahit movie.

EMOTION WORDS

There is a distinction between **telling** the audience what emotion the character is feeling, and **showing** the audience the character feeling the emotion. This is a very important distinction for screenwriters.

To *tell* the audience the emotion a character is experiencing involves nothing more than having the character state the emotion word in dialogue, such as "I am angry," or to have another character state this about the first character, as in "You are angry."

To *show* the audience the emotion that a character is feeling is to write the **situation** in which the character finds himself or to write the **behavior** of the character that expresses the emotion. *Showing* the emotions is much more effective dramatically because it causes the emotion to also be experienced by members of the audience. This is the way to write a story which will eventually produce a **satisfying emotional experience in the audience.**

But it is often very helpful for a writer to **tell** what emotion the character is experiencing in the story treatment to ensure that they are writing an emotional reaction for each character for every event. Then, in the first draft of the screenplay, the writer should concentrate on writing scenes that **show** the character experiencing the emotion.

Below is the list of emotion words. Associated with each basic emotion word is a list of synonyms obtained from a thesaurus. These are the words that a writer should use when **telling** which emotion a character is expressing. In the following sections, we will discuss techniques used for **showing** these emotions.

ANGER: rage, outrage, fury, wrath, ire, temper, gall, bile, indignation, resentment, exasperation, vexation, annoyance, displeasure, hostility

ANXIETY: uneasiness, unease, apprehension, misgivings, foreboding, distress, concern, tension, anguish, angst, dread

APATHY: indifference, unconcern, lack of interest, inattention, unresponsiveness, passiveness, lethargy, lack of feeling, numbness, emotionless, coolness, impassivity

CONFUSION: bewilderment, stupefaction, bafflement, perplexity, puzzlement, mystification, disconcertment, discomposure, abashment, disorder, disarrangement, disarray, untidiness, shambles, upheaval, mess, muddle, clutter, jumble, hodge-podge, snarl, tangle, riot, tumult, madhouse, turmoil, pandemonium, hullabaloo, hubbub, commotion, ferment, disturbance, bedlam, uproar

CONTENTMENT: satisfaction, content, contentedness, gratification, happiness, pleasure, peace, serenity, ease, comfort

CURIOSITY: inquisitiveness, interest, questioning, prying

DESIRE: crave, want, wish, long for, yearn for, hunger for, thirst for

DESPAIR: hopelessness, discouragement, desperation, despondency, gloom, depression

EXCITEMENT: thrill, adventure, stimulation, interest, animation, enthusiasm, elation, action, activity, furor, ferment, commotion, brouhaha, turmoil, tumult, agitation, flurry, flutter, frenzy, stir

FEAR: fright, dread, foreboding, terror, panic, threat, horror, apprehension, alarm, dismay, trepidation, consternation, disquietude, quaking, perturbation, qualm

FONDNESS: tenderness, affection, attachment, devotion, care, love, amorousness, desire, passion, ardor, liking

GRATITUDE: gratefulness, appreciation, thankfulness, thanks, acknowledgement, recognition, obligation

GRIEF: grieving, sorrow, sadness, heartbreak, heartache, misery, agony, woe, wretchedness, suffering, anguish, distress, despondency, despair, desolation, affliction, tribulation

GUILT: guiltiness, guilty conduct, criminality, culpability, wrongdoing, misconduct, misdoing, misdeed, misbehavior, wrong, turpitude, transgression, sinfulness, sin, vice, trespass, delinquency, dereliction, shame, disgrace, self-disgust, humiliation, degradation, dishonor, infamy

HAPPINESS: gladness, joy, delight, felicity, contentment, content, sense of well-being, pleasure, enjoyment, satisfaction, light-heartedness, rejoicing, elation, jubilation, high spirits, bliss, beatitude, blessedness, rapture, ecstasy, gaiety, exultation, exuberance, merriment, cheer, cheerfulness, cheeriness, glee, jollity, mirth

HATE: dislike, despise, detest, abhor, loathe, abominate, execrate, hold in contempt, bear malice toward, be hostile to, not be able to bear, have no use for, recoil from, shrink from, be repelled by, be sick of, be tired of, give one a pain

HOPE: faith, confidence, belief, assurance, reassurance, encouragement, trust, reliance, conviction, optimism, expectation, great expectations, expectancy, anticipation

HOSTILITY: belligerence, animosity, antagonism, antipathy, enmity, opposition, contrariness, malice, viciousness, malevolence, bitterness, spleen, unfriendliness, ill will, rancor, hatred, vindictiveness, venom

IRRITATION: annoy, vex, anger, make impatient, peeve, provoke, nettle, exasperate

JEALOUSY: envy, envious, resentment, covetousness

LONELINESS: lonely, companionless, alone, friendless, forlorn, desolate, forsaken, alienated, aloof, detached, withdrawn, insular

LONGING: strong desire, yearning, craving, hungering, thirst, wish, aspiration, ardent

LOVE (PARENT-CHILD): devotion, adoration, fondness, tenderness, affection

LOVE (ROMANTIC): passion, passionate affection, rapture, amorousness, ardor, amour, infatuation,

PASSION: emotion, feeling, warmth, heart, ardor, fervor, fire, intensity, sentiment, rapture, ecstasy, intoxication, enthusiasm, earnestness, gusto, eagerness, vehemence

RESIGNATION: submission, submissiveness, passiveness, nonresistance, acquiescence, equanimity, stoicism, fatalism, patience

RESTLESSNESS: restiveness, agitation, fretfulness, disquietude, inquietude, edginess, fitfulness, jitters, jumpiness, nervousness, uneasiness, unrest, discontent

REVENGE: vengeance, paying back, retaliation, reprisal, satisfaction, retribution, requital, repayment, eye for an eye, tooth for a tooth

SADNESS: unhappy, cheerless, joyless, grieved, grief-stricken, dispirited, downcast, low, crestfallen, disconsolate, desolate, despondent, melancholy, inconsolable, depressed, dejected

SHAME: guilt, remorse, self-disgust, self-abomination, embarrassment, humiliation, mortification, chagrin, shamefacedness, unworthiness, disgrace, dishonor

SURPRISE: astonish, astound, startle, amaze, flabbergast, shock, stun, dumbfound, stagger, strike with awe, defy belief, stupefy, confound, boggle the mind

SUSPICION: distrust, mistrust, jealous apprehension

SYMPATHY: concord, accord, harmony, congeniality, understanding, agreement, rapport, affinity, communion, consonance, unanimity, concert, regard, amity, fellow feeling, fellowship, friendship, concern, compassion, feeling, commiseration, empathy, grief, sorrow, pity

TENDERNESS: softness, gentleness, delicacy, mildness, kindness, kindliness, loving-kindness, compassion, sympathy, goodness, benevolence, beneficence, humanity, mercifulness, fondness, warmth, affection, lovingness, love

WORRY: be anxious, feel uneasy, be apprehensive, be disturbed, be troubled, be distressed, agonize, fret, despair, lose heart, be downhearted, be heavy-hearted, be afraid, dread, brood over, stew

THEORIES OF EMOTION

The **emotions** have been the subject of much philosophical and scientific debate. Cheshire Calhoun and Robert Solomon, in *What is an Emotion? Classical Readings in Philosophical Psychology*, distinguish five models of emotion: **sensation theories, physiological theories, behavioral theories, evaluative theories, and cognitive theories.**

> Both sensation and physiological theories begin from the observation that mental and physical agitation, excitement, and arousal frequently, if not always, accompany emotional experiences... Sensation theorists are only interested in the psychology of emotion—how people experience their emotions. By contrast, physiological theorists pursue the physiological basis of emotional experience—what we feel when we are angry are various physiological changes and disturbances...For behavioral theorists, "observable behavior, not private experience, is the basis for analyzing emotions... 'Emotional behavior' is actually an umbrella term covering not only deliberate or voluntary verbal and physical actions, such as shouting joyously or embracing a friend affectionately, but also innate or reflexive 'behaviors', such as weeping for grief or starting at a surprising sound.

Robert Plutchik, in *Emotion, A Psycho-Evolutionary Synthesis*, offers the thesis that emotions "are universal, biologically adaptive, prototypic patterns." Plutchik identified the following patterns:

> the destructive pattern associated with **anger**
> the protection pattern associated with **fear**
> the rejection pattern associated with **disgust**
> the deprivation pattern associated with **sorrow**
> the reproduction pattern associated with **joy**
> the incorporation pattern associated with **acceptance**

Changes from one emotional state to another do depend on the changes in the meaning of the situation to the perceiver. One fact about emotions that has importance for story construction was stated by Jon Elster in *Nuts and Bolts for the Social Sciences*, "The cessation of an emotional state—be it positive or negative—does not simply bring us back to the earlier emotional plateau. Rather, it tends to generate another emotional state of opposite sign."

This explains why the cessation of love can lead to hate and why the interruption of joy can result in terror. One of the most effective techniques used to create enmity for the antagonist is to have him destroy a joyous celebration, as does the Wicked Witch in *The Wizard of* Oz during the Munchkin liberation party and the Joker in *Batman* during Gotham City's 200th Anniversary.

THE COGNITIVE THEORY OF EMOTION

The most fruitful theory of emotions for story construction is the *Cognitive Theory*, as developed by Ortony, Collins, and Clore. Their analysis divides emotions into three general classes: reactions to events, agents and objects. Emotions arise because of the way situations are construed by a perceiver. "...some emotions (e.g., disgust), involve much less cognitive processing and structure than others (e.g., shame)... the claim that emotions always involve some degree of cognition is not the same as asserting that the contribution of cognition is necessarily conscious."

SUMMARY OF THE COGNITIVE THEORY OF EMOTION

Emotions are valenced (pro, con) reactions to:

Consequences of Events
Consequences for Self
Consequences for Others

Actions of Agents
Self as Agent
Others as Agent

Aspects of Objects

Events are appraised by **desirability** with reference to **goals**

Actions are appraised by **praiseworthiness** with reference to **standards**

Objects are appraised by **appealingness** with reference to **attitudes**

This theory constructs a classification of distinct emotion types and provides a **situational description** of the conditions under which the emotion can be generated. These emotion types will be explained in greater detail in the following sections, with examples for each type drawn from scenes in the megahit movies.

FACTORS AFFECTING THE INTENSITY OF EMOTION

Four global variables that affect the **intensity of the emotions**.

(1) **Sense of reality**: how much one believes the situation is real.
(2) **Proximity**: how close in terms of psychological space one feels to the situation.
(3) **Unexpectedness:** how sudden the event occurs and how surprised one is by the situation.
(4) **Arousal**: how sensually aroused one is to the situation.

These four factors affect all the emotions.

EMOTIONAL REACTIONS TO EVENTS

Reactions to Events: Consequences for Self

If a character is pleased about a desirable event, then the resulting emotion will be joy. If a character is displeased about an undesirable event, then the resulting feeling is distress. In general, to the extent that the character sees the event as contributing to the realization of his goals, he will tend to experience the positive emotion we call joy. Similarly, to the extent that the person sees the event as interfering with the realization of his goals, he will tend to experience the negative emotion of the kind called distress.

Joy Emotions: pleased about a desirable event
(emotion words: contented, cheerful, delighted, ecstatic, euphoric, feeling good, glad, happy, joyful, jubilant, pleasantly surprised, pleased)
The Ghostbusters are ecstatic about surviving their battle with Gozer.

Distress Emotions: displeased about a undesirable event
(emotion words: depressed, distressed, displeased, dissatisfied, distraught, feeling bad, feeling uncomfortable, grief, homesick, lonely, lovesick, miserable, regret, sad, shock, uneasy, unhappy, upset)
Dorothy is upset about the guard not allowing her to see the Wizard.
Indiana Jones is miserable about the death of Marion.

Reactions to Events: Consequences for Others

If the character is pleased about an event desirable for some other character, then he will experience a **happy-for** emotion. If a character is pleased about an event undesirable for some other character, then he will experience a **gloating** emotion. If a character is displeased about an event desirable for another character, then he will have a **resentment** emotion. If a character is displeased about an event undesirable for another character, then he will have a **sorry-for** emotion.

Happy-for Emotions: pleased about an event that is desirable for someone else (emotion words: delighted-for, happy-for, pleased-for)
Dorothy is happy for Toto when he escapes from Elmira Gulch and also later when Toto escapes from the Wicked Witch of the West.

Sorry-for Emotions: displeased about an event that is undesirable for someone else
(emotion words: compassion, pity, sad-for, sympathy)
Elliott and Michael are sorry for E.T. when he is ill. Dorothy is sorry for her Aunt Em, who she believes is sick.

Resentment Emotions: displeased about an event presumed to be desirable for someone else
(emotion words: envy, jealousy, resentment)
The Joker resents Batman for getting all the publicity. The Witch resents Dorothy getting the ruby slippers.

Gloating Emotions: pleased about an event presumed to be desirable for someone else
(emotion words: gloating, Schadenfreude-delighting in the misfortune of others)
The Wicked Witch gloats as she watches Dorothy's desperation as the sand runs out of the hourglass. Belloc gloats as he orders the natives to kill Indiana Jones.

Hope Emotions: pleased about the prospects of a desirable event
(emotion words: anticipation, anticipatory excitement, excitement, expectancy, hope, hopeful)
The Ghostbusters are excited about the hope of capturing a ghost. Dorothy and her friends hope to see the Wizard of Oz.

Fear Emotions: displeased about the prospects of an undesirable event
(emotion words: apprehensive, anxious, cowering, dread, fear, fright, nervous, petrified, scared, terrified)
The Lion cowers in fear before the Wizard of Oz. The Ghostbusters run in fear from the ghost in the library.
Satisfaction Emotions: pleased about the confirmation of the prospect of a desirable event
(emotion words: gratification, hopes-realized, satisfaction)

Venkman is satisfied that Dana will finally have dinner with him. Indiana Jones is gratified that he will be able to search for the Ark of the Covenant.

Fears-Confirmed Emotions: displeased about the confirmation of the prospect of an undesirable event (emotion words: worst fears realized)
Elliott watches E.T. die. Dorothy loses Toto to Elmira Gulch in the *Wizard of Oz*. In *Ghostbusters*, the grid explodes after the power is shut off and all of the ghosts escape.

Relief Emotions: pleased about the disconfirmation of the prospect of an undesirable event (emotion words: relief)
Belloc and Marion are both relieved they were not tortured by the sadistic Nazi.

Disappointment Emotions: displeased about the disconfirmation of the prospect of a desirable event (emotion words: despair, disappointment, frustration, dashed-hopes, heartbroken)
Vicki Vale is disappointed when she discovers that Bruce Wayne lied to her about having to go out of town. Dorothy is disappointed by the reaction of the Wizard when she brings him the broomstick.

EMOTIONAL REACTION TO THE ACTIONS OF CHARACTERS

If a character is appraising his own actions, he will approve of his own praiseworthy actions (resulting in pride) and disapprove of his own blameworthy actions (resulting in shame). If a character is appraising another character's actions, then he will either approve of the other character's praiseworthy action (resulting in admiration), or disapprove of the other character's blameworthy action (resulting in reproach). Emotional reactions of members in the audience to the behavior of characters in the story will also be based on their values and the praiseworthy or blameworthy actions of the characters.

Pride Emotions: approving of one's own praiseworthy action
Elliot is proud of helping E.T. get home. The Scarecrow, Lion, and Tin Man are proud of receiving the symbols of achievement from the Wizard.

Self-Reproach Emotions: disapproving of one's own blameworthy action (emotion words: embarrassment, feeling guilty, self-blame, shame)
The Scarecrow is ashamed that he is a failure at frightening crows.

Appreciation Emotions: approving of someone else's praiseworthy action (emotion words: admiration, appreciation, awe, esteem, respect)
The New York community appreciates the Ghostbusters' efforts to save the world from Gozer. The Mayor of Gotham appreciates Batman's efforts to defeat the Joker.

Reproach Emotions: disapproving of someone else's blameworthy action (emotion words: appalled, contempt, despise, disdain, indignation)
Dean Yaegar despises Venkmen's para-psychological research. Dorothy expresses indignation at the Wizard's refusal to keep his promise after she returns with the broomstick of the Wicked Witch of the West.

Gratitude Emotions: approving of someone else's praiseworthy action and being pleased about the related desirable event
(emotion words: appreciation, feeling indebted, thankful)
The Rebel community expresses their gratitude to Luke Skywalker for destroying the Death Star.

Anger Emotions: disapproving of blameworthy action and being displeased about the related undesirable event
(emotion words: annoyance, exasperation, fury, incensed, livid, offended)
Elliott is angry with the doctors, who are examining E.T.

Gratification Emotions: approving of one's own praiseworthy action and being pleased about the related desirable event
(emotion words: pleased-with-oneself, self-satisfaction)
The Joker is pleased with himself about allowing the Gotham Anniversary Celebration to occur. Elmira Gulch is smug about getting Toto.

Remorse Emotions: disapproving of one's own blameworthy action being and displeased about the related undesirable event
(emotion words: penitence, remorse, self-anger)
Indiana Jones feels remorse because he believes he caused the death of Marion. Stantz expresses sincere remorse at destroying the chandelier in the ballroom.

EMOTIONAL REACTIONS TO OBJECTS

Objects that cause pleasant feelings, joy, pleasure, or comfort are liked. Objects that cause pain, unpleasant feelings, fear or discomfort are disliked. These likes and dislikes are built upon our attitudes.

"Appealingness is rooted in attitudes that are dispositional likes and dislikes. These dispositions are associated with representations of or categories of objects—one may feel disposed to like dogs and to dislike snakes. Momentary liking (or disliking) thus often derives from how one categorizes an object and what one's disposition is toward objects in that category, as well as from characteristics of the individual object itself."
— Ortony, *The Cognitive Structure of Emotions*

Liking Emotions
(emotion words: adore, attracted-to, like, love)
Marion likes the monkey in *Raiders of the Lost Ark*.
Dorothy loves Toto in *Wizard of Oz*.

Disliking Emotions
(emotion words: aversion, detest, disgust, dislike, hate, loathe)
Indiana Jones hates snakes in *Raiders of the Lost Ark*.
Marion is disgusted by the dead bodies she bumps into while in the Well-of-Souls. The Scarecrow loathes fire in *Wizard of Oz*.

DIALOGUE & EMOTION

"Drama is action. What drama is not is a bunch of characters sitting around talking, twiddling their thumbs, doing nothing."
—Richard Walter, *Screenwriting*

"The writer who wants to learn how to use dialogue in the motion picture should try to make his story understandable without the spoken word."
—Eugene Vale, *The Technique of Screen and Television Writing*

Lew Hunter's *Screenwriting 434* book has some good points to make about writing dialogue in screenplays. "Never write dialogue that only a few people will understand…Be simple, but not simplistic." Don't try to make your characters speak above or below their education level. Don't have a janitor speak like someone with a Ph.D. in English Literature, or your scientist speak like the junkman. Also, of course, there is a reason to play them out of type or for humor. For example, the intellectual who is unemployed and now waiting on tables, or the lower-class working man studying at night school in an effort to improve his status in life. As Lew Hunter says, "let your characters be your characters." The speech patterns should flow naturally from their personalities.

Hunter also recommends that writers avoid "snappy sayings and witty patter" if it is a substitute for weak story lines, conflict, or lack of tension between the characters. But, if your story is about a group of schoolboys competing in "The Best Oscar Wilde Imitation Writing Contest," then being "witty" is essential for them to be in the scene. The best advice is to use language that is appropriate to the character and the situation.

"Good dialogue is dialogue that illuminates what the characters are not saying" and "less is more" are other pieces of advice offered by Hunter. Never say the obvious. Never have characters describe actions in the scene that the audience can see. Have what the characters say be an expression of their feelings and reactions to what is occurring around them, **not a description** of what is happening to them. To write descriptions is to write dialogue that is "on-the-nose." Hunter also recommends that one should not write dialogue in which people discuss their past and memories. "In movies, it's a bore, and a snore." Also, avoid writing dialects. This is really the domain of the actor and director, not the screenwriter, who should be concerned with action and story design.

Some characters will talk around a problem, rather than dealing with it directly. This is a way of avoiding having to confront something that is emotionally difficult. But here the language reflects the psychology of the character, rather than describing the events of the scene.

One book that is dedicated just to the topic of writing dialogue is Tom Chiarella's *Writing Dialogue.* In this book, the author focuses on methods "to create memorable voices and fictional conversations that cackle with wit, tension and nuance."

Chiarella discusses the use of misdirection in dialogue in which the characters are not dealing directly with what each are saying. This form of dialogue appears "realistic" to the audience. Some forms of misdirection are changing the subject; directing the dialogue "offstage"; answering questions and answers that aren't quite answers but sounds like them; allowing characters to speak to themselves and for themselves; and carrying on more than one conversation at the same time.

Chiarella believes that "There is no secret, except to learn how to *trust* the language you hear, to learn to *hear* the people around you and to *expose yourself* to as many voices (and techniques) as possible." The voice of a character is the idioms he selects and the metaphors he uses in conversation. The pace and rhythm of the dialogue is a function of the character in conflict with other characters in a situation.

> "when I speak of the energy and direction of a story, I am referring to its tone and emotion (energy) and tension (direction). Writers craft, or shape, patterns of energy and direction in dialogue. In many ways these become the signatures of their dialogue, the things that make the voices of the characters recognizable and sustainable...what your characters says is directed by the needs of the story."

Chiarella asserts that, "The way people speak defines who they are," but I would argue that, "the way people are defines the way they speak." The writer should focus on the emotional state of the character in the moment of the scene. They move and react to actions of other characters and events that happen. "Speaking" is just another body and emotional reaction to stimuli. It is the utterance of sounds that often do nothing more than express the feelings of the character, although sometimes also to express a thought, intention,or desire. But it is the underlying emotion, intention, and desire that are of primary interest to the audience.

Chiarella does state that, "when writing dialogue, you should begin with character. What does each character want? Determining this should allow some sense of pace and rhythm. Examine tension next. What is holding these people together or keeping them apart? Then look at setting. What's brought them to the same place? Where are they?"

Often silence is the best response for a character in a situation. Sometimes it is best to use silence over words. But fill the silence with a gesture: dramatic gesture, particular gesture, and incidental gesture. A writer should learn how to communicate using non-verbal body language and write that for your character's behavior.

Each character has a unique speech pattern. There are many non-sequiturs in conversations, and people very often talk past each other. Most people are not very good listeners and often talk at, rather than to, their partners. People speak in half phrases, characters sound different, and realistic dialogue is jumpy. Speeches usually are not longer than three continuous lines. If they are longer than this, the audience will begin to lose interest. Most films avoid long speeches unless they are in exposition scenes.

Characters don't always tell the truth, and definitely not the whole truth. They will hold back many things. Most of the time people lie for social reasons; to keep the peace and minimize problems. It is only in moments of anger and pain that the whole truth is usually expressed. It is important to realize that it is a character's mood and emotion that precede his action; words are just a means to express these feelings.

With mounting action, sentences become shorter and simpler. The characters don't need to talk about what will be visually displayed within the scene action. Most of the megahit films minimize the use of dialogue, and most of the images do not consist of just talking heads. The actions of a character reveal him, not just his words.

Joel Kupperman, in his book, *Character*, states that "any scientific study of the psychology of character is most revealing if it focuses not on what people say, but on what they do. Furthermore, what a person does in commonplace situations may be much less indicative of character than what he or she does when severely tempted or pressed."

The best dialogue is that which goes against, or is contrary to, the action of the scene. Dialogue or statements uttered by the characters, but are contradicted by their body movements and actions, create the most dramatic and emotionally effective scenes. Much more can be said with gestures and the techniques of non-verbal communication than with words. In realistic situations, most people never say what they really feel. Powerful scenes reflect this truth.

HUMOR
RELEASE THE TENSION AND MAKE THEM LAUGH

Emotion & Humor

Theories of Humor

Humorous Dialogue

Humorous Situations

Humorous Characters

Humor in the Megahit Movies

EMOTION & HUMOR

"Somehow laughter is connected with emotions—we laugh with glee, with scorn, with giddiness, etc. ...Laughter often involves major physiological disturbances. There is an interpretation of breathing and the loss of muscle tone; in heavy laughter there may be a loss of muscle control."
—John Morreall, *Taking Laughter Seriously*

In *Argument of Laughter*, D.H. Monro discusses the relationship of laughter to the instincts:

> Normally, when an instinct is stirred, it finds its outlet in the cognative activity appropriate to the instinct. Laughter occurs when this activity is, for some reason, checked. The stirring of the instinct means the organism has been, physically and psychically, mobilized for action. Laughter is, on the contrary, a demobilization of forces. Normally this occurs gradually in the course of the activity toward which the instinct is striving. But when this activity is prevented, the release is sudden and explosive...the change must be sudden, and must swing from one viewpoint to its direct opposite. A systematic, logical examination of the object, involving a continuous change of ground, is not enough; there must be a direct and violent opposition...Further, the opposition must be complete. If you shift your viewpoint to another, only slightly opposed to the first, the laughter is not whole-hearted.

The need to change from "one viewpoint to its direct opposite" becomes essential in designing jokes that produce laughter. On the emotional impact of attitude-mixing, Monro, in *Argument of Laughter*, states "We all of us practice a mental compartmentalism: we sort out the facts of our environment into different mental compartments, and decide that a particular attitude and emotion is appropriate to each. The linking of disparates may mean the shattering of this orderly system. We then have an attitude-mixing or universe-changing."

The famous French philosopher, Henri Bergson, stated that, "Laughter is incompatible with emotion. Depict some fault, however trifling, in such a way to arouse sympathy, fear or pity; the mischief is done, it is impossible for us to laugh." This is true only if the situation concludes by being a state of affairs truly eliciting sympathy, fear, or pity. But it is **not** true if there is a sudden change of interpretation of the situation that it concludes by being non-threatening. Then, the pent up energy is released, which in itself is a pleasurable feeling. Emotions and laughter are not incompatible, as Bergson held. On the contrary, strong emotions are necessary for the greatest outbursts of laughter. It is only certain types of emotions, like pity, fear, or anger, if they persist in a situation, will block laughter.

There seems to be a structure to the emotional dynamics underlying the laughter producing process. The viewer perceives a situation. Suddenly, he notices an "incongruity"; something is occurring that is inappropriate in this type of situation. There is a deviation from the patterns the viewer has come to expect in this situation. This produces tension and stress because this deviation can be threatening. The viewer physiologically becomes energized, and he starts to develop the emotions of fear or anger, depending on his perception of the deviation. He concentrates and further analyses the situation, which demands more psychic energy. Suddenly, there is a new change in the pattern that allows the viewer to interpret the situation as non-threatening. There is no longer a need for the energy that he has been accumulating. He then releases this energy in laughter. The greater the perceived threat, the greater is the accumulated energy, and the greater the outburst of laughter when this energy is finally released.

THEORIES OF HUMOR

Humor is an experience that causes people to laugh. **Humor** is generated by a *sudden radical deviation from expected patterns of behavior in a situation that concludes by being non-threatening to the perceiver*. Upon reflection, these situations are characterized as containing *incongruous* elements or exhibiting behavior patterns that are *inappropriate* in this type of situation.

Before applying this definition to the analysis of popular films, it would be valuable to explain how this constructive theory integrates elements from other theories of humor.

Many people question whether there can be a theory of humor. For example, John Morreall, in *Taking Laughter Seriously*, states that "...we are still without an adequate general theory of laughter. The major difficulty here is that we laugh at such diverse situations that it seems difficult, if not impossible, to come up with a single formula that will cover all cases of laughter."

As Victor Raskin, in *Semantic Mechanisms of Humor*, states, "Different people will not necessarily find the same things equally funny—many things which strikes one group as funny may bore another group; some jokes are private or individual, i.e., restricted in their funniness to just one or very few individuals. However, the ability to appreciate and enjoy humor is universal and shared by all people, even if the kinds of humor that they favor differ widely. This universality of humor is further reinforced by the fact that surprisingly many jokes or situations will strike surprisingly many, if not all people as funny."

The project of a constructive theory of humor is not to explain the cause of every instance of laughter, but instead to arrive at a few fundamental concepts that a writer could use to construct humorous situations; situations that will make **most** of the audience laugh. It cannot guarantee that everyone will laugh (although it will provide reasons that explain why everyone doesn't laugh). These methods are intended to be an extension to the general theory of story construction in that it is consistent with and uses most of the concepts already explicated.

The following division of theories of humor is a modification of the research presented in the book, *The Psychology of Humor* by Jeffrey Goldstein and Paul McGhee.

The Self-Knowledge Theory of Humor (Pretense)

This theory was originally proposed by Plato, who stated that a necessary condition for humor is the presence of "a failing, one that tales its name from a state of the character, and is that specific form of failing with the characteristic quite opposite to what the oracle of Delphi recommends." What the oracle of Delphi recommends is that a person "know thyself."

This theory of humor can be characterized as the theory of *pretense*. We laugh at those characters that **lack self-knowledg**; we laugh at ourselves when we recognize our faults, and at others when they fail to recognize their faults. We laugh at those whose behavior is fraudulent, who attempt to present themselves as something different than their actions show them to be. Usually, these characters attempt to present themselves as having an "authority" which in reality they do not possess. We laugh when this incongruity suddenly becomes evident, when the fraud is exposed, and the characters unsuccessfully try to "cover up" their exposure. This is a sudden deviation from the expected patterns of character that the individual has presented to the audience. Once his fraud is exposed, he is no longer a threat to the audience.

Biological, Instinct, and Evolution Theories

Theories in this group place emphasis on the biological benefits of laughter and humor. "Laughter and humor have been hailed as 'good for the body' because they restore homeostasis, stabilize blood pressure, oxygenate the blood, massage the vital organs, stimulate circulation, facilitate digestion, relax the system, and produce a feeling of well-being."

Some believe that laughter evolved as a biological corrective to the effects of sympathy. "Without a sense of the ludicrous, nature's antidote for minor and depressing and disagreeable spectacles confronting men, the species might have not survived." Laughter gradually became a substitute for assault. The similarity of bodily stance (exposed teeth, contorted face, sprawling movements of the limbs) in both fighting and laughter is pointed to as evidence. Present day ridicule can be traced to the primitive thrashing of enemies. "Laughter has also been viewed as the means of maintaining group standards in primitive times."

The primary focus of these theories is the impact of laughter on the biological state of the individual, and **not** the construction of humorous situations that will generate laughter, which is the enterprise of the present book.

Surprise Theories

The element of surprise is a necessary element for humor and laughter. The constructivist theory incorporates **surprise** in the feature of "sudden" deviation of expectations. The film's audience is constantly monitoring the movie for change in an effort to comprehend the story. "Our whole sensory apparatus," writes Gombrich, "is basically tuned to the monitoring of unexpected change. Continuity fails to register after a time, and this is true both on the physiological and psychological level."

In order for laughter to result, a necessary condition is that the change be sudden. In *Taking Laughter Seriously*, John Morreall states, "For a sudden change there must be a relatively large difference between the two states, and the time separating these states must be short." Suddenness is necessary to disrupt the tranquility of continuity in order for the physiological process of laughter to begin.

Superiority-Disparagement Theories

The **Superiority** theories assert that laughter is the result of feelings of triumph over other people. We laugh when we compare ourselves to others, and feel less stupid, less ugly, less unfortunate, or less weak. These theories assert that mockery, ridicule, and laughter at the foolish actions of others are central to humor.

In *Comedy Writing Secrets*, Melvin Helitzer argues for the position that humor is reducible to superiority, hostility, aggression, and malice.

> To those we consider superior, because they are in positions of authority or are more famous, richer, or more intelligent, physically stronger, or socially admired, we delight in publicizing their every shortcoming, perceived or real. The greater the prestige of the individual, the greater is our desire to equalize. The largest category of contemporary humor and witticism is insult humor.

But Helitzer's thesis is **not** fully justified by the types of humor found in popular movies, for only a small number of humorous instances include elements of superiority and derision. This form of humor, while it does occasionally generate laughter, expresses attitudes and behavior that are inappropriate within contemporary culture. It is, therefore, a mode of behavior characteristic of the antagonist and his supporters, best exemplified by the Joker in *Batman*.

Hostility is not a necessary aspect of humor, although it is often found in many situations that produce laughter. This is because the character is usually attacking a norm or standard he hates. If the audience believes that the norm is oppressive, then they will have great empathy for the character that attacks this norm. But hostility is not necessary to produce laughter. A sudden deviation from the expected pattern is the sufficient condition.

Given the mixed feelings that hostility produces, the mocking and ridiculing form of behavior is best associated with the antagonist and his supporters. Examples of this behavior are Belloc in *Raiders of the Lost Ark*, the Joker in *Batman,* and the Wicked Witch in *The Wizard of Oz.*

Bergson's Theory of Humor

Henri Bergson, the famous French philosopher, "attributed laughter to the 'mechanical encrusted on something living'." He meant that when man becomes rigid, machine-like, and repetitive, he becomes laughable, since the essence of humanity is its flexibility and spirit. While Bergson's theory may explain the behavior of the Tin Man in *The Wizard of Oz*, it is not helpful in explaining the humor of the Scarecrow and the Cowardly Lion, plus many other laughter producing situations found in popular movies. "The mechanical encrusted on something living," is a type of "deviation from expected patterns of behavior," that of excessive rigidity. Another form of deviance is excessive plasticity, which is expressed by the Scarecrow. While a third is that of deviating from the expected attributes of a stereotype, in the case of the Cowardly Lion, because the stereotype of a lion has the feature of a courageous and ferocious beast. Therefore, Bergson's theory is a limited special case of the more general constructivist theory.

Another of Bergson's ideas may be more fruitful in the development of humorous constructs: the idea of a "reciprocal interference of series." To draw a quote from D.H. Monro's *Argument of Laughter*:

> A situation…is invariably comic when it belongs to two independent series of events and is capable of being interpreted in two entirely different meanings at the same time. Thus we have the stage made misunderstanding, in which the actors put one interpretation on events, while the audience knows the real one.

This is an idea that is later developed, with variations, by researchers working within the **incongruity theory**, such as Koestler and Paulos. It is also a predecessor of Victor Raskin's "script-based semantic theory" of humor construction. In general, this is a deviation from pragmatic rules of language use and the expectation that people will understand each other and discuss the same topic whenever they engage in conversation.

Ambivalence

In *The Psychology of Humor*, the authors state that

> Ambivalence theories (or "conflict-mixture" and "oscillation") hold that laughter results when the individual simultaneously experiences incompatible emotions or feelings... we laugh whenever, on contemplating an object or situation, we find opposite emotions struggling within us for mastery. Although there is obvious similarity between ambivalence and incongruity theories, incongruity theories tend to stress ideas of perceptions, whereas ambivalence theories stress emotions or feelings.

This theory focuses on the emotional reactions of the individual viewer and **not** the structure of the situation that produced these emotions. Not considered is the interactive process that produces these incompatible motions in the perceiver. These are the concerns of the constructivist theory of humor.

The Relief Theory

The **Relief Theory** emphasizes that laughter is due to an overflow of surplus energy that results when the serious expectations of the person laughing are not met and his attention is diverted to something less dangerous. In other words, the energy the person accumulated because of a "serious expectation" suddenly turns out to be inappropriate for the situation. This "serious expectation" could have been the intense concentration needed to solve a puzzle or problem, the arousal that occurs with anger, fear, terror, or the energy needed either to fight or for flight. John Morreall, in *Taking Laughter Seriously,* discusses the Relief Theory:

> Any prohibition can cause a person to build up an increase desire to do what has been forbidden, and this frustrated desire may manifest itself in pent-up nervous energy...Freud thought that sex and hostility were the only drives whose repression led to laughter, but any taboo can set the stage for relief laughter.

The release of energy, then, may be of nervous energy built up before the person entered the laughter situation. The other kind of release we mention is the release, not of pre-existing energy, but of energy built up by the laughter situation itself. When we listen to certain nonsexual, nonhostile jokes, for example, the narrative may arouse certain emotions in us toward the characters in the story. But then at the punch line the story takes an unexpected turn, or the characters are shown not to be what we thought they were, and so emotional energy that has been built up is suddenly superfluous and demands release. The release of this energy, according to the simplest version of the theory, is laughter.

Although this theory also focuses on the physiological reactions that occur in the viewer of a situation, it does **not** point out the role that tension plays in generating the energy that is later released in laughter. Tension in a situation is the result of *conflict* and *jeopardy for a character for which the audience has empathy.*

The greater the tension, conflict, and jeopardy in a scene, the greater the amount of energy accumulated in the viewer, and the greater the laughter when this energy is released. When there is a sudden radical deviation from expectations in the scene, the emotions built up are shown to be irrelevant and then released in laughter. These factors are essential elements of the constructivist theory of humor.

Freud and the Psychoanalytical Theory of Humor

Freud's theory is a variation of the relief theory embedded within the conceptual framework of Freudian psychoanalysis. Freud's theory explicates humor within the intra-psychic dynamics of the individual, using his concepts of id, ego, and superego. What may be useful for screenwriters in his theory has already been discussed in the analysis of the superiority and relief theories. Freud's emphasis on the use of ambiguity and double meanings to disarm one's "censors" can be incorporated in some types of humorous constructions. But Freud's principle that "in humor there is an economy in the expenditure of feeling" is not a constructive principle that helps a screenwriter design humorous characters or situations in a story.

The Incongruity Theory

John Morreal, in *Taking Laughter Seriously*, states that, "the basic idea behind the incongruity theory is very general and quite simple. We live in an orderly world, where we have come to expect certain patterns among things, their properties, events, etc. We laugh when we experience something that does not fit into these patterns."

The idea that *incongruity* forms the basis of humor was originally developed by the critic Hazlitt and the philosophers Kant and Schopenhauer, whose statement of the theory is the most fruitful.

> Humor often occurs in this way: two or more real objects are thought through one concept; it then becomes strikingly apparent from the entire difference of the objects in other respects, that the concept was only applicable to them from a one-sided point of view.

John Monro, in *Argument of Laughter*, emphasizes the concept of *inappropriateness*:

> We have returned continually to the linking of disparates, to the collision of different mental spheres, to the obtrusion into one context of what belongs to another. We have found this to be an element in many kinds of humor…if we want a convenient single word for it, we may call it inappropriateness.

The concepts of *incongruity* and *inappropriateness* are essential to the constructivist theory of humor and are found to be the most fruitful in constructing humorous situations and explaining the humorous situations found in popular films.

Configurational Theories of Humor

That humor is experienced when elements originally perceived as unrelated suddenly fall into place is the basis for configurational theories of humor. There is a relationship between the concepts found in incongruity and configurational theories. Each stresses the cognitive and perceptual attributes of humor, but the main difference lies in the point at which humor emerges. In the Incongruity Theory, it is the perception of "disjointness" that produces the laughter. In the Configurational Theory, it is the "falling into place" or sudden "insight" that produces the laughter. Laughter in both cases comes from the release of "mental tension" generated by the effort to make things "make sense."

Both are "sudden radical deviations from expected patterns" of interpretation of the events in the story. The authors of *The Psychology of Humor* present Schiller's explanation of configurational humor:

"Dynamic Duality" theory proposed jokes to be a variety of problem solving. Jokes are analogous to ambiguous figures which can be seen in different ways. The comic feeling is a logical joy aroused by a sudden change in the configuration of a thought pattern of unstable structure, showing the double aspect of a moment in its dynamic duality.

These ideas are compatible with a "dual script" theory that is the basis of the humor of misunderstanding, which is a fruitful device in constructing humorous situations.

An Integration of the Theories of Humor

In his book, *Semantic Mechanisms of Humor*, Victor Raskin offers the following synthesis of theories of humor:

> In general, while the history of humor research has been marked by a great deal of fighting, with loud claims and counter claims, examples and counterexamples, theories and anti-theories, the three large groups of theories ... are not at all incompatible, and much feuding and animosity in the fields has often been based on the mutual misunderstanding of each other's goals, premises and, of course, terminology. The three approaches actually characterize the complex phenomena of humor from very different angles and do not at all contradict each other—rather they seem to supplement each other quite nicely.

In our terms, the **incongruity**-based theories make a statement about the **stimulus**; the **superiority** theories characterize the **relations** or **attitudes** between the **speaker** and **hearer**; and the **release/relief** theories comment on the **feelings** and **psychology** of the **hearer** only.

To state this within the conceptual framework of the constructivist theory:

> *Incongruity*-based theories are useful in constructing *situations* that generate laughter in members of the audience.
>
> *Superiority*-based theories are useful in characterizing *attitudes* in members of the *audience* that *humorous situations* may produce.
>
> *Release/Relief* theories are useful in characterizing the *feelings* and *psychology* of members of the *audience* that *humorous situations* may generate.

Since, as screenwriters, we are concerned with designing humorous situations in stories, the insights developed within the *incongruity* tradition should be the most fruitful for this enterprise.

Morreall's Theory of Humor

In *Taking Laughter Seriously,* John Morreall, working within the incongruity tradition, develops a theory of humor, which is the thesis that "laughter results from a pleasant psychological shift."

The constructivist theory agrees with much that Morreall has to say in his book, but emphasizes not the state of the individual laughing, but the **situation** that caused the laughter. Instead of focusing on the pleasant shifts that occur within the individual, it concentrates **on the construction of the tension producing sequence of events in the situation that are suddenly transformed and conclude by becoming non-threatening to the perceiver.**

The Constructive Theory of Humor

The definition of the constructivist theory of humor is restated below. *Humor*, is an experience that causes people to laugh. *Humor* is generated by a *sudden radical deviation from expected patterns of behavior in a situation that concludes by being non-threatening to the perceiver*. Upon reflection, these situations are characterized as containing *incongruous* elements or exhibiting behavior patterns that are *inappropriate* in this type of situation.

The "behavior" in the phrase "a sudden deviation from expected patterns of behavior," can be:

> Linguistic behavior (grammar, word usage, pragmatics)
> Character and social behavior (deviations from stereotypes, attacks on authority)
> Situational or Visual associations (incongruities)

Or it can be any other "pattern" that the perceiver has come to expect will be continued in the situation, and where "expected" means conforming to what is normal or accepted as standard by the community. The audience must have a common knowledge of these standards and norms, or they will not laugh. In other humorous situations, "expected" means the pattern presented to the audience during the setup portion of the joke. The notion of "pattern" is also important, for sequence items usually must be constructed in order to create expectations in the audience.

The deviation must be original and sudden, otherwise, it will not produce laughter. Often, it is the exact opposite of what is expected. The element of surprise is also an essential ingredient of humor. People rarely laugh at a joke the second time they hear it.

The deviation to the expected pattern can be an exaggerated response, an understated response, or an irrelevant response to the situation. All are deviations from the normal behavior expected, and all will produce tension in the viewers, who know what the expected behavior should be. These responses will cause the tension to be relieved though laughter, if no real harm is done to the characters for which the audience has empathy. The audience will also laugh if harm is done to a character that the audience hates, as demonstrated by the behavior of the burglars in *Home Alone*.

The deviation should also be "radical" in the sense of being extreme. Very often, it is the exact opposite of what was expected. If the deviation is small or only of a minor degree, then the surprise will be minimal and the resulting laughter greatly diminished.

Humor in the midst of conflict relieves tension, and this release is pleasurable for the audience. To entertain the audience is to make them laugh in the midst of danger. This gives the audience the thrills and excitement of vicariously being in jeopardy, while still having a pleasurable experience.

HUMOROUS DIALOGUE

Humorous dialogue are linguistic and logical structures that produce laughter. They are different from **humorous situations**, which deal with objects, events, actions, and their relationships that produce laughter, and **humorous characters** whose behavior patterns involve some incongruity that causes people to laugh.

In this section, we will present some of the constructions of language that tend to generate laughter. John Allen Paulos in *Mathematics and Humor,* states

> Logic, pattern, rules, structure—all these are essential to both mathematics and humor, although of course the emphasis is different in the two. In humor the logic is often inverted, patterns are distorted, rules are misunderstood, and structures are confused. Yet these transformations are not random and must make sense on some level. Understanding the "correct" logic, pattern, rule, or structure is essential to understanding what is incongruous in a given story—to 'getting the joke.'

The assertion of logical contradictions will always generate laughter, especially if the character asserting it doesn't realize that he is contradicting himself. Associated with this is the non-sequitor, an illogical statement that is humorous because the second statement (the sequitor) is in no way conceptually connected with the first statement. This is the George Burns-Gracie Allen style of humor and is also often found in the dialogues between Chico and Groucho Marx.

Switching between conceptual frameworks during a dialogue will also generate laughter, especially if there are words in the different frameworks that sound alike. Any violation of a rule of logic will cause people to laugh, provided that they understand which rule is being violated. Koestler, in *Acts of Creation*, states that laughter results from "the perceiving of a situation or idea in two self-consistent but habitually incompatible frames of reference."

So-called "modal jokes" are the result of a deviation from an utterance and the normal expected attitude associated with that type of utterance. An example of this is a hysterical person screaming that they are relaxed, or a person yelling at the top of their lungs that they are speaking softly.

Laughter is often generated when a character assumes an *inappropriate attitude* for an issue which the audience will interpret as the character perceiving the situation from a *radically different perspective.* One example of this technique is to discuss a topic with "mocking insincerity," a method often used by David Letterman on his late night television show.

Another construction that extends the modal form occurs when a joke fails to make the audience laugh. An experienced comedian will then respond with ridiculing his own delivery or the writer of the material, or chastising the audience for their lack of comprehension. Johnny Carson was a master of this technique.

Linguistic incompetence, in all of its variations, will generate laughter. The audience understands the appropriate language use and will laugh at any deviations. Puns are often not successful because the speaker usually does not sincerely expresses the second use of the word in the sentence. The audience does not believe that the speaker could really be confusing the two different meanings of the word.

To misinterpret the intended metaphoric meaning of a word for its literal meaning will generate laughter, especially if the audience understands the context of conversation. Ambiguity is a fruitful source for humor. The setup line makes a true statement using one of the possible meanings of a word. This establishes the audience's expectations within this context. The punch line then states another true statement based on a radically different meaning of the same word. This produces the deviation from expectations that causes people to laugh.

The comic "rule of three" forms another standard construction, consisting of two setup lines followed by the punch line. The first case introduces the situation and the pattern of behavior to the audience. The second case reinforces the pattern within this situation, so that the audience will come to accept this as a standard and normal pattern. This effectively builds up the audience expectation about what will happen next. The third case will be a surprise radical deviation from this pattern, but a deviation that does not threaten the audience. If the audience feels threatened, they will feel fear and anger, instead of laughing.

In *Comedy Writing Handbook*, the professional Hollywood comedy writer, Gene Perret, explores the various linguistic constructions that create humor by deviating from expected patterns of linguistic usage. Some of the suggestions offered by Perret are discussed below.

The punch line should be kept hidden until the very last word. This will prolong the audience's expectations and make the deviation sudden.

Sentences using words that generate bizarre images within the minds of the audience will create incongruity by making them visualize unexpected patterns. Exaggerate an impossible image. The more absurd or outlandish the image, the greater the incongruity in the mind of the audience, and the greater the resulting laughter. Use very 'concrete' and particular images, because the more visual it is, the more the audience will become emotionally involved and the more energy will be expended in laughter when they can't make the image fit into their normal framework of things.

Humor is often generated when one character misinterprets the meaning of the words and sentences uttered by another character. The laughter will be even greater if the hearer then ascribes the opposite attitude to the speaker than the speaker intended.

Language that exaggerates and distorts objects will generate laughter. This is accomplished when an object is viewed from a radically different perspective, and its traits are magnified to the extreme. For example, the small becomes the infinitesimally small, and the large becomes the gigantic. Distortions of the dimensions of space and time will create absurdity.

Transforming clichés and quotations is another important technique that constructs humor. The Joker, in *Batman,* often uses the inappropriate use of clichés to produce humor. As Helitzer states, "one definition of a cliché is a phrase so predictable you can finish it after you have heard the first few words." Both quotations and clichés are effective because the audience knows what to expect, so the comic writer will then suddenly deviate from that expectation in the punch line.

Breaking the pragmatic rules of language use in communication situations will also generate laughter. In *Taking Laughter Seriously,* John Morreall discusses the work on the rules of conversation developed by the philosopher Paul Grice and demonstrates how humor can be generated when we deviate from these rules.

Pragmatic Rules of Conversation
1. Make your contribution as informative as is required for the purposes of the exchange.
2. Do not make your contribution more informative than is required.
3. Do not say what you believe to be false.
4. Do not say that for which you lack adequate evidence.
5. Avoid obscurity of expression.
6. Avoid ambiguity.
7. Be brief.
8. Be orderly.

Deviations from Pragmatic Rules of Conversation That Will Generate Laughter
1. It is humorous when a person's contribution to a conversation is not informative or helpful.
2. The person who gives too much information is comic. (Louis in *Ghostbusters*).
3. We are often amused by lies and characters who lie.
4. The wild speculation or guess inserted into a conversation can be funny.
5. Obscurity of expression humorously hinders or prevents communication.
6. Ambiguity can be the cause of humorous misinterpretations.
7. The person who doesn't know when to stop talking is funny (Louis in *Ghostbusters*).
8. A confused person is often a comic character.

HUMOROUS SITUATIONS

"Drama is not the opposite of comedy; it is part of it. In any situation comedy there is always jeopardy. It heightens the humor. So in any story you tell—even a funny story—you need to look for trouble. You look for the worst thing that could happen."
— Gene Perret, *Comedy Writing Handbook*

D.H. Monro, in *Argument of Laughter,* asks the following questions. "What is the common element in laughable situations? How does the common element in laughable situations fit in with human behavior in general? What is the relation between the common element in laughable situations and the physical concomitants of laughter? Monro classifies *humorous situations* into the following ten types, all of which can be conceived to involve sudden radical deviations from expected patterns of behavior:

1. Any breach of the usual order of events. This is a sudden radical deviation from the natural order of things in the world.

2. Any forbidden breach of the usual order of events. This is a sudden radical deviation from the social norms of appropriate behavior.

3. Indecency, which could be considered as a deviation from the moral codes of appropriate behavior.

4. Importing into one situation what belongs to another situation. Universe changing is a very important factor for humor. Things that are normally associated with one context appear in another radically different context.

5. Anything masquerading as something that it is not. This is a deviation from expected role behavior or type behavior.

6. Word-play, a deviation from expected linguistic behavior.

7. Nonsense, which is a deviation from the expected linguistic behavior of semantic meaningfulness.

8. Small misfortunes. We laugh because things could be much worst, and no one was seriously harmed.

9. Want of knowledge or skill, which is a deviation from the expectation that a character should not be ignorant when dealing with a situation.

10. Veiled insults, which is a deviation from the rules of appropriate social interaction.

One technique that can be used to construct a humorous situation from a non-humorous state of affairs is to reverse the intention of the primary character to the opposite intention. For example, if a man appears extremely angry, reverse his intention to that of trying to help the other character in the scene. The misunderstanding generated by the other character will cause people to laugh. Humor is generated by incompetent actions that characters do when trying to overcome obstacles to their objectives. The characters could under-prepare for an obstacle that turns out to be enormous, over-prepare for an obstacle that turns out to be insignificant, or irrelevantly prepare for an obstacle that turns out to be completely different from anticipated.

HUMOROUS CHARACTERS

In morality plays, characters "were named after, and made to personify, human vices and virtues: Lust, Sloth, Hypocrisy, Pride, Avarice, Honor, Prudence, Temperance, Charity, and so on."
— Raymond Hull, *How To Write A Play*

"What my comedy is all about is envy, greed, malice, lust, narrowness and stupidity – John Cleese."
— Melvin Helitzer, *Comedy Writing Secrets*

A source of character humor is found in deviations from expected role behavior or social behavior. In *Taking Laughter Seriously,* Morreall discusses humorous characters.

> We also laugh at the absentminded professor, who is intelligent in theoretical matters, but who is forgetful or doesn't have practical intelligence. A stock way of getting a laugh in a play is to have some character speak or act in ignorance of some fact that we in the audience are aware of.

> Moral shortcomings, too, have been a standard object of laughter throughout history: the miser, the liar, the drunkard, the lazy person, the lecher, the gossip, the coward, the hypocrite – these are all stock comedic characters.

Bergson, commenting on the comic plays of Moliere, states that the "comic character is simply a man with an obsession. The joke is to see how this obsession crops up again and again in the most varied situations, so that he always behaves in a manner inappropriate to the circumstances as others see them, but entirely appropriate to his own ruling passion."

Pretense is a common trait of many humorous characters. The audience will laugh at any character who lacks self-knowledge, who are frauds, or who try to publicly present themselves as something other than what they really are.

Humans that take on animal characteristics and animals who act like humans, such as the Cowardly Lion and many of the Walt Disney and Warner Brothers cartoon characters, are also examples of deviations from expectations. Their behavior deviates from what is expected of different kinds of creatures, humans, and animals.

Characters involved in embarrassing situations, pratfalls, and small misfortunes, are humorous and will generate laughter. Chevy Chase made a career from this type of comic behavior. Successful comedians develop a *persona*, a character with an essential incongruity at the core of their personality. Judy Carter, in *Stand-up Comedy, The Book*, states that "a persona is when a comic has one specific emotional attitude for their entire act, and all of the material hangs on that hook." As examples, she includes Rodney Dangerfield ("I don't get no respect"), Jay Leno ("Here's something stupid"), and Richard Lewis ("I'm in pain").

But this does make the characters one-dimensional. Other successful comedians posses an incongruity at the core of their personality, such as Steve Martin ("the would-be sophisticate who is socially inept"), Bill Cosby ("an adult with child-like enthusiasms") and Bob Hope ("the womanizer who never gets the girl").

Mark Stolzenberg, in *How To Be Really Funny*, discusses types of behavior that generates laughter: silly walks, silly faces, silly sounds, silly body movements, and funny gestures. A character can also suddenly deviate in the way that he speaks by playing with rhythm, pitch, tempo, volume, and timing. He could also speak gibberish while presenting it as a meaningful utterance. Incongruity can also be expressed in his makeup, hairstyle and wardrobe.

Besides deviant behavior patterns, humor is also generated whenever a character expresses exaggerated or understated reactions to a situation, absentmindedness, aimlessness, superfluous motions, and mechanical or automatic movements, as long as these behaviors suddenly break established patterns, and conclude by being non-threatening to the audience.

Continual repetition of any behavior is also a deviation from the norm and will produce laughter. Another common comic type is the bumbler, best exemplified by Peter Sellers as Inspector Clouseau in the *Pink Panther* movies. This character poses as an authority figure, a police detective, who in actuality is an incompetent fool.

One process for designing comic characters that radically deviate from expected norms of behavior is to work with the framework of Aristotelian ethical theory. Aristotle, in *Nichomachean Ethics,* designed a theory of virtues and vices. For each "sphere of action" he indicates a "mean", which is the norm or appropriate behavior for that type of situation. From this "mean," he then constructs an "excess" which represents the exaggerated behavior pattern for a type of situation, and a "deficiency," which represents the understated behavior pattern for this kind of situation. Extreme cases of either type of deviation from the "mean" will produce laughter.

ARISTOTLE'S ETHICAL CONCEPTS
Table of Virtues and Vices

Action or Feeling	Excess	Mean	Deficiency
Fear and Confidence	Rashness	Courage	Cowardice
Pleasure and Pain	Licentiousness	Temperance	Insensibility
Getting and Spending (minor)	Prodigality	Liberality	Illiberality
Getting and Spending (major)	Vulgarity	Magnificence	Pettiness
Honor and Dishonor (major)	Vanity	Magnanimity	Pusillanimity
Honor and Dishonor (minor)	Ambition	Proper Ambition	Un-ambitious
Anger	Irascibility	Patience	Lack of Spirit
Self-Expression	Boastfulness	Truthfulness	Understatement
Conversation	Buffoonery	Wittiness	Boorishness
Social Conduct	Obsequious	Friendliness	Cantankerous
Shame	Shyness	Modesty	Shamelessness
Indignation	Envy	Righteous Indignation	Malicious Enjoyment

Following are examples of comic characters from the popular films classified in terms of the Aristotelian virtues and vices

ARISTOTLE'S ETHICAL CONCEPTS
Excess Character Traits

Rashness (Courage-Fear)
Forrest (*Forrest Gump*): Running in the jungle to rescue his fellow soldiers in Vietnam.

Licentiousness (Temperance-Pleasure/Pain)
Venkman (*Ghostbusters*): Lusts after the female student during the ESP experiment.

Prodigality (Liberality-Getting/Spending)
Joker (*Batman*): Throwing money into the crowd at the Gotham City parade.

Vanity (Honor/Dishonor)
Joker (*Batman*): Admiring himself in the mirror as his girlfriend Alicia watches.

Ambition (ProperAmbition-Honor/Dishonor)
Joker (*Batman*): Wants his face on the one dollar bill.

Irascibility (Patience-Anger)
Joker (*Batman*): Easily angered and prone to violence.

Boastfulness (Truthfulness-Self-expression)
Joker(*Batman*): Boss Grissom could not run Gotham City without him.

Buffoonery (Wittiness-Conversation)
Ray Stantz (*Ghostbusters*): Over-enthusiastic whenever he talks about the supernatural.

Obsequiousness (Friendliness-Social Conduct)
Hotel Manager (*Ghostbusters*): He tries to placate clients waiting to use the Ballroom.

Shyness (Modesty-Shame)
Forrest (*Forrest Gump*): Forrest is shy when Jenny first makes a sexual advance towards him in her college bedroom.

Envy (Righteous Indignation-Indignation)
Joker (*Batman*): He is envious of Batman getting all the publicity.

ARISTOTLE'S ETHICAL CONCEPTS
Deficient Character Traits

Cowardice (Courage-Fear)
Sallah (*Raiders of the Lost Ark*): When Sallah sees snakes in Well of Souls, he tells Indiana Jones to go first.

Insensibility (Temperance-Pleasure/Pain)
Louis (*Ghostbusters*): At the end of the story, Louis is oblivious to the danger he has just experienced.

Cheapness (Liberality-Getting/Spending)
Uncle Frank (*Home Alone*): He will not pay for the pizzas.

Pettiness (Magnificence-Getting/Spending)
Kevin's Sisters (*Home Alone*): They don't help Kevin pack his suitcases.

Timidity (Magnanimity-Honor/Dishonor)
Cowardly Lion (*The Wizard of Oz*): He is afraid to go in the Witch's Castle to save Dorothy.

Un-ambitiousness (Proper Ambition-Honor/Dishonor)
Kevin (*Home Alone*): All he wants is to be left alone at home.

Lack of Spirit (Patience-Anger)
Egon (*Ghostbusters*): Egon is a scientific nerd who is passive and indifferent to the sexual advances of the secretary.

Understatement (Truthfulness-Self-expression)
Venkman (*Ghostbusters*): Almost all of his reactions are understated.

Boorishness (Wittiness-Conversation)
Egon (*Ghostbusters*): Egon is a scientific nerd who only talks about his research topics.

Cantankerousness (Friendliness-Social Conduct)
Mr. Peck, the EPA Inspector (*Ghostbusters*): Self-righteous.

Shamelessness (Modesty-Shame)
Burglars (*Home Alone*): Marv brags that they are "the wet bandits."

Malicious Enjoyment (Righteous Indignation-Indignation)
Marv (*Home Alone*): Blocks sinks so water will overflow onto the floor.

HUMOROUS CHARACTERS IN THE MEGAHIT MOVIES

Wizard of Oz
Scarecrow (with exaggerated mannerisms), Tin Man (the human encrusted in the mechanical), the Cowardly Lion (the king of the jungle who lacks courage), and the Wizard (a man who pretends to have magical powers that he really lacks)

Star Wars
R2D2 and C3PO (the human encrusted in the mechanical with exaggerated worrisome and bickering behavior)

Raiders of the Lost Ark
The Nazi Agents in Cairo (they exhibit idiot behavior by saluting monkeys and wearing inappropriate wardrobe: short ties and pants).

Ghostbusters
Peter Venkman (understated behavior), Ray Stantz (exaggerated enthusiasm), Egon Spengler (nerd scientist), and Louis (socially inept)

Batman
Joker (a mass murderer with a child-like sense of humor)

E.T.
E.T. and Elliott (when drinking beer or wearing inappropriate clothes)

Home Alone
The Burglars (the audience laughs whenever these characters get beaten up because of their immoral behavior, yet neither is ever seriously harmed)

The Phantom Menace
Watto (the greedy junkman eventually loses the bet with the Jedi Knights and has to let Anakin go free)

Jurassic Park
Dennis, the fat computer technician (his greed places all the people in Jurassic Park in danger, and ends up getting him killed)

Forrest Gump
Forrest (because his non-normal behavior always leads to success)

Lion King
Timon and Pumba romp through the jungle and show Simba the ways of a carefree life

Return of Jedi
Ewoks (funny little furry creatures that help Luke triumph over the Imperial forces)

Independence Day
Russell Casse (the drunk who ends up saving the world) and Captain Steve Hillier (who exhibits a sense of humor as he fights the aliens)

The Grinch
The Grinch (filled with rage and resentment, his exaggerated and obsessive meanness becomes humorous)

Men in Black
K (the understated character who is always "cold" in a situation) and J (who always exaggerates and over-reacts to a situation)

HUMOR IN THE MEGAHIT MOVIES

General Categories of Humor

These general categories apply to all three sources of humor: language, situations, and characters.

Inappropriateness: Deviations from expectation of appropriate patterns of behavior.

Home Alone
"Where are the passports and tickets?" asks Kevin's mother.
"I put them in the microwave to dry them off," answers Peter.

Incongruity: Deviations from the expected patterns of objects in situations.

Home Alone
The family is in Rob's apartment in Paris. The movie, "IT'S A WONDERFUL LIFE," is playing on the television, but the movie dialogue is spoken in French.

E.T.
"Be good, be good," Gertie says to E.T. as she closes her closet doors. Elliott pushes Gertie aside and opens the doors. Elliott sees E.T. dressed in girl's clothes with a blonde wig on his head. He has a rabbit fur around his neck and wears a black hat with flowers. The visual incongruity of E.T. dressed in a girl's clothes causes the laughter.

Irony: Deviations from the expected intended meaning of a statement. Usually, the exact opposite meaning is expressed from the normally understood meanings of the words.

Batman
Suddenly, the museum door slams open. The bodies of dead patrons lie on the museum floor. The Joker enters wearing a French artist's cap. The Joker is surrounded by his band of thugs. "Gentlemen, let's broaden our minds. Lawrence!" Lawrence turns on the large radio that he is carrying as the Joker leads a dance parade into the museum. They proceed to knock statues off their platforms and spray paint on the works of art.

Misdirection: Deviations from the expectation of honesty and unambiguous communication.

Raiders of the Lost Ark
Belloc and Marion are alone in a tent in the desert. Marion says to Belloc that she has already told him everything she knows. She says she has no loyalty to Jones, who has brought her nothing but trouble. Marion walks out from behind the screen. She looks beautiful in the white dress. She radiantly smiles at Belloc as she spins around to show him the dress. She places her red pants over a knife that lies on the table. "I don't think we need the chaperon," she says as she picks up the wine bottle. Belloc gestures the guard away. The audience already knows Marion's capacity for liquor. This important trait was established during her introduction scene in Nepal. That was the setup, and in this scene it pays off. The audience expects that Marion plans to get Belloc drunk, take the knife hidden under her pants, and escape through the unguarded exit. What the audience doesn't realize is that Belloc has developed a tolerance for this liquor because it's from his family stock, and he's been drinking it for years. When revealed, this unexpected information surprises the audience, confounds their expectations, and generates the humor in the situation.

Ghostbusters
The Ghostbusters are on the top of Dana's building. Gozer's voice speaks out, demanding that they choose and perish: they must 'choose the form of the Destructor. Venkman understands. He explains that whatever they think of will appear and destroy them. He orders the rest to empty their heads and think of nothing. Then, the voice of Gozer states that the choice has been made. Everyone had emptied then minds except Ray. Suddenly, the giant, Mr. Stay Puft Man, rumbles through the city streets. He has a big happy grin on his face and is dressed in a little sailor's uniform, as he turns the corner at Columbus Circle. Taxis collide into each other in an effort to escape. The audience was expecting the most horrible creature that they could imagine, but instead they got the comically absurd figure of the Stay Puft Marshmallow Man. This character, in normal size, is the most harmless creature imaginable.

Rule of Three: Deviations from the expected pattern established in the first two cases. The punch line, which is the surprise radical deviation from the pattern, occurs in the third case.

Batman
The Joker is broadcasting his message to the Mayor of Gotham City. "Now you fellows have said some pretty mean things, some of which was true under that fiend Boss Grissom," says the Joker.

"He was a thief and a terrorist, but on the other hand, he had a tremendous singing voice."

Linguistic Categories of Humor

Misinterpretation of Ambiguous Words: Deviations from expected word meaning.

Ghostbusters
When the Ghostbusters finally reach the roof of Dana's building, they watch as the supernatural powers transform her into a primitive demon-beast. Venkman turns to the others and says, "Okay, she's a dog."

Double Entendre: Deviations from the norm of not discussing sex explicitly in public.

Batman
The newspaper reporter Knox has just returned to the newsroom. When he approaches his desk, he sees a woman's legs on the desktop.
"Hello, legs," says Knox.
"I'm reading your stuff," says the woman from behind the newspaper.
"Well, I'm reading yours," responds Knox.
The blonde woman, wearing reading eyeglasses, puts down the newspaper and says, "Hi, I'm Vicki Vale."
"Vicki Vale, yeah, photographer. Vogue. Cosmo. Look, you want me to pose nude, you're going to need a long lens," says Knox. This was Knox's attempt to avoid small talk.

Contradictions: Deviations from the expectation that a person will utter consistent and truthful statements.

Home Alone
Kevin stands alone on the balcony then shouts as he jumps up and down. "This house is so full of people it makes me sick. When I grow up and get married, I'm living alone. DID YOU HEAR ME? I'M LIVING ALONE! Humor is generated by the contradiction of "being married" and "living alone," plus Kevin's exaggerated reactions while having a temper tantrum.

Logic Violation and Incorrect Reasoning: Deviations from the expectation that characters will be reasonable and make correct inferences.

Wizard of Oz
While traveling on the road to Oz, Dorothy comes to a crossroad and must decide in which direction to continue. A Scarecrow hangs from a post in the field. He speaks out, suggesting first that she go in one direction, then the opposite, then finally in both directions. He explains that he can't make up his mind because he hasn't got a brain. Humor is generated because the Scarecrow's advice to Dorothy is logically impossible. The exaggerated actions and movements of the Scarecrow also generate humor in the scene, for he's a walking, talking, and singing incongruity.

Ghostbusters
The Ghostbusters are considering leasing a building for their business from a middle-aged female real estate agent. Egon and Venkman walk through the rubble of a dilapidated building. Venkman thinks the building is overpriced, while Egon believes it should be condemned. Ray Stantz suddenly slides down a fire-pole. He's excited by the building and wants to spend the night. Venkman then tells the agent that they'll take it. The humor of the sequence is based on the stupidity of making a bad decision for childish reasons after Venkman and Egon have established the realistic grounds for rejecting the building.

Ghostbusters
Dana exits from the elevator, says hello to a man, then walks down the hallway. A door opens and her neighbor, Louis, enters the hallway. He says hello to Dana and tells her that he thought she was coming from the drugstore. He reveals himself to be a hypochondriac. Louis explains how he taped a twenty minute workout on his video machine then played it back at high speed so that it only took ten minutes to do. This enabled him to get a great workout.

An Incorrect Definition or Explanation: Deviations from the expectation that characters will utter true and correct statements and explanations.

Ghostbusters
Venkman explains to Dana that "Gozer" was "big" in Sumaria.

A Literal Truth Inappropriately Stated: Deviations from the expectation that characters will only make informative statements.

Ghostbusters
The burnt door falls to the floor as the Ghostbusters enter Dana's apartment. The apartment has been completely destroyed. They walk toward

the ledge. To the side is a staircase. "Where do the stairs go?" asks Ray. "They go up!" replies Venkman. Venkman stating an uninformative literal truth generates humor.

Batman
Bruce Wayne is speaking to Vicki Vale and Knox. "I've seen your photographs from Corto Maltese," replies Bruce. "You have a wonderful eye," continues Wayne. "Some people think she has two," interjects Knox.

Ghostbusters
Dana tells the Ghostbusters about the supernatural experiences she had with her refrigerator. She heard a voice call out the name Zuul. To this, Venkman responds, "Generally, you don't see that kind of behavior in a major appliance." This is a literal truth that is inappropriately stated in this situation.

Exaggeration: Deviations from the expectation that characters will react to a situation with an appropriate emotion or behavior.

The Wizard of Oz
When the Wizard yells at the Cowardly Lion to go, the Lion turns, runs down the hallway as quickly as possible, and jumps through the window to escape the wrath of the Wizard of Oz.

Understatement: Deviations from the expectation that characters will react to a situation with an appropriate emotion or behavior.

Ghostbusters
The giant Mr. Stay Puft Marshmallow Man rumbles through the city streets. He has a big happy grin and is dressed in a little sailor's uniform. As he turns the corner at Columbus Circle, taxis collide into each other in an effort to escape. Screaming crowds of people run through the streets. "Now there's something you don't see everyday," says Venkman. True to his character, Venkman uses a hackneyed cliché to utter a major understatement when confronted with an extraordinary situation.

Wizard of Oz
Dorothy arrives in Munchkin land. Beautiful colors and the musical theme inform the audience that Dorothy is now "over the rainbow." Dorothy walks around the colorful garden then utters her classic line to Toto, "I've a feeling we're not in Kansas any more."

An Irrelevant Comment: Deviations from the expectation that characters will make statements relevant to a situation.

Raiders of the Lost Ark
Marion and Belloc are getting drunk in the tent in the desert. Marion tries to pour herself another drink but completely misses the glass and pours the liquor onto the table. Belloc takes the bottle and refills their glasses. Marion again laughs then quickly lunges for the knife under her red slacks. She holds the knife up to Belloc. He looks at it then bursts out in laughter. Marion tells him that she has to go, as she holds the knife in front of her and backs away from the table. Belloc laughs as he waves goodbye. Marion says she likes him, and hopes they will meet again under better circumstances. Suddenly, the smile drops from Belloc's face. Marion quickly turns and comes face-to-face with the sadistic German. "We meet again, Fraulein," he says. She struggles, but he forces the knife out of her hand. "You Americans are all the same. Always overdressing for the wrong occasions." This comment is so inappropriate to this life and death situation that the audience bursts out in laughter.

Raiders of the Lost Ark
Jones runs down an alley after the Arabs. He sees them in the distance as they carry Marion away in the wicker basket. "You can't do this, I'm an American. INDY!" screams Marion. Of course, saying she is an American is irrelevant to her situation.

Ghostbusters
Louis, encrusted within a stone statue, yells out for help. The Ghostbusters free Louis as Venkman cares for Dana. Louis looks around at the damage and says, "Boy, the Superintendent's going to be pissed." After being told the people saving him are the Ghostbusters, Louis asks who does their taxes. The joke is that Louis is socially inept and always thinks of others as potential business clients. In this situation, the appropriate response should have been gratitude, not a request for business.

An Ineffectual Statement: Deviations from the expectation that characters will make statements effective to solving the problem in a situation.

Ghostbusters
Louis is running through the park as he tries to escape from the demon dog. He tries to get into a restaurant, but the doors are locked. He pleads for their help, but no one in the crowd moves. Louis then turns to confront the approaching creature. "Nice doggie, cute little pooch. Maybe I got a milk bone."

Clichés Incorrectly Stated: Deviations from the expectation that characters will state clichés correctly or not use them at all in conversations.

Ghostbusters
Venkman is on the street talking to a group of reporters. "24 hours a day, seven days a week. No job is too big, no fee is too big" (instead of saying too small).

Clichés Inappropriately Applied in Situations: Deviations from the expectation that characters will apply clichés to appropriate situations.

Batman
The Joker is telling Boss Grissom's syndicate that he is now in charge of the operations.
"Why don't we hear this from Grissom?" asks a fat gangster.
"Yeah, and what's with that stupid grin?" asks Antonio.
Jack is wearing flesh colored makeup to cover his white skin. He is also wearing a purple hat and an orange shirt. "Life's been good to me," laughs the Joker.

Misspellings: Deviations from the expectation that characters will spell words correctly.

Raiders of the Lost Ark
Jones is lecturing to his class as he writes on the blackboard. He is having trouble spelling the word "NEOLITHIC." The students in the class laugh.

Malapropisms and Mispronunciations: Deviations from the expectation that characters will use words correctly.

Ghost
Oda Mae Brown completes filling out the account signature card, then hands it to the bank officer.
"Please make sure that this goes up to the third floor file because I have a transfusion that I have to make," says Oda. She mistakenly says "transfusion" instead of "transaction."

Nonsense presented as being sensible: Deviations from the expectation that characters will use the language correctly and think correctly

Ghostbusters
The Ghostbusters are questioning Dana about her paranormal experience. Egon says that Dana is telling the truth, or at least she believes she is. The Ghostbusters offer alternative explanations for her experience: past life experience intruding on present time, race memory stored in the collective unconscious, clairvoyance, or telepathic contact. Dana replies that she doesn't believe in any of those things, to which Venkman responds that he doesn't either.

Deviations from Patterns of Items in a List: Deviations from the expected consistency of the category of items established in the list.

Ghostbusters
The Ghostbusters tell the Mayor that he can believe Peck, or accept the fact that the city is headed for a disaster of Biblical proportions. Real Wrath of GOD type stuff: fire and brimstone coming down from the sky, four years of darkness, earthquakes, volcanoes, the dead rising from the grave.
"Human sacrifice, dogs and cats living together, mass hysteria!" adds Venkman. Humor is generated by Venkman's deviation from the list. He includes the "dogs and cats living together" with disasters of "Biblical proportions."

Dialects: Deviations from the expectation that characters will speak correctly.

Wizard of Oz
As Dorothy leaves the campsite in order to return to the farm before the Tornado hits, Marvel breaks out of character and his phony dialect when he says, "Poor little kid! I hope she gets home all right."

Pragmatics: Deviations from the conventions of communication.

Ghostbusters
Louis is constantly trying to get Dana to take an interest in him. He ignores all the rules of conversation and having a dialogue whenever he sees her in the hallway. He talks at high speed ignoring her attempts to communicate that she has no interest in him, including her slamming the door in his face.

Repartee: Deviations from the expectation of not being hostile. Repartee is an expression of veiled hostility.

Ghostbusters
Venkman enters Dana's apartment and searches for supernatural phenomena. He walks toward the bedroom. Dana tells him that nothing ever happened in there. "What a crime," responds Venkman.
"You know, you don't act like a scientist," says Dana.
"They're usually pretty stiff," replies Venkman.
"You're more like a game show host," replies Dana.

Information that Arrives Too Late to be Beneficial: Deviations from the expectation of communicating effectively.

Back To The Future
Marty has just overloaded the speaker. The blast has thrown him across the room. He picks himself up off the floor. Suddenly, the phone rings. It is Doc Brown. Doc tells Marty not to hook up the amplifier. "There's the possibility of an overload."

Modal Jokes: Deviations from the expected rules of discourse. The norm in popular movies is to show the actions of the characters not to comment on the mode of presentation.

E.T.
E.T. and Elliott stand in the back of the van, as Mike and his friends sit on their bikes.
"Okay, he is a man from outer space and we're taking him to his spaceship," says Elliott.
"Why can't he just beam up?" asks Greg.
'This is reality, Greg," answers Elliott.
Of course, the joke is that it isn't reality. It is a fantasy movie with characters expressing an emotionally realistic response to a fantastic situation. Right?

Interplay of Dual Scripts: Deviations from the expected rules of communication and discourse needed to facilitate understanding. The norm is not to talk about two different topics at the same time. Humor is created because two truths are expressed from two radically different perspectives at the same time.

E.T.
E.T. has gotten drunk by drinking the beer in the refrigerator. He wobbles across the kitchen floor and walks into a counter. Elliott, sitting at his desk in the schoolroom, also becomes drunk. The sequence is intercut between E.T. in the kitchen and Elliott in the classroom. The dual script sequence ends with E.T. watching John Wayne kiss Maureen O'Sullivan in the television movie and Elliott kissing the little girl in the classroom.

Situation Categories of Humor

Bizarre Images: Incongruities that are deviations from expected visual patterns.

The Wizard of Oz
The image of a spinning house rising up into the tornado is superimposed over Dorothy's face. Outside her bedroom window, images of characters appear. Chickens and a hen house float past her window. Dorothy sits up in bed and stares at the objects. Aunt Em, knitting as she sits in her rocking chairs, floats by. A cow also flies through the air, followed by two of the farm hands rowing a boat. The incongruity of these bizarre images generates laughter.

Deviations from a Natural Norm: Deviations from the standard laws of nature.

The Wizard of Oz
Dorothy and her companions approach the Haunted Forest on their way to the Witch's castle. The Tin Man is suddenly lifted up into the air by some invisible spirits and dropped to the ground, defying the laws of nature.

Deviations from an Established Visual Pattern

E.T.
Mary walks into the closet and looks around. The camera pans across the large faces of all the stuffed dolls: Raggedy Ann, a Bear, a Monkey, E.T.'s face, a Lion, etc. Mary doesn't notice E.T. She closes the closet door and leaves. Humor is generated because of the incongruity of a living creature among the dolls and the inability of Mary to distinguish between them.

Relief from Danger: A Deviation from the expectation of jeopardy. The tension is released in laughter.

Raiders of the Lost Ark
Jones and the German soldier struggle for control of the truck. They both grab the wheel as the truck scrapes the side of a wall under construction and knocks over ladders, planks, and the construction workers. One Egyptian worker falls onto the hood of the truck, then rolls off onto the road. Jones and the German laugh and smile at each other in relief of avoiding a disaster.

Avoiding a Near Misfortune: Deviation from the expectation of jeopardy. The tension is released in laughter.

Home Alone
From the top floor, Jeff throws a packed bag down the staircase. "BOMBS AWAY!" The bag lands at the feet of the policeman. The audience laughs because of the avoidance of a disaster.

A Small Misfortune: Deviations from the expectation things will turn out all right if we follow standard procedures. The tension is released in laughter.

Home Alone
Kevin walks down the sidewalk carrying two plastic bags filled with groceries. Suddenly they both break and all the food falls to the ground.

A Confusing Situation Suddenly Makes Sense: A Deviation from the expected resolution of a situation.

Home Alone
The burglar's van pulls up in front of Kevin's house. Harry and Marv see silhouettes of people moving inside the house. They all seem to be dancing to the music of *Rocking Around the Christmas Tree.*
"Did they come back?" asks Marv.
"Paris?" responds Harry.
Inside the house, Kevin has rigged up mannequins with pulleys. He manipulates their movements by pulling on ropes as he dances to the music. A small toy train moves a cardboard cutout of a basketball player around the railroad tracks.

Character Categories of Humor

Pretense: Deviations from the expectation that a character is what he presents himself to be.

Ghostbusters
Venkman asks the librarian, Alice, if she is habitually uses drugs, stimulants, alcohol, or is menstruating now. The male librarian interrupts and asks Venkman what these questions have to do with Alice's experience of seeing a ghost. Venkman responds, "Back off man! I'm a scientist!" The audience laughs because they know that Venkman is a fraud.

The Wizard of Oz
Dorothy meets Professor Marvel. An establishing shot of the Professor's wagon tells the audience where they are. This information is needed since there is a radical change in scenery. The sign on the carnival wagon states: "PROFESSOR MARVEL ACCLAIMED BY THE CROWNED HEADS OF EUROPE." Dorothy wants to travel with the Professor to see the Crowned Heads of Europe. He responds to this request by asking her if she knows any, thereby revealing himself to be a fraud.

Inappropriate Social Behavior: Deviations from the norms of polite society.

Batman
The newspaperman, Knox, introduces himself to Bruce Wayne. "Oh, I read your work. I like it, like it a lot," says Bruce Wayne. "Can I have a grant?" replies Knox.

Ghostbusters
At his party, Louis exhibits incompetent social skills by telling his guests that he invited clients to his party instead of friends. When the doorbell rings, Louis opens it. In walks a fat homely woman with her tall lanky husband. Louis introduces them to the other people at the party. Again, he displays his social ineptness by discussing this couples bankruptcy with the other party guests.

Deviations from Moral Norms: Deviations from the expected rules of moral behavior.

Home Alone
On the plane to Paris, Uncle Frank notices that the crystal is real and tells his wife to put it into her purse.

Lying: Deviations from the expected norm of telling the truth.

Ghostbusters
A male undergraduate and a beautiful coed sit in Venkman's office. Venkman smiles at the female student, holds up a card, and asks her to guess the image on the card. She guesses a star. Venkman tells her that she is right, but the camera reveals that the true image on the card is a circle.

Cowardliness: Deviation from the expectation that people will be courageous.

Raiders of the Lost Ark
Sallah leans forward to get a closer look at the snakes on the floor. "Asps, very dangerous," says Sallah. He shakes Jones' arm. "You go first."

Ghostbusters
Venkman starts up the stairs to the rooftop of Dana's apartment building. Lightning flashes from the sky above. Venkman suddenly stops and waves the others forward. "Okay, you go ahead," he says.

Cheapness: Deviations from the expectation people will be generous.

Home Alone
The delivery boy arrives with the boxes of pizza. Uncle Frank sees the pizza and takes the boxes from the delivery boy.
"That's $122.50"
"Ah, it's my brother's house. He'll take care of it." Frank walks away with the pizza.

Exaggerated Behavior: Deviations from the expectation that people should remain calm.

Home Alone
Kevin runs through the house waving his arms with joy when he realizes that his family has abandoned him.

Understated Behavior: Deviations from the expectation of displaying appropriate behavior in a situation.

Ghostbusters
Egon warns the Ghostbusters not to cross the power streams. To do so would cause a total protonic reversal, and every molecule in their bodies would explode at the speed of light. "That's bad. Okay. All right. Important safety tip! Thanks Egon."

Expressing an Inappropriate Attitude Deviations from the expectation that characters will express attitudes appropriate to a situation.

Batman
Jack looks at himself in the mirror and laughs. Alicia, his girlfriend, approaches him and places her hand on his shoulder. "You look fine," she says. "I didn't ask," replies Jack Napier as he removes her hand.

Inappropriate Actions: Deviations from the expectation that characters will perform actions appropriate to a situation.

Home Alone
Kevin jumps up and down on his parent's bed while eating popcorn.

Self-Mocking Attitude: Deviations from the expectation that characters will not hold themselves up to public ridicule.

Ghostbusters
"Funny," says Ray, "us going out like this. Killed by a one-hundred foot marshmallow man."

Deviations from Expected Character Behavior: Deviation from the expectation that characters will exhibit stereotypical behavior patterns.

The Wizard of Oz
In this movie we have a scarecrow that cannot scare away crows, a lion that is a coward, and a wizard that has no magical powers.

Mimicking Another Characters Behavior: Deviation from the expectation that a character will not become someone else.

Home Alone
Kevin combs his hair and mimics Frank Sinatra's voice playing on the record. Kevin sings into his comb as if it was a microphone.

Exaggerated Facial Expressions: Deviations from the expectation that characters will display the appropriate emotional facial expression in a situation.

Home Alone
"He was in the garage again playing with the glue gun," Kevin's mother says to his father. Kevin makes a grim face and signals to his mother to stop talking by pretending to cut his throat with his hand.

Repetition of Stupid Actions: A Deviation from the expectation that characters will learn from their mistakes.

Home Alone
Kevin combs his hair and mimics Frank Sinatra as he sings into the comb. He sprays deodorant under his arms, and then splashes BRUT33 onto his face a second time. Kevin screams out from the stinging pain.

Ghostbusters
Venkman has just been rejected by Dana and thrown out of her apartment. Louis walks out of his apartment and steps into the hallway. Louis becomes embarrassed and turns to go back into his apartment, but he has locked himself out. This becomes a recurring joke in the movie.

Incompetent Professional Behavior: Deviations from the expectation that characters will be professionally competent.

Ghostbusters
The Ghostbusters have made contact with the ghost in the library. "A full torso apparition, and it's real," says Ray.
"So, what do we do?" asks Venkman. Ray and Egon just stare at each other. Ray announces that he has a plan. He tells the others to stay close as he walks towards the ghost. Suddenly, Ray yells "GET HER!" As the three men rush toward the ghost, it transforms from a sweet old lady into a screeching banshee with a horrifying skeletal face. Ray, Egon, and Venkman scream in terror as they run from the ghost.

Not Following Explicitly Stated Instructions: Deviations from the expectation that characters will follow instructions.

Ghostbusters
When they are about to capture their first ghost in the hotel ballroom, Ray warns everyone not to look directly into the trap. He pulls goggles over his eyes and puts his foot on the trap. A flash of bright glaring light shoots out of the box. Egon then says, "I looked into the trap, Ray."

Inept Behavior that Results in Destruction: Deviations from the expectation that characters will be competent and non-destructive.

Ghostbusters
Their objective is to find and eliminate the ghost in the hotel. The Ghostbusters each activate their power supplies. Ray leads the way down the hallway. A cleaning woman pushing a cart enters from the opposite direction. They quickly turn around and fire their weapons at her. They blast the cart. Several rolls of burnt toilet paper fall onto the floor.

Inept Behavior Which Results in Self-Destruction: Deviations from the expectation that characters will not destroy themselves.

Raiders of the Lost Ark
An Arab swings a bat at Jones but misses and hits an Arab standing next to Jones. Jones punches the Arab who is holding the bat. He grabs Marion and tells her to get out of there. An Arab attempts to stab Jones with a sword but ends up stabbing another Arab instead.

Wanton Destruction of Property: Deviations from the expectations that characters will respect and protect property.

Home Alone
Marv, one of the burglars, stuffs cloth into a sink drain, then turns on the water. He laughs with glee at the irresponsible destruction that he is about to cause.

Ghostbusters
The Ghostbusters destroy the ballroom in the hotel during their efforts to capture their first ghost.

Taking Pride in Expressing Negative Traits: Deviations from the expectation of morally or socially acceptable behavior.

Batman
Bruce Wayne confronts the Joker. "I know who you are," whispers Bruce. "Let me tell you about this guy I know, Jack. Mean kid. Bad seed. Hurts people." "I like him already," laughs the Joker.

Fooling an Authority Figure: Deviations from the expectation that characters will respect people in authority.

E.T.
Mary covers Elliott with a blue sleeping bag as Elliott puts the thermometer back into his mouth. Laughter is generated because the audience knows that Elliott heated the thermometer by holding it against the light bulb. They know he is fooling his mother and getting away with it.

Ridiculing An Authority Figure: Deviations from the expectation that characters will respect people in authority.

Home Alone
A policeman, with his back to the camera, stands in the hallway of a house. He tries to get someone to pay attention to him, but everyone ignores him.

Playing a Practical Joke on Another Character: Deviations from the expectation that a character will not intentionally humiliate another character by making him look foolish in public.

Ghostbusters
Venkman and Ray approach Spengler, who is sitting on the floor of the library reading room. Spengler is wearing earphones as he uses an instrument designed to measure psychic energy. Venkman knocks on the table above Spengler's head, makes strange noises, and then drops a book on the table. He does this to mock Spengler and his psychic research.

Triumphant Laughter: Deviations from the expectation that characters will not gloat over defeating their opposition.

Raiders of the Lost Ark
Belloc gestures to the native Indians to cut Jones' throat. The natives get up and chase after Jones. Belloc laughs with pleasure as he admires the golden idol in his hand.

Batman
The Joker laughs after incinerating the gangster, Antonio.

Raiders of the Lost Ark
In Nepal, a native suddenly enters the bar, grabs Jones, and throws him against the wall. The sadistic German laughs at Jones.

Sadistic Behavior: Deviations from the expectation of not taking joy in hostility and violence. Audiences will laugh as long as the characters for which they have empathy are not harmed.

Ghostbusters
Venkman administers minor electrical shocks to the male student during his ESP ability test.

Disgusting Behavior: Deviations from the expectation of normal behavior concerning bodily wastes. The audience will often laugh, but are also often left with feelings of disgust and distaste.

Ghostbusters
As the Ghostbusters walk down the aisle stacked with bookshelves, they come upon card catalogues that are covered with oozing slime. Ray characterizes this slime as "ectoplasmic residue" generated by "telekinetic activity." They ask Venkman to get a sample of this. Egon hands him a plastic container. "Somebody blows their nose and you want to keep it," says Venkman.

Physically Punishing the Villains: Deviations from the expectation that characters will not physically harm other characters. The audience will laugh if the characters are **not** seriously harmed.

Ghostbusters
Debris falls on the crowd in the street below. Peck, the Environmental Protection Administrator, stands in the midst of the debris. Suddenly, he looks up and screams as wads of hot sticky marshmallow fall on him.

Home Alone
The complete third act of this movie consists of scenes showing the burglars receiving physical punishment from Kevin because of their efforts to rob Kevin's house.

The Misinterpretation of a Situation: Deviations from the expectation that a character will correctly understand a situation.

Batman
Bruce Wayne is trying to tell Vicki Vale that he is Batman. "There is something I have to tell you. You know how people have different sides of their personality. Sometimes a person will have to lead a double life," says Bruce.
"Oh no, you're married!" says Vicki.

Star Wars
Luke and his companions are about to be crushed in the garbage disposal unit. Suddenly, the walls stop moving because R2D2 has shut down the unit. The prisoners shout with joy at not being crushed to death. C3PO hears the sounds and believes that they are dying.

Behavior Appropriate in One Type of Situation becomes Inappropriate When Performed in a Different Situation: Deviation from the expectation that behavior will be appropriate to a situation.

Batman
The ACTION NEWS is being broadcast on the television monitor. Suddenly, the Joker appears on the screen. He dances down the aisle of supermarket. "New and improved Joker products with the new secret ingredient, SMYLEX. Let's go over to our blind taste test," says the Joker. "Love that Joker!" announce two models with hideous smiles. A man is tied to a chair. Titles stating, "NOT AN ACTOR," flash across the screen. This is a parody of a standard television commercial.

Characters Who are Oblivious to What is Really Occurring in a Situation: Deviations from the expectation that characters will be aware of what is occurring around them.

E.T.
Mary, with her arms filled with grocery bags and clothes from the cleaners, walks into the kitchen. She is followed by Gertie, who sees E.T standing near the refrigerator. Mary opens the refrigerator door, and knocks E.T. in the head. He falls backwards onto the floor. Gertie helps E.T. up off the floor. He walks past Mary as he goes back to the refrigerator. Mary still doesn't see him. This increases the audience's tension. Gertie keeps telling her that she wants Mary to meet somebody, but Mary ignores her as she talks about how much the price of food has gone up in one week. E.T. grabs a can of coffee from the kitchen table, then again walks past Mary as she goes in the opposite direction. He goes back into the TV room. The laughter is produced by Mary's failure to see the alien who's right under her nose.

SEQUENCES
DESIGNING A SERIES OF SCENES

Entertaining the Audience

Visual Material

Excitement

Surprise

Suspense

The Chase

Ticking Clocks

Using Props

Exposition

ENTERTAINING THE AUDIENCE

"Movies are for audiences...Don't be boring!!!"
—Richard Walter, *Screenwriting*

"If the spectators are interested, they will sit still and be silent; if they are amused, they will laugh; if they are pleased, they will applaud."
—Raymond Hull, *How To Write A Play*

Entertainment is something that is performed to amuse an audience. Amusement causes people to laugh or smile and to make time pass pleasantly. To entertain an audience means to give them the thrills and excitement of vicariously being in the midst of danger while still having a pleasurable and humorous experience.

"A correct dramatic construction presents the story content in the most effective manner. It should prevent the spectator from feeling boredom, fatigue, dissatisfaction, and lack of speed. It should cause surprise, hope, fear, suspense, and forward movement."
—Eugene Vale, *The Technique of Screen and Television Writing*

Every scene should be constructed in terms of its effect on the audience. Each character's action or any event that occurs in the story should be designed in terms of its impact on the audience. The audience's emotional reactions should be carefully designed to maintain the intended character empathy, along with the appropriate levels of tension, stress, fear, surprise, and laughter.

"We must learn to so construct a story that it will arouse, sustain, and steadily increase the interest of the spectator. To achieve this, we must make use of the spectator's capacity and ability to anticipate."
— Eugene Vale, *The Technique of Screen and Television Writing*

Humor in the midst of conflict relieves tension, and produces pleasure in the audience. To entertain an audience is to make them laugh in the midst of terror and excitement. The audience desires thrills and the experience of seeing fascinating images that they have never seen before. What they want is a sense of adventure: to journey somewhere they've never gone before. Most of the popular films considered contain elements of adventure in which all the characters are in great danger and jeopardy in a strange environment. But most importantly, the audience will be entertained if they have a pleasurable and **emotionally satisfying experience**.

VISUAL MATERIAL

"One picture is worth a thousand words...for this reason it may be wise for the writer to depend on the visual sources of information than on dialogue."
—Eugene Vale, *Technique of Screen and Television Writing*

Film is a visual medium. It is not radio, an audio medium, nor is it literary, in which all information is expressed with written words. The visual image is essential to the cinematic form.

A story must be told through images. In narrative films, the story is dominant, and the images must be chosen and ordered to construct a story that is emotionally effective. Story is more fundamental than image, even though the story is necessarily communicated through the use of images. A sequence of vivid images will not constitute a story unless the essential elements of story structure, such as character, objectives, values, decisions, obstacles, and emotional conflicts organize these images.

Embedded in the most powerful images will be characters embroiled in human conflict; caught in situations in which they must make difficult choices concerning primal human relationships. Special effects, while visually overwhelming and exciting to the senses, are not as powerfully engrossing for the audience as a situation in which a character for whom they have great empathy is in jeopardy.

It is important to realize that in the early years of the film industry, all of the films were silent movies. Yet, they were still extremely effective in being able to communicate a story without dialogue and with the minimum use of titles. Even today, many filmmakers are successful in making popular movies using a minimum amount of dialogue. Not more than fifteen lines of dialogue are spoken within the first fifteen minutes of *Raiders of the Lost Ark* or *E.T.*, yet by the time these sequences are over, the audience knows much about the characters and the story.

The audience loves to have new experiences, to see things that they have never seen before, and to experience images that they cannot find in their everyday lives. Special effects, exotic locations, or different historical periods all contribute to providing the audience with a unique and exciting experience. To select cinematic material means to choose a plot arena or story setting that lends itself to visual imagery not available in everyday existence.

Titanic
This film provides a view of an aristocratic life aboard a ship that existed almost 100 years ago.

Star Wars
This is a film with high-tech special visual effects exploding across the screen in the midst of a rebellion against an evil empire in outer space.

Phantom Menace
This is a futuristic film with high-tech special visual effects taking place during a war against the planet, Naboo, by an invading Trade Federation army of droids.

E.T.
The most mundane of all environments, contemporary suburban America, creates an environment where the most engrossing extraordinary visual image of all is a three-foot tall telepathic and psychokinetic alien.

Jurassic Park
This story takes place in a prehistoric park where dangerous dinosaurs roam.

Forrest Gump
This story takes place in the United States during the 1950s, 1960s, and 1970s, with segments also occurring in Vietnam, a history that many people in the audience also experienced.

The Lion King
This is a jungle fantasy filled with animals that have human personalities and conflicts.

Return of the Jedi
This is a film with high-tech special visual effects exploding across the screen in the midst of a rebellion against an evil empire in outer space.

Independence Day
This story takes place throughout the United States and inside an alien spaceship that is attempting to annihilate the human race.

The Sixth Sense
This story takes place in Philadelphia neighborhoods, where a little boy sees dead people.

Empire Strikes Back
Like the other films in this series, it is a high-tech futuristic special effects production set in the story of a rebellion against an evil empire.

Home Alone
This film, set in a conventional middle-class neighborhood, becomes most cinematic when Kevin uses commonplace household objects to combat the burglars who invade his home.

The Grinch
This story takes place inside a snow flake where the community of Whoville exists.

Jaws
The beach is the most natural of environments for the young during summertime. It is this peaceful fun-filled environment that is terrorized by a man-eating shark.

Batman
The dark streets of Gotham City and a Gothic Cathedral establish the visual motifs for an underground battle between good and evil.

Men in Black
This story takes place in the New York City metropolitan area inhabited by refugee space aliens and one mean spirited alien, Edgar-Bug.

The Wizard of Oz
The story takes place in the magical Land of Oz, populated by witches, wizards and flying monkeys, a Scarecrow and a Tin Man who talk, and a Cowardly Lion that yearns for courage.

Shrek
This story takes place in a Fairy Tale Kingdom.

Spider-Man
This story takes place in contemporary New York City, where a young man wearing a red-blue spider costume swings between skyscrapers and climbs up the side of buildings.

Finding Nemo
This story takes place in the ocean and in a fish tank, experienced from the point-of-view of the fish.

Monsters, Inc.
This story takes place in a world where funny monsters scare little children.

Bruce Almighty
This story takes place in a city where an average guy gets to play God.

Matrix Trilogy
This story takes places in the futuristic world of the Matrix.

Pirates of the Caribbean
This story takes place in the world of cursed pirates, who are ghosts.

Harry Potter-The Sorcerer's Stone
This story takes place in the magical world of Hogwarts: a school for young magicians.

Lord of the Rings Trilogy
This story takes place in the magical world of the warring Wizards, Hobbits, and Kings of Middle-earth.

EXCITEMENT

To excite a person is to arouse in them an intense emotion. Normally, this emotion will involve terror, desire, or joy. Most of the megahit movies do not rely on sex to create excitement in the audience.

In the top-grossing popular films, the audience becomes excited when a character with whom they have empathy for is placed in jeopardy. This danger can be either to his own person or to someone or something that the audience knows that the character holds dear: a favorite possession, a friend, a family member, a wife, a lover, or a child. In *The Wizard of Oz*, the dog, Toto, plays this role for Dorothy.

The relationship of the character to this object of affection must be clearly established in the early scenes, so that the audience will unequivocally know the character's affection for the object. Then, whenever the object is placed in jeopardy by the antagonist, the audience will have empathy for the character. The audience becomes "thrilled" when the character is able to rescue the endangered object from jeopardy. This gives them the feelings of joy and happiness at seeing the love interest saved. The danger that the protagonist confronts must be believable for the audience. The filmmaker can establish this by having companions close to the protagonist die violent and horrible deaths.

In order to keep the story exciting, there must be an order to the objects placed under jeopardy, starting from those the protagonist cares least about to those that he loves more than life itself. The last object of affection (usually the "love interest;" a child or a very close friend) is typically placed in jeopardy of death in the climax scene. Here, the values and abilities of the protagonist are finally tested to determine if he can defeat the antagonist and obtain the dramatic objective, while still preserving the life of the person he most cherishes.

Situations are thrilling to an audience when the protagonist confronts impossible odds and the threat of imminent death, yet still outwits his opponent and survives in an unexpected way. The films that are the most exciting, such as *Star Wars* are those in which the protagonists are constantly in jeopardy. This is accomplished by continuously throwing dangerous obstacles in their paths and their near misses with death. Even in a "children's film," like *The Wizard of Oz*, Dorothy is in jeopardy in almost every single scene.

The amount of excitement in a scene is equal to the intensity of the danger to a character, with the greatest intensity resulting from life-threatening situations. Characters overcoming dangerous obstacles make these films thrilling to watch. This, with the addition of unexpected obstacles to a protagonist's plans and actions, provides excitement that an audience is willing to pay to experience time and time again.

SURPRISE

"Tragedy is an imitation not only of a complete action, but events inspiring fear or pity. Such an effect is best produced when events come on us by surprise; and the effect is heightened when, at the same time, they follow as cause and effect."
—Aristotle, *Poetics*

"... the selection of information can make a story more interesting than it actually is. Because we do not give all the facts, but only the essential ones, the story becomes more poignant and effective. Because information may be given at its most decisive moment, the surprise may shock the spectator. Because information may be withheld, the spectator can be made curious."
—Eugene Vale, *The Technique of Screen and Television Writing*

Surprise is generated when **the expected does not occur**. This emotionally shocks the audience. One method of creating false expectations in the audience is to have a character intentionally mislead another as to his real plans and subgoals. Since this is all the information that the audience has about the situation, they are surprised when the outcome is other than expected.

SUSPENSE

"Suspense is not an element of the story, but a reaction of the spectator to the story. Suspense is the doubt of the spectator as to the outcome of an intention of an actor in the story."
—Eugene Vale, *Technique of Screen and Television Writing*

Suspense creates emotional tension within the audience, causing the viewers to become engrossed in the story. Suspense is created when the characters which the audience empathizes with are placed in danger. The audience wants them to escape unharmed. Jeopardy is an essential element that each scene must contain. The characters must always have something at risk. If not, then the audience loses interest.

Suspense is also created when the audience knows more about what will occur in the scene than the protagonist does. They gain this knowledge whenever the antagonist reveals his plans to destroy the hero or when the audience knows of imminent danger of which the protagonist is unaware (e.g., the killer is hiding in the closet).

Suspense involves audience uncertainty about the outcome of future events. This is different from *mystery*, in which the audience knows less about what is taking place in the story than the characters.

The structures of a *chase* and *ticking clocks* are methods of creating suspense, and both rely heavily on the use of obstacles.

THE CHASE

One method of creating suspense is to construct a classic **chase** scene, where the life of the protagonist and his supporters are placed in jeopardy. In these situations, the protagonist attempts to overcome distance and the obstacles placed in his path that prevent him from reaching his destination. Obstacles are effective time-stalling devices that help to keep the audience in a state of frenzy.

Fast paced action differentiates the chase scene from a scene where the character is solely in pursuit of his objective. In the chase scene, it is necessary that the protagonist constantly be in peril. Usually, at the end of the major chase scenes, the protagonist confronts the antagonist in the life and death climatic battle.

Titanic
Cal chases Jack and Rose and tries to shoot them as Titanic sinks.

Star Wars
Darth Vader and the Imperial Storm Troopers chase the rebels. Darth Vader chases the rebel planes trying to destroy the Death Star.

Phantom Menace
Two Jedi Knights and Jar Jar Binks are chased by giant underwater creatures.

E.T.
The United States Government Agents chase Elliott and E.T.

Jurassic Park
Ellie, Ian, and the Australian Security Guard are chased by a T-Rex as they drive away in a jeep. The Raptors chase the children, Dr. Grant, and Ellie throughout the complex.

Forrest Gump
The chase scene does not occur at the end of the film, but in the beginning when Forrest is being chased by the young boys on bicycles, then later by the young men in the car.

The Lion King
Simba chases Scar up the rock cliff overlooking the Pride Lands.

Return of the Jedi
Imperial Troops chase after Han, Princess Leia, and the Ewoks as they try to destroy the power generator that provides the shield for the Death Star.

Independence Day
Alien fighters are chasing the American planes that are trying to destroy the mother spaceship before it can fire its prime weapon.

The Sixth Sense
There are no chase scenes in this movie. All the dead people, including Dr. Malcolm Crowe, walk slowly as they haunt Cole Sears.

Empire Strikes Back
Darth Vader chases Luke Skywalker and confronts him in a laser sword duel.

Home Alone
The burglars chase Kevin and capture him in a neighbor's house.

The Grinch
The Whos chase the Grinch, who has destroyed their Whobilation.

Jaws
Quint, Brody, and Hooper chase the shark, then the shark turns around and chases them.

Batman
Batman chases the Joker to the top of the Cathedral.

Men In Black
J and K chase the Edgar-Bug and try to prevent it from leaving the Earth with the Galaxy that was around Orion's neck.

The Wizard of Oz
The Wicked Witch chases Dorothy and her friends around the walls of the Castle during the climax scene.

Shrek
The Dragon chases Shrek, Donkey, and Fiona through the castle. Shrek and Donkey run to save Fiona from marrying Farquaard.

Spider-Man
Spider-Man chases after the thief who stole his Uncle Ben's car.

Finding Nemo
Marlin chases the boat that has taken Nemo.

Monsters, Inc.
Randall chases Sulley, Mike, and Boo as they try to get to Boo's door.

Bruce Almighty
The street gang chases Bruce.

Matrix Trilogy
The Machines chase the rebel's spaceship.

Pirates of the Caribbean
The Black Pearl chases the Intrepid.

Harry Potter-The Sorcerer's Stone
Fluffy, the three-headed dog, chases Harry, Ron, and Hermione.

Lord of the Rings Trilogy
The RingWraiths chase Frodo and Arwen.

TICKING CLOCKS

Ticking Clocks are another technique for building suspense. The protagonist must race against time to either achieve his objective, save his life, or both. The suspense is intensified as more and more obstacles are thrown into his path as he is running out of time. This creates "urgency" and keeps the audience on the edge of their seats, wondering if the protagonist will achieve his objective and survive.

Titanic
Titanic has struck an iceberg and will sink in only one hour. Will Jack and Rose survive?

Star Wars
Time ticks away on the digital computer screen as the moon moves out of its orbit, and the Death Star will have a clear shot at the rebel planet. Luke must lob the torpedo into the shaft and destroy the Death Star before the rebel home planet is destroyed.

Phantom Menace
Queen Amidala must launch a counter-attack against the Trade Federation before they completely conquer Naboo. Anakin Skywalker must destroy the control ship and disable the battle droids before they destroy the Gungan army.

E.T.
Elliott and E.T must get to the forest, communicate with his home planet, then return to Elliott's house by 10:00pm.

Jurassic Park
Dennis, the computer technician, must get the dinosaur embryos to the ship before it leaves the dock.

Forrest Gump
Forrest must carry all of his soldiers to safety before the air strike hits.

The Lion King
Simba must reclaim his right to be King before the Pride Lands is destroyed by the Jackals.

Return of the Jedi
Han Solo and his team must disable the power source so that the attack on the Death Star will be successful. They must do this before all the rebel ships are destroyed.

Independence Day
The President must take off in his plane before the clock runs out and the aliens launch their attack. The American fighters must destroy the alien's prime weapon before it destroys their headquarters.

Empire Strikes Back
Luke must save his friends before they are killed by the Imperial Soldiers.

Home Alone
The family overslept and must get to the airport before their plane leaves for Paris. Kevin's mother wants to get home in time to spend Christmas with Kevin.

The Grinch
The Grinch must return all the gifts before the Christmas Day is over.

Jaws
Quint, Brody, and Hooper must kill the shark before their boat sinks and the shark eats them.

Batman
There is no explicit timelock device in this story besides the issue of whether Batman can destroy the Joker's balloons before the poisonous SMYLEX gas is released and kills all the spectators at the parade.

Men In Black
The Arquillian Spaceship gives the MIB only one hour to deliver the Galaxy, or the Earth will be destroyed.

The Wizard of Oz
Time runs out of the sand clock as the Scarecrow, Tin Man, and the Lion try to break down the door and free Dorothy.

Shrek
Shrek must save Fiona before she marries Lord Farquaard.

Matrix Trilogy
Neo must destroy the Agent Smiths before the Machines destroy Zion.

Finding Nemo
Nemo must escape before Darla arrives to take him as a gift.

USING PROPS

Props are useful for the non-verbal communication of a character's feelings. These props take on a symbolic significance in the story, and often become the objects for which the protagonist and antagonist fight. The number of significant props should be held to a minimum; otherwise, the audience may become confused as to which are the most important.

Sometimes props are concrete objects that may be the needed components to obtain the final objective. This is the case in *Raiders of the Lost Ark* in which the amulet that is "the headpiece of the staff of Ra," is needed to locate "the well of souls." These props are often the tools needed to complete a task.

At other times, props are used to "tag" or to individuate a character in order to make him unique and memorable. The whip and hat used by Indiana Jones in *Raiders of the Lost Ark* play this type of role.

Titanic
"The Heart of the Ocean" jewel is the most important prop in this movie.

Star Wars
The design plans for the Death Star and the Jedi laser swords are props.

Phantom Menace
The Jedi Knight laser swords are individuating props. The electric energy balls used as weapons by the Gungan soldiers are props.

E.T.
The geranium plant that symbolizes E.T.'s well-being is an important prop.

Jurassic Park
The computer system the children use to turn on the security grid is an important prop.

Forrest Gump
The ping pong paddle is a prop, as is the feather which represents the spirit of Forrest.

The Lion King
The staff of Rafiki, the mystical baboon, is an individuating prop.

Return of the Jedi
The Jedi laser swords are individuating props.

Independence Day
David Levinson's computer that tracks the alien countdown is an important prop.

The Sixth Sense
The toy figurines that Cole Sears uses to ward off the dead people who terrorize him are props.

Empire Strikes Back
Darth Vader's black helmet is an individuating prop. The Jedi laser swords are individuating props.

Home Alone
The appliances and other home objects that Kevin uses to fight the burglars when they invade his home are props.

The Grinch
The Santa Claus suit worn by the Grinch is an ironic prop.

Jaws
The chum that is thrown into the ocean to attract the shark is a prop, as are the metal containers of compressed oxygen used to destroy the shark.

Batman
The Joker's poison balloons are important props.

Men In Black
The Neuralyzer that destroys memories, alien guns, MIB Ford LTDs, and black sunglasses are all props.

The Wizard of Oz
The Witch's broomstick and the ruby slippers are props.

Shrek
The Deed to Shrek's Swamp.

Spider-Man
Spider-Man's Webbing.

Finding Nemo
The Diver's Mask.

Monsters, Inc.
The piece of Boo's door.

Bruce Almighty
The Prayer Beads.

Matrix Trilogy
Agent Smith's Ear-Piece.

Pirates of the Caribbean
The Aztec Gold Coin. The Green Apple.

Harry Potter-The Sorcerer's Stone
The Golden Snitch. The Sorcerer's Stone.

Lord of the Rings Trilogy
The One Ring. The Elf Charm given to Aragorn by Arwen.

EXPOSITION

"The screenwriter must arrange the story information in such manner as to cause anticipation if he wants to obtain the valuable effects of expectancy and surprise, fear and hope, disappointment and relief."
—Eugene Vale, *The Technique of Screen and Television Writing*

Exposition is the presentation of necessary background information about characters, relationships, and events, or the presentation of plans for the future. This information is essential for the audience to follow the story.

It is important to realize that information is constantly being presented to the audience and is usually conveyed through images and actions. Sometimes, it is more economical to have the characters present the background information with dialogue. When this is the case, the characters should not bore the audience by lecturing them, but instead, the vital information should be presented in a visually interesting manner.

Exposition is most effectively transmitted when the characters in the scene are in conflict with each other. The audience then sees and experiences the character's feelings and reactions. Rage, frustration, and anger are the emotions that are often used by characters presenting exposition. It is under these emotions that characters often tell each other the truth. Humor, laughter, and jokes are also ways of conveying background information in an interesting manner. Using suspense and mystery, while conveying the information, also hold the audience's attention. Sometimes incidents in the past cannot be effectively shown but only discussed.

Exposition scenes are often used to setup expectations in the audience about future events in the story. This can be used to create excitement and unpredictability when how the events actually unfold are different from the expectations created through the exposition scene. Sometimes, this becomes an effective tool for misdirecting the audience's attention for the sake of giving them a more exciting and emotionally satisfying experience.

Titanic
The crew on the ship searching for the jewel on the sunken Titanic present a computer graphics rendition of the sinking and breaking apart of the Titanic to Rose.

Star Wars
The holograph of Princess Leia explains the importance of the Death Star design plans to the rebellion.

Phantom Menace
Padme, Captain Panaka, Qui-Gon, Obi-Wan, and Boss Nass discuss plans to wage war against the Trade Federation and to capture the Viceroy.

E.T.
Exposition about E.T.'s home planet is presented to the children through his psychokinetic powers as he makes the planet-like objects rotate in mid-air.

Jurassic Park
An animation sequence in the Jurassic Park theater-ride explains how the DNA code was obtained to make a baby dinosaur.

Forrest Gump
The school principal explains to Mrs. Gump that Forrest is not normal because his IQ is only 75, and he doesn't meet the standards for being admitted to the school. He uses a chart to present this information.

The Lion King
Mufasa shows his kingdom to Simba and explains his role in the circle of life.

Return of the Jedi
The Rebel Commander presents the battle plans and discusses the need for Han Solo to disable the power source on the Ewok's planet so that the rebel fighters can destroy the new Death Star.

Independence Day
The President and his military advisors discuss the plans to use nuclear weapons in Houston to destroy the alien spaceship.

The Sixth Sense
Cole Sears finally tells Dr. Malcolm that he sees dead people.

Empire Strikes Back
Luke conveys his strategy and plans to destroy the AT-AT walkers of the Imperial forces by circling their legs with cable and making them trip and fall to the ground.

Home Alone
Kevin's mother explains to the policeman (thief) that the family is going to Paris for the Christmas holidays as the rest of the family runs through the house.

The Grinch
Clarinella and Rose Whobiddie tell Cindy Lou Who the history of the Grinch through a memory flashback.

Jaws
The Mayor conducts a town meeting to discuss how best to handle the shark threat during the July 4th weekend.

Batman
Boss Grissom explains why he wants Jack Napier to clean out the safe at AXIS CHEMICAL so that they will not be connected to criminal activity.

Men in Black
K explains to J that the MIB facility monitors the aliens in the New York area by tracing their movements on a computerized screen.

The Wizard of Oz
Exposition concerning the Yellow Brick Road and the Wizard of Oz is communicated by the Munchkins during a dance and musical routine.

Shrek
Lord Farquaard discusses choosing a Princess as a Game Show situation.

Spider-Man
The Museum Spokesperson talks about the genetically altered spiders.

Finding Nemo
Marlin and Dory converse as they search for Nemo.

Monsters Inc
Mr. Waternoose explains the need for the energy obtained from children's screams after the opening scene.

Bruce Almighty
God explains the rules of divine power as he and Bruce walk on water.

Matrix Trilogy
Morpheus explains the history of the war between Humans and the Machines to Neo while they are standing in the Desert of the Real.

Pirates of the Caribbean
Barbossa tells Liz about the curse of the Aztec Gold while showing her that she is now in a "Ghost Story."

Harry Potter-The Sorcerer's Stone
The Centaur explains the crimes of Voldemort after he saves Harry in the forest.

Lord of the Rings Trilogy
The story of the forging of the Ring is told in the opening sequence of the movie.

THEMES
CREATING UNIVERSAL APPEAL

Mythic Structures

Megahit Movie Themes

MYTHIC STRUCTURES

"Don't be afraid to create variations on the myth, but don't start with the myth itself. Let the myth grow naturally from your story. Developing myths are part of the rewriting process. If you begin with the myth, you will find that your writing becomes rigid, uncreative and predictable. Working with the myth in the rewriting process will deepen your script, giving it a new life as you find the story within the story."
—Linda Seger, *Making A Good Script Great*

Linda Seger is correct in that if you use Joseph Campbell's archetype approach as a method of story construction, "**your writing becomes rigid, uncreative and predictable**." It may be useful after you have designed your story and plot and have written the first draft of the screenplay to read books about mythic structures. They may stimulate your creative imagination and help to enrich your story by adding universal features to your characters or to your scene situations. But if you try to design a story using these methods, the story will no longer be "organic" in the sense of flowing naturally from the needs, desires, and objectives of your characters. You will also lose focus and not concentrate on the important **emotional reactions** of your characters and the audience to actions in the movie. For if your intention is to develop a **popular** movie, as opposed to a "universal" movie, giving the audience an **emotionally satisfying experience** is much more important than having your story follow the mythic structures promoted by Joseph Campbell in *Hero of a Thousand Faces*.

Below are the titles of books that promote the mythic structure approach to story analysis and story development.

Bonnet, James. *Stealing from the Gods: A Dynamic New Story Model for Writers and Filmmakers.* Michael Wiese Productions

Campbell, Joseph. *Hero of a Thousand Faces.* Princeton University

Campbell, Joseph and Moyers, Bill. *The Power of Myth.* Anchor

Seger, Linda. "Creating the Myth" in *Making a Good Script Great.* Samuel French Trade

Vogler, Chris. *The Writers Journey: Mythic Structures for Writers.* Michael Wiese Productions

MEGAHIT MOVIE THEMES

"Theme is the universal statement the movie makes about the human condition. It is the screenwriter's underlying prescription for how one should live one's life in order to be more evolved, more fulfilled, more individuated, more moral person. It's the filmmaker's way of saying, 'This is how to be a better human being.'"
— Michael Hauge, *Writing Screenplays That Sell*

Themes are statements about the values characters choose when confronting obstacles and conflicts while in pursuit of their objectives. Western culture believes that individuals freely pursuing their vision of happiness is the supreme political value. We believe that people have free will, and their lives are not pre-determined. We believe their success depends upon the choices they make and the actions they take. Our popular stories reflect these beliefs. Tom O'Brien, in *The Screening of America*, states:

> ...most movies, even the bad ones, have some social content. Films, in general, are not only fun, but a vital part of the educational and psychological adjustment of many Americans to reality. They give us models to imitate and images to love; sometimes they even give us standards by which we unconsciously measure our real life relations.

Characters in popular movies are the role models with whom we try to identify and want to emulate. They have goals and objectives. Often, the objects they desire are unique and are also desired by others. This generates conflict. The obvious case is that in which two men desire the same woman. For dramatic purposes, one of the characters is the protagonist, and the other is the antagonist. The protagonist will possess the values and attributes that the dramatist believes desirable while the antagonist will perform acts that are socially reprehensible. The craft of the dramatist enables him to manipulate the audience emotionally so that they will have empathy for the protagonist and enmity for the antagonist.

Audience empathy for the protagonist, critical for making the movie popular, is greatest in stories where the protagonist attempts to achieve his dreams by overcoming innumerable obstacles. The greatest emotional involvement is created when obstacles are generated by other characters that should be supporting the protagonist (lovers, spouses, parents, siblings, and friends). *The Wizard of Oz* exhibits these features. Dorothy attempts to save the life of her dog, Toto. Her aunt and uncle are unwilling to help her. They even give Toto to the villain, Elmira Gulch, in order to save their farm. Dorothy dreams of a place "over the rainbow," where no problems exist. When caught up in a tornado, Dorothy is "transported" to the magical land of Oz. Once she discovers that she also has serious problems here, her objective then becomes to return home to Kansas. The Munchkins tell her that the Wizard of Oz will help her, and she embarks on a journey to the Emerald City.

On this journey, she makes friends with a Scarecrow, a Tin Man and a Cowardly Lion. Each has his own objective, and each decides to journey with Dorothy to Oz. But this journey is not free from dangers, for a Wicked Witch wants the magical ruby slippers attached to Dorothy's feet. When they reach the Emerald City, the Wizard demands they obtain the broomstick of the Witch before he will help them. Overcoming many obstacles and dangers, they finally get the broomstick. Upon returning to the Wizard, they discover that he really doesn't have the power to give them what they want. All that he can do is give them the public acknowledgment that they do possess the intelligence, compassion, and courage that they desire. Dorothy is able to "return" home to Kansas once she realizes and accepts that she always had the power to do so. The film ends with a very simple message: there is no place like home.

The fundamental themes and objectives found in *The Wizard of Oz* also occur in most of the popular films analyzed in this book. The desire to return **home** is the primary objective not only for Dorothy, but also for the Extra-Terrestrial in *E.T.*

In the other films, the primary objective is not to return home, but to protect the home from destruction. This is evident in *Star Wars* where Luke destroys the Death Star in order to save the rebel home base. His own home and the planet, Alderan, were destroyed earlier in the story. Preservation of freedom from the Empire is the theme continued in *Empire Strikes Back* and *Return of the Jedi*. Freedom from the tyranny of the Trade Federation is a variation on this theme developed in *The Phantom Menace*. In *Independence Day,* all the primary characters want to save the world from destruction by the Aliens. This is also the primary objective of J and K in *MIB*. Batman wants to save Gotham City from the insane Joker who wants to poison the community and Kevin, in *Home Alone*, wants to protect his home from the burglars. In *Jaws,* police Captain Martin Brody wants to save the community of Amity from the great white shark. While in *Jurassic Park,* the primary objective is not to save the world, but to save the grandchildren of Dr. Hammond and the remnants of the human species left in Jurassic Park from destruction by the dinosaurs.

The Grinch plays on a variation on these standard themes. While isolated from the Whos in his cave on Mt. Crumpit, the Grinch nurtures the rage he feels from the humiliations he experienced from the Whos as a child. But ultimately he does rejoice and celebrate his reunion with the community, once all the grievances have been remedied, and all conflicts been resolved. At the end, the Grinch is once again home, and Whoville is once again safe from his attacks of vengeance.

The theme of *The Sixth Sense* revolves around a small boy's efforts to feel safe with himself and his ability to see dead people. It is this special skill that terrorizes him. Once he realizes that the dead people do not mean to harm him, but instead need his special skills to help them solve their problems (and finally, like the dead man Dr. Malcolm Crowe, rest in peace), he feels safe with himself, or "at home with himself." In *Forrest Gump,* another protagonist must come to accept that he is different and be at home with himself. Forrest does this by being completely focused on the moment, and concentrating totally on whatever he is doing in the present. This then transforms his "difference" from that of an underperformer on the IQ tests to a person who excels in whatever activity he embarks on, be it football, ping pong or shrimp fishing. Forrest, in the beginning and end of the movie, is forever at home with himself. Finally, there is *Titanic,* the greatest box office grossing film to date. The theme of this film, of course, is that true love is eternal, and if found in life, will even continue after death. Perhaps this is the greatest sense of security, and of "being at home" that anyone could ever achieve.

The movie *E.T.* demonstrates that box-office success does not depend on the casting of superstars. The actors who performed in this film were not famous before it was released into the theaters, nor have any of them starred in megahit movies since then. There are no exotic locations or expensive sets in this film. The action takes place in an ordinary suburban community, in a conventional family home, with some scenes in a school classroom and others in a forest. There is no explicit sex or gratuitous nudity. The special effects are limited to a spaceship that appears briefly in the opening and closing scenes. It does contain one amazing alien, although it is not the physical appearance of the alien that wins the audience's heart, as much as his childlike behavior. This is fundamentally a simple story about innocence, friendship, learning to communicate with different beings, and helping a friend to get back home. Targeted to children throughout the world, it contains two very simple messages: call home and be good.

Friendship is another common theme that is found in many of these films. In *The Wizard of Oz* and *E.T.*, friends place themselves in great jeopardy in order to help the protagonist return home. In films such as the *Star Wars* trilogy and *Independence Day,* friends help each other protect the home from destruction, even if it means that they might be killed in the process. *Batman* is different. Batman is a loner who is willing to place himself in jeopardy to save the community from destruction, though he does depend on his butler and friend, Alfred. Loyalty to friends is a common attribute possessed by the protagonists.

The wanton destruction of human life is a common attribute for most villains. Besides destroying their enemies, they also will destroy their most loyal supporters when it suits them. This is clearly exhibited by the Joker in *Batman*, who kills his cohort Bob, who had saved his life many times throughout the film.

The antagonist desires power and control over the lives of the other characters and will break all accepted codes of human conduct in order to achieve this. Terror is their standard mode of operation. The one bit of behavior that is guaranteed to turn the audience against the antagonist is his mocking laughter as he gloats over his helpless victim. The antagonist's lack of mercy and his joy at anticipating the destruction of another human being causes the audience to hate him. This is a standard moment in most popular films: the Wicked Witch laughing at Dorothy's cries of help to her Aunt Em, the two burglars laugh as they are about to harm Kevin, Belloc laughing after he has instructed the natives to kill Jones, and the Joker as he watches Batman and Vicki hanging over the edge of the cathedral in fear for their lives.

In many of these films, supernatural powers come to the aid of the protagonist during their moments of desperation. Glinda, the Good Witch of the North, saves Dorothy by creating a snowstorm when Dorothy succumbs to the drugs in the poppy field. The voice of the deceased Obi-Wan Kenobi instructs Luke to place his faith in "the force" as Luke attacks the Death Star. E.T.'s telekinetic powers save Elliott and his friends by lifting their bicycles over the police barricade. In *MIB,* the friendly aliens have provided K with a Neuralyzer that erases the memories of seeing aliens from the minds of human beings. Therefore, beings with supernatural powers play an essential positive role in many of the most popular films ever made.

Themes exhibited in some of the megahit movies are listed below:

Titanic
True love means being willing to sacrifice your life for the person you love, as Jack does for Rose.

Star Wars, Empire Strikes Back, Return of the Jedi
Freedom from tyranny necessitates fighting for control of the absolute power of the universe.

Phantom Menace
Freedom from tyranny necessitates fighting for control of your home.

E.T.
Friendship sometimes means helping the person you love to achieve his desires, even if it means separation.

Batman
Preservation of the community from crime necessitates fighting the source of evil.

Home Alone
A person must use all his intelligence and resources in order to protect his home from destruction.

Jurassic Park
To obtain family security, one must preserve the lives of the young and protect them from destruction.

Jaws
Preservation of the community from terror necessitates fighting and destroying the source of evil.

Forrest Gump
To obtain happiness in life one must "go with the flow," be flexible, but also be completely absorbed in the moment.

Independence Day
Preservation of the community from terror necessitates fighting and destroying the source of evil.

Men in Black

Preservation of the world from destruction necessitates fighting and destroying the source of evil.

Sixth Sense
To obtain freedom from terror, one must confront and understand that which terrorizes them.

The Grinch
To become part of a community sometimes means having to apologize and change your behavior.

The Wizard of Oz
Freedom from fear is found in the power of self-confidence used to confront life's problems.

Shrek
To achieve happiness, one must share one's home with others.

Spider-Man
With great power comes great responsibility. Preservation of the community from crime necessitates fighting and destroying the source of evil.

Bruce Almighty
Happiness can be obtained by rejecting selfishness and making sacrifices.

Finding Nemo
To obtain family security, one must preserve the lives of the young and protect them from destruction. To make a child happy, you must give them confidence in their abilities.

Monsters, Inc.
Friendship means helping the person you love to achieve her desires, even if it means separation.

Pirates of the Caribbean
A person can both be a pirate and a good man.

Matrix Trilogy
Preservation of the community from destruction necessitates fighting and destroying the source of evil, even if this requires self-sacrifice.

Harry Potter-The Sorcerer's Stone

Sometimes, one needs to break all the rules to save the world.

Lord of the Rings
Preservation of the community from terror necessitates fighting and destroying the source of evil.

The Passion of the Christ
Preservation of the community from evil necessitates self-sacrifice.

In conclusion, for many protagonists, the primary motivation is to have the emotional security of a safe home. Being at home with people who love you provides a character with a sense of safety and well-being. In *The Wizard of Oz*, Dorothy learns that she has always had the power to be in this place, she just had to believe that she possessed the ability to solve her problems. She learns that with the help of intelligence, compassion, courage, and friends she can overcome any problem. This is the secret, and the meaning, of the ruby slippers.

In *Acts of Meaning*, the cognitive psychologist, Jerome Bruner, states:

> When and if we pass beyond the unspoken despair in which we are now living, when we feel we are again able to control the race to destruction, a new breed of development theory is likely to arise. It will be motivated by the question of how to create a new generation that can prevent the world from dissolving into chaos and destroying itself. I think that its central technical concern will be to create in the young an appreciation of the fact that many worlds are possible, that meaning and reality are created and not discovered, that negotiation is the act of constructing new meanings by which individuals can regulate their relations with each other. It will not, I think, be an image of human development that locates all of the sources of change inside the individual, the solo child...man is not an island of itself, but part of the culture that he inherits and then recreates, the power to recreate reality, to reinvent culture, we will come to recognize, is where a theory of development must begin its discussion of mind.
>
> What will see us through is the writing of poems and novels that help perpetually to recreate the world, and the writing of criticism and interpretation that celebrate the varied ways in which beings search for meaning and for its incarnation in reality, or better, in such rich realities as we can create.

SCENE-BY-SCENE ANALYSIS
OF A POPULAR MOVIE

THE WIZARD OF OZ

THE WIZARD OF OZ

OPENING SCENE: COUNTRY ROAD

DOROTHY runs down a country road that is surrounded by desolate fields. There are wire fences on either side of the road. With her runs her dog, TOTO. Dorothy looks back to see if she is being followed. She speaks to TOTO:

> DOROTHY
> She isn't coming yet, Toto. Did she hurt you?
> She tried to, didn't she! We'll tell Auntie Em.

[Empathy is immediately created for the young girl by showing her terrorized by someone who is pursuing her and has tried to hurt her dog. The audience's curiosity is aroused by this situation. They are curious to know who is pursuing the girl and why is she being chased? What does the pursuer look like? This is a standard method used to force the audience to pay attention to the story.]

[This scene establishes Dorothy as the protagonist with the object she loves, Toto, placed in jeopardy by some yet unknown villain. Dorothy's objective is to escape from her pursuer.]

KANSAS FARM

Her aunt and uncle are busy with their chores and ignore Dorothy. The incubator has broken, and they are about to lose their baby chickens. Dorothy displays sympathy for a small baby chick, then tells her aunt and uncle that Miss Gulch hit Toto over the head with a rake because Toto went into her garden after her cat. Miss Gulch is going to get the sheriff. Aunt Em responds that she's too busy to deal with Dorothy's problem. [Here's a situation where exposition, the background information needed to understand the story, is presented to the audience by a character under emotional stress and in a conflict with other characters who don't have time to help her.]

[The conflict in this scene is between the protagonist and her relatives whom the audience expects to show concern for the child. Most children can immediately identify with Dorothy. They too are often ignored when their parents are busy. This creates immediate empathy for Dorothy, not only in the children, but also in the adults who also have memories of their own childhood experiences.]

[This empathy generating structure is also used in *E.T.*, where Elliott is ignored and belittled by his older brother, and in *Star Wars*, where young Luke's concerns are ignored by his aunt and uncle. Luke, like Dorothy, doesn't have natural parents. In *E.T.*, there is only one parent.]

[This scene establishes the relationship between Dorothy and her guardians, that of not having her needs satisfied. Her objective is to communicate her problem. She fails, and this propels her into the next scene to seek help from friends.]

DOROTHY AND THE FARM HANDS

[This scene establishes Dorothy's relationship with her friends.]
Three farm hands are fixing a wagon. Accidentally, they drop the wagon onto the hand of one of the men, Hunk. Another character, Zeke, criticizes Hunk for not getting his finger out of the way, thereby implying that Hunk is stupid and brought the pain upon himself.

[This is a quick characterization (lack of brains) for Hunk, the person who will become the Straw Man in Dorothy's fantasy. This is accomplished by showing the character in action and not just by having other characters talk about him.]

[This is the first instance of humor. The audience loves to laugh at stupidity. There is a theory of humor called the superiority theory which states that people laugh at characters in order to show their sense of superiority. But stupidity can also be considered as a surprising deviation from the standard behavior expected in a situation. People are not expected to hit their fingers with hammers.]

Dorothy asks Zeke for help with Miss Gulch, but he's too busy getting the hogs in.

[Again, Dorothy is rejected when she pleads for help. This serves to increase the audience's empathy for her: a child in need neglected by her friends, the farmhands, who should be helping her.]

Hunk advises her to use her head, which isn't made of straw, when dealing with Miss Gulch. Hunk tells her not to take Toto by Miss Gulch's house and, thereby, avoid the trouble. Hunk then proceeds to hit his finger with a hammer.

[This, of course, is a foreshadowing of his "brains/intelligence" concern. This is an example of a slapstick comic structure in which the person offering the advice doesn't follow it. This character lacks the ability to carry out his own advice.]

Dorothy then walks on the pigpen railing as Zeke offers some advice. He tells her to have courage, and that she doesn't have to be afraid of Miss Gulch. Dorothy then falls into the pigpen. She screams for help as she's about to be trampled by the Hogs. Zeke jumps in and saves her. He is shaken up by the incident. Dorothy tells Zeke that he's just as scared as she is, and Hunk reinforces this by asking Zeke if the pig made a coward out of him.

[Again, a character trait is indicated and foreshadowed. Here the trait is courage. So far, each of the farmhands actually falls short of the virtue he advocates: First Hunk, with intelligence and now Zeke, with courage.]

Aunt Em tells them to get back to work. She reprimands Hickory for tinkering with his contraption instead of doing the farm work. Hickory holds his arm up, assumes a pose, and says that some day they'll erect a statue to him.

[This characterization is not as clear as the others. Hickory will become the Tin Man, who desires a heart. But here he seems to express a desire for social status and the respect of the community. There is an association between the metal contraption that he is building and his later transformation into a Tin Man, but that's the foreshadowing of a physical manifestation, not a virtue. The key to understanding this characterization is that at the end of the film, the Wizard awards the Tin Man a testimonial for the good deeds that he has performed, which were the result of his kind, generous heart. Compassion and doing good for others appear to be the virtue foreshadowed here, though in a manner less precise than that of intelligence and courage.]

Aunt Em then gives them each a freshly baked bread to eat as she shoos them back to work.

[This is important because it creates empathy for Aunt Em. Although she is stern, feeding them shows that she cares. She's just an overworked farmer. Without this action, she might be characterized as a mean spirited, uncaring old woman.]

Aunt Em then admonishes Dorothy to stop imagining things and exciting herself over nothing. She tells Dorothy to find a place where she won't get into any trouble.

[This is a precise characterization of Dorothy as a person with an active imagination, something most children have heard said about themselves. Dorothy is depicted as someone with a tendency to get upset over minor things. Like Elliott's concern about the monster in his backyard in E.T., the legitimate concerns of the protagonist are not considered by the other characters to be realistic, and this creates more empathy for the protagonist. Dorothy's primary objective is recommended to her by her aunt: find a place where there won't be any trouble.]

[It's important to realize the economy of characterization in this scene. There is not a wasted line nor action. Each word and movement is directly revealing of some trait of one of the characters, a trait central to the story that will be elaborated in more detail as the film continues.]

DOROTHY'S PRIMARY OBJECTIVE (HER DREAM)

To find a place where there isn't any trouble; where there will never be a problem. Somewhere over the Rainbow. She expresses this goal in a song.

INTRO THE ANTAGONIST (ELMIRA GULCH)

Elmira Gulch rides down the desolate country road on her bicycle, accompanied by ominous sounding music. She's a stern, angry, stiff-backed, righteous woman. She parks her bike in front of Dorothy's house and informs Dorothy's Uncle Henry that Toto has bit her on the leg. Uncle Henry opens the gate for Miss Gulch then lets it swing back and hit her in the backside.

[This action is Uncle Henry's non-verbal expression of contempt. Actions are the best way to cinematically express the relationship between two characters, instead of using explicit dialogue.]

AUNT EM'S LIVING ROOM

Dorothy, Toto, Aunt Em, Uncle Henry, and Elmira Gulch are gathered together in the parlor. Miss Gulch says that Toto is a menace to the community, and she wants to have him destroyed. She'll bring a suit against them and take away the farm if Toto isn't handed over to her. There's a law against dogs that bite. Dorothy desperately clings to Toto.

[This creates tremendous empathy for the protagonist (Dorothy) and hatred for the antagonist (Elmira Gulch), for Gulch wants to destroy the animal that Dorothy loves.]

Gulch presents the sheriff's order to Aunt Em, who concedes defeat by stating that she "can't go against the law." Aunt Em hands Toto over to Elmira Gulch, as Dorothy runs out of the room crying. "For Twenty-three years I've been dying to tell you what I thought of you, Elmira Gulch, but now, being a Christian woman, I can't," says Aunt Em.

[This establishes that Gulch has a bad reputation in the community and that her conflict with Dorothy is not an isolated incident. This affirms the audience's right to hate Elmira Gulch.]

Gulch puts Toto into the wicker basket and leaves the house.

[Scene Structure:
Crisis: Gulch has a legal writ from the sheriff to take Toto.
Concrete Stake: Toto's life or death.
Confrontation: Between Gulch and Dorothy, who refuses to release Toto.
Climax: Dorothy and Gulch struggle for Toto. Aunt Em tells Uncle Henry to place Toto in the basket.
Resolution: Aunt Em obeys the law, Uncle Henry gives Toto to Gulch, and Dorothy, defeated, runs out of the room.]

TOTO ESCAPES

Return of the ominous music, as Elmira Gulch rides her bicycle back down the country road with the wicker basket strapped to the back. Toto pokes his head out of the wicker basket. Toto looks down at the moving bike then up at Elmira Gulch as she pedals. Toto jumps out of the basket onto the road. He escapes, running back along the road that he and Dorothy were on in the opening scene of the movie.

DOROTHY AND TOTO RECONCILED

Dorothy lies crying on the bed in her room. Toto barks and jumps up on the bed. Dorothy is overjoyed with his return. But then she realizes that Gulch will come back for Toto and that she can't fight the law. So, she decides to run away. Dorothy and Toto walk down the road.

[This scene resolves the inciting event and expresses the major decision of the protagonist. The inciting event was Gulch taking Toto. The major decision for the protagonist is to leave home in order to save Toto from extermination. Dorothy realizes that if she stays, Miss Gulch will return for Toto, and Dorothy will have to give him back to her. The inciting event often destroys the established world and relationships of the protagonist. Her home and family no longer provide the safety and security it once did. Her family and friends cannot or will not help her, therefore her world is shattered, and she must start anew somewhere else]

PROFESSOR MARVEL

[An establishing shot of the Professor's wagon tells the audience where they are, especially since this is a radical change in scenery.]

Written on the sign of a carnival wagon are the words "PROFESSOR MARVEL: ACCLAIMED BY THE CROWNED HEADS OF EUROPE." Professor Marvel is cooking a hot dog by the fire as Dorothy, with suitcase in hand, and Toto by her side, approaches. Professor Marvel quickly analyzes the situation and informs her that he knows that she is running away because they don't understand her at home, they don't appreciate her.

[Again this creates more audience empathy for Dorothy, for people in the audience have also had the similar experience of not being understood or appreciated. It also makes Marvel a sympathetic character for the audience because here is an adult who understands and empathizes with Dorothy's problems. He appears to sincerely want to help her.]

Toto eats the Professor's hot dog. Dorothy scolds Toto, but the Professor just laughs it off.

[This again establishes more empathy for the Professor as a kind man with a sense of humor. He is a character who forgives the dog for stealing his supper, as opposed to Elmira Gulch who wants to destroy Toto. Since Dorothy and Toto already have the audience's support, and he's kind to them, he thereby receives the audience's empathy.]

Dorothy wants to travel with the Professor to see the crowned heads of Europe. He responds to this by asking her if she knows any, by which he reveals himself to be a fraud. But he's a kind and likable rogue. Professor Marvel decides to consult his crystal ball about Dorothy's future.

INSIDE PROFESSOR MARVEL'S WAGON

As he consults his crystal ball, he tells Dorothy that she must first close her eyes. When she does this he looks through her purse and finds a photo of her with Aunt Em. Looking back into the crystal ball he tells Dorothy that he sees a woman standing in front of a house with a white picket fence. She's crying, because someone has hurt her deeply, someone has broken her heart. Dorothy interprets this as Aunt Em being sick, and she decides to return to the farm. As she runs from the wagon, a storm starts up.

[Marvel's character of a fraud is confirmed, but he's a fraud who does good instead of using his deceptions for personal gain. This foreshadows the character of the Wizard of Oz. Here Dorothy makes another decision, to return to help a sick family member instead of running away. She decides not to bring sorrow and grief to her family and to care for Aunt Em who had nursed her when she was sick.]

[Scene Structure:
Dorothy's Objective: To get away and go to Europe with Prof. Marvel.
Professor: To get Dorothy to return home.
Prop: The crystal ball.
Conflict: Dorothy's self-conflict between values: Save the life of her dog or the life of her aunt.
Protagonist Decision: Dorothy decides to return home.
Professor wins by playing on Dorothy's sense of loyalty to her family.]

TORNADO SEQUENCE

Twister looms ominously in the distance as the farmhands try to save the horses from danger. Aunt Em and the farmhands call out for Dorothy, but she's nowhere to be found. They all enter an underground shelter and close the door over them.

Dorothy returns to the farm. She tries to open the cellar door, but its locked.

[There are many obstacles in this scene that prevent Dorothy from returning to the security of her home: the threatening tornado, the locked cellar doors, the howling wind that drowns her calls for help.]

She returns to her bedroom. The Tornado approaches. She calls for her aunt. Suddenly, the wind blows the window off the hinges. It hits Dorothy in the head and knocks her onto the bed. The room begins to spin.

DOROTHY WITHIN THE TORNADO

The image of a spinning house rising up into the tornado is super-imposed over Dorothy's face. Through her bedroom window, images of characters appear. Chickens and a hen house float past. Dorothy sits up in bed and stares out the window.

Aunt Em floats by, knitting as she sits in her rocking chair. A cow flies by, followed by two of the ranch hands rowing a boat through the air. Dorothy looks down to see the twister spinning. Then, Elmira Gulch rides by on her bike. But after a few moments, she transforms into a hideous cackling witch on a broomstick.

The room spins and the house falls to the ground. Dorothy gets up out of bed, picks up Toto, then walks to the door. She opens it and steps out into the colorful world of Oz.

[This is a montage transition scene which takes Dorothy from Kansas into the land of Oz. Is it a dream, or was she really picked up by the tornado and transported to the Land of Oz? Both interpretations are possible.]

DOROTHY ARRIVES IN OZ

Beautiful colors and the musical theme conveys to the audience that Dorothy is now "over the rainbow." The white and blue dress on Dorothy is indicative of her innocence, this being the traditional production design meaning of the white-blue color combination. Dorothy walks around the colorful garden and utters her classic line to Toto, "I don't think that we're in Kansas any more."

From within the flowerbeds little people, the Munchkins, stand up and stare at Dorothy. Suddenly, a pink bubble appears in the sky. It then floats down to the ground. A beautiful woman, dressed in rose colors, steps out of the bubble, approaches Dorothy, and asks if she's a good witch or a bad witch. The Munchkins called her because a house fell from the sky and killed the Wicked Witch of the East.

Dorothy tells her that she's not a witch, and that witches are old and ugly, to which the woman responds that she herself is a witch, Glenda, the Witch of the North. Dorothy has become a heroine to the Munchkins because she has killed their tyrannical ruler. The Munchkins celebrate the liberation that she has brought to their community with song and dance, which emphasizes the death certification process.

[It's important that when the protagonist kills another character, the killing must be justified, otherwise, the audience will lose empathy for the protagonist. In this case, the Wicked Witch's desire for revenge for the death of her sister would be emotionally legitimate and win some of the audience's empathy, if it weren't for the fact that the Munchkins, who are adorable little people, characterize the Witch of the East as a tyrant and celebrate her death with song and dance. In any story, a death must be completely justifiable from the point of view of the audience, otherwise, the character that caused the death will lose all empathy.]

Suddenly, in the midst of the celebration, the Wicked Witch of the West appears, accompanied by a loud explosion and an orange cloud of smoke. Dressed from head to foot in black and with a blue-green face, she approaches Dorothy. All the Munchkins scream in terror as they fall to the ground. Glenda tells Dorothy that this is the Wicked Witch of the West, who is worse than the deceased Witch of the East.

The Witch demands to know who killed her sister. Dorothy responds that it was an accident. The good witch, Glenda reminds, her of the ruby slippers. The Wicked Witch rushes to take possession of them but, suddenly, the slippers vanish only to reappear on Dorothy's feet. They rightfully now belong to her since she killed the Wicked Witch of the East. Glenda advises Dorothy to "stay tight inside them. Their magic must be very powerful, otherwise she would not want them back."

[In the prelude, it was Toto in jeopardy, now it's Dorothy. This increases the audience's concern. The Ruby Slippers becomes the object which binds together the protagonist and antagonist in a life and death struggle, the bond that they cannot break. Dorothy doesn't really desire the slippers. She wants only to get "home," to that place where she is safe and secure. At this stage, she doesn't realize that it will be the slippers, and the power that they hold that will allow her to achieve her objective.]

Glenda laughs at the other witch, reminds her that she has no power here, and advises that she better leave or a house might fall down upon her. The Wicked Witch threatens Dorothy by saying that she'll get her and her little dog, too. The Witch then disappears in a burst of orange smoke.

[You can't get much meaner than that. The Witch's comments, of course, will increase the audience's empathy for Dorothy and hatred for the antagonist. Audience empathy for Dorothy is also increased by the accidental killing of the Wicked Witch of the East. She is in this mess now due to no real fault of her own. Audience empathy is always increased for a character that becomes endangered due to circumstances beyond their control, as in the case of Dorothy. But again, the audience's natural tendency to support the desire for justice over the death of a family member (the witch's sister) has to be strongly counterbalanced.]

[The opening sequence of *The Wizard of Oz*, all the black and white scenes that occur in Kansas can be considered a prelude to the main story where all the major characters and objectives are presented. Once "over the rainbow," the characters and objectives are once again introduced, and the story proceeds. For example, Elmira Gulch, called a "witch" by Dorothy, was introduced as the antagonist. Here, we have the second introduction of the antagonist, Dorothy's nemesis, in a more explicit form. Both want to destroy Toto. Also introduced is the object (the ruby slippers) which binds them.]

Glenda tells Dorothy that she has made a bad enemy of the Wicked Witch of the West, and that the sooner she gets out of Oz, the better she'll be. Dorothy responds that she'd give anything to get out of Oz and asks for the way back to Kansas. She is told that only the Wizard of Oz would know how to do this, and he lives in the Emerald City. To get to the Emerald City, she must follow the Yellow Brick Road. She is also told by Glenda never to let those ruby slippers off her feet or she'll be at the mercy of the Wicked Witch of the West.

[The protagonist now has a new primary objective: to get back home to Kansas. In order to accomplish this, she has to accomplish a subgoal: get to the Emerald City and seek the help of the Wizard of Oz, for he's the only one who can help get her back home.]

In order to get to the Land of Oz, Glenda tells Dorothy to follow the Yellow Brick Road. Glenda then departs in her bubble as the Munchkins sing a chorus of "Follow the Yellow Brick Road." Dorothy leaves them all behind as she dances down the road.

[*The Wizard of Oz* is primarily a "morality story" which presents a set of virtues that will help a person deal with problems that confront them in life. Within this context, it is appropriate to interpret the Yellow Brick Road as representing "the golden path through life" or "the golden mean": treat others as you would have them treat you.]

DOROTHY MEETS THE SCARECROW

Dorothy comes to a crossroads and must decide in which direction to continue. A Scarecrow hangs from a post in the field. He speaks out, suggesting first that she go in one direction, then the opposite, then finally in both directions. He explains that he can't make up his mind because he hasn't got a brain.

[Humor is again created here by a surprising deviation from standard patterns of behavior. The stereotypical role of a scarecrow is that of an artificial being, one that cannot talk, dance, or sing. A scarecrow that can do all three is incongruous to our standard pattern. Added to this is his stupidity, advising Dorothy to go in both directions, compounds the humor in the situation.]

Dorothy helps him down from the post. He is completely made of straw. He has flimsy movements, no skeletal structure, always flopping around and falling down onto the ground, like a bumbling idiot. He didn't scare Dorothy and can't scare the crows. He's a failure in life as a scarecrow because he hasn't got a brain. He then sings a song telling what he would accomplish if he only had a brain.

[A character who sincerely admits that he is a failure usually gets the audience's empathy. This is because most members of the audience probably believe themselves to be failures or at least not as successful as they once dreamed of becoming. Therefore, they secretly identify with the Scarecrow. The Scarecrow's primary objective is to get a brain.]

The Scarecrow wonders if the Wizard could get him a brain. Dorothy tells him that the Witch is after her, and that it might be dangerous.

[This also reminds the audience that Dorothy is in jeopardy.]

He responds that he's not afraid of anything, except perhaps, fire.

[A standard technique used to generate empathy for a character is to show what he fears most in life. This humanizes him, and makes it easier for the audience to have sympathy for the character. Then before he is able to achieve his primary objective, show him overcoming this fear as the last obstacle in his path. The audience will be rooting for him to win as they empathize with his situation. This is especially true if the thing that he fears could cause his death, such as fire for the Scarecrow.]

Scarecrow agrees to make the journey with Dorothy, and together they dance down the Yellow Brick Road.

[The moral being, that in order to fulfill your objectives, you may have to help another achieve theirs.]

FOREST OF APPLE TREES

As Dorothy and the Scarecrow enter a forest of Apple Trees, the Witch watches them from behind a tree. When Dorothy picks an apple from one of the trees, the tree moves. It's alive. The tree grabs the apple, slaps Dorothy's hand, then reprimands her for taking the apple. Dorothy responds by saying that she's hungry.

[This scene could have been humorous. It has many of the same elements found in the scene when the Scarecrow is introduced: the surprising incongruity of a normally inanimate object that speaks. But in this instance the tree is dangerous. It slaps Dorothy. This destroys the possibility of laughter.]

The Scarecrow pulls Dorothy away, telling her that she doesn't want those apples because they have little green worms in them. He then whispers that he'll show her a way to get apples. Scarecrow makes a face at the tree. The Tree becomes angry and throws some of his apples at the Scarecrow. Dorothy and the Scarecrow retrieve the apples.

[The lesson to be learned from this scene is that when confronted with obstacles to an objective, the objective can sometimes be achieved by using intelligence and not just brute force. The irony is that the Scarecrow exhibits the intelligence and "brains" that he doesn't believe he possesses. He is not lacking brains, only the belief that he has them. In the prelude back in Kansas, the characters really don't have the attributes that they desire, but in Oz they reveal these attributes under conflict. What they all seem to lack is the realization that they already possess the qualities they desire.]

THE TIN MAN

Dorothy reaches down to pick up an apple and finds a Tin Man. He's immobile, as he stands frozen like a statue, a statuesque poise reminiscent of Hickory's stance in the farmyard. The Tin Man mumbles for the oilcan. Dorothy picks up the oilcan and squirts oil into his mouth. The Tin Man then explains that one day while chopping wood in the forest, it began to rain and he got rusted. Dorothy continues to oil his joints, stating that now he's perfect. But the Tin Man sorrowfully tells her to bang on his chest if she thinks he's perfect. She does, and it produces a hollow sound. He explains that when he was made, they forgot to give him a heart.
He sings about his dream, listing all the things that having a heart means to him. He could be human if he had a heart; tender, gentle, and sentimental, not a man of tin metal. Friend of sparrows and cupid, the boy who shoots the arrows, able to love, register emotion, jealousy, devotion, would stay young and chipper. Dorothy suggests that the Tin Man comes with them to see the Wizard and perhaps the Wizard will give him a heart.

[This is his primary objective: to have a heart. Yet his initial sorrow and grief at lacking a heart indicates his lack of realization that he already may have that which he seeks.]

WITCH IN THE FOREST

Suddenly, they hear the cackling of the Witch. Standing on a rooftop, she warns the Scarecrow and Tin Man to stay away from Dorothy and to stop helping her. She then creates a ball of fire and throws it at the Scarecrow. The Tin Man takes off his metal cap and uses it to quickly put out the fire. The Witch then disappears in a burst of orange smoke.

[This shows the audience that the characters are in jeopardy and are in danger of being destroyed. This increases the tension and heightens the sense of excitement in the audience.]

The Scarecrow overcomes his fear of fire and makes a commitment to help Dorothy get to the Emerald City, even if he doesn't get his objective (a brain). The Tin Man makes a similar commitment. Dorothy is overwhelmed by their loyalty and tells them that they are the best friends she's ever had.

[Within this scene, the virtue of friendship is introduced. Friendship means putting the interest or needs of the friend before your own, even if it places your own objectives in jeopardy. This type of behavior increases the audience's empathy for the Scarecrow and Tin Man in that they are willing to put themselves in mortal danger to help Dorothy. The audience likes those characters that display friendship and support for the protagonist for whom they have already developed empathy.]

THE COWARDLY LION

Dorothy, Scarecrow, and Tin Man fearfully enter a dark forest singing the "Lions and Tigers and Bears" song, when suddenly, a Lion jumps out from the trees. He challenges the Scarecrow and Tin Man to a fight, but when they both refuse, he runs after Toto. Dorothy picks up Toto and slaps the Lion on the nose. The Lion begins to cry and admits that he's really just a big coward. His dream is to have courage. They invite the Lion to come with them to see the Wizard, and he accepts.

[It's Dorothy who overcomes her fear and confronts the threat when Toto, the character she loves most, is threatened. The others cower in fear of the Lion. Yet through confrontation, one can transform an enemy into a friend, especially, if along the way, you can help him achieve his own objectives.]

[At this stage each of the five major characters has revealed their individual primary objectives. For Dorothy, it's to get home, the Scarecrow wants brains, the Tin Man a heart, the Lion courage, and the antagonist, the Witch, wants the ruby slippers that are in Dorothy's possession. The subgoal, getting to the Emerald City and meeting with the Wizard who will provide them with their individual objectives, has also been established.]

WITCH WITH CRYSTAL BALL

As the foursome dance through the woods, they appear within the crystal ball of the Witch. She has been watching their every movement. Since they wouldn't take her warning, she plans to stop them by poisoning the poppy fields. She states that once she has the ruby slippers, her power will be the greatest in Oz.

[This scene establishes the real objective of the Witch, which is to have absolute power in the Land of Oz. The ruby slippers are a tool to that end. This is an instance of a character pursuing a concrete object (the ruby slippers) that really represents an abstract value (absolute power). It is standard that the antagonist's objective is an object that will give them absolute power and control over the community.]

THE POPPY FIELDS

Dorothy and her three companions reach the end of the forest. In the distance, they can see the Emerald City. But in order to reach the city, they must past through a field of poppies. They start to run across the field, but before they get halfway, they start to succumb to the poison. First Toto, then Dorothy, and then the Lion collapse from the drugged poppies. Only the Tin Man and the Scarecrow remain standing since the drugs do not affect metallic or straw creatures. The Tin Man begins to cry which shows that he does have a heart. They begin to yell for help, calling out against all hope. Their cries are answered by Glenda, the good witch of the North. She makes it snow over the poppy field, and this dampens the effects of the drug. Toto, Dorothy, and the Lion awake. They all then continue on with their journey to Oz.

[The objective in this scene is to get to the Emerald City. The prime obstacles are the distance and the poison in the poppy fields. It is important to realize that in this scene, the characters do not overcome the obstacles by the powers within them, but instead by an appeal to a supernatural power. They call to Glenda for help, and she saves them.

This is common in many of these fantasy films. The will and ability of the characters are not always sufficient to overcome all obstacles, and they need help from beings beyond the human dimension.]

[A similar situation occurs with Luke Skywalker relying on the spirit of Obie-Wan Kenobi and the "force" to overcome the Empire in *Star Wars*, Indiana Jones being saved by the spirits in the Ark of the Covenant that also destroy the Nazis in *Raiders of the Lost Ark*, and Elliott with E.T. eventually being saved through the non-human powers of E.T. himself and by his extraterrestrial friends. At the end of the *The Wizard of Oz*, it is Glenda that reveals to Dorothy how to use the slippers to return to Kansas.]

The witch is angry because someone is always helping Dorothy. She grabs her broomstick and flies off the balcony towards the city of Oz. Dorothy and friends leave the poppy field, accompanied by a joyous song that celebrates their salvation.

GATE TO THE EMERALD CITY

They knock on the door to Oz. A guard appears. He has a mustache and wears a blue-green uniform. Blue and green are the magical colors of the Emerald City and are used as a visual motif. They are nature colors: possibly blue for the sky and green for the fertile earth. When Dorothy and the others request to see the Wizard, they are turned away. The Guard refuses to let them in, stating that no one gets to see the Wizard. Dorothy shows the guard the ruby slippers, and he lets them in the Emerald City.

[In this scene the objective is to enter the Emerald City, but the obstacle is a guarded locked door. They finally are allowed to enter after displaying their own magical possessions.]

INSIDE THE GATES OF THE EMERALD CITY

Dorothy and friends ride on a carriage that is pulled by the "horse of a different color." This is a case of a cliché becoming visually manifested. Dorothy, Tin Man, Scarecrow, and Lion then get primed and prepared to be presented to the Wizard. A musical number reveals how the inhabitants "laugh the day away in the merry old land of Oz."

At that very moment, the sound of the Witch cackling explodes the air. The crowd looks upward to see the Wicked Witch of the West on her broomstick writing the words, "SURRENDER DOROTHY," across the sky. The crowd panics as they run to the Wizard's house in search for an answer. They are met by the guard who tells them that the Wizard has everything under control, and that they all should go back to their homes.

[Now the whole community is placed in jeopardy because of the protagonist. This is a classic "setup" structure where terror strikes in the midst of a joyous occasion, just when the protagonist believes that the battle is won, and all is well with the world. This creates hatred in the audience for the villains since their feelings of joy have been turned to terror.]

Dorothy and companions approach the guard and tell him that they want to see the wizard. After being told to go away, they explain that this is the witch's Dorothy. The guard leaves to inform the Wizard.

GUARD BLOCKS ENTRANCE TO WIZARD'S PALACE

The Lion, anticipating that he will receive courage, sings his "Long Live the King" song. The guard returns and tells them that the Wizard says they should all go away. They all become depressed. Dorothy, in sorrow, despairs to the others that now she'll never get to see her sick Aunt Em. The guard overhears this, takes pity on them because he too also once had an Aunt Em, and lets them into the city.

[In this case, it is the guard who is the obstacle that blocks access to their objective, which is to see the Wizard. Dorothy's honesty and sincerity in expressing her motivations affects the guard and removes the obstacle. The obstacle is overcome by her sharing of a common human desire, to be with a loved one who is ill. This touches the humanity of her opposition, and the obstacle dissolves.]

INSIDE THE WIZARD'S PALACE

Dorothy, Scarecrow, Tin Man, and Lion walk down a long intimidating hallway inside the Wizard's palace. The Lion loses his courage and wants to wait outside, but the others persuade him to continue. They all hold hands and cautiously proceed. Suddenly, the Wizard's voice booms out: "Come forward!" In a large room orange flames shoot up from the floor, as the blue-green enormous disembodied head of the Wizard appears elevated above Dorothy and her companions.

[Once again all the characters feel in jeopardy, for in this scene their objectives are at risk: will the Wizard fulfill their needs? The colors of the flames alter whenever the head of the Wizard appears. This creates emotional associations within the audience. At this stage, the Wizard is meant to be a mysterious creature. The orange flames are naturally associated with the orange flames around the Wicked Witch of the West, which symbolizes high energy and power. The pink and rose color flames are natural associations with the color of Glenda's bubble. So at this stage, subconsciously, the audience is still not sure whether the Wizard is evil or good. This is the effect the filmmaker desires at this stage of the story. In the last scenes, the Wizard's flames become baby blue, which is Dorothy's color, the color of innocence.]

The Great and Powerful Wizard of Oz questions them, then explains that he knows why each of them has come to him, as the pink-rose colors of Glenda now filter in with the orange flames. The Tin Man wants a heart, the Scarecrow a brain, and the Lion wants courage. He intimidates them all, but the Lion faints when it becomes his turn. The Lion thereby physically demonstrates his lack of courage. Dorothy becomes outraged with moral indignation. This is the second time she behaves this way, the first being in the forest when confronting the Lion.

[Dorothy has a strong code of ethics which expresses itself as outrage and moral indignation when she believes that some injustice is being committed.]

She reprimands the Wizard for frightening the Lion who came to him for help. The Wizard orders her to be silent, then states that he has every intention of granting their requests. Upon hearing these words the Lion awakes. But first they must prove themselves worthy by bringing him the broomstick of the Wicked Witch of the West.

The Scarecrow (once again thinking ahead) states that they'd have to kill her to get it, and the Lion fears that she may kill them first. But, in response, the Wizard shouts that they should go! The terrified Lion runs down the hallway and jumps through a window.

[The last lines of the scene concentrate on the jeopardy and great danger involved in getting the Witch's broomstick. It may indeed be a life and death situation.]

[The structure of *The Wizard of Oz* is divided into a prelude and three acts. The prelude consists of the opening scenes shot in black and white, with Dorothy in Kansas. This introduces all the basic characters along with their individual objectives and the dramatic objective of the protagonist: to find a place where there are no problems. The first act contains Dorothy's arrival in Oz, meeting her antagonist, the Wicked Witch of the West, establishing her new objective, which is to get back home, and her primary subgoal, which is to get to the Emerald City and have the Wizard of Oz help her home. Also in this act, she meets the three companions who have their own objectives of obtaining the qualities of intelligence, compassion, and courage that will be needed for Dorothy to eventually get home ("home" being a sense of safety and security)].

[At the end of the first act, we have the first "plot twist" or what some screenwriters have called a "plot point." Accomplishing their subgoal (i.e., arriving at Oz and meeting the Wizard), they discover that this subgoal does not help them to achieve their primary objectives. This is the twist. What was expected to happen does not. Instead, they are assigned another subgoal by the Wizard: bring him the broomstick of the Wicked Witch of the West, and then he'll grant them their primary objectives. This will constitute the second act. But we know at the end of the second act, another "plot twist" will occur, because even though they bring the Wizard the broomstick, he still cannot give them what they desire.]

[The broomstick is a concrete object that Dorothy and her companions must obtain. The abstract value associated with this is "worthiness" (or having proved their "virtue" under trial). This object also intensifies the struggle, because now it becomes a matter of high danger and life or death, since they may have to kill the witch to get her broomstick. The bond between the protagonist and antagonist is now solidified even more. Dorothy has something that the Witch wants, the ruby slippers, and the Witch has something that Dorothy needs to get home, the broomstick. This foreshadows the confrontation and climax between Dorothy and the Witch and intensifies the audience's emotional involvement in the story.]

Dorothy and companions fearfully walk through a dark forest up to a sign that states: HAUNTED FOREST. WITCHES CASTLE 1 MILE. I'D TURN BACK IF I WERE YOU.

[Establishes that the characters are in extreme jeopardy.]

Lion reads this sign and immediately tries to run away. He growls but then is frightened by two owls. He starts to leave but is picked up by the Tin Man and Scarecrow and turned around. They talk about spooks. The Tin Man asserts that he doesn't believe in spooks. Suddenly he is lifted up into the air, then dropped from the heights and hits the ground with a clang. The Lion, terrorized, closes his eyes and prays: "I do believe in spooks, I do, I do!"

[Establishes danger from the supernatural-mysterious unseen forces that can do harm. This heightens the audience's state of excitement.]

INTERCUT - WITCHES CASTLE

The forest scene is displayed in the Witch's crystal ball. She cackles with glee then orders her flying Monkeys to attack the group, capture Dorothy, and bring back the ruby slippers. The winged monkeys, dressed in blue-red uniforms, jump off the balcony and fly across the sky.

They attack the group in the forest, tear up the Scarecrow, then fly away with Dorothy and Toto.

[The antagonist succeeds in accomplishing her subgoal: getting Dorothy with the ruby slippers. Now she must get the ruby slippers from Dorothy. Traditionally, the second act belongs to the antagonist. In these scenes, the Witch has most of the victories and holds the dominant position.]

The Tin Man and Lion try to put the Scarecrow back together, while having a bit of humorous dialogue.
Tin Man: "That's you all over."
Lion: "Sure knocked the stuffings out of you."

[Here is an example of using humor to relieve tension after a terrifying scene. The audience needs to relax and laugh, especially since Dorothy, the character for whom they have the most empathy, has just been carried off to her doom. The comments of the Tin Man and the Lion are "surprising deviations from normal patterns of social behavior," for one doesn't joke about a friend who has just been torn apart, unless, as in this case, the damage is easy to repair and no real harm was done.]

WITCH'S CASTLE

The Witch holds Toto in her hands, then, she places him in a basket as she speaks with Dorothy. This is reminiscent of the earlier scene when Elmira Gulch placed Toto in a basket. The Witch offers to trade Toto for the Ruby Slippers. Dorothy refuses. The Witch then tells her winged-monkey to take the basket and throw it into the river and drown the dog. Dorothy relents and tells the Witch that she can have the slippers.

[This is an example of using a "prop" (in this case, Toto) to reveal the emotional conflict within a character. The audience clearly knows how Dorothy feels about Toto, and they empathize with her.]
[The protagonist is forced to make a decision between two things that she values: the life of the faithful dog she loves, or the slippers that Glenda said would protect her from the Witch. She chooses the life of her faithful companion and, thereby, places her own life in jeopardy. It is in these

situations, when characters are forced to choose between objects of value, that the true nature of the person is revealed (i.e., their value system with its priorities).]

The Witch tries to take the slippers from Dorothy, but as she reaches down for the shoes, she receives an electrical shock. The Witch remembers that the shoes will never come off Dorothy as long as she is alive. She then decides to kill Dorothy. Her only concern is that the murder be done delicately, so as not to destroy the power of the ruby slippers.

[This is a standard value system of the antagonist; ruthless disregard for human life when it's an obstacle to their objective. In her lust for absolute power, the Witch will kill anyone who stands in her way.]

Toto jumps from the basket and runs out of the room. The Witch orders the monkey after the dog. Toto runs down the staircase, over the drawbridge, then jumps to the other side of the embankment. Dorothy cries with joy at his escape.

[Another standard value of the protagonist is joy at seeing a friend survive, even if they themselves are doomed]

The Witch fumes with anger and turns over an hourglass that is filled with red sand. She tells Dorothy that she'll die when the sands run through the hourglass. The background music plays a mocking version of "Over the Rainbow," as if laughing at the prospects of an ideal world that's problem free. The red sand in the hourglass trickles away, a metaphor that possibly foreshadows the flow of Dorothy's blood from her body when she dies.

[The hourglass is a case of the "ticking clock" technique that increases suspense in the audience. They know that when the time runs out, the protagonist will be killed. They become anxious for her and hope for her rescue before it's too late.]

DOROTHY-AUNT EM-CRYSTAL BALL

Dorothy despairs and is filled with remorse that she ever left home. Without hope, she cries out to her Aunt Em in desperation: "I'm frightened Auntie Em. I'm frightened."
Within the crystal ball an image of Dorothy's Aunt Em appears, calling out Dorothy's name. Dorothy tries to communicate with her Aunt, but the image is then transformed into the mocking cackling face of the Wicked Witch of the West. Dorothy's face becomes filled with terror, and the

scene ends with a shot of the red sands sifting down through the hourglass.

[This is an extremely effective technique that creates empathy for the protagonist and hatred for the antagonist. Here, in a moment of privacy, Dorothy, in despair, reveals her deepest fears to a person she most trusts, only to have that confession ridiculed by the witch. This can be generalized: have the villain destroy the protagonist's last bit of hope in a mocking, contemptuous manner. This invasion of privacy and the last stripping away of human dignity irreversibly solidifies the audience's empathy for Dorothy and hatred for the Witch.]

HAUNTED FOREST

Toto climbs down a steep mountain slope then runs into the haunted forest. There he meets up again with the Lion, Tin Man, and Scarecrow. They follow Toto to find Dorothy. They climb back up the mountain slope from which Toto had just descended. From behind some boulders they watch the guards in front of the Castle of the Wicked Witch of the West.

[Here the characters have to overcome a series of obstacles in the natural world to reach their new subgoal: save Dorothy. While overcoming these obstacles, they display the very qualities that were their primary objectives. The Tin Man displays compassion as he cries when he thinks about Dorothy in the Witch's castle. The Scarecrow displays brains as he plans to get into the castle to save Dorothy. The Lion displays courage by committing to go into the castle, even though he may not come out alive. He is still frightened and would like his friends to talk him out of it, but he doesn't run away from the fight. They always had the qualities that they desired. They just needed the right situations, the right conflicts, through which these qualities could be expressed. When they forget about themselves, their own personal objectives, and commit to help another character in need, they then manifest the qualities they desire.]

HOURGLASS

[A shot of the sand running through the hourglass creates suspense. This reminds the audience that time is running out, which increases their tension. The audience wonders if they will have enough time to get into the castle to save Dorothy for this is really a do or die situation. Again, an example of how the "ticking clock" functions within a story.]

MOUNTAINSIDE

Suddenly, the Scarecrow, Tin Man, and Lion are attacked by three of the Witch's guards. After a brief scuffle, Dorothy's friends emerge victorious. They dress up in the guards' uniforms then quickly walk down the mountainside. They join the end of the line of guards as the guards cross over the drawbridge and enter the castle. The Lion, with long tail swaying out from under the uniform, brings up the rear.

[The filmmaker creates as many obstacles as possible for characters to overcome in their efforts to obtain an objective. Whatever can go wrong must go wrong. In this sequence, in order to save Dorothy, they must put the Scarecrow back together, climb the side of a steep mountain, overcome three attacking guards, and deceive a company of guards in order to gain entrance to the Witch's castle.]

INSIDE CASTLE

Toto leads the Tin Man, Scarecrow, and Lion up the stairs to the room in which Dorothy is held captive. They call out to Dorothy, and she responds. The hourglass is almost empty. This increases the suspense because the audience knows that the Witch will soon return. The Tin Man uses his ax to chop open the door.

[The door is another obstacle to their goal.]

They take off the uniforms, unite with Dorothy, and run down the staircase. Suddenly, the castle gate slams shut, and the air is filled with the cackling laughter of the Witch. They are trapped within her fortress. They are all surrounded by the Witch's guards. The Witch taunts them then throws the hourglass to the ground. It bursts into flames at their feet.

[This is a great use of prop to convey information. It was established that when the sands run out Dorothy will be killed. The destruction of the hourglass by the Witch signifies that the time for death has come!]

But once again, the Scarecrow, using his intelligence, devises a plan. He eyes the rope that holds up the chandelier filled with lit candles, then quickly uses the Tin Man's ax to cut the rope. The chandelier falls onto the guards as Dorothy and friends make their escape. They are chased by the remainder of the Witch's guards.
[The capture and death of the protagonist also cannot be achieved easily. He must exhaust all possible options to escape.]

CASTLE BATTLEMENTS

Dorothy and friends run along the battlements. They are chased by guards coming from two different directions. Finally, they are cornered and surrounded. Once again, the Witch taunts them.
Witch: "The last to go will see the first three to go before her, and her little dog, too!"

[Important to make the villain as vicious and as mean as possible. Right down to the last moment, the antagonist displays no mercy. Mercy is never one of the villain's qualities. The audience nows hates her and feels that her death is justified.]

The Witch takes her broomstick and places the bristles into the flame of a nearby torch. This ignites the bristles which she then uses to set the Scarecrow's arm on fire. It bursts into flames. In order to save her friend, Dorothy picks up a nearby bucket of water and throws it on the Scarecrow's arm. Her objective here is to put out the flames, not to kill the Witch. But the Witch is standing in front of the Scarecrow's arm and gets splashed with the water. The Witch then utters one of the classic lines of cinema.
"Ahhh, you cursed brat, look what you've done. I'm melting, I'm melting. Ahhh, what a world, what a world. Who would have thought that a little girl like you could destroy my beautiful wickedness."
She then melts, and dissolves into a puddle. Toto sniffs among her remaining black cape but finds nothing underneath.

[This is the second death caused by Dorothy. By helping her friend survive, she accidentally destroyed their enemy. The character thereby retains "innocence" in the destruction of the antagonist. In order for the audience to accept a protagonist killing another human being, a strong case must be visually made that the antagonist is deserving of death. If not, the audience will reject the protagonist. Killing an enemy in order to save the life of a loyal friend is acceptable, especially if that enemy is intent on killing you. So, in order to maintain Dorothy's quality of girlish innocence, the witch's death is an unintended consequence of her attempt to save the life of a friend.]

[The death of the antagonist often is not the result of a direct action of the protagonist, but instead on the unintended consequence of something that the antagonist himself does in the climax scene. This case, of the Witch setting the Scarecrow's arm on fire, is one example. Belloc performing Hebrew rituals over the Ark of the Covenant in *Raiders of the Lost Ark* is another, the Green-Goblin intending to have his vehicle impale Spider-

Man, and the Joker's fall to his death because of the weight of the gargoyle tied to his foot in *Batman*.]

The guards kneel before Dorothy. They are overjoyed at the Witch's death, for it releases them from bondage. They salute Dorothy. She requests the Witch's broomstick, which the guards happily give her.

[They have accomplished the second major subgoal of the story: get the broomstick of the Wicked Witch of the West. They also accomplished this while retaining fundamental human values of loyalty to friends and being willing to put oneself in danger and self-sacrifice to help a friend in distress.]

GREAT HALL OF THE WIZARD

Dorothy and friends return to the Wizard. They present him with the broomstick, and he congratulates them for "liquidating" the Witch. They request that he fulfill his promise. The Wizard commands that they all go away and come back tomorrow. The Scarecrow replies that the Wizard has had plenty of time already, to which the Wizard repeats out that they should come back tomorrow. The flames are the color blue. The orange color, symbolic of the Witch, has disappeared. Dorothy, again with righteous moral indignation, tells him that, if he were really great and powerful, he'd keep his promises.

Toto runs to the corner of the room and pulls back a soft blue curtain to reveal a man who resembles Professor Marvel. He is pulling levers on a mechanical apparatus; the technology behind the facade of magic. He confesses that he's the Wizard of Oz.

Disappointed, Dorothy tells him that he's a "very bad man." He protests, explaining that he's a good man, but a terrible wizard. Dorothy demands that he keeps his promise, which he does. To the Scarecrow, who desires brains, he gives a diploma, to the Tin Man, who desires a heart, he gives a testimonial, and to the Lion, who desires courage, he gives a medal.

[The Wizard doesn't give any of them the quality itself, but only an object that symbolizes or represents the public recognition that the character does possess this quality. It was the characters themselves who manifested the desired qualities during the conflict situations. They always had them, they just had to realize that they possessed them. All the Wizard could do is help them realize this through public acknowledgment.]
For Dorothy, the Wizard responds that the only way to get her home is for him to take her there himself. The Wizard reveals that he's an old Kansas

man himself, a balloonist, who one day floated down into the land of Oz and accepted the job as Wizard. He'll take her back in his balloon.

[This is the completion of the second major subgoal, and it also ends in a "plot twist," because although they brought back the Witch's broomstick, they did not achieve their individual objectives in the manner expected.]

THE WIZARD'S BALLOON

A gigantic hot air balloon sits in the center of Emerald City. A large crowd, dressed in blues and greens, surround the balloon. Within a gold-green basket (perhaps the end of the yellow brick road) stands the Wizard and Dorothy, with Toto in her arms. The Wizard makes a speech in which he tells the residents that while he's away, the Scarecrow, by virtue of his brain, the Tin Man, by virtue of his heart, and the Lion, by virtue of his courage, shall rule Oz.

Toto sees a cat being held in the arms of one of the residents and jumps out of Dorothy's arms. Dorothy jumps out of the basket in order to get Toto. Suddenly, the ropes holding the balloon become loose and the balloon drifts away. Dorothy calls out to the Wizard to wait for her, but he explains that he can't control the balloon. He waves goodbye as he floats away. Dorothy is depressed. She depended on the Wizard to get her back to Kansas. Now that he's gone she'll never get home. Suddenly, the Scarecrow looks up to the sky and points to Glenda floating downward within her rose-colored bubble.

Dorothy asks Glenda for her help, but Glenda replies that she doesn't need to be helped any longer, and that she has always had the power to go back to Kansas. Glenda didn't tell Dorothy before because "she wouldn't have believed me." She had to find out for herself.
"What have you learned, Dorothy," asks the Tin Man. "Well, I think that it wasn't enough to want to see Uncle Henry and Aunt Em, and that if I ever go looking for my hearts desire again, I won't look any further than my own back yard, because if it isn't there, I never really lost it to begin with. Is that right?"
"That's all there is. You had to find that out for yourself. Now those magic slippers will take you home in two seconds," says Glenda.
Dorothy says goodbye to her friends. Tin Man now knows that he has a heart because it's breaking. The Lion never would have found courage if it wasn't for Dorothy. Dorothy will miss the Scarecrow most of all. Glenda: "Close your eyes, tap heels together three times, and think to yourself, "There's no place like home, there's no place like home."

[This is the resolution of the OZ section of the story. Here all problems are resolved, and all conflicts end. It ends with the message that "there's no place like home." This in itself should make it obvious why the film is a classic and in perpetual demand. It's the type of film that parents will always want to see with their young children, if for nothing else, but this important message. As long as the humans survive, and there are parents with children, *The Wizard of Oz* will always be one experience that parents will want to share with their children.]

DOROTHY RETURNS HOME

Dorothy re-enters the vortex of the falling house and ends up back in her bed in Kansas mumbling, "there's no place like home." Aunt Em places a cold compress on her head. Dorothy wakes up and sits up in the bed. Uncle Henry comes to her bedside. Professor Marvel comes to the open window. Dorothy tries to tell them about her adventure in Oz, but they all interpret it as a dream. Then Hunk, Hickory and Zeke come to her bedside. Toto jumps up to Dorothy.
Dorothy: "But anyway, Toto, we're home, home. And this is my place. And you're all here. And I'm not going to leave home ever, ever again, because I love you all, and, Auntie Em, THERE'S NO PLACE LIKE HOME."

THE END

In Logic, there is a method often used to prove the truth of a proposition called, "Reductio Ad Absurbdum." It uses the assumption that for every proposition, either it is true or its negation is true. You assume the truth of the negation of the proposition that you want to prove, then demonstrate that the negation leads to a contradiction and, therefore cannot really be true. Since for every proposition, either it is true, or it's negation is true, and we've just shown that the negation is false, we've proven the original proposition to be true.

The *The Wizard of Oz* can be interpreted to follow a similar process.

To prove the premise:
THERE IS NO PLACE LIKE HOME.
Assume the negation:
THERE IS A BETTER PLACE OVER THE RAINBOW.
Demonstrate:
WORST PROBLEMS COULD EXIST OVER THE RAINBOW.
Therefore:
THERE IS NO PLACE LIKE HOME.

Dorothy's dramatic objective is the security of a home where there are no problems. Being at home, surrounded by people who love you, normally provides one with a sense of safety.

But there is jeopardy in almost every scene of the story. Either Dorothy is in danger, or someone she loves, such as Toto or the Scarecrow. These are all life-and-death situations. It is this constant jeopardy that keeps the audience engrossed in the action.

Another motif in this story is the joy and happiness the characters share along the road of life. They have fun while on their quest. These are characters with whom the audience enjoys spending time. They are humorous and good-natured. They display loyalty to each other while pursuing their individual objectives. Dorothy especially displays the traits of decency, kindness, generosity, fairness, obliging when another is in need, and doing what is right.

It may ultimately be true that others cannot give you what you desire; they may only be able to help you obtain it. This may be the true message of the Wizard's inability to give the characters what they want. Ultimately, each character has to accomplish his objective on his own and can't expect another to give it to him.

Dorothy, Lion, Tin Man, and Scarecrow all suffer from the same basic problem: a lack of confidence in themselves and the understanding that they already possess those attributes that they seek. They just need the right situations or conflicts under which these qualities will become manifest. The power of belief-in-self will help you solve your problems and get you wherever you want to go, even home, if it is accompanied by intelligence, compassion, and courage. Belief-in-self is also that which those who wish to control and have power over you, must steal.

This is the value associated with the **RUBY SLIPPERS: THE POWER OF BELIEF-IN-SELF**. This is not "blind self-confidence," but the belief that one has the ability to solve his problems and accomplish that which he sets out to do. And it is this that the Witch hopes to steal from Dorothy. Her objective is to gain control of the Ruby Slippers, which will give her the ultimate power, the power over others belief in themselves. It doesn't matter whether you are in a "dream" or "reality." The values that you utilize when dealing with others under extraordinary conditions are what's important. There will always be new experiences, new environments, and new conditions of life. To be grounded in reality throughout these alterations means to live according to a set of principles of interpersonal behavior that will sustain life.

STORY STRUCTURES in MEGAHIT MOVIES

Chicago

Shrek

Shrek 2

Spider-Man

Spider-Man 2

Pirates of the Caribbean

Finding Nemo

Monsters, Inc.

Bruce Almighty

The Matrix Trilogy

The Passion of the Christ

Harry Potter and The Sorcerer's Stone

Harry Potter and The Prisoner of Azkaban

The Lord of the Rings Trilogy

CHICAGO

Who is the protagonist of *Chicago*?

Roxie. Roxie Hart. What is Roxie's dream? To be a famous dancer. To live the life of Velma Kelly. To be a nightclub dancer and to be as famous as Velma Kelly. How many minutes into the movie do we see her dream? About 3 to 5 minutes into the movie we see the protagonist and her dream. Roxie is standing in the audience as she watches Velma perform on stage. Then we have a fantasy image of Roxie imagining that she was up there...that she is Velma.

This is the standard Hollywood structure for popular movies. The audience has to know the dream-motivation of the protagonist as soon as possible, inside the first five pages. Then, Roxie restates her dream when Fred Casey pulls her out of the club. They were in the club to meet someone who would help Roxie get on stage. That is her primary objective throughout the film: to become a famous popular night club performer, and through many twists and turns, that is what she finally achieves in the closing scene.

Who is the antagonist of the movie?

Not Velma, nor the court? In some ways, Roxie is her own antagonist. She stands in her own way. But the real antagonist of this movie is the people of Chicago. That is why the movie is called *Chicago*. It is the people that Roxie must finally triumph over. Yes, the court is a representative of the people, but what Roxie wants is to become famous...to have the people love her...and for that she does anything. Velma is part of the problem in the first act; an obstacle that Roxie must overcome. But in the end, Velma becomes Roxie's partner to help her triumph over the people of Chicago. Roxie wants to be popular.

Fame is what Roxie wants, and it is the fickleness of fame that Roxie has to deal with. She wins her court case by lying, but as soon as she is found innocent, and another woman murders some man on the street, Roxie is off the front page. She was hoping that the court victory would be a boost to her dancing career, but when she auditions in the next scene, she is rejected. She is just another woman who murdered a man.

Billy Flynn is a protagonist supporter. He helps Roxie defeat the people of Chicago in court. So while he is corrupt, he is not the antagonist.

The best way to analyze this story and to construct any story is to start with a character that has a dream-goal then create as many obstacles as possible to achieving that goal. Some characters will help her, some will block her, and some will switch sides and back again, as they do in this movie. Then, see how your character changes when reacting to the oppositions to her goal. Roxie did go through lots of changes; lying and cheating all the way to the top. Yet, the final scene is of the two man killers (Roxie and Velma) celebrating their fame in a dance hall where the audience, the people of Chicago, applaud.

All that jazz....

This is truly classic structure simply set against a musical, in fact, the plot continues through the musical numbers. But Roxie has one goal and never loses sight of it. Within the first ten pages, you have to get the audience to care about the protagonist. They have to have empathy for the protagonist. How do they do this for Roxie? She's being used by Fred. They have a scene in which Fred Casey admits that he was lying to her and just using her for sex. He did not value her dream or talents. This is also the inciting event of the movie; this is what changes her whole life, because in her moment of rage, she shoots him.

Yet it is this killing that in an ironic way helps her achieve her real goal: FAME. There is another scene which reinforces the empathy for Roxy. It is the musical number done by the six women on death row; the "He got what he deserved" musical sequence.

Roxie is an outcast in prison; the women don't accept her into their circle. The switch comes when she gets Billy Flynn to be her lawyer. All the women want Billy to be their lawyer. The values promoted in this movie are all very corrupt. Roxie does what she has to do to survive in a world that is corrupt.

Then, there is loyal Amos, the devoted husband, who becomes the patsy for all the other characters. Amos nearly destroys the audience's empathy for Roxie. But it was the music and the dancing that kept us entertained by her...the Razzle Dazzle! Without music and dance, the audience would not have been entertained, and the movie would not have been that successful in the box-office. It would have been a dark Film Noir story with limited audience appeal.

Nothing comes easy for Roxie. Just when she thinks she has it made, another major obstacle is thrown in her path. Every victory is followed by a defeat. Just when Roxie thinks she has the complete attention of Billy, an heiress does a triple murder and takes him away. How does Roxie deal with that? She fakes being pregnant for the sympathy it will bring. She wins the hearts of the people of Chicago.

Billy Flynn's fickle nature mirrors the public's fickle nature. Billy is the perfect representative of the heart and soul of Chicago. He is as fickle as fame itself.

The story is filled with plot twists. Morton's reversal is one. She even dyes her hair blonde and has it cut like Roxie's. Morton changes because she believes Roxy has dropped her, but at the end we find out that the diary was part of Billy's plan. Billy sent it to Morton to give to Velma so that Billy could use the diary to get both Velma and Roxy off. Then, the plot twist comes when Roxy wins her court case and she is blown off the front page of the newspapers. Achieving the subgoal does not get her what she thought it would. We also have the twist that she has to accept Velma's help to become famous, even though they hate each other.

Many story twists, but the primary objective always stayed the same. Roxy wanted to be famous...adored by the people of Chicago...her face on the Front Page, no matter what she had to do to get there.

To get the motivation expressed early in the story you have to drop the back story. The back story should only be told if something in the character's past causes problems for the character when they try to obtain their goal. Roxie doesn't tell her own back story until way into act two when she is trying to put together her act. We never hear her real back story: just the past year or so. It is the sequence when she is dressed in silver and dances on the stage alone while telling the audience about her past. But we know all we need to know about Roxie's character by the time she sets up her husband to take the fall. We don't have to know all the facts about her past...just her present character. Roxy will say and do whatever has to be done to get what she wants. Billy Flynn doesn't change that character, he just provides her with new material: new stories that will help her win her trial.

The first ten minutes of a good script should have four core scenes: introduce the Antagonist in 3 pages; introduce the Protagonist in 3 pages; show the protagonist's dream-goal, and the inciting event. In act one and act two you take more time to develop the characters and story, but start the script with a bang. *Chicago* opens with Velma's Dance scene, Roxie's Dream scene, police coming in for Velma, further development of Roxie, then Roxie killing Fred Casey.

The character arc for Roxie is all downhill: from bad to worst, except that she finally accepts the friendship and offer of help from Velma. Once she does that, together they conquer the people of Chicago.

Chicago is *All That Jazz*! Razzle-dazzle and fancy foot work with the moral being, as Morton says, "Truth is the fastest way to the Death House."

Chicago did not become a megahit movie because of the values that the movie promoted. This is not a family movie; not the type of film that parents will take their children to see. It lost a large segment of the market and repeat audience potential. But the producers probably knew that going into the project. It was a successful stage play that they chose to make into a feature film. $170 million dollar box-office gross is very good, but it is still $80 million short of the $250 million needed to become a megahit movie.

SHREK

Unique Object: The Swamp (Shrek's Home)
Protagonist: Shrek
Antagonist: Lord Farquaard
Love Interest: Princess Fiona
Protagonist-Supporter: Donkey

"Once upon a time there was an enchanted princess who lived in the top of a castle tower, guarded by a fire-breathing dragon, waiting to be saved by her true love's first kiss," Shrek reads from a Fairy Tale book.

Shrek, the big green ogre, rips this page from the fairy tale book and uses it as toilet paper. This shows his contempt for fairy tales. Shrek leaves the outhouse and takes his morning mud bath. Shrek paints a sign: OGRE – BEWARE! Shrek eats his breakfast.

Villagers wander through the countryside. They light their torches and head for Shrek's swamp. He hears them coming. They plan their attack, with Shrek standing behind them. When they notice him, he tells them what he is about to do to them. The Ogre roars. The villagers scream. "This is the part where you run away," says Shrek. The villagers run for their lives. Shrek picks up a piece of paper; a poster on which is written "Wanted: Fairy Tale Creatures."

In a camp in the forest, bounty hunters are bringing FairyTale creatures to the soldiers. A witch is captured. Pinocchio protests that he is really a boy, but his nose grows, proving him a liar. An old lady drags her donkey to the table and tells the soldier that it is a talking donkey. But the donkey refuses to talk. The donkey is hit on the head with a cannister that breaks and fairy dust falls over him. He begins to fly. He talks as he rises up into the air. When the fairy dust disperses, he falls to the ground. The soldiers try to grab him, but the donkey runs away into the forrest.

Donkey runs into Shrek. Soldiers follow and try to arrest them by the order of Lord Farquaard. Shrek scares off the soldiers. Donkey wants to be friends with Shrek. He follows him and sings to him. They climb over a hill and see a house in the swamp: Shrek's home. Shrek likes his privacy. Shrek allows Donkey to stay for one night, but not inside, outside.

Shrek eats his dinner. He pulls wax out of his ear and uses it as a candle. Donkey watches from the window. Suddenly, three blind mice start walking on Shrek's table. He tries to get rid of them. Dwarves place a coffin holding Snow White on the table. "Dead broad off the table," yells

Shrek. There is a wolf in Shrek's bed. His swamp is filled with Fairy Tale creatures. Shrek yells at them to get out. They were forced to come to the swamp because Lord Farquaard evicted them from their lands. Shrek vows to go to Farquaard and get them their homes back so that he will be left alone in his swamp. Donkey goes with him.

This is the Inciting Event: Fairy Tale Creatures invade Shrek's Swamp. His primary objective is now to safeguard his home and get back his privacy. To accomplish this, he must go to Lord Farquaard and persuade him to give the Fariy Tale creatures their homes back.

Lord Farquaard (the short) enters the torture chamber where the Gingerbread Man lies with his legs broken off. "Who is hiding the fairies?" demands Farquaard. "Do you know the muffin man?" sings the Gingerbread Man. A guard comes into the room carrying the magic mirror. Farquaard asks the mirror whether this is not the most perfect kingdom of them all. The mirror replies that it is not yet a kingdom, because he is not a King, since he is not married to a princess. But that can be easily fixed. The mirror gives him a choice of three bachelorettes: Cinderella, Snow White, and Princess Fiona. Farquaard chooses Princess Fiona. The mirror tries to tell him what happens to her after dark, but Farquaard orders the mirror to remain silent! He plans to hold a tournament to find a knight, who will bring him back his princess. Lord Farquaard's primary objective is to become a King. To accomplish this, he must achieve the subgoal of marrying a princess. To marry a princess, he must find a knight who will free Princess Fiona from the dragon.

Donkey and Shrek approach DuLoc, the castle of Lord Farquaard. The streets are empty. It is too quiet. Donkey goes to an Information Booth and opens the door. "It's a Perfect Place" song plays. Trumpets sound. Shrek and Donkey head toward the town square where Farquaard is making a speech. He sees Shrek and orders the knights to kill him. The fight begins, and Shrek beats up all the knights. The crowd roars to celebrate Shrek's victory. Farquaard names Shrek his champion. Shrek wants his swamp back. They make a deal. If Shrek brings him the princess, he gets the deed to the swamp.

Shrek and Donkey journey to the Enchanted Castle. They walk through a field of sunflowers. Shrek says that he is layered, like an onion. They argue. They climb up the side of a mountain that smells like brimstone. In front of them they see a black castle surrounded by a river of red lava below a wooden rope bridge that leads to the castle. Donkey is afraid. They walk across the bridge, and Shrek tricks Donkey into overcoming his fears. They enter the castle.

Shrek puts on a helmet with a face mask and searches for the princess while Donkey looks for the dragon. Donkey meets the eye of the dragon…the fire breathing dragon. He screams and runs away. The dragon corners Donkey, but Shrek grabs the dragon by the tail. The dragon tosses Shrek up into the air. He lands in the tower room of Princess Fiona. She pretends to be asleep. Fiona puckers her lips expecting to be kissed. Instead, Shrek shakes her to wake her. Shrek then drags her down the tower steps. She protests all along the way.

The dragon roars. Shrek leaves Fiona to rescue Donkey. During the action, the dragon mistakenly kisses Shrek's butt. The chained chandelier falls around the dragon's neck. The chase is on! Shrek, Donkey, and Fiona run for their lives while being chased by the fire-breathing dragon. They run across the bridge. The dragon sets the bridge on fire. It collapses. Donkey almost falls to his death but Shrek saves him. The dragon leaps across the bridge but is restrained by the chain around his neck Shrek, Donkey and Fiona make it to safety on the other side of the abyss, while the dragon cries.

Fiona thanks them for rescuing her. She wants Shrek to remove his mask and kiss her. She is filled with romantic thoughts and thinks that Shrek is her true love. Shrek and Donkey laugh. Shrek explains that he just came to get her for Lord Farquaard. Shrek takes off the helmet, and Fiona sees that he is an Ogre. She is disappointed. "I am supposed to be rescued by a prince," says Fiona. Shrek picks her up and carries her away toward DuLoc.

Donkey and Shrek make "size" jokes about Lord Farquaard. It is getting dark. Fiona demands that they make camp for the night. Fiona hides in a cave. Shrek and Donkey lie outside and look at the stars. Shrek tells stories about the characters in the stars. Shrek tells Donkey that there is no we! After this is over, Shrek is going back to his swamp alone! Shrek wants to keep everyone out, because the world has always rejected him. Fiona hears all of this from her cave.

Lord Farquaard is in his bedroom. He tells the mirror to show him Princess Fiona again.

Fiona comes out of her cave and sings to a blue bird. When she hits a very high note, the blue bird explodes. Fiona then takes the bird's eggs and cooks them. She makes breakfast for Shrek and Donkey. They walk toward DuLoc. Shrek burps. Fiona burps, too. Robin Hood swings from the trees and sweeps Fiona away. He announces that he has saved Fiona from the Ogre. He is Robin Hood. He introduces his Merry Men who do a song and dance routine. Robin Hood gets punched in the face. Fiona uses her martial arts techniques to defeat Robin and his men. Shrek gets an arrow stuck in his butt. Fiona tells Donkey to find a blue flower with red thorns. Finally, Fiona pulls out the arrow. Donkey faints.

Shrek, Fiona, and Donkey continue on their journey. Finally they see DuLoc in the distance. Fiona doesn't want to reach the castle, so she stalls. She says that Donkey does not look well, and that they should all stay where they are for the evening. Donkey agrees. Shrek cooks them a dinner. The sun begins to set. Fiona goes into the nearby cabin for the night. Donkey and Shrek talk about Shrek's feelings for Fiona.

Donkey goes into the cabin looking for Fiona. When he finds her, he sees that she has transformed into a fat ugly ogre-like creature. This is a surprise plot twist. It happens to her every night since a witch cast a spell on her when she was a child. This is not how a princess is supposed to look. Only true love's kiss can break the spell!

Shrek overhears the conversation, but misunderstands. He thinks that Fiona is saying that he is too ugly to love. Shrek turns and walks away.

In the morning, Fiona is debating with herself about whether she should tell Shrek she loves him: "Tell him, tell him not!" Fiona comes out of the cabin and approaches Shrek. He is angry because of the misunderstanding. "Who could love a hideous, ugly beast!" says Shrek.

Lord Farquaard rides up. Shrek turns Fiona over to him and takes the deed to the swamp. Farquaard laughs. "It's not like the Ogre has feelings!" Fiona accepts Lord Farquaard's proposal and rides away with him. Shrek argues with Donkey, telling him that he lives alone. Shrek rejects Donkey.

Montage of Shrek and Fiona separated as she prepares for her wedding, and he lives alone. This is the end of act two, with the classic desperation sequence in which the hero's cause seems hopeless. The love interest is in the possession of the antagonist, and it appears that there is no way that the protagonist can win her back. The "Hallelujah Song" plays over the montage. Dragon and Donkey also meet again.
Donkey makes a wall in the center of the swamp. He argues with Shrek, saying that half the swamp is his since he went on the journey to get the princess. Donkey calls Shrek "Onion Boy." Fiona was not calling you ugly," says Donkey. Donkey forgives Shrek, and Shrek forgives Donkey. They are friends. They remember the wedding. Donkey whistles for the dragon that swoops down and flies them to LuDoc.

The marriage ceremony between Lord Farquaard and Fiona is taking place.

Shrek and Donkey go to the church door. Donkey tells the dragon to wait until he whistles for her. Donkey says that they have to wait for the right moment when Shrek should run in and say, "I object!" Shrek throws Donkey up into the sky so that he can see through the church window. Donkey realizes that it is too late. Shrek drops him and runs into the church. Shrek runs down the aisle screaming "I object!!!"
"Now you want to talk?" says Fiona. Shrek shouts out that Lord Farquaard is not her true love! He just wants to marry her in order to become King!" Lord Farquaard and the people in the church laugh at Shrek. Farquaard tells Fiona to kiss him. She stops, as she sees the setting sun. It transforms her into the ugly ogre-like creature. Farquaard is repulsed by the sight of her. He orders his guards to take her and Shrek away. A fight starts up. Donkey whistles for the dragon, which flies through the church window and swallows Lord Farquaard. Dragon spits out his crown.

"I love you," Shrek says to Fiona. They kiss. Fiona is lifted up into a swirling vortex of magic dust. She is transformed and then gently falls down to the floor. Shrek goes to her side. She has not changed. She is still the plump little green ogre. This is another surprise twist in the story.
"I was supposed to become beautiful," says Fiona.
"You are beautiful," says Shrek.

Resolution Scene: Big party in the swamp. Everyone is singing and dancing, including the Gingerbread Man and Donkey with Dragon.
This is the standard resolution scene in which the community celebrates the triumph of the protagonist and love interest: Shrek and Princess Fiona. But the celebration is made unique by the antics of the Fairy Tale creatures. But, in the end, "They live happily ever after."

THE END

SHREK 2

Logline
Shrek 2 (a.k.a. The Princess Fiona Story)
"Meeting the Parents meets The Magic Kingdom"
"The Trials and Tribulations of the Ogres' First Year of Marriage"
"How I Learned I Married an Ogre and How I Learned to Love the Ogre I Married"

Theme
You must be willing to make changes for the one you love (Shrek), but if you really love someone, you must accept them as they are (Fiona).

Introduction of the Antagonist
Prince Charming rides through the rain and blazing sun, storming the castle to get to the top and rescue the fair maiden. He is the bravest and most handsome knight of all. He will win his bride with a kiss. But there is no sign of Princess Fiona, nor a fire-breathing dragon. Instead, there is a wolf in a granny gown, who tells him that Fiona is on her honeymoon at the Gingerbread House. Surprise twist: the stereotypical Prince Charming does not get to kiss the sleeping princess.

Introduction of the Protagonist, Love Interest, and Protagonist-Supporter
The sequence begins with a montage of Shrek and Fiona on their honeymoon. Back in the swamp, Shrek carries Fiona over the threshold, only to find Donkey sitting in the living room chair, singing a song expressing his loneliness. He has left home because his Dragon love has been too moody. Donkey doesn't want to leave. Shrek says that he and Fiona are now a married couple and want to be alone. This is the protagonist's primary motivation and dream. When Donkey finally lives the cottage, he finds more guests on the front lawn.

Inciting Event
A royal page, accompanied by heralds with trumpets, invites them to a royal ball being held by the King and Queen, Fiona's father and mother. Fiona and Donkey want to go, but Shrek believes it is a bad idea and refuses. The next morning, they embark on their journey in an Onion carriage. This is the inciting event which changes their lives and starts them on the journey to the magic kingdom to become part of the family. There is now a conflict of primary objectives. Shrek wants to stay at home with his wife while Fiona wants to visit her parents.

Fairy Tale creatures run into Shrek's home to house sit as Shrek, Fiona and Donkey embark on the journey to the magical kingdom of Far, Far, Away. They travel through mountains, rain, snow, and the wilderness. Since this is a transition scene, the scenery needs to be visually diverse in order to keep the audience from getting bored. Shrek is not happy and has to deal with Donkey's incessant talking and his annoying question: "Are we there yet?" The straw that finally breaks the Ogre's back is Donkey's "popping of his lips."

They finally reach their destination, and the kingdom is as wonderful as anyone can imagine. When Shrek and Fiona step out of the carriage, the crowd is aghast and becomes silent. They were expecting Prince Charming and Princess Fiona, but instead they got two ogres. Doves are released into the air. But one dove is so disoriented at the sight of the ogres that it flies into the side of a building and drops down to the feet of King Harold. Shrek and King Harold both display discomfort and unhappiness at meeting each other.

At the welcome dinner, Shrek and the King openly show their disdain for each other. The silence is deafening. Harold is appalled that his only daughter has married an ogre and has become an ogre herself. Shrek is disgusted that the King would lock his daughter up in a castle. Donkey, who comes to dinner late, and by watching Shrek learns not to drink out of a finger bowl. Donkey blurts out that Shrek lives in a swamp which upsets King Harold. Then the conversation moves on to the topic of grandchildren, and the King is repulsed by the thought that they would be ogres. "Nothing wrong with that," says the Queen. "Of course not," says the King, "assuming that you do not eat your young." The King and Shrek simultaneously grab for the roasted pig in the center of the table. The pig is heaved up into the air then slams down on the table. The argument between Shrek and King Harold intensifies until finally Fiona becomes upset and runs out of the dining room. Everyone else becomes deathly silent.

Fiona hides in her childhood bedroom. She believes her parents will never accept Shrek in the family which also means they will never accept her. All the people in the kingdom would shun Shrek and her for the rest of her life. A single teardrop falls from her eyes. Suddenly, a pink bubble appears. Inside is the Fairy Godmother. It is Fiona's fallen tears that have called her. When the Fairy Godmother sees that Fiona is an ogress, the bubble burst. She is shocked. The Fairy Godmother tries to make her happy by changing her dress, making the furniture dance, showing her the type of handsome man she will attract, and giving her a little puppy.

Then, Shrek and Donkey arrive. The Fairy Godmother learns that it was Shrek who saved Fiona from the castle and not her son. Shrek takes the Fairy Godmother's business card. The audience at first believes that the Godmother is supportive of Fiona, but the twist will come when it is revealed that she is really the antagonist of the story. The writers chose to take a traditionally supportive character and twist the stereotype to make her the villain, thereby surprising the audience.

Shrek wants to pack up and leave. Fiona argues with him. "You're unbelievable, you are behaving like
an …" says Fiona. "Like what? An Ogre?" shouts Shrek. "And guess what Princess, that is not going to change," says Shrek. "I made changes for you," replies Fiona. With a heavy heart, she leaves the room.
This introduces the basic theme of the movie.

In their bedroom, the King and Queen argue about Shrek. The Queen wants to accept him, but the King does not. The King goes out onto the balcony to brood. Suddenly, the Fairy Godmother appears in a floating carriage. The King goes for a ride with her, accompanied by two brutes and her son, Prince Charming. He tells King Harold that he journeyed to the castle but found that Fiona had left. This makes the Fairy Godmother very angry and forces her to break her diet. They stop at Friar's Fat Boy, the Fly-by Deli in the sky. Prince Charming orders the Medieval Meal that comes with a battle-axe. This is the way to write effective humor to which the audience can relate: take an ordinary situation (fast-food eating) and place it into a different context (fairy tale story).

The Fairy Godmother is not pleased and commands King Harold to fix the situation. "We made a deal, and I assume you don't want me to go back on my part?" she threatens. This creates a mystery. What was the deal? It is also a setup for the surprise payoff in the climax scene when King Harold turns back into a frog, revealing that he was the original Fairy Tale Frog Prince. "Believe me Harold, it is what is best, not only for your daughter, but also for your kingdom." Now, it is not only two characters that are at risk but the whole community. This raises the stakes for the audience.

Under the disguise of a cloak, King Harold visits The Poison Apple pub. The pub is filled with characters from the dark side of the Fairy Tale world, including a talking frog that seems to recognize him. The King speaks with the wicked step-sister barmaid in order to find the only killer vicious enough to take on an ogre. When the King visits the killer in his room, he can only see a pair of boots and glowing eyes. They make a deal to kill the ogre. We do not see the face of the killer which keeps mystery in the story.

Back at the castle, Shrek cannot sleep so he walks around the bedroom. He finds Fiona's diary which she wrote as a young girl. Shrek reads about her wanting to be a beautiful princess and marry a Prince Charming. Shrek begins to have doubts about their marriage. Perhaps he is not the best thing for Fiona. Suddenly, there is a knock at the door. It is King Harold who invites Shrek to go hunting with him the next day so that they can bond.

In the morning, Shrek and Donkey go into the forest but cannot find the King. Suddenly, Shrek is attacked by the hired assassin, Puss in Boots. When Puss gets a hairball in his throat, Shrek defeats him.

Puss In Boots tells them he was hired by the King to kill Shrek. Shrek is sad because he wants to make Fiona happy. Then, he pulls out the Fairy Godmother's business card. Puss makes Donkey shed a tiear by stepping on his foot. The tear drops on the card and the Fair Godmother appears in a bubble. But this is her "answering machine" message since she is not in her office. Shrek sets off to seek the Fairy Godmother's help to be accepted by his in-laws and win back Fiona's heart. Puss requests to accompany Shrek and Donkey. He pledges to help them until he has saved Shrek's life since Shrek has spared his.

Back at the castle, the Queen is making preparations for the royal ball. She asks Harold to help her choose the fabric for the event. The King is uneasy because he assumes that there will be no event since he believes that Shrek has been killed by Puss in Boots. Fiona joins the group and asks if anyone has seen Shrek. They argue again about Shrek. "Shrek loves me for who I am. I would think you could be happy for me." "Darling, I'm just thinking about what is best for you. You are a Princess and deserve much better than this," says King Harold. This sets up the character arc for King Harold, because he eventually comes to realize that Shrek is best for Fiona.

Shrek, Donkey, and Puss go to the Fairy Godmother's Potion Factory. It is a massive factory with several smokestacks filling the air with billowing magical soot. The male receptionist tells them that the Fairy Godmother is not in, but then she calls on the intercom and orders coffee. Shrek, Donkey, and Puss sneak into the Fairy Godmother's lab and find her mixing together a magic potion. Shrek tells her that Fiona is not happy.

She tells Shrek that princesses and ogres do not mix. She then tells Shrek to go! They pretend to leave but actually they go into the Fairy Godmother's private potion room. There, they steal a bottle of the "Happily Ever After" potion. "For you and your true love. Drink of this potion and bliss will be thine. Happiness, comfort, and beauty divine." They are discovered, the alarm goes off, and security elves run after them. They run from the guards and escape from the factory. The Godmother and Prince Charming discover that Shrek has stolen the potion, but the Fairy Godmother thinks that this could work to their advantage.

Once in the woods, Donkey and Shrek drink the 'Happily Ever After" potion, but nothing happens.
Then it starts raining. As they walk down the road, a drop of the potion transforms the toadstool into a rose, foreshadowing the changes that will take place in the other characters. They take shelter in a barn. Shrek and Donkey then pass out.

Back at the castle, Fiona tells her mother and father that as soon as she finds Shrek, they will leave the kingdom and return to the swamp. She leaves the room, with the King and Queen following. When Fiona reaches the open front door, she faints. The King and Queen place her in her bed.

The next morning, Shrek wakes up inside the barn to find he is surrounded by beautiful farm girls who
are clinging to him. Normally, women run away when they see him. He sees his reflection in a bucket
of water and realizes that he is handsome. Donkey has also changed and become a gleaming white stallion. Puss in Boots reads the label on the bottle and discovers that the effects of the potion are not permanent unless Shrek can kiss his true love before midnight. "Midnight! Why does it always have to
be midnight?" says Shrek. This introduces the "ticking clock" structure to build suspense for the climax scene. Shrek needs some new clothes, so they hold up a carriage and steal the clothes from an elder man. Shrek looks ridiculous in the outfit. But then the son pokes his head out of the carriage, and Shrek takes his clothes instead.

Shrek, Donkey, and Puss go to the castle and tell a guard to get Fiona because her husband, Shrek, wants to see her. Fiona wakes up and she is beautiful again. The potion that Shrek drank had an effect on her, too. Fiona screams. Shrek hears the scream and runs to find Fiona, only to be met by the Fairy Godmother, who blocks him from leaving the room. Fiona runs out to the castle courtyard where she meets Donkey (as Noble Steed). Fiona then runs back into the castle to find Shrek and meets Prince Charming, who pretends to be the transformed Shrek. Back in the bedroom, the Fairy Godmother shows Shrek Fiona talking to Prince Charming, who is pretending to be the handsome Shrek in order to win Fiona's heart. Shrek thinks that Fiona is happy with Prince Charming. "If you really love her, you will let her be," says the Fairy Godmother. He leaves the castle dejected.

As Shrek drowns his sorrows at The Poison Apple pub, along with Donkey and Puss In Boots, King Harold goes into the back room for a secret meeting with the Fairy Godmother and Prince Charming. Shrek overhears their plans to make Fiona fall in love with Prince Charming. The Fairy Godmother gives King Harold a potion to give to Fiona. Once she drinks it, she will fall in love with the first man she kisses. The Fairy Godmother spots Shrek, Donkey, and Puss. She sends the Knights after them. They are captured and put in jail. This is the moment of desperation for the protagonist, for the antagonist has control of the love interest and is about to gain possession of the Kingdom (the unique object).

King Harold brings the magic potion for Fiona to drink which will make her fall in love with Prince Charming. But when they meet and speak, he realizes that Fiona really does love the old Shrek. King Harold is hesitant to give Fiona the potion. The audience is unsure whether or not he gave her the potion. This ambiguity is needed to make the climax scene where Prince Charming kisses Fiona more dramatic.

Back at the castle, the wedding party for Fiona and Shrek (Prince Charming) has begun. The Red Carpet has been rolled out and the celebrities are introduced. During a television commercial for "The Knights" TV "Cops" Show, the Fairy Tale creatures in Shrek's house watch the capture of Shrek, Donkey, and Puss on television. They realize that Shrek is in trouble.

Shrek, Donkey, and Puss are in jail. The Gingerbread Man, Pinocchio, the Three Blind Mice, and the Fairy Tale gang bust them out. Pinocchio is lowered down from the ceiling, but in order to release Shrek, he must tell a lie to make his nose grow. Pinocchio tells the lie that he is not wearing woman's underwear, which he really is. Shrek, Donkey and Puss are released. They plan to storm the castle. Shrek has the Muffin Man create a monster gigantic gingerbread man called Mongo.

With the musical song "I Need a Hero" playing on the soundtrack, Shrek rides Mongo into battle against the castle. The guards launch milk at Mongo, but Shrek still manages to get inside the castle and lowers the drawbridge. They are in the castle and charge forward to save Fiona.

Inside the banquet hall, Prince Charming is trying to kiss Fiona. Shrek bursts in to stop him. The Fairy Godmother attacks him with her powerful wand, but Shrek dives out of the way. The Fairy Tale creatures fight to gain possession of the wand.

Fiona realizes that she has been tricked and that the handsome man who has just arrived is the real Shrek. But before she can do anything about it, Prince Charming forces a kiss on her lips.

A victorious smile spreads across the Fairy Godmother's face.

To Shrek's horror, Fiona steps back and lovingly takes Prince Charming's head into her hands. She then rears back and head-butts him so hard he crumbles to the floor. Shrek and Fiona run into each other's arms. The Fairy Godmother is angry, and with the wave of her magic wand, directs a bolt of energy at Shrek. King Harold jumps in front of Shrek and takes the blast full-on. The wicked magic deflects off the King's shiny metal armor and bounces right back at the Fairy Godmother. It hits her and she disappears in a thunderous explosion.

King Harold is now a frog, the original Frog Prince. But Queen Lillian still loves him, and accepts him. This foreshadows what will happen with Shrek and Fiona.
The clock strikes midnight. Puss reminds Shrek about the message on magic potion bottle.
"Fiona, is this what you want? Kiss me now, and we'll stay this way forever," says Shrek.
"You'd do that for me?" says Fiona
"Yes," answers Shrek.
"I want what any princess wants, to live happily ever after." He bends to kiss her, but she stops his kiss with his hand. "...with the ogre I married." This is Fiona's big decision. This is the story climax: she decides to accept Shrek for the ogre that he is.
"Whatever happens, I must not cry!" Puss bit his paw as tears welled up.
"You cannot make me cry!"
This comment from Puss suggests how the audience should feel at this moment.

The last chime of midnight sounds. Fiona and Shrek hold each other tightly as the transformation begins, lifting and spinning them high into the air. Strange light shoots out of their bodies. The crowd stares as Donkey is also lifted up and changes. When they all land, they are back to their former selves, Shrek and Fiona as ogres and Donkey as a donkey.

Resolution Scene
The celebration party begins. It's a Fiesta. They all get up on stage and sing! It is a happy, joyous event.
Shrek is a fun movie filled with music and joy that the whole family can enjoy. There is plenty of humorous material for both children and adults. The credits roll with another rendition of the song,
"I Need a Hero" on the soundtrack.

After part of the credits roll, Puss, accompanied by two beautiful women, discovers Donkey alone on the stage. Puss invites Donkey to join them, but he turns Puss down. Suddenly, Donkey is surprised by his Dragon love, along with all her little flying mutant donkey-dragons. He is happy to see them, but now Donkey has to get a job, and we have the premise for **Shrek 3**: Shrek, Fiona, and Baby Shrek. Is the swamp really the best neighborhood to raise the children? What's the educational system like?

THE END

SPIDER-MAN

Protagonist: Peter Parker (Spider-man)
Protagonist-Supporter: Uncle Ben (Mentor) and Aunt May
Love Interest: MJ – Mary Jane Watson
Antagonist: Norman Osborn (Green Goblin)
Antagonist Supporter: Harry Osborn, J.J. Jameson (Newspaper Editor)

Protagonist Empathy Scene: Peter runs after the school bus. The other students and driver laugh at him. He is publicly humiliated.

Inciting Event: A spider bites Peter while he is on a field trip to a museum. This changes Peter's life:
1. Peter is stronger. He no longer needs glasses.
2. He becomes amazingly agile. He can run super fast.
3. He can shoot webbing from his wrist.
4. He can cling to walls and climb up the sides of buildings.

Peter loves MJ. He decides that he can use his new superpowers to make money to buy a car. That would make him popular. He enters an amateur wrestling contest. The ad says that he will win $3,000 if he stays in the ring for three minutes. He must also be a colorful character. Peter designs a costume for himself: red hood mask with a spider's web design. Blue pants and red shoes.

Uncle Ben drives Peter downtown: "You are feeling this great power, and with great power comes great responsibility."

Peter wins the match, but the owner will not give him all the money: only $100 instead of $3000. When Peter complains, the owner says "I miss the part where that's my problem." This is the first plot twist. Peter accomplishes the subgoal, but does not get what was expected. A thief then breaks in and steals money from the owner. He runs past Peter and into the elevator. Peter does not try to stop him. When the owner complains, Peter says "I miss the part where that's my problem."

But it becomes his problem because the thief steals Uncle Ben's car and shoots him. Peter finds Uncle Ben dying on the street. He runs after the killer. Peter rips off his clothes and wears only his Spider-Man costume. After a wild car chase Peter corners the thief in a warehouse. After a fight, the thief accidentally falls out of a window to his death.

Norman Osborn wants to turn men into super-soldiers by altering natural evolution. His company, Oscorp, is being funded by the DOD. Yet, the army will cancel the contract funding if Osborn can not produce a successful test experiment that validates his theories.

Osborn decides that it is time for a human trial. He will be the test subject. The test goes badly, and Osborn kills his research assistant.

Spider-Man uses his powers for good:
1. He captures criminals.
2. He rescues innocent people.
3. He foils bank robbers.
4. He protects the community from danger.

Spider-Man becomes famous. He takes photos of himself in action and sells them to the newspapers to make money. The newspaper editor, J.J. Jameson, is a corrupt sleaze, but he believes that pictures of Spider-Man sells newspapers. Jameson writes exploitative headlines: "Spider-Man: Hero or Menace!"

The love interest in this story is MJ (Mary Jane). She has lived next door to Peter since he was six years old. MJ moves into the city to become an actress. Peter meets up with MJ one day and discovers that she is working as a waitress. He also discovers that she is dating his best friend, Harry Osborn, the son of Norman Osborn.

The Board of Directors of Oscorp decides to sell the company to their competitors. They remove Norman Osborn as CEO of the company. He vows revenge!

Peter is taking photos downtown on the World Unity Day Celebration. Suddenly, the Green Goblin appears, flying through the sky and wreaking havoc on the celebration. He throws bombs onto the ledge and kills the Oscorp Board members. The balcony collapses, and MJ clings on the ledge for her life. Peter changes into Spider-Man and fights with the Green Goblin. Peter damages the Goblin's flying machine, then saves MJ's life. He flies away with her and leaves her in a garden on top of a skyscraper.

When Peter is in the newspaper office selling Editor Jameson Spider-Man photos, the Green Goblin attacks. He is looking for the man who took the photos. Peter changes into Spider-Man and fights the Goblin. But the Goblin sprays knockout gas into Spider-Man's face and takes him up to the rooftop. The Green Goblin wants Spider-Man to become his partner. Together they can rule the city. But Peter decides to protect the city from crime.

Aunt May is cooking a Thanksgiving dinner for Peter, MJ, Harry, and Norman Osborn. Peter is late. When he finally comes down to the table, Aunt May notices that his arm is bleeding. Peter says that he was clipped by a bike messenger. Norman does not believe him and realizes that Peter is Spider-Man. Norman Osborn walks out of the dinner, followed by his son Harry. Norman then degrades MJ and tells Harry to get rid of MJ after he has had his way with her.

That night the Green Goblin attacks and terrorizes Aunt May. This was his way to get at Spider-Man; attacking those that he loves. Aunt May is sent to the hospital. Peter visits her. Peter realizes that the Green Goblin knows who he is. Peter calls MJ, but it is too late. The Green Goblin laughs at him over the telephone. This is the second major empathy scene that most megahits have before the climax scene. It helps to get the audience to emotionally support the protagonist and his desire to destroy the antagonist.

Spider-Man rushes to save MJ. She is being held captive by the Green Goblin on the top of the Roosevelt Tower Bridge. The Green Goblin gives Spider-Man a choice: save MJ, the woman he loves, or save a tram filled with children. The Green Goblin releases both MJ and the cables at the same time. Spider-Man saves them both, even while he is being attacked by the Green Goblin. He safely lowers the tram and MJ onto a barge that is floating up the river.

Spider-Man fights with the Green Goblin and finally appears to defeat him. The Green Goblin reveals himself to be Norman Osborn. When Spider-Man lets down his guard, the Green Goblin activates his glider in an effort to kill Spider-Man. But in the last moment, Spider-Man jumps aside, and Norman Osborn is impaled by glider! With his last dying death, Norman begs Peter not to tell Harry that he was the Green Goblin. Again, this type of climax scenes is standard in megahit movies. The antogonist is killed not by the protagonist, but by actions he initiated in his attempt to kill the protagonist boomeranging back and destroying him.

The final scene takes place in the cemetery at the funeral of Norman Osborn. Harry Osborn says that he knows Spider-Man killed his father, and that he will spend the rest of his life hunting him down. MJ tells Peter that when she thought she was going to die, the face that came to her was Peter's. She realizes that she loves Peter. But Peter, though he, too, loves her, cannot tell her. He cannot tell her because he is afraid that doing so would place her in danger. So he walks away from the tearful MJ, with the thought echoing through his mind that "with great power comes great responsibility."

This is not your happy ending. It takes place in a cemetery, never a happy setting. The hero is not integrated back into the community. His best friend pledges to destroy him, and he rejects the love of the woman he loves. Yet, the movie still grossed over $404 million dollars. Some say that this ending was okay with the audience because they knew a sequel would follow with a happier ending for all the characters. Perhaps. But this closing still breaks all the rules of the standard Hollywood ending.

The last scene of the movie are the exhilarating images of Spider-Man swinging among the skyscrapers and above the streets of New York City, giving the adolescents in the audience a vicarous joyful experience.

THE END

SPIDER-MAN 2

Protagonist: Peter Parker (Spider-Man)
Nothing comes easy for Peter Parker. He is forced to balance his studies as a college student at the city university, a part-time job delivering pizzas, and his freelance job as a photographer for the *Daily Bugle* newspaper. He is always late or sometimes does not show up at all. But he is the only photographer in the city that can get photos of Spider-Man. Peter is always short on money. While attending a demonstration on genetically engineered spiders at a museum, Peter was bitten by one of the spiders. He then under went a transformation and became Spider-Man. Peter is madly in love with Mary Jane Watson, the girl next door.

Protagonist-Supporter: Aunt May
She lives alone in Queens. She has always acted as Peter's mother. Peter works hard to keep his secret from Aunt May, and to keep her out of harm's way. Peter always has the fear that Aunt May could become a victim of his enemies. In the two years since Uncle Ben's death, things have gotten tougher for her. She lives on a fixed income and has trouble paying her mortgage.

Protagonist-Supporter: Uncle Ben
He was killed in the first movie. His death cause much guilt for Peter.

Love Interest: Mary Jane Watson
She has a dream of becoming an actress. MJ was given a modeling job for a magazine, then ended up on the billboards throughout the city as the face of Emma Rose Parfumerie. Next, MJ got the job of playing Cecily Cardew in an off-Broadway production of *The Importance of Being Earnest*. Mary Jane always liked Peter Parker, the boy next door. Often she wondered if Peter felt the same, but Peter always seemed too busy. MJ is dating a young astronaut, John Jameson.

Antagonist-Supporter: Harry Osborn
He was born into a life of wealth and privilege. After the death of his father, Norman Osborn, Harry became the head of Special Projects at OsCorp. Harry blamed Spider-Man for the death of his father. Harry considers Peter Parker to be his best friend and Spider-Man to be his enemy.

Antagonist: Doc Ock (Dr. Otto Octavius)
Dr. Octavius married his loving wife, Rosie while they were in college. Dr. Octavius' latest research is being funded by OsCorp. The Doctor's research caused him to handle dangerous radioactive material. Because these materials are too dangerous to handle with bare hands, Dr. Octavius created a mechanical harness containing four metal arms. Using these arms, he can handle any kind of dangerous material safely. But the experiment goes wrong and he becomes a monster.

Antagonist-Supporter: J. Jonah Jameson
He is the publisher of the *Daily Bugle* newspaper. Jameson is cheap, blustery and grouchy. Jameson hates Spider-Man, and runs stories characterizing him as a menace. Peter Parker works for Jameson at the Bugle and takes photos of Spider-Man.

Minor Character: John Jameson
John is the son of Jonah and Mary Jane's new boyfriend.

Minor Character: Dr. Curt Connors
Peter's college professor who is a friend of Doc Ock

Minor Character: Robbie Robertson
Bugle's Editor-in-Chief. He believes that Spider-Man is a hero.

Minor Character: Betty Brant
Jameson's secretary at the *Bugle* who pays Peter for his photos.

Opening Credits:
Cartoon images of Marvel Comics and Still Images from the first Spider-Man movie. This allows to audience to remember the important events from the first *Spider-Man* movie.

Voice over of Peter Parker. "She looks at me every day." Peter sits on his motorbike in NYC. In front of him is a huge billboard of Mary Jane, her eyes literally gigantic, gazing out. The logo reads, *"Emma Rose Parfumerie."* "With me she was always in danger from those who fight against me. Without her, I travel a lonely road. My story will always be about the loss of a girl." Peter believes that he has lost the girl of his dreams. This produces sympathy in the audience for Peter.

Peter drives his motorcycle up to JOE'S PIZZA. The manager, Rahi Aziz, was very angry.

"In eight minutes I am defaulting on Joe's twenty-nine minute guarantee." Peter is told that this is his last chance. If he fails to deliver the pizza, he will be fired. Peter is placed in danger of losing his job.

Peter rides through the traffic of NYC. His motorbike stalls out in the middle of traffic. He puts on the Spider-Man outfit, then, having webbed the pizza boxes together, he fires a web-strand to an overhanging ledge. It snagged on the underside. An instant later, he was drawing himself up the web-line as fast as he can go. The audience admires his abilities.

Spider-Man saves two little children (boy and girl) from being hit by a truck. This scene generates sympathy for Spider-Man. A man on the street below thinks that Spider-Man has stolen the kid's pizzas. A man tries eat some pizza left on the ledge. Spider-Man grabs it from him.

Peter Parker, back in his regular clothes, emerges from a janitor's closet. He struggles with the mops and brooms. This is a bit of humor showing him to be incompetent as Peter Parker. Peter holds the pizzas aloft and called out, "Pizza Time!" The receptionist stared up at him like a dead fish as he brushes away strands of web. She says nothing but simply glances in the direction of the clock over her head. It read 2:03. "You're late. I'm not paying for those pies. Peter leaves them with her. The audience feels empathy for Peter because they know how hard he tried to get the pies delivered on time.

"Joe's twenty-nine minute guarantee is a promise!" Aziz was shouting in Peter's face. "I know a promise means nothing to you, Parker, but to me it is serious! You're fired!" This produces sympathy for Peter because the audience knows that he is being treated unfairly.

He got the same message at the Daily Bugle. "You're fired!" Jameson screamed at Peter. "I pay you because for some reason that psycho Spider-Man will pose for you!" Jameson flips through a portfolio of photos that Peter has given to him." Peter again is placed in danger of losing another job.

"Spider-Man will not let me take any more pictures of him because you turned the whole city against him!" replied Peter. Peter then gives Jameson one more picture of Spider-Man, for which Jameson finally agrees to pay $300.

They argue about payment, but Jameson gives Peter a voucher. He takes it to Betty, the secretary. "Sorry, Pete, this doesn't even cover the advance you got two weeks ago."
Peter is broke. This generates empathy for Peter. No matter how hard he tries, he cannot win.

New York University: Arriving at the campus Peter runs into Dr. Connors, but he is too late for his class. Peter tells Connors he is planning on writing a paper on Doctor Otto Octavius, who is a friend of Connor's. Connor tells Peter to write the paper or he will fail him. Peter is in danger of failing the course.

Peter jumps on his motorcycle and rides to Aunt May's house. It is night-time. SURPRISE! It is his birthday. Harry Osborn and Mary Jane are there with Aunt May. The audience shares in the joy of seeing Peter with his friend and the girl he loves.

"Long time no see," says Mary Jane. Mary Jane is in a play off-Broadway.
"Spider Man's photographer! How's the bug these days?" asks Harry. Harry is in charge of Special Projects at OsCorp. "We're funding one of your idols, Otto Octavius," says Harry.
"I am writing a paper on him," says Peter.
"Want to meet him?"
Harry promises to arrange for Peter to meet Octavius. Peter has hope for success.

"Be honest," said Harry. "If you knew who Spider-Man was, would you tell me?"
"You'd only want him dead."
"Of course I would! The same way you'd want the man who killed your uncle Ben dead. My father loved you like a son, Pete." The audience feels sympathy for Peter. They know that Harry's father was the Green Goblin, who tried to kill Peter. It is unfair for Harry to blame his father's death on Spider-Man.

Peter sees a "Pre-Eviction Notice" from Aunt May's mortgage company on the table. This is another problem for Peter, who does not have enough money and just got fired from his job.
His aunt might get evicted. This creates more sympathy for Peter.

After Harry left the party, Peter was hauling out a bag of garbage and discovered Mary Jane sitting on a stoop on the other side of the fence. "I wish you would come see the play. You are the one who always encouraged me," said MJ. The audience sees how happy Peter is to be with MJ.

"I'm seeing somebody now," she said. Peter is in danger of losing the woman he loves to another man. "Hey, I'm going to see your play tomorrow night!" says Peter.
"Do you want me to put a house seat aside for you? Third row center? Prime spot?"
"Absolutely."
Don't disappoint me!"
"I won't," says Peter.

Peter went back inside and woke up Aunt May, who was sleeping at the table. She gives him a twenty-dollar bill for his birthday. She wants to face the one responsible for what happened to Uncle Ben. Peter feels guilty about causing his death. The audience sees how much Peter is loved by Aunt May, and they have sympathy for his situation.

Peter goes back to his run down apartment and is confronted by his landlord, Mr. Ditkovitch. Peter is a month late with the rent. The landlord takes the twenty-dollar bill from Peter's hand. Peter takes another loss.

Next morning, Peter knocks on the Rest Room door in the hallway. The landlord comes out and goes in before him. This is a bit of humor which releases the tension in the audience.

Octavius is working in his laboratory when Harry and Peter enter. Harry introduces Peter to Octavius. "Nobel Prize, Otto, Noble Prize. We will all be rich!" The audience anticipates great success for Harry and Otto. This is a setup which will make the audience even more disappointed when they all fail.

"It's not about prizes, Harry. It's not about money."
"But you need money," says Harry. You need OsCorp."

After Harry leaves, Octavius talks to Peter. "Let me tell you something. Being brilliant is not enough. You have to work hard. Intelligence isn't a privilege, it's a gift. It's not yours to waste. We've been given the power of intelligence for a purpose: to use it for the good of mankind."
Otto and Peter bond. This shows the audience that Otto is really a good guy. This makes the audience have sympathy for him when he is taken over by the intelligent arms. Otto becomes a tragic figure, another scientist destroyed because he pushed the limits of technology in the hope of benefiting mankind with an unlimited source of energy.

He introduces his wife to Peter. "This is my wife, Rosie." This scene shows Otto to be a loving husband, who is also loved by his wife. Another setup to make him a tragic figure.

"I understand that you use harmonics of atomic frequencies," says Peter.
"Sympathetic frequencies. Harmonic reinforcement—"
"An exponential increase in energy output," says Peter

"But are you sure that you can stabilize the fusion reaction?" asks Peter. Peter introduces the possibility of danger in the experiment.

Rosie and Otto talk about their relationship: "He tried to explain the theory of relativity and I tried to explain T.S. Eliot. "Poetry will win a woman's heart," says Otto to Peter. Those in the audience who like poetry will now like Otto.

Peter is in the Laundromat washing his clothes as he reads a book of poetry; Hiawatha by Longfellow. He takes his Spider-Man suit out of the washing machine. The red and blue colors ran into his white shorts. Peter's incompetence produces laughter.

Peter is back in his apartment getting dressed. He takes his shirt off in front of the window. He looks in his closet and sees two suits: Spider-Man and blue dress suit. (These are his two life options.) He puts on the blue-suit. He takes the play ticket from his mirror.

Peter buys a bouquet of flowers, but he only has money for three flowers. His lack of money to buy the girl he loves a beautiful gift generates empathy for him with the audience.

MJ is putting on makeup for the play, *The Importance of Being Earnest* by Oscar Wilde. She is jittery that night because she expects Peter to attend. This shows that MJ really does care for Peter.

Peter is on his way to the theater when he hears gunshots. He becomes Spider-Man and chases after the criminals. Peter is able to stop a police car from crashing into a crowd of people. They urge him on. Peter finally captures the two criminals, spins a web around them and hangs them from a lamppost. This scene generates admiration for Peter because of his ability to capture the criminals while also saving the lives of innocent bystanders.

MJ notices that he is not in his seat! She is upset. The audience becomes anxious because the lovers may not get together.

The traffic cop in front of the theater threatens to tow away Peter's car, which he had taken from the criminals. Another obstacle for Peter to overcome, but the scene is humorous because it is not Peter's car.

Peter gets to the theater too late and the usher will not let him through the doors. Peter's relationship with MJ is placed in jeopardy by the usher because MJ will be disappointed that he does not see her performance. Again, Peter cannot win for all his trying. This generates empathy for him with the audience.

Peter stands outside the theater as a street musician sings a song: "Spider-Mon, Spider-Mon, does whatever a spider con." This is a bit of comic relief for the audience. Peter watches as MJ leaves the theater. She is met by a young man. He kisses her. She leaves with him. Peter is sad, and the audience shares his sadness.

Peter swings through the dark alleys, but his Spider-Man powers begin to fail him. He falls onto the street. He tries to climb up the side of a building, but falls into the pool of water in the alley. Peter is losing his powers at the same time he is losing the love of his life.

Peter is in an elevator with another young man who is walking his dog. "Cool Spidey outfit. It looks uncomfortable." "It kind of itches and rides up in the crouch sometimes," replies Peter. Another humorous scene to break the tension and make the audience laugh.

Peter calls up MJ from school. She walks into her apartment, hears the phone ring, then her answering machine picks up. Peter starts talking and apologizes for missing the play, but MJ does not pick up the phone. He runs out of time and the telephone disconnects.

Peter makes his confession into the phone about how he loves MJ but cannot be with her because he is afraid that he will place her in danger. He is a lonely man in the midst of a campus crowded with people. The audience shares this moment of honesty with the protagonist and will care for him because they know that he loves MJ but will not tell her the truth because he is trying to protect her.

Rosie and Octavius prepare for the Fusion Power demonstration. Harry and Peter are present. The audience anticipates success. Otto makes a joke by asking if anyone lost a roll of money with a green rubber band around it. Otto found the rubber band. The humor makes the audience laugh. It also makes Otto a more likeable character at the moment before his transformation into a monster.

Otto then whips off a drape revealing the rig and its contents: four long metal arms attached to a wide, lightweight harness. At the end of the arms is a set of pincers serving as that arm's "hand." The arms terrify the audience. They look like metallic snakes with red eyes.

"My smart arms are controlled by my brain through a neural link. Nanowires feed directly into my cerebellum, allowing me to use the arms to control the fusion reaction in an environment no human hand can enter," says Octavius.

"If the artificial intelligence in the arms is as advanced as you suggest, couldn't that make you vulnerable to them?" asks a spectator. The audience becomes fearful that Otto is in danger.
"That's why I developed this inhibitor chip to protect my higher brain function. It makes sure I maintain control of the arms, instead of them controlling me," says Otto.

The arms come to life and move toward the Tritium target. The audience becomes excited with the anticipation of a successful experiment. The plasma igniters on each of the four towers simultaneously fire on the Tritium capsule in a continuous blast, exciting the core. A fine circular beam of plasma forms. Then spokes like a wheel extend and—after a few seconds – a bright glowing sphere of energy about fourteen inches in diameter flares into existence in the center of the array.
"We have the equivalent of one thousand megawatts," says Octavius. "The power of the sun in the palm of my hand."

Peter watches a metal paperclip slide against the floor toward the fusion ball of fire. This is becoming a dangerous situation. Matters began to spin out of control. From all around there are screams and shouts, and people evacuating the room. "Are you sure you can stabilize the fusion reaction?" asks Parker.

Peter turns into Spider-Man. Harry Osborn sees him. Spider-Man saves Harry's life by pulling him away from a flying metal cabinet. Harry hates him for that. "This changes nothing," shouts Harry. This produces more empathy for Spider-Man because the audience knows that whatever Spider-Man does, he will still be unjustly hated by his best friend. This is an effective use of the dual personality structure. The best friend of one personality (Peter Parker) hates the other personality (Spider-Man).

Otto still believes that he can stabilize the fusion reaction, but the audience knows that everybody is in great danger.

The fusion source is creating a gravitational field which pulls metal objects into it. Rosie is killed by broken glass flying across the room. Spider-Man yanks cables out of the device and the fusion reaction began to subside. Otto sees his dead wife Rosie and then passes out. The audience feels sympathy for Otto as he becomes tragic by unintentionally causing his wife's death.

The body of Rosie is taken away. Harry blames Spider-Man for all his problems, yet his bodyguard says that Spider-Man saved his life. "He humiliated me by touching me," says Harry. Peter walks out of the building. More sympathy for Peter because the audience sees that he is hated by the man whose life he has just saved.

At the Midtown Hospital Operating room doctors are preparing to cut the metal arms off Dr. Ock which have fused to his spinal cord. Although the Doc is out cold, the arms become alive and kill all the medical doctors. Dr. Ock with metal arms in control breaks out of the hospital.

At the Daily Bugle, Jameson is excited. "Panic in the street… if we are lucky. Crazy scientist destroyed his own lab, turned himself into some kind of monster. Four mechanical arms welded right into his body!" Jameson names the monster "DOC OCK." The audience laughs because Jameson takes credit for the name that was suggested to him by his employee.

Jameson forces Peter to be the photographer at a high society party for his son, the hero, the astronaut, at the Planetarium tomorrow night at 8 pm. The audience gains more sympathy for Peter because they watch this heroic figure being treated abusively.

Doc Ock talks to his metallic arms in the broken down wharf by the river. The arms take over the mind of Doc Ock because his inhibitor has been damaged. They persuade him to rebuild the fusion system. The power of the sun will be in the palm of his hand. Nothing will stand in his way! Otto has been taken over by the evil arms. He has now become the villainous antagonist of the story.

Peter and Aunt May go to a Bank to get a loan. She has just opened an account, but the Social Security and the insurance from her late husband are not enough to qualify her for a loan. Sympathy for Aunt May and Peter because their request for a loan is rejected by the Bank and Aunt May will lose her house.

While they are in the bank, Doc Ock tries to rob it. He uses his arms to pull off the safe door. Peter runs to change into Spider-Man. The loan officer thinks he is a coward and is running away. Peter returns as Spider-Man and confronts Doc Ock, who hurls bags of money at him.

Doc Ock grabs Aunt May as a hostage and carries her up the side of the building. Aunt May hits Doc Ock with her umbrella, and he drops her. Spider-Man rescues her from the fall and sets her down on the street. Doc Ock gets away with bags of money.

Peter goes to the High Society Ball. Harry is drunk and confronts him about Spider-Man. John Jameson walks down the stairs with Mary Jane on his arm. More sympathy for Peter as he is falsely accused by Harry, and he watches the woman he loves on the arm of another man.

Peter talks to MJ on the balcony. She is angry at him for not coming to her play, then walks away from him. More sympathy for Peter because the audience knows how hard he tried to get to see her play.

Harry is drunk and confronts Peter again, saying that he is more a friend of Spider-Man than him. Harry slaps Peter in front of the crowd of people. Peter is humiliated in public. This generates a lot of empathy for him with the audience, especially since he does not strike Harry. The audience knows that Peter (Spider-Man) could easily defeat Harry.

John Jameson takes the podium and announces to the crowd that MJ has agreed to marry him. This results in applause. Peter is stunned. This produces even more sympathy for Peter. Jameson tells Peter to take a picture of his son and MJ. This is the final humiliation for Peter.

Peter's web abilities start to fail him. He cannot get his webbing to work, and he falls off a wall. He is losing all his special powers as he is losing the woman he loves.

Doc Ock puts together his new equipment in the wharf building. The antagonist will now place the city of New York in jeopardy.

Peter goes to see a doctor, Doctor Wally Davis. "You seem okay to me," says the Doctor.
"My diagnosis? It's in your head. Maybe you are not supposed to be climbing the wall. Maybe you should not be Spider-Man. You have a choice, Peter," says the Doctor.
"I have a choice!" says Peter. There is hope for Peter. The only way he will become well is if he changes his life and gives up the desire to be Spider-Man.

Peter sits in bed and imagines a conversation with Uncle Ben. They talk about "with great power comes great responsibility." Peter tells Ben that he loves MJ and does not want to be Spider-Man any more. Peter decides to be Spider-Man no more! Peter chooses love over power.

Peter walks up to a trash can in the alley, opens it, then dumps the Spider-Man costume in. The audience feels that he has made the right choice and that he will become happy.

Peter is happy as he walks through the park. He fixes his bicycle tire in his room. The tire spins off the stand, off the balcony, and onto the street below. The audience experiences and shares his happiness. The humor of the tire going over the balcony makes them laugh.

Peter has a hot dog in the park. He is now relaxing and starting to enjoy his life. He watches the police chase after a criminal, but Peter does not join them.

Peter goes to Connor's class at the college and gives the correct answer. The Professor congratulates him for being a good student. Peter is starting to get the respect he deserves.

Peter goes to see MJ in the play. MJ says the lines of Cecily: "I hope you have not been leading a double life, pretending to be wicked and being really good all the time. That would be hypocrisy." Suddenly, MJ realizes that Peter is in the audience. This line in the play also applies to Peter's life.

They talk after the play as they walk through China Town. Peter tells her that he has changed, but she says it is too late. She is getting married. She walks away from him, but then turns and says: "You are different." He is starting to regain the love of MJ, but it may be too late. Their relationship is still in jeopardy.

At the *Daily Bugle*, Betty Bryant leads the street bum into Jameson's office. The bum has Spider-Man's costume in a bag. Jonah is excited. "He's out. He's given up! Thrown in the towel! He abandoned his sad masquerade." The bum sells the costume to Jameson, who is overjoyed. The audience laughs at his extreme behavior.

The Daily Bugle headlines blares at him: *Spider-Man No More!* Peter walks past an alley and sees two men beating up on a third, but he walks away because he is no longer Spider-Man and no longer wants to get involved. The audience becomes concerned, because Peter's decision now has a cost to the community.

Peter and Aunt May are at the grave of Uncle Ben. Two years have passed. This creates sympathy for Aunt May and Peter. Back at Aunt May's house: "It was not fair that he was taken this way. He was a peaceful man. It's my fault." She blamed herself, when she had been sitting at home not involved in any of it. "You wanted to take the subway, I told him to drive you," she says. "I'm responsible," says Aunt May. The audience has sympathy for Aunt May because they know she is not really responsible.

Peter confesses to her. "I could have stopped the thief, but I let him go. I even held the door open for him. He stole Uncle Ben's car, and shot him." says Peter. He was seeking absolution. Peter takes Aunt May's hand, but she pulls away. Aunt May gets up and walks up the stairs to her room. She tells Peter that she wants him to go! The audience has more sympathy for Peter because he is rejected by his Aunt, one of the only true friends that he has in his life.

At Harry Osborn's apartment, the butler Bernard leaves him for the night. Doc Ock comes into the room. He wants more Tritium.

"We'll make a deal," says Harry. "Kill Spider-Man and I'll give you what you need!" says Harry. "On second thought, don't kill him. I'll never have closure if this ends like this, with the chance of never seeing him again. Bring him back to me…alive. Do that, and I promise you can have all the Tritium you want!"
"How do I find him?" asks Doc Ock.
"Peter Parker. He takes pictures of Spider-Man. Make him tell you where he is."
But don't hurt Peter! He is my best friend!" yells Harry at the departing Doc Ock. Peter is now in grave danger.

Newspaper Headlines: "Crime up 75%." The community is now in grave danger because of Peter's decision not to be Spider-Man.

Peter is on the street. He sees that a house is on fire. One man is positive that there is a kid on the second floor. *Spider-Man no more!* But he was still Peter Parker. That would never change and Peter Parker has to do something. Peter runs into the burning building. The audience respects and admires Peter for going into a burning building to save the life of a child.

Peter saves the life of the child. A paramedic gives him oxygen then says "some poor soul got trapped on the fourth floor and never made it out!" Peter feels bad for not being able to save the man that died.

"Am I not supposed to have what I want? What I need?" What am I supposed to do?" says Peter to himself when he is back in his apartment alone. The audience feels sympathy for Peter.

Ursula, the landlord's daughter, knocks on Peter's door. "Would you like a piece of chocolate cake?" she asks. They eat together. When they are done she tells him that his aunt called for him.
This act of friendship shows Peter that he is not alone, and there are other people in the world who like him.

When he arrives at his Aunt May's house, she is packing boxes in her driveway. She has found a small apartment. "You made a brave move. And I am proud of you, and I thank you, and I love you, Peter…so very, very much." The audience is relieved that Aunt May has forgiven Peter. If she forgives him, then they can forgive him, too.

Henry Jackson is a little boy helping Aunt May. "You take Spider-Man's pictures, don't you?" he asks Peter. 'Where is he?"
"He quit."
"Why?"
"Wanted to try other things," says Peter.
"You'll never guess who he wants to be. Spider-Man. He knows a hero when he sees one. There are too few characters out there flying around like that and saving old girls like me. And Lord knows, kids like Henry need a hero. Courageous, self-sacrificing people, setting examples for us all," says Aunt.

"Everybody loves a hero. People line up for them, cheer them, and scream their names. And years later tell how they stood for hours in the rain just to catch a glimpse of the one who taught them to hold on a second longer. I believe there is a hero in all of us who keeps us honest, gives us strength, makes us noble, and finally allows us to die with pride, even though sometimes we have to be steady, and give up the thing we want the most. Even our dreams! Spider-Man did that for Henry, and he wonders where he has gone. Henry needs him." Peter feels good about himself because he realizes that his efforts have been appreciated, and the sacrifices that Spider-Man has made have not been in vain.

Eight stories up in the heart of New York City, Peter stares at the twenty-foot chasm that stretches between himself and the next rooftop…he keeps telling himself that his strength is back. Peter is trying to demonstrate to himself that his powers have returned.

Peter runs and jumps off the building, but realizing that his arc was not sufficient to clear the distance, Peter Parker emits a high pitched scream. Then he drops like a ballast bag tossed from a balloon, flailing his arms about, trying to find something to grab onto. He slams down onto the cars below. He hurts his back. His powers have not returned because he has not gotten back the love of the woman he loves.

As Peter walks away he touches one of the cars. This sets off a car alarm. The audience laughs at this bit of humor.

MJ is looking at her wedding invitations. John Jameson is stretched out on the couch in MJ's apartment. "Are you sure that you don't want to invite your friend Peter Parker?"
"Peter Parker is a great big jerk." says MJ. She is still angry at Peter. "Put your head back," she tells John. She comes around to the other side, then leans in and kisses his upside-down face. She has never kissed him like this before. But it is not the same. The audience has empathy for MJ because they do not want her to make a mistake and marry the wrong man. This is why she has to make sure and kiss Peter.

Mary Jane sits at a table in the window of Ari's Village Deli and Bakery. Peter approaches the table. They talk, and Peter tells her he made a mistake. He cannot be there for her. MJ is upset.
There is danger in this scene. The audience is afraid that Peter and MJ will not get back together.

"Kiss me," says MJ. "I need to know something." She draws closer to him, and he to her. The audience hopes they will be reunited.

Suddenly she sees his eyes go wide in alarm. The restaurant's plate glass restaurant window shatters and a car hurls directly at them. The audience is terrorized by the situation.

Peter slams to the ground with Mary Jane and desperately rolls to the side, just avoiding having the car's back tire run over his face. The vehicle fishtails, and then crashes to a halt at the back of the restaurant. The audience is relieved that Peter and MJ are not killed.

It is Doc Ock. He confronts Peter. "I want you to find your friend Spider-Man." He picks up Peter and slams him into the wall. The ceiling collapses on Peter. "Find him or I'll peel the flesh off her bones." The audience hates Doc Ock for threatening MJ. Peter becomes enraged. Doc Ock throws Peter against the wall. Doc Ock grabs Mary Jane and carries her away, laughing all the while. Peter jumps out from under the debris and in a rage starts after Doc Ock. Peter takes off his glasses. He doesn't need them any more. Peter's rage and the love of MJ has empowered him.

At the Daily Bugle Robbie says, "No news of your son's fiancée."
"It's all my fault," said Jameson. "I drove him away."
"He was the only one who could have stopped Doc Ock," says Robbie. Jameson is now in jeopardy due to his false accusations.

Peter quickly leans into the room and takes his costume from the wall. "Spider-Man was a hero. I just couldn't see it," says Jonah. Jameson screams when he realizes that Spider-Man has taken back his suit. He starts verbally attacking Spider-Man again. The audience laughs at Jameson's quick change of attitude.

Ock sits perched on a giant clock tower, waiting patiently, as Spider-Man swing closer and closer. "Where is she?"
"She's nearby. Quite safe."

Spider-Man fights Doc Ock. Together they fall onto a train as they continue to fight. Two of Doc Ocks tentacles wrap down and around and crashed into the front cab. The engineer falls back, screaming in alarm, as one of the arms slam the accelerator into overdrive and then snapped off the lever. With another swift blow, the emergency brake system is shattered. The train begins to speed up. The community is now in jeopardy.

Doc Ock grabs two people from the train, and throws them into the air. As Spider-Man struggles to save them, Doc Ock gets away. Spider-

Man returns to the train. His mask catches on fire, so he takes it off. "I can't stop it," says the engineer. "The brakes are busted!"
Peter looks up ahead to see that beyond the station lay a dead end. Worse, some yards beyond the dead end, the track just stops. The result is an eighty-foot drop-off beyond the dead end.
The lives of all the people in the train are now at stake.

Spider-Man tries to stop the train by putting his feet on the tracks, but that does not work. His first efforts have failed. The audience's anxiety level increases since they do not know how he will be able to stop this runaway train.

The train is not slowing down. Spider-Man could have jumped clear; it would have been no problem. Instead he starts firing those fantastic web-strands of his. He snags onto the passing buildings, but all that he seems to accomplish was to rip off chunks of brick and mortar and ledge. The train slowed, but not remotely enough. The edge of the track is looming. It is hopeless. The audience is driven to a frenzy of excitement. But Spider-man keeps trying. Right up to the edge the train rolls, and almost over, but then it stopped. The audience is relieved that no one has died.

At the precipice the train stops. But Spider-Man, exhausted, is about to fall forward. The conductor grabs him and with help from others pull him back into the car. They lift him up and carried him above their heads. Someone takes the mask off Spider-Man. The conductor looks down at the battered and bruised face of their unlikely savior. "He's just a kid, no older than my son." The members of the train care about Spider-Man, and so does the audience because they watched his efforts to stop the train from going over the edge.

Doc Ock appears. "Stand back, He's mine!" Everyone on the train closes ranks over the fallen hero. "You don't scare me pal," says one beefy fellow. "You want him you have to come through me?"
"Very well," said Doc Ock. He descended upon them and knocked them all aside. He scoops up the unconscious Spider-Man and carries him away. The audience is anxious about what will happen to Spider-Man.

Back at Harry Osborn's apartment, Doc Ock appears with Spider-

Man dangling from his tentacles. He is wrapped in some sort of barbed wire. Doc Ock drops him carelessly onto the chaise. Doc Ock takes the Tritium from the safe, then leaves.

Harry picks up a dagger and approaches Spider-Man. He steps next to him and lifts the dagger high. Then he stops and asks, "First, let's see who's behind the mask. Then I can look into your eyes as you die, Spider-Man." This is Spider-Man's most desperate moment. The audience believes that Harry will kill him.

As he pulls off Spider-Man's mask, a blast of lightning chooses that moment to strike, and Harry stares down in stupefaction at the face of Peter Parker, illuminated in the harsh glare of the lightning. "Peter." Harry staggers back as the dagger falls from his hand. "No, it can't be!" Spider-Man jumps up and frees himself. The audience is relieved that Harry does not kill Spider-Man.
"Harry, he took Mary Jane!"
"All he wanted was the Tritium."
"Tritium? Harry, he is making the machine again. When that happens MJ will die, along with half of New York! Now, where is he?"
"Peter, you killed my father!"
"There are bigger things happening here than me and you, Harry. Please…."
The community is a stake now, not just the lives of three people: Peter, Harry, and MJ.

At the old wharf Doc Ock is working with his fusion machine. He has MJ tied to a post. The life of the protagonist's love interest is at stake.
"You got what you needed for your little science project, now let me go!" she yells.
"I can't let you go. You'll bring the authorities. Not that anyone can stop me, now that Spider-Man is dead."
"He's not dead! I don't believe you."
"Believe it," he assured her.

Doc Ock fires up his machine to an even more earsplitting level. The stuff hanging in the middle suddenly ignited, and to Mary Jane's wonderment, it takes on the aspect of a tiny golden sun, no bigger than an orange, forming in the middle of the machine. The pulsating light reveals Spider-Man crawling along the ceiling.

"Shut it down, Octavius! You're going to hurt a lot more people this time!" says Spider-Man. The whole of New York City is at risk.

Mary Jane sees the glowing ball continue to grow, and she pulls at the chains with rising desperation. All at once she was lifted off her feet, and finds her ankles being pulled toward the fiery ball. The only things holding her in place are the chains that bound her wrists to the rusted pipe. The audience is excited because it looks like MJ will be killed.

The chains around her hands snap off the rusted pipe, and Mary Jane is yanked through the air directly toward the glowing ball. One of Spider-Man's web-lines has snagged her wrists, halting her, suspending her horizontally in midair. The aggressive machinery is pulling her in one direction while Spider-Man is doing everything he can to haul her in the other. The excitement rises to a frenzy level.

Doc Ock is knocked down. Then, as if emerging from a dream, Doc Ock wakes up. Peter tries to persuade Doc Ock to destroy the machine. Doc Ock fights the metal snake arms for control of his mind.
"Don't listen to them," says Peter.
"But it was my dream."
"Sometimes we must give up our dreams to do what is right!"
This is the moral of this movie. Doc Ock agrees.

"Now tell me how to stop it," says Peter.
"It can't be stopped, unless...the river. Drown it."
"I'll do it," says Doc Ock. The audience regains admiration for Otto. He was just temporarily crazy. He still has time to redeem himself.

MJ sees Spider-Man without his mask and knows he is Peter! A golden halo glow surrounds them. She expresses her love and joy at realizing that Peter and Spider-Man are one. The audience is also happy. But in this moment of happiness, disaster strikes. The wall suddenly falls down toward MJ. Spider-Man struggles to keep it off them, but it is very heavy. They profess their love for each other.

Octavius pulls the fusion ball down over him. "I will not die a monster!" says Doc Ock as he drags the ball of fire into the river. Spider-Man then throws the wall off them. He picks up MJ then jumps over a metal frame that is rolling towards them.

MJ and Spider-Man sit on a grid above the river.

"I think I always knew, all the time, who you were," says MJ.

"You know why we can't be together. Spider-Man will always have enemies. I can never let you take that risk. I will always be Spider-Man. You and I can never be." This is a moment of sadness for the audience because it appears that the lovers will not be united. He lowers her to the ground. The audience shares MJ's sadness. Police cars arrive below. John Jameson comes out and hugs her. He is relieved that she is not harmed. They kiss. Spider-Man jumps into the night.

Harry Osborn is home alone. He hears the voice of his father telling him to kill Peter. He wants Harry to avenge him. Harry screams "NO!" He throws a dagger into the mirror, which is reflecting his father's image. There, in the space revealed by the broken mirror, the face of the Green Goblin is starring back at him. The audience is happy that Harry will finally learn the truth about his father and the Green Goblin.

The mask is not moving or talking to him. It merely hangs there. There is an entire hidden workshop behind the mirror. There was a familiar glider on its stand and the armored suit in a case. The confusion gives way to growing horror, then to the realization that totally reordered his world. The audience is concerned that Harry will also become crazy like his father and perhaps still try to kill Spider-Man.

At the church MJ is preparing for her wedding. She is dressed in white and looks at herself in the mirror. John is at the church altar. Music starts playing "Here comes the Bride!" The audience is afraid that MJ will make a mistake and marry the wrong man. One of the maids of honor runs down the alley and gives John a note. J.J. Jameson reacts. He tells his wife to call Jackie, the caterer, and tell her not to open the caviar. The joke breaks the tension and allows the audience to laugh.

MJ, in her white wedding dress, runs through the park. She is happy, and the audience shares her happiness.

Peter is sitting on the bed in his apartment. Suddenly MJ, is in the doorway wearing her wedding gown. "Had to do what I had to do! Peter, I can't survive without you! I know that there may be risks, but I want to face them with you. It's wrong that we should only be half-alive, half of ourselves. Isn't it about time that somebody saved your life?"

"Thank you Mary Jane Watson." The emotional tension the audience feels is released, and they are happy that MJ and Peter will express their love for each other. Peter takes MJ into his arms and kisses her.

Suddenly, the howling of sirens floated through the window. Mary Jane simply smiles. "Go get them, tiger," she says. The audience is happy that MJ will let Peter be Spider-Man.

Spider-Man hurls above the streets of New York City. The audience is exhilarated by Spider-Man's actions. Mary Jane stands by the window of Peter's apartment and looks out after him.

Spider-Man hurls above the streets of New York City, followed by two helicopters. The audience vicariously shares the experience of swinging among the skyscrapers high above the streets of New York City. This is a joyous thrill!

THE END

COMMENTARY

One of the largest theater going audience is the 18-22 year old males. The *Spider-Man 2* movie was made especially for them.

"There had never been a teenage superhero. There had never been a hero who had personal problems. And there had never been a hero who, even though he triumphed over a villain, would never achieve a full victory because there was always something that he regretted or felt guilty about. In fact, that guilt, that belief that he has to do penance as Spider-Man for not preventing the death of his uncle Ben, sets Peter apart from every other Lycraclad crime fighter. Revenge is a typical motivation, but I don't think that there's another comic-book superhero that is completely driven by trying to pay some debt, a debt that cannot be paid, as Spider-man is." (*Newsweek June 28, 2004 page 52*)

The B-Story dominates the A-Story in *Spider-Man 2.* In this movie Peter Parker's inner conflicts are at least as interesting as his outer conflicts. Peter could never reveal his secret identity to his beloved Mary Jane Watson lest that knowledge put her in danger. He understood that he must hide his true self from his dear old widowed Aunt

May, plus keeping it a secret from his best friend, Harry Osborn, who believes that Spider-Man killed his father. Peter struggles with ambivalence, loneliness, resentment, and jealousy. All the mental confusion and divided loyalties manifest themselves in comic book terms but still give us a superhero with doubts. Peter is a tortured young man with secrets, increasingly alienated from everyone he cares about, battles demons inside and out. He eventually learns that secrets need to be shared.

Why does Peter have to be so weak? It essential to Spiderman's character that Peter be a mild-mannered nebbish who gets stepped on (literally) on campus by the other students. He is weak so that the 16-18 yr old boys in the audience will be able to identify with Peter and enjoy the fantasy of being Spider-Man. Having the audience care and have empathy for the protagonist is very important because the audience will experience the movie through the protagonist.

Guilt is an important factor in Peter's character. He feels responsible for the death of his Uncle Ben. Overcoming this feeling of guilt is why we have the fantasy scene of Peter talking to Uncle Ben in which Peter tells him that he doesn't want the power, he only wants to love MJ.

In *Spider-Man 2* every character, even J. J. Jameson, has a story arc that makes us care for them. Jameson admits that he drove Spider-Man away, and that Spider-Man was always a hero. But his changed opinion of Spider-Man doesn't last for too long. We even like the antagonist, Otto Octavius and are horrified by his transformation into the villainous Doc Ock. We are forced to care about Peter Parker because we realize that this is a guy who, no matter how good he is, is never going to get any respect. Despite the wonderfully done super heroics, the writers never forget that this is a story about people: more a drama of emotions than a reason to string together action. It is the story about characters confronting themselves. It's a tortured coming-of-age story about love and fear, regret and loneliness.

Why did the police have a problem finding Doc Ock when everyone else could hear him coming from blocks away? Why didn't anyone report him when he bought all that high tech equipment? You would think the UPS guy would have been a bit suspicious delivering it to a sunken wharf.

In popular Hollywood movies it is not the logic of the situation, or the plot that matters...but the emotional involvement of the audience with the characters. This movie is about the trials and tribulations of a young man who believes he has to give up love in order to be responsible. The film took its time working through the character arc. Peter had many more empathy scenes in this movie than in the first. It was only in the last thirty minutes of the movie that action dominates.

What about the scene with the landlord's daughter bringing cake and milk to Peter? It was there to show friendship, companionship, and to demonstrate that there was a woman attractive to Peter as Peter. He didn't need to be Spider-Man to have someone fall in love with him

Once Peter lost his love, he lost his power. No Mary Jane, no web slinging. But Peter had a great character arc. He goes from being Spidey, to giving up being Spidey, to learning that the city needs Spidey, and finally to winning the girl he loves and being Spidey again! The audience learns that you can fulfill your duty (being responsible) and have love, too! Everyone loves a superhero. That's what Aunt May said, and it made Peter finally feel good about himself again, good enough to want to jump off a roof.

In the climax scene Spidey fights Doc Ock, with Mary Jane dangling again. Yes, the love interest is tied to a post once again. But this is a climax scene with a twist. Spidey fights Doc Ock, but it is the nasty little snake arms that are the real villains. Doc Ock is a pussy cat. The snake arms took over nice Doc Ock's mind. They made him do it. Then we have the classic scene: "I'll do it, I'll sacrifice myself to save the world" speech delivered by the Doc to Peter. Doc tears down the girders. He'll destroy myself because it's the right thing to do! Then he looks back at Spidey woefully, "I wish it didn't have to end this way...I really did like you a lot." Then Doc Ock pulls down the fiery ball of fusion into the water and together they float so slowly away, redeeming himself by drowning in (and with) his sin. It is important to recognize that the protagonist does not kill the antagonist in the climax scene. The antagonist does himself in. This absolves the protagonist of any guilt for the death of the antagonist. Because Spider-Man was able to reach out to his higher nature, the audience gets what they want (kill the villain) but in an unexpected and emotionally satisfying way. A classic megahit movie climax!

This leaves us with Peter and MJ. She sees him without his mask, as she bathes in the glowing amber of the nuclear ball of fiery fusion, and it is complete love at long last sight! But then the roof falls down on her and Spider-Man (Peter) again comes to the rescue. She now knows why he's been skipping out on their dates and missing all her stage performances. But it is not over yet. They tell each other that they love each other. Peter then regains the strength to throw the metal roof away from them. It is amazing what the power of love can do!

Peter picks her up and they jump over the rolling metal frame that would crush them both the death. But it is still not over yet. Together, inside the spider-web on the top of the girders overlooking the river they profess their love for each other. But alas, it cannot be, because Spidey must be Spidey, and a guy's gotta do what a guy's gotta do (which MJ says back to him later). Spidey "lets her down" easily into the arms of another man, accepts his fate, and jumps into the night sky, once again swinging away.

Why did the writer and director write the story this way? How does the audience feel about the characters at this moment? They are on tenterhooks! Could it be that these two, who should end up together, wont? The audience can't stand that thought! But there she is, in her white gown, in the church, with the wrong guy waiting for her at the altar. This increases the emotional tension for the audience. They deserve each other, they love each other. Can't this somehow work out?
It is more dramatic if, at the last moment, she runs to the man she loves, as they did in the movie, *The Graduate*. It is emotionally more effective to have the audience feel that all is lost then have the lovers get together at the very last moment. The emotions become more intense, and the ending is more satisfying, filled with relief! This is good dramatic structure if you want to make a popular movie.

Spider-Man 2 focused more on the B-Story (relationships and character changes) than the A-Story (action, excitement, and thrills) which was the primary focus of the first *Spider-Man* movie. But the first movie grossed $404 million, while *Spider-Man 2* only grossed $355 million. It remains to be seen which of the two will become the most popular movie over time.

PIRATES OF THE CARIBBEAN

The Opening Scene: Fog, a Ship, and a Young Girl at the bow. Elizabeth Swan is singing a song about Pirates. A sailor, Mr. Gibbs, warns her against pirates. Norrington and Captain Swan, Elizabeth's father, engage in conversation. Suddenly, we see an umbrella in the water, then a boy on a raft, then a burning ship. This is the introduction of the antagonist: pirates! Captain Swan tells Elizabeth to watch over the boy. Elizabeth sees a Pirate's Aztec coin on a chain around the boy's neck. She takes it from him.

The **Unique Object** has been introduced: **the Aztec Gold Coin!**

The girl and boy introduce themselves to each other: Elizabeth Swan and Will Turner. Norrington then has Will carried below. Elizabeth keeps the Aztec coin. She then sees the pirate ship and the black flag.

TEN YEARS LATER

Elizabeth awakes from her dream. She opens a drawer and takes out the Aztec coin. Liz places it around her neck. There is a knock on her door. Her father, now Governor Swan, walks into the room with a present for Liz. It is a new dress. He wants her to wear it for the ceremony at which Captain Norrington will be promoted to Commodore Norrington. The dress is much too tight. Liz has problems breathing.

Downstairs, Will Turner waits in the hallway. He tries to fix a wall lamp, but it breaks off in his hand. He hides the broken piece. He brings a sword to the Governor which will be a gift to Commodore Norrington.

Liz sees Will and tells him she had a dream about him. Will is tense. It is inappropriate for them to be familiar because of class differences. The Governor and Liz leave the house and ride a coach through the gates.

Captain Jack Sparrow makes his entrance. He stands on the top of the mast and he rides into port on a sinking ship. He sails past pirates who have been hung. Near them is a sign: PIRATES BEWARE. Jack salutes the dead pirates. Jack rides his sinking boat up to the dock. He is approached by the docksman who asks Jack for his name and the docking fee. Jack does not give him his true name. Instead, he pays the docksman a few extra coins for his discretion.

The ceremony to honor Norrington is taking place in the courtyard. Liz has a problem breathing because of her tight dress.

Jack walks toward one of the British ships but is stopped by two soldiers. They talk about the Black Pearl being the fastest ship on the sea versus the Interceptor. The two soldiers continue to argue. Jack plays logic games with the soldiers about telling the truth and lying.

Norrington and Elizabeth walk to the edge of the fort. She continues to have trouble breathing, faints, and falls off the ledge into the water. Jack sees this and jumps in to the water to save her.

The Aztec gold coin hits the water. Winds howl. A storm starts up. This is the Inciting Event of the story. The Aztec coin hitting the water signals the cursed pirates on the Black Pearl. Now they know where the coin is.

Jack saves Elizabeth. He sees the Aztec coin around her neck. "Where did you get that?" he asks. British soldiers surround them. They take Jack captive. Jack has a pirate "P" tattooed on his arm and a compass that does not point north. Norrington says, "Worst Pirate I have ever heard of." Jack takes Elizabeth hostage. "This will be remebered as the day you almost caught Captain Jack Sparrow," says Jack.

Jack runs to escape but does so ineptly. He swings up on a rope which then spins him around in circles. This gives the soldiers below a chance to shoot at him. Jack hides in Brown's sword shop. Brown is drunk and asleep on the floor. Jack cuts off his chains. Will Turner comes into the shop and fights with Jack because he threatened Miss Swan. This is a comic swordfight scene. Will throws a sword at Jack which sticks in the door next to his head. Jack struggles to pull out the sword. Brown hits Jack on the head and knocks him out. "This will be remembered as the day that Jack Sparrow almost got away," says Norrington.

Elizabeth is in bed and talks with her maid. The maid says that Norrington would be a smart match, but that Will Turner is a fine man, too!" Liz touches the Aztec coin. Suddenly, the flame on her candle goes out.

The Black Pearl pirate ship approaches the harbor and begins firing on Port Royal. Jack is in jail when he hears the sounds of the guns. "I know those guns. It's the Black Pearl." Pirates from the ship attack the city. Two comic pirates lead the charge against the Governor's mansion. They kill the butler and chase Liz around the house, finally catching her in the closet. "Parley," says Liz. She wants to meet their Captain.

A cannonball hits the jail wall. The other prisoners escape, leaving Jack in his cell. He tries to get the dog to bring him the key. Two pirates enter the jail and confront Jack. When a cloud passes away from the moon, the moonlight reveals the skeletal arm of the ghost pirate.

Liz is taken to the Black Pearl. She meets Barbossa and his monkey. Liz negotiates with Barbossa. She wants him to leave the city. She threatens to drop the Aztec coin into the ocean. She tells him her name is Elizabeth Turner. "Bootstrap," says one of the Pirates. Barbossa agrees to her demands. But when Liz wants to be taken to the shore, Barbossa tells her that was not part of the bargain.

Back at the fort, Will goes to Norrington. He says that the pirates have taken Liz, and that they must go after her. Will says that Jack Sparrow knows the location of the ship.

Will goes to the jail and confronts Jack. He wants to save Liz. Will does not want to be a pirate. He tells Jack that his name is Will Turner. Jack agrees to help Will save Liz. Will gets Jack out of jail. They plan to steal one of the British ships. They overturn a row boat and walk underwater toward the ship. They take control of the Dauntless. They are chased by the British sailors on the Interceptor. Then, Jack and Will switch ships and take control of the Interceptor! "That's got to be the best pirate I have ever seen," says a sailor standing next to Norrington.

Jack and Will argue while sailing away on the Interceptor. Jack tells Will that his father was a pirate, Bootstrap Turner. Will cannot accept this. He refuses to become a pirate. They sail toward Tortuga, the Pirate City. There Jack wakes up Gibbs, who is sleeping with the pigs. Jack tells Gibbs that he wants to go after the Black Pearl. He says that he has the child of Bootstrap Turner.

On the Black Pearl, Liz is invited to wear a new dress and dine with Barbossa. If she refuses, she will have to dine naked with the crew. Barbossa and Liz have dinner. He offers her a green apple which she fears is poisoned. He tells her about the cursed Aztec treasure, and that the only way to end the curse is to return all the pieces. Liz has the final coin. Liz stabs Barbossa and tries to escape. She runs out onto the ship deck and in the moonlight sees that all the sailors are ghosts. She screams in terror. Barbossa confronts her and says: "You best start believing in ghost stories, because you are in one!"

Gibbs recruits a crew for Jack Sparrow. They are a bunch of inept rejects. When Jack approaches Anna Marie, she slaps him and accuses him of stealing her boat. He admits to doing so. They sail away in the ship. They get caught in a storm. Jack's compass does not find north, but they do find Tortuga.

The pirates take Liz into the cave where the Aztec treasure is hidden. Jack sails his ship through the sea of sunken boats. Gibbs tells Will the story of the mutiny of the Black Pearl, and how Jack was left to die on a deserted island.

Barbossa takes Liz to the Aztec treasure chest.

Will and Jack enter the cave. They watch Barbossa and Liz by the treasure chest. The monkey sees them. Barbossa cuts Liz's hand and drops the gold coin into the treasure chest. To see if they are now mortal again, Barbossa shoots one of the sailors. But he does not die. They discover that Liz is not the daughter of Bootstrap Turner. The curse is not broken! Cut her throat. Spill all her blood, yell the pirates. Jack walks toward Barbossa. He is surrounded by pirates. "Parley," he says.

Liz and Will escape with one of the coins. They leave Jack behind. They reach the ship and want to get the others to save Jack, but Mr. Gibbs reminds them of the Pirate's code: those who fall behind are left behind.

Barbossa decides to kill Jack, but Jack tells him that the girl's blood will not work, although he knows whose blood will.

Liz and Will are together in a love scene. Liz gives Will back the Aztec coin and tells him that she took it off him when he was saved years ago. It was a gift from his father. It is Will's blood that the pirates need to end the curse. Will is the son of a pirate: Bootstrap Turner.

Jack and Barbossa negotiate.

The Black Pearl gives chase to the Intrepid. Barbossa throws Jack into the brig. The ships engage in a battle. The Aztec coin drops below deck. Will goes for it, but the monkey grabs the coin. Water fills up the cabin, and Will is about to drown. Jack chases the monkey to Barbossa. The monkey's name is also Jack. The Intrepid is blown up. Liz thinks that Will is dead. Will comes onto the Black Pearl and demands the release of Liz. Will puts a gun to his head, and threatens to kill himself if Liz is not set free. If he dies, the pirates will live with the curse forever! Barbossa accepts.

Once Barbossa has the Aztec coin, he makes Liz walk the plank. She gives him the dress back, then she is knocked into the water. Jack is also made to walk the plank. Before him is the island on which he was marooned before. He is given only one gun with one bullet. Barbossa thows it into the ocean.

Liz and Jack swim to the island. Jack tells her that he was saved by rum runners after lying on the beach drinking for three days. That night they drink rum together near a fire. Jack tells Liz that the Black Pearl means freedom to him. They drink to the Black Pearl and to Freedom!

The next morning Jack awakes to see Liz burning up all his rum. She is making a big fire with billowing smoke in order to attract any British ships in the area that are searching for her. Jack runs down the beach and sees a British ship approaching. Norrington and Liz's father save her and capture Jack. Liz persuades Norrington to search for Will, as a wedding present.

The comic pirate tells Will about the death of his father, Bootstrap Turner. Barbossa killed him because he did not like the mutiny that took the Black Pearl away from Captain Jack Sparrow.

British soldiers in row boats sail with Jack toward the Pirate's cave. Jack makes a plan. Liz is locked in the ship's cabin by her father. Jack then rows into the cave alone.

Jack approaches Barbossa and Will. Barbossa is about to cut Will's throat, but Jack explains that once he does that, the pirates will all become mortal and the British sailors waiting for them will kill them. The pirates should defeat the sailors while they still cannot die! They make a deal. Barbossa will get two ships. Jack will become the captain of the Black Pearl once again. Barbossa will become a Commodore.

Barbossa orders his men to attack, but not by using the row boats as Jack expected. The pirates walk underwater and attack the British ships, thereby, bypassing the waiting sailors in the rowboats.

The Governor talks to Liz through the cabin door. He opens it to discover that Liz has escaped. The cursed pirates attack the British ship. The Governor fights a skeleton arm. Liz saves Gibbs and his crew. She wants them to help her save Jack, but they refuse. Liz row towards the pirate's cave alone.

Liz returns to the fight. Jack fights with Barbossa. But since Jack has stolen one of the coins, he is now also cursed and cannot be killed. In the climax scene, Liz runs toward Barbossa. He points a gun at her. Jack points a gun at Barbossa. Will cuts his hand and drops the two Aztec coins into the chest. Jack shoots Barbossa, who is now mortally wounded and dies. All three characters, Liz, Will, and Jack, together bring about the destruction of Barbossa. Therefore, all three should be considered protagonist of this story.

All the pirates on the ship become mortal. They surrender to the British sailors. Liz, Will, and Jack are alone in the cave. Will tells Liz that Norrington is waiting for her. "If you are waiting for the appropriate moment that was it!" says Jack to Will as Liz walks away.

Back at Port Royal, Jack is on the gallows waiting to be hung. Will walks through the crowd. Liz watches the scene. Will tells Liz that he loves her. The gallows door drops open. Will throws his sword against the gallows wall. Jack stands on the sword and struggles not to fall. Will frees Jack. Jack and Will grab a rope and trip up several soldiers. Finally, they are surrounded. This is the final confrontation scene between Jack, Will, Liz, Norrington, and the Governor. Will accepts that he can be both a pirate and a good man. Jack bids his farewell and trips over the edge of the fort. He falls into the water below. Norrington gracefully frees Liz from her vows to him. Norrington gives Jack one day's lead. "But he is a blacksmith," says the Governor about Will to Liz. "No, he is a pirate," answers Liz.

The Black Pearl sails into the harbor and pulls Jack onboard. Anna Marie gives Jack his hat back. Jack takes control of the wheel, looks at his broken compass which does not point north, sings a pirate's song, then says "Now give me that horizon!"

THE END

COMMENTARY

In the first ten minutes of the movie, what do we see? What is the first image? The very first image? A ship in the fog, young girl on the bridge. Meeting of the young girl and boy. The girl rescues the boy. So, who is the protagonist? Is it Captain Jack Sparrow? But Will Turner is the one with a character arc, while the opening scene makes you focus on the girl, Elizabeth Swann, who has a fascination with pirates.

Liz is the one who takes the Aztec coin from the neck of Will Turner. You could argue that there are three protagonists in this story: Liz, Will, and Jack. They each take the lead at different parts of the movie, and they are all together and necessary in the climax scene where they defeat the villain Barbossa.

There definitely is only one antagonist! Barbossa. The pirate captain of the cursed crew. Will and Jack also have Norrington as an antagonist. Norrington creates problems in the love triangle, but he is not the real villain of the story. It is Barbossa that killed Will's father, tries to kill Liz, tries to kill Will, tries to kill Jack, and led the mutiny that stole the Black Pearl from Jack. So there is no doubt he is the villain.

Liz, Will, and Jack all function as the protagonist. Will tries to save Liz from the Pirates, but then Liz tries to save Will from the pirates. This is a movie with many, many twists... which makes it exciting.

Now back to the opening scene. A ship comes out of the fog (this sets up the mystery) with a young girl at the front of the boat, Liz. She talks of pirates with Gibbs and her father. The antagonist is introduced first by conversation. Liz expresses her fascination with pirates. They next find Will on a raft, and they bring him on board. Liz sees the pirate coin around his neck. This coin becomes the unique object of the story: the object that everyone wants to possess. Then, they see a ship destroyed by pirates which introduces danger and jeopardy for all the characters. These are the basic elements of the story, and they are all introduced during the first five minutes.

Then we jump years ahead...maybe ten or more. Continuity is maintained by the unique object: the pirate Aztec coin. Liz wakes up from a nightmare...much older now...and reaches for the coin which she then places around her neck.

Next, the basic love triangle is introduced. Liz loves Will and Will desires Liz, but he is not in her class and feels he cannot court her. The father wants Liz to marry Norrington, Norrington wants to marry Liz, and Captain Jack Sparrow wants to get back his ship: The Black Pearl!

Why does Will break the candle holder? Why did the writers put that scene into the movie? It shows that he is out of place in that household and it is meant to make us laugh. But it also creates sympathy for Will. We care about Will in his awkward moment. The scene was written to elicit an emotion from the audience for this character. We later discover that he's good at sword fighting. Swords are his trade.

Each protagonist gets their own empathy scene: Liz because she has to wear a tight fitting corset and cannot be with the man she loves, Will because he cannot court the woman he loves, and Jack Sparrow because he is a silly pirate on a sinking ship.

Let's talk about Johnny Depp's entrance as the pirate, Captain Jack Sparrow. He rides a sinking boat into the dock. How fearsome a pirate can he be? He sails past the skeletons of pirates who were hanged, so there is danger in his situation. Jack gallantly salutes them which shows that he is indifferent to the threat of death. He rides into the midst of a British naval fleet. He is a quick witted thief which is shown in the scene where he pays a corrupt official for docking his sunken ship.

Each character has an objective: each character wants something. This is how you design characters in your stories. Norrington wants to marry Liz and Liz wants to marry Will. Jack Sparrow wants a ship, but more than that, he wants to get back his ship, the Black Pearl. Barbossa wants to be released from the curse of the undead. To do this he needs the last Aztec Coin and the blood of a Turner. This becomes the unique object that ties the villain to Will and Liz.

The writers play with this structure to create plot twists. Because Liz wants to marry Will, when she is captured, she tells the pirates that her name is Liz Turner, and they think that she is the daughter of Bootstrap Turner, therefore, the source of their salvation. They believe that once they return the last Aztec coin and spill some of her blood, they will become mortal again.

The writers did a great job in crafting this story because they only gave the audience the information that that wanted them to have when they need it. Most of the time it was misinformation or incomplete information meant to deceive. That is why the audience is constantly surprised. This is how you create your plot twists and mystery...create anticipations in the audience which are then not realized. The audience never knows for sure what is going on. This keeps the audience engrossed in the story. It's finding that fine line of what is needed to move the story along and yet keep the mystery and surprise coming around the next twist in the road. The writers did a great job in crafting not only a story, but expectations for the audience. The pirates didn't go on boats to the ships, but walked underwater to attack, thereby upsetting Jack's plan. Another plot twist!

The writers kept coming up with surprises right up to the very end of the story. Jack becomes one of the cursed undead, so Barbossa cannot kill him in the sword fight from hell.

Although Liz has a fascination with pirates, she can't go on the Black Pearl with Jack because the Black Pearl means freedom to Jack. Will accepts that he is the son of a pirate, and Liz decides to marry him.

What was the climax scene of this movie? Or, how many climax scenes do we have in this movie? There was one for each major story line. Who kills the villain? This was the big swordfight in the cave. Jack, Will, and Liz together bring about the death of Barbossa: Liz forces Barbossa to point his pistol at her and not Jack, Jack shoots Barbossa, and Will drops the bloodied coin into the Aztec chest, which removes the curse, makes Barbossa mortal, and enables him to die! The three in unison bring about the defeat of the antagonist. This was climax number one!

But Will loses his moment with Liz, and she returns to Norrington. Climax two occurs when Jack is to be hanged as a pirate by Norrington but is saved by Will and Liz. Norrington accepts defeat when Liz chooses Will over him, and he allows Jack to "fall free."

The resolution? Liz and Will get each other. Liz not only gets a pirate, but the respect of her father and Norrington, while Captain Jack Sparrow gets back his ship, the Black Pearl, and the open seas of freedom.

All's Well that Ends Well on the Pirate Seas of Yore!

FINDING NEMO

Classic Hollywood story design has one protagonist trying to overcome dangerous obstacles to achieve a goal.

Finding Nemo has two protagonists: A father in search of son (Marlin), and a son who wants to get back home (Nemo).

This structure does work for the mass audience since *Finding Nemo* has grossed over $339 million in the U.S. Domestic Box Office.

Let's review the opening sequence, which is a standard Spielberg type of opening. A happy husband (Marlin) and wife (Coral) watch over the brood of new eggs. Then comes the hook...the JAWS...the RAPTOR. In the case of *Finding Nemo*, it is the Barracuda who knocks out Marlin then eats Coral and all the eggs except one. Nemo with the wounded fin!

As Spielberg does in many of his megahit movies, this story starts with the introduction of terror in order to emotionally hook the audience! It creates sympathy and empathy for the dual protagonists: the wounded sole surviving child and the father, who has seen his family destroyed.

Now the audience cares for the characters and wonders what will happen to Nemo! This is part of the important first ten pages of any script. Next, we jump forward to the future. Nemo has to go to school. Marlin is over protective about his son with the broken fin. First day of school they go to the drop off. Nemo decides to swim to the boat, and he is captured by a fisherman.

This is the inciting event. Nemo's and Marlin's world changes! Nemo is taken away from his home! We are still in the first ten minutes of the movie. We now have two protagonists with two objectives: Marlin wants to find Nemo and bring him back home; Nemo wants to get back home. It is the same inciting event for both protagonists. The rest of the story is designed around a series of problems-obstacles that both characters have to overcome in order to achieve their primary objectives.

Marlin and Nemo are given equal time on the screen. That is why the Nemo story is hard to classify as a subplot. I would rather say that they are the dual protagonists. Some movies have multiple protagonists. *Independence Day* is an example with four protagonists, all of whom have the same primary objective: save the Earth from destruction. Each of the protagonist finds a protagonist-supporter; a character who helps them on their journey. For Marlin, it is Dory; for Nemo, it is Gill. Dory helps Marlin find Nemo. Gill helps Nemo to escape from tank.

Dory is the comic relief: *Memento* as a fish story. Dory has short-term memory problems which create problems for Marlin. But that is how to create an interesting story: create a supporting character that creates problems for the protagonist they are supposed to be helping.

This is also the case with Gill. He has his own agenda. He wants to use Nemo to help him escape. He almost gets Nemo killed in the process. It is the scarred face on Gill makes him sympathetic to the audience, plus the fact that he almost sacrifices himself to save Nemo in the dentist's office during the climax scene. The fact that Gill, too, had a wound is not an accident. It was part of story design to create empathy for Gill.

Carla, the little girl, is the ultimate villain, even though it is the Dentist, who captures Nemo, who is the antagonist. She is the critical problem (the life-and-death villain), that Nemo will have to deal with in the climax scene. But the little girl is not the antagonist throughout Nemo's story. It is Dr. Sherman who caught Nemo and holds him captive.

What was one of the plot twists of the story? Sharks that are fish friendly is a bit of humor that works. This is a twist on our stereotypes! And that is how you create humor. We all expect sharks to be flesh eating creatures. That is the expectation. But then as writers we create the contradiction...the opposite of the expectation, the opposite of the norm. The shark in this story, Bruce, is a vegetarian who believes "Fish are our Friends!" This basic humor design is old as creating a Lion who is a coward (since we all know that lions are the symbol of heroic courage), as in *Wizard of Oz*. But although he is a reformed shark, he relapses now and then when he gets really hungry. Funny stuff!

Another plot twist has to do with the fish tank. The audience is led by the writers to believe that once the tank gets dirty, the fish will be able to escape. So the fish in the tank overcome many obstacles to stop the filter and dirty the tank...then what happens? A plot twist! The subgoal achievement fails. A new upgraded filter is placed into the tank. Dr. Sherman installs a high tech filter and cleans the tank. Understand the basic structure: the writer creates expectations in the audience that he knows will not be realized. This is to create surprise and maintain a state of suspense in the audience.

The climax scene for Nemo occurs in the dentist's office. Will he achieve his objective, escape from Dr. Sherman and the fish tank and return home, or will Nemo be taken away by Dr. Sherman's niece, Darla, the evil fish killing villainess? This is a life-and-death moment for Nemo, because the last fish that Darla took home in a bag, she shook to death.

In the climax scene we expect twist upon twist, and we are not disappointed. Everything does not go according to the expectations set up in the mind of the audience by the writers. Many unexpected events occur before Nemo is finally free. This is good story design, because it gives the audience what they want (Nemo is freed), but in an unexpected way.

Father and son are finally rejoined after Nemo shows Dad that he has the smarts to save Dory. We have the classic reconciliation scene that lasts no more than five minutes at the end of the movie. There is no place like home! Marlin finally has the faith in Nemo that he lacked at the beginning of the film. Marlin and Nemo go back at School. Bruce and the Sharks stop by to say hi! Nemo says: Love you, Dad. Marlin says: Love you son! End of movie! $339 million at the Box Office!

While the deep structure is the same, the emotional subtext is the same, the context and setting of the story is very different. We must always be taken into an extraordinary world where "no man has gone before."

These stories are designed to provide the audiences with an "emotionally satisfying experience." They take the audience through an emotional roller coaster ride with lots of danger, jeopardy, and thrills, but take them home safely at the end. The kids want to see it again and again, but they are too young to go themselves, so the parents have to take them, and the parents don't mind seeing the story again. This is the kind of repeat audience needed to make a film a megahit movie.

MONSTERS, INC.

First Image: An Open Door.

VO of parents talking to a child: "Good night."

A little boy is sleeping in his bed. Clock indicates it is 9:00 pm.
The window is open…a strong breeze blows the curtains. A door opens. A monster from under the bed rises up and hovers over the child. The child wakes up and SCREAMS! This is a standard Spielberg type of opening: start with terror to hook the audience. But since this is a comedy, we have to release the fear and stress through laughter. How is this done? The source of terror becomes non-threatening. The terrorist becomes terrorized. The monster screams in terror. The monster reacts in shock and falls down onto tacks lying on the floor. The monster shrieks in pain. Suddenly, the simulation is terminated. Nobody really got hurt. The audience laughs.

The monster, Mr. Vial, is reprimanded by the instructor. Other monsters are watching the simulation. They learn that the major mistake was to leave the door open.

Mr. Waternoose, a spider-like creature and the owner of Monsters, Inc., is a tarantula dressed in red and black. These are the standard colors of the villain. This is the introduction of the antagonist scene. He explains that a human child is deadly and cannot be let into their world. Yet they need the screams of the children as an energy source to power their world. Mr. Waternoose announces that he will bring the best monster he has, James P. Sullivan, to give a demonstration to the others on how to scare children and make them scream.

Sully, the turquoise bear-like creature, is asleep in his bed. Mike
 (of the green eye) wakes up Sulley and makes him exercise. Mike is Sulley's trainer. TV Commercial about Monsters, Inc. and the Super Scream…pure energy. "We Scare because We Care!" Sulley's mom calls because she saw Sulley on TV. Mike answers the phone call.

There is a scream shortage. This is the protagonist's main problem. His primary objective is to increase the energy supply for Monsters, Inc. and the city. Sulley and Mikey walk to work.

Inside Monsters, Inc. Sulley is listed on the wall as the Scarer of the Month. Mike runs up to the receptionist, Celia, and says "Happy Birthday!" Celia has snakeheads for hair. Mikey promises to take her out to Harry Hausen's Restaurant for Dinner.

Mike and Sulley go into the locker room. They are confronted by nasty Randall, the lizard, and rival of Sulley. Randall wants to beat Sulley's record. Randall appears to be the antagonist for the rest of the movie, until the very end, when it is revealed that he is really working under the direction of Mr. Waternoose. This becomes a surprise twist at the end of the movie. The Harry Potter movies also use the structure of keeping the real villain hidden until the end of the third act.

The Scarers walk into the door room like the astronauts from "The Right Stuff" movie. The Scarers parade by like they are ready for battle.

Sully has over 99,222 points. Randall has 99,111 points.

The clock strikes 9:00 and they all go to work! They work the day away. More doors, more screams. A child almost touches a monster and scares the monster to death. The workers shred that door into little pieces. "Kids just do not scare like they used to," says one of the doormen.

An announcement comes over the intercom. There is a new Scare Leader! Randall! But then, suddenly, the points change again, and Sulley is back as the leader! The rivalry keeps tension in the story.

Monster George comes out of the door with a child's sock on his back. The attendant screams code 2319! The CDA run in and grab the sock, then they destroy it. Next, they decontaminate George by shredding all his hair. Monster George stands naked on the assembly floor.

Mr. Waternoose, the boss, is afraid that the Monsters, Inc. company will go under. It is the end of the work day. Sulley and Mike go into the locker room. They go into the main hallway. Mike is about to leave for his date with Celia, when Roz, the timekeeper, reminds him that he did not turn in his paperwork. Sulley goes back to get the paperwork.

One door is still on the factory floor. It is not closed. Sulley enters the room, but no one is there. He finds an empty bed. He walks out and closes the door. A child in pigtails stands on the floor next to him. She plays with Sulley's tail. Sulley quickly places her back into the room. This is the Inciting Event. Sulley's world is about to change!

Sulley tries to flush the child's stuff down the toilet, but the water backs up. The child is on his back. Sulley runs away, but the child chases him. Sulley tries to return the child to the room, but Randall is in the warehouse. Randall presses a button and sends the door back into storage.

In the restaurant Mikey is courting Celia. Tells her she should get a haircut. The snakes that are her hair panicand hiss. Sulley comes in carrying a bag. He talks to Mikey. The child walks away with the bag over its head. The other monsters in the restaurant panic when they see that there is a human child wandering freely in the room. They run out of the restaurant as the CDA enter in order to decontaminate the area. There is a child security breach!

The human child is in Sulley's and Mikey's apartment. The monsters do not want to touch the child, who takes little Mikey from the shelf. The child laughs and causes an energy surge which leads to a blackout! Mike and Sulley argue about what to do with the child.

The child is in Sulley's bed. Randall is the child's monster. Sulley goes into the closet to show that it does not hold a monster. Sulley tries to get the child to go to sleep. Sulley goes out of the room.

Sulley wants to put the child back into her room and send her back home. This becomes his new objective. They walk back to Monsters, Inc. with the human child disguised as a little monster. The factory is filled with CDA agents.

Mike and Sulley take the child into the men's locker room. The child has to go to the bathroom. The child sits in the stall and sings. Sulley opens the door with the child now behind him. They play hide and seek.

Mikey comes into the bathroom and confronts Sulley with the child. Suddenly, they hear Randall. They hide. Randall comes in and searches the stalls. Randall becomes invisible.

Sulley, Mikey, and the child go into the door room. Mikey gets the wrong door. He argues with Sulley. "Boo" is the human child's name. Mikey and Sulley bump into Randall.

Celia confronts Mike. Randall sees Mikey behind the human child in the restaurant picture on the front page of the newspaper. Randall now knows that Mike is involved. Randall confronts Mikey, and together they plan to return the child to her room during the lunch break at 12:00 pm.

The child, Boo, runs loose and jumps into a garbage can. CDA agents confront Sulley, but they only want his autograph. Boo jumps out of the can seconds before the garbage men dump its contents down the garbage chute. Sulley believes that Boo has been thrown down the chute and chases after her. He runs down the stairs and watches the garbage compressor pack the trash into squares. Sulley faints. Mike is looking for Sulley. He finds Sulley walking down the hallway carrying a square of compressed garbage.

Sulley then finds Boo with the kindergarten class. Boo laughs. There is another power surge! It is now 12:30 noon. They all run toward Boo's door. Sulley does not trust Randall. He thinks that it is a trap. Mikey decides to prove him wrong and enters the room. Randall jumps him, and places Mikey into a container. Randall wheels the container out of the room and out of the factory. Sulley follows Randall.

Boo opens the hidden door. She and Sulley travel down a tunnel. Randall and Fungus strap Mikey to a chair then activate the Scream Extraction machine. The machine's funnel approaches Mikey's mouth. He struggles to avoid it.

Sulley pulls the plug and cuts off the power. Randall searches for the problem. Mikey pulls a switch and places Fungus in the chair. Sulley, Mikey, and Boo run down the hallway.

Waternoose is in the Simulation Room. Sulley runs into the room. He tries to tell Waternoose what Randall has done. Waternoose forces Sulley to demonstrate his scare tactics. Sulley scares Boo, who cries and runs away from him. Mikey tells Waternoose all that has happened. Waternoose is sad, excuses the others from the simulator room, then brings down a new door. Randall comes in. He opens the door…to the artic mountains…then pushes out Sulley and Mike. They are now banished! Another plot twist. They thought that telling Waternoose the truth would solve their problems. But they were wrong. They were betrayed, and now things are worse. This is the end of act two desperation scene. The antagonist controls the love interest and unique object.

The Abominable Snowman welcomes Sulley and Mikey to banishment. He offers them snow cones. Mikey wears mittens on his ears. Sulley learns that there is a local village nearby…with children. "Never go out in a blizzard," says the Snowman. Sulley builds a sled. He argues with Mike, who does not want to go back to rescue Boo. Sulley pushes the sled into the snow, leaving Mike behind. Sulley slides down the mountain then crashes. When he looks up, he sees the village below. The windows in the cottages light up. Sulley gets up and runs into one of the cottages. Boo is tied to the Scream Extraction machine. Waternoose watches the operation. Sulley runs in and breaks up the machine. Randall becomes invisible and beats up Sulley. Mikey returns carrying a snowball and engages Sulley in conversation while he is getting beat up by the invisible Randall. Mikey throws the snowball at Sulley and hits Randall. Randall becomes visible. Sulley hits Randall, knocking him out.

Sulley drags Boo and Mikey down the hallway. Celia jumps on Mikey. Mikey tries to explain as they are chased by Randall. Mikey explains, but Celia falls to the ground. Celia makes an announcement that Randall is the new leader. All the workers surround Randall to congratulate him. This blocks his efforts to catch Boo. They activate the door machine and see Boo's door coming toward them, but Randall breaks free and runs after them.

THE CHASE IS ON! The excitement drives the audience into a frenzy!

Sulley jumps up onto the conveyor belt with Mikey and Boo and goes after Boo's door. Randall follows. They all go on a rollercoaster ride. They become trapped in a dead end. Mikey makes Boo laugh. There is another power surge. They jump through a door on a tropical island then through another door into Japan. Randall still chases them. They next go into a Paris apartment with a view of the Eiffel Tower. Randall grabs Boo! Sulley then gives chase. Sulley and Randall fight. Boo hits Randall and knocks him out. Randall is thrown through a door by Sulley and Mikey. Randall lands inside a trailer in a swamp. There he is beaten by a woman who lives in the trailer. Sulley and Mike destroy the door so that Randall can never return to Monsters, Inc.

Waternoose brings back Boo's door. Mikey uses a dummy Boo to fool Waternoose into confessing. He would kidnap a thousand children to save his company. They get this on videotape. The CDA burst into the room and arrest Waternoose. The #1 CDA agent is Roz. Sulley wants to take Boo home. Roz allows this, but then the door must be shredded. That's the way it has to be.

Boo leads Sulley into her room. Sulley puts Boo into bed. "Goodbye, Boo, Kitty has to go." They hug goodbye. Sulley walks through the door and closes it. Boo gets out of the bed and opens the door. It is just a closet.

Boo's door is shredded. Mike gives Sulley one piece of the door. "None of this ever happened! And I do not want to see any paperwork on this!" says Roz.

Back in the Simulation Room, Mike, with a microphone in his hand, is sitting on a stool doing a standup comedy routine. Mike swallows his microphone. The child in the bed laughs. Laughter is more powerful than screams. Celia and Mike kiss. Sulley and Mike are on the front cover of a magazine. On the Laughter Board, graphs show an upward trend in energy production.

Sulley carries a scoreboard in his hand. Under the papers he has the picture that Boo drew of them. Taped to the picture is the last piece from the door. Mike has a surprise for Sulley. He shows him Boo's door that he has pasted together. But he needs the one last piece to make it work. Sulley gives Mike the piece. Sulley slowly opens the door. "Boo?" he says. "Kitty," says Boo. Taking away a character's source of joy, then unexpectingly bringing it back to them, gives the audience a happy ending once again.

THE END

BRUCE ALMIGHTY

The opening scene: Bruce must cover the "Buffalo's Biggest Cookie" news story. Bruce has to wear a hairnet for the TV newscast, while the baker picks his nose in the background. This scene is designed to create empathy for Bruce by exposing him to public humiliation. It also shows Bruce's major problem and weakness: he blames others for the state of his life, especially God. "GOD, why do you hate me?"

Bruce and Grace watch the TV commercial while sitting on the couch in their apartment. The love of our family, our town…Buffalo. Grace wants Bruce to help her put together the photo album. Bruce wants to watch himself on TV again.

The theme of the movie is also introduced: Altruism versus Selfishness. Selfishness versus Family and Community! What is Bruce's Dream? He wants to be the Anchorman on the TV news show. Bruce blames his problems on God! This is Bruce's antagonist, although the real antagonist of the movie is Bruce himself.

The next morning, Grace is going to give blood. She has a rare AB type. Bruce does not want to give blood. This is a setup that will later be used to save his life. Grace also gives Bruce the prayer beads, a theme prop that is passed between characters throughout the movie.

Bruce is caught in traffic. He is going to be late for work. It is "Sweeps Week." A lot is at stake this week for Bruce. This produces tension and jeopardy for the protagonist. His dream is at stake. Bruce drives his Datsun to work. The meeting starts without him. He sees a beggar holding a sign: R EWE BLIND.

Jack is supervisor at the TV station. Bruce and Evan are rivals for the anchor position. They insult each other. Jack gives Bruce a chance for a live feed from Niagara Falls. Grace is working at school with little children. One child eats paste. Her sister Debbie comes in and picks up the phone. We get the message that Debbie believes Bruce is wasting Grace's life. Bruce believes he has a chance at winning the anchor spot.

Bruce is at Niagara Falls with a rainbow color umbrella on his head. It is then announced that Evan gets the anchorman job. Bruce freaks out! Live with Wacky Bruce. Bruce's world changes when he gets fired from Channel 7. This is the INCITING EVENT.

Bruce sees a gang beating up the old man. He yells at the gang, and they beat him up and smash his car. Again, Bruce blames God for his problems. The beggar holds up sign saying LIFE IS JUST!

Grace says "EVERYTHING HAPPENS FOR A REASON." Bruce complains about his mediocre life. He and Grace have a fight. Bruce leaves. He is very upset. He calls out to God to give him a sign as he passes a truck filled with signs such as STOP, DEAD END, etc. Bruce drops his prayer beads in the car. He bends down to pick them up and crashes into a pole. Bruce throws the beads into the lake as he yells at God: "The only one here NOT doing his job is you!"

The next day, the dog is again on the sofa. Bruce throws his pager out the window because it is getting a message from 776-2323, a number he does not recognize. It hits the ground and a car rolls over it, but it still rings. Bruce dials the number and gets a message to go to an empty warehouse for a meeting.

He see a janitor mopping the floor. The janitor asks Bruce to help, but Bruce just laughs. Says he will have some free time on the 7th at 7pm. He says okay. Bruce gets to the 7th floor and sees a white ladder going up to the ceiling. A bright light is turned on. The janitor walks down the ladder wearing a blue-overall suit. He takes that off to reveal an all white suit and announces that he is God. This scene is a confrontation between the protagonist and the antagonist.

God has a file on Bruce. Magically, the filing cabinet extends across the room. Bruce asks God to tell him how many fingers he is holding up in his hand. God always has the right answer. The final joke is that God says Bruce has 7 fingers. Bruce laughs, but when he looks, he does have 7 fingers. This freaks out BRUCE. God then gives Bruce God's powers. Bruce enters an extraordinary world.

Bruce is able to start his stalled car. He wishes he was Clint Eastwood then becomes Clint Eastwood. With a GUN! He then runs into a diner. He desires a spoon and one comes out of his mouth. He then parts the red soup. A windstorm blows through the diner. God appears in the diner. Together, they go for a walk.

God explains the rules:
1- You can't tell anyone that You are God.
2- You can't change Free Will.

A boat moves across the screen and shows that they are standing on water. Jim Carrey loves to walk on water (see THE TRUMAN SHOW). God retrieves the prayer beads out of the water then goes on a holiday. It appears that Bruce, the protagonist, has triumphed over the antagonist. He has God's power. This is the end of act one.

MUSIC: "I got the power" theme. Bruce creates a gust of wind which blows up a girl's dress. He looks at neat clothes in a store window and magically they appear on him. Bruce beats up the gang that beat him up. Bruce makes a monkey pop out of the butt of the gang member. Bees fly from his mouth and stings the other members of the gang.

BRUCE ALMIGHTY—MY WILL BE DONE!

Bruce decides to romance Grace. He pulls the moon closer to the earth. They kiss. In the morning, Bruce begins to hear voices calling out for help. He hears prayers.

Bruce causes his dog, Sam, to pee in the toilet. Grace notices that her breasts are bigger. Bruce wants to get his job back. Bruce transforms his Datsun into a high tech sports car.

Bruce is caught in a traffic jam, but magically separates the cars and opens a path through which he can drive.

Bruce uses his powers to make himself famous. Bruce discovers the body of Jimmy Hoffa. He fills the van for Channel 5 with drugs. Police arrest the other news team. At the Mark Twain Cookout, Bruce makes a meteor strike the earth. He gets the news story. Bruce becomes MR. EXCLUSIVE and gets his own Billboard on Main Street.

His dog, Sam, sits on the toilet and reads the newspaper as Grace walks in. This freaks her out.

Grace and Debbie get body massages in preparation for a night at the Blue Palm restaurant. Grace expects to get a proposal from Bruce.

Bruce manipulates Evan when he is on TV, forcing him to make weird sounds and look foolish in front of the audience. Bruce is becoming evil. He is using his powers to humiliate others in public.

Tony Bennett is singing at the Blue Palm restaurant. Instead of proposing marriage, Bruce tells her he got the promotion as the TV Anchorman. Tony sings "If I Ruled the World." SELFISH BRUCE! Bruce hears loud voices in his head. He screams at people around him for talking so loud, then he runs out of the restaurant.

God takes Bruce to Mt. Everest. "How many people have you helped?" asks God. Bruce has to manage the prayers. He starts with file cabinets, then yellow pasties. Then, he creates a computer system. "YAHWEH – The Revelation Super Highway!"

Juan Valdez comes to the window so that Bruce can get some java. Bruce becomes a speed typist and types "YES!" to all the prayers.

PARTY SCENE: Everyone wants to be with Bruce! He turns water into wine and hangs out with the Golden Calf. But Grace will not go to the Party and celebrate with him. "It's a Wonderful Life" is playing on the TV. It is showing the scene where Jimmy Stewart promises to lasso the moon for Donna Reed. Grace comes to the party and sees Susan kissing Bruce. Grace breaks up with him. Bruce rains on his own party.

Bruce cannot get Grace to take him back. It is a problem of "free will." He does not have the power to force someone else to love him.

We now see the consequences of Bruce's actions as an announcer reports the disasters occurring around the world.

Bruce has his anchorman debut, but it is interrupted by the announcement that the Sabers have won the Stanley Cup. There is a sudden loss of power in the studio. They cut to a live interview in the sports arena. Bruce causes a cork to pop and knock out the sports announcer, so that the cameras cut back to him. The power goes off again, and again Bruce turns it back on. Bruce is frustrated on his big night!

People are rioting outside the news station. Bruce decides to leave the anchor position and go outside to help. Bruce is on the streets with the rioters, who are stealing goods from the bakery and the diner. The homeless man hangs up the sign: "Thy Kingdumb Come." A rioter complains about the lottery. Others push over the billboard sign. The photo of Bruce goes up in flames. Bruce screams!

Suddenly Bruce finds himself back in the empty warehouse, looking for help from God. He looks up the ladder, but no one is there. God, dressed as the janitor, returns. He has two mops with him. It is 7:00pm on the 7th. "Not as easy as it looks, this God business," says God.
"They are all out of control. It is mayhem. I do not know what to do!" says Bruce.

God gives Bruce a mop. Together they clean the floor.
"No matter how filthy something gets, you can always clean it up!" says God. "You want to see a miracle, be the miracle. The problem is you keep looking up." Bright lights go on as God walks up the ladder.

Bruce is by himself and looks up at the moon, as order is restored to the city. Bruce is stuck in traffic. He helps push a motorist's car that has stalled. Bruce disconnects the computer so that people can solve their own problems. Bruce apologizes to Evan and congratulates him on getting the anchorman job. Bruce accepts the position as the comic news reporter. Bruce stands up next to the homeless man and holds up his own sign: "What he said."

Sam will not pee on the sidewalk. Bruce runs upstairs and carries down the chair so that the dog will pee. Grace's sister comes to collect her things from the apartment. Bruce gives her the photo album. She tells him Grace prays for him every night.

Bruce searches for messages from Grace at the computer. "Dear God, help Bruce," appears. Bruce watches Grace cry as she prays for him.

Bruce walks in the rain in the middle of the street. He gets down on his knees to pray. "I don't want to be God! I want you to decide what is right for me! I surrender to your will!" Bruce gets hit by a big truck! A surprise plot twist. This is also the protagonist desperation scene that usually occurs at the end of act two.

CLIMAX SCENE

Bruce walks through the clouds of heaven and meets God, who says that "Bruce has the divine spark: the gift of bringing joy and laughter". God gives Bruce back the prayer beads. He wants Bruce to pray for what he really cares about. Bruce wants Grace to be happy. That is his prayer! God says that he will get right on it, then pokes Bruce in the chest with his fingers. This shocks Bruce back to life!

RESOLUTION SCENES

Bruce is now on the street where he was hit by the truck. He is receiving electrical shocks. Bruce next wakes up in a hospital bed with a doctor standing over him, telling him that he is lucky to be alive. Over the side of his bed is a bag of blood: AB Positive.

Grace comes into the room and hugs Bruce. He apologizes, then realizes that he has the prayer beads in his hands.

The last scene takes place at the "Be the Miracle" Community Blood Drive. Bruce is covering the story for the TV news. He introduces Grace as his future wife to the audience. They are surrounded by members of the community.

"BE THE MIRACLE!" says Bruce.

Grace pushes Bruce forward to donate blood.
The homeless man holds up a sign: "Armageddon Outta Here."
The face of the homeless man morphs into the face of God.

THE END

COMMENTARY

Bruce Almighty is a non-sequel megahit; an original story without a built-in audience. It is the kind of story that any writer could develop without having to worry about obtaining rights to existing material. *Magic and Humor* are the key to success. Show the audience things they do not see everyday and make them laugh.

Does this movie fit the standard first ten minutes of a classic Hollywood story design? What is the inciting incident? Bruce loses the anchor job he wanted. He flips out and gets fired. Now let's go back to the very first scenes to see what information the writer gave the audience.

What is Bruce's goal? His objective? Material things. Fame. Life on his terms. He wants one thing more than anything else. Bruce wants to be the TV anchorman. This is a concrete goal, but it is also a unique objective: only one person can be the anchorman. Bruce has competition because Evan also wants to be the anchorman. The way to guarantee conflict in a movie is to create a unique object that only one character can possess, have the protagonist and the antagonist both desire it, then have them fight for it. This is setup in the first ten pages of the script; the first ten minutes of the movie.

What is Bruce's personal problem? His Achilles heal? His weakness? Bruce is very selfish! Bruce only cares about himself and his desires. How is this established in the first ten minutes? What is the relationship with his girlfriend Grace like? He blew off his girlfriend over the picture book in the beginning of the story because he was worrying about his job. His character arc goes from selfishness to giving to others. Bruce goes from being completely selfish to giving his blood at the community blood drive.

And the writers did a great job in developing this character arc in small incremental steps. They set him up as being selfish because he will not help Grace with the family photo album (a "we" thing), because he wants to see his TV newscast one more time (again and again).

We have the classic Hollywood ten minute opening:
Introduce the protagonist with an empathy scene (in a hairnet).
Show the protagonist's dream (he wants to be the anchorman).
Show the antagonist (Bruce complaining about God).
Create an inciting event which changes his world (Bruce gets fired).

Who is the real antagonist of BRUCE ALMIGHTY? Bruce! Bruce is his own worst enemy and the character he must overcome before he can find happiness. He blames God for all his problems. What about the prayer beads? This is a great prop that was used by the writers to convey much meaning in the story, especially as it was moved from character to character. This is a great cinematic device. Grace gives Bruce the beads in the car. Bruce uses the beads to pray for a sign from God. He drops them on the floor of the car and, when he tries to find them, he crashes the car into a pole. Then he gets angry and throws the beads into the lake. Later, when Bruce and God are walking on water, God picks up the beads and takes them with him. In the end Bruce has the beads with him in the hospital when Grace comes back to him. It is an object that represents faith and hope in this story.

Once Bruce got God's power, what did he do with it? He abused it. Bruce got back at everyone he was mad at. He used the power for his own pleasure and personal gain. Selfishness to the max again! But then he discovered that he did not have the power to make Grace love him again. It was only when he realized that he could not win her back by power that he begins to change.

How does Bruce win back Grace? He wins her back through an act of selflessness. He wants Grace to be happy, even if that means her being with someone else. So God gives Grace the man who loves her most and will make her happy, which is Bruce. She prayed to God to help him. It was God answering Grace's prayers for Bruce to be contented with life and their love all along. So this was a nice plot twist, where the hero wins by letting himself lose.

THE MATRIX TRILOGY

MATRIX	$171,479,936
MATRIX RELOADED	$281,553,689
MATRIX REVOLUTIONS	$136,924,212

The first MATRIX movie was not a megahit, but it did create an audience for the second movie of the trilogy. *Matrix Reloaded* grossed over $280 million in the U.S. Domestic Box-Office. This was a highly anticipated movie that everyone had to see, yet, it was also universally proclaimed to be a critical disappointment. Many believe that the failure of *Matrix Reloaded* doomed the third part of the trilogy, *Matrix Revolutions*, which has grossed less than the first movie. Although not all three gained megahit status, much can be learned by studying the story structures found in these movies in the hope that they may lend some
light as to why this trilogy failed to maintain a mass audience appeal.

The first movie introduced the main characters and their primary objective: free the human race from the Matrix. Neo was deemed to be the ONE who would be able to do this. The movie is a "coming of age" story in which the hero develops the powers to save the race from enslavement to the Machines. Morpheus took on the role of the protagonist supporter, who helps Neo become the man he is destined to be, while Trinity is cast as the traditional "love interest." The antagonists are the Machines which have conquered the humans and enslaved their minds within the Matrix while using their bodies as an energy source for the machine world. The antagonist supporters are the agents, led by Agent Smith. He is the primary villain of the first movie. Neo chooses to fight the agents in order to save Morpheus's life, even though the Oracle has prophesied that one of the two must die. Neo is killed by Agent Smith, but then is brought back to life by Trinity's kiss, becomes the ONE, manipulates the Matrix, and destroys Agent Smith. The resolution scene of the movie shows Neo in the Matrix but warning the powers that be that he will challenge them to free mankind.

The first movie follows standard Hollywood story design with Neo as the protagonist overcoming obstacles to save the world from villains, who desire to enslave mankind. There are plenty of surprise twists, including Neo coming back from the dead, but ultimately in the climax scene, he prevails and destroys his opposition. The film is filled with amazing special effects and a stunning production design that made it the must see film of 1999. These factors led to the initial popular success of the second movie. Everyone wanted to see the sequel. They had to see this movie. But the reason that the second movie failed was that the characters became much less emphatic: Neo, with his Superman capabilities, became a comic book character with whom the audience could no longer identify. He was no longer personally in jeopardy. Neo was not at risk. It was Trinity, the love interest, who seemed destined to die. Yet, Neo also had the ability to bring her back to life by removing a bullet and massaging her heart with his hand. Neither of the characters are really in jeopardy in this movie. The audience no longer cared or remained emotionally involved. The climax scene had a classical Hollywood structure: the protagonist was given a choice of either saving the world, or the woman he loved. Neo chose not to save the world. He chose to save Trinity. So much the worst for Zion. To make matters even worse, at the end of the *Matrix Revolutions* Neo no longer believes that he is the ONE. He abdicates from his mission. This conclusion was emotionally disappointing for many people, and the word of mouth got out. After a great opening weekend, the box-office dropped 60 percent for the second weekend.

How many Agent Smiths can you fit in one courtyard? If Neo always had the ability to fly away from a courtyard filled with Agent Smiths, what took him so long? How many Agent Smiths can Neo defeat leads to the question of how many Agent Smiths can a teenager destroy playing the video game? The *Matrix Reloaded* theatrical release became nothing more than an advertising promo for selling *Matrix* video games and DVDs, which now have a greater profit margin (and gross revenues) for the Hollywood Studios than money received from theatrical releases alone. It is no wonder that the theater audiences could no longer become emotionally involved with characters that were reduced to video game action figures. Warner Bros. was determined to build on the momentum of the first two movies, but they realized that there would be problems with audience acceptance of the third movie of the trilogy. In order to avoid bad word of mouth they released the movie worldwide on the same day. It had a great first global weekend, but then audiences failed to return during the second week. The U.S. Box-Office Grosses for *Matrix Revolutions* is the lowest of the trilogy.

The *Matrix* trilogy is often complimented for introducing metaphysical discourse to the general movie public. Issues concerning appearance versus reality and determinism versus free-will are thrown into the dialogue between the action filled sequences. Books such as *The Matrix and Philosophy* edited by William Irwin, are dedicated to discussing philosophical issues raised in the movie. The Oracle was introduced in the first movie to bring up issues of Free Will and Determinism. She continued to play a pivotal role in the second and third films. There is a symbiotic relationship between humans and machines. Humans have become dependent on machines and technology for their survival. This is shown and discussed in the city of Zion when Neo speaks with one of the Elders. But in Zion, it is humans that are transforming the technology more than the technology transforming itself. It was the creation of Artificial Intelligence by humans that empowered the Machines to revolt. Both the *Terminator* and *Matrix* movies start from the same premise: Intelligent Machines declare war on the human race. But the Matrix movies takes this premise to the extreme in having machines enslave humans and use them as an energy source.

The *Matrix Reloaded* continued to explore the journey of a futuristic messiah who would save the human race from enslavement. But Neo's objective changes from the first to the third movies: in the first Matrix movie his mission is to save humanity from the Matrix, but by the end of the third movie the best that he can accomplish is to end the war between the machines and the humans: the Matrix survives and the machines dominate the world after Neo's sacrifice. In this sense, the ending is an emotional disappointment for the audience.

In the climax scene of the second movie, the Architect explains that Neo was the sixth anomaly, and that this would be the sixth time that Zion gets destroyed. Neo then no longer believes that he is so special. What is so great about being THE ONE when there were five other ONES before you? Why bother to save Zion when it has been saved, then destroyed, five times before. Why not instead save the life of Trinity, the woman he loves? This is the choice that Neo makes at the end of the second movie.

The Matrix is a virtual reality world constructed by the Machines in order to keep the humans sedated so that they can be used as batteries to fuel the energy needs of the Machines. The Architect is a program in the Matrix, as is the Oracle. The Architect is the program that creates and maintains the Matrix system as an efficient order that will generate the most energy possible from the farm of human batteries. The Oracle is the program that generates the belief in some humans that they have free choice in order to keep them functioning within the Matrix. Neo is not a program, he is a human that has been released from the Matrix by the efforts of Morpheus, Trinity, and the other free humans. He is believed by Morpheus to be the reincarnation of the first human who freed himself and others from the Matrix. These free humans have escaped to the city of Zion. Here, they bred other humans who have not been born as servants to the machines and stage a resistance to the control of the machines. Morpheus believes that Neo will be able to control the Matrix, free the enslaved humans, and end the war with the Machines. The Machines have been fighting this war for over a hundred years. They have destroyed the city of Zion many times before, but they have not been able to create the perfect Matrix which will enslave all humans. Some humans always escape and free others. An Anomaly to the Matrix designed by the Architect is always generated each time a new Matrix system is created: this Anomaly is just intrinsic to the Matrix design process. A perfect Matrix that does not generate an Anomaly cannot be created. But if an Anomaly becomes too powerful, and starts to free too many humans, the Matrix becomes a failure for the Machines. It is the Oracle's task to point the Anomaly back to the source of power controlled by the Machines so that he can be recycled, Zion can be destroyed, and the optimal generation of battery energy from the human farms can be maintained. Neo is just the sixth Anomaly in the history of the Matrix system.

Humans want to believe that they are free; that they can make choices in their lives. This is the function of the Oracle: to help some believe that they can make choices. Ninety-Nine percent of the humans can be happy with the illusion of choice. The other fraction breaks out of the Matrix and goes to Zion. These are the ones that free themselves from the Matrix, the world of machin- generated illusions. Cypher was one such character, who then came to regret his choice. Cypher was not happy living in 'the Desert of the Real" and betrayed Morpheus and the others so that he could return to the Matrix and live a life of bliss in ignorance.

Then, there is the Anomaly, the ONE (or A ONE), like Neo. He is the One that can alter the Matrix and shift the balance; free more humans than the system can withstand. That is his threat to the machines and the reason why, if he is too powerful, he must be returned to the Source. This is also the function of the Oracle; to show an Anomaly the way back to the source so that the Anomaly can be assimilated and transformed back into human nutrition.

Neo is different from the others because this time he has released a new force which threatens to destroy the power of the Machines: Free Agent Smiths. Agents are sentinel programs created by the Machines to live within the Matrix and to prevent humans from escaping from bondage. Agent Smith was just one of these programs. But when Neo destroys him in the climax scene of the first *Matrix* movie, Neo also transforms Agent Smith. Neo unwittingly leaves something of himself in Smith, enabling

Agent Smith to also become free of the Matrix and the Machines. This is revealed when Agent Smith gives his control communication ear piece to Neo as a gift. Like Neo, Agent Smith is now a free agent but with the ability to reproduce at will. He is also instilled with a hatred for humans. Not only do the Agent Smiths want to destroy Neo, but they also want to destroy ALL the humans. This poses a critical threat to the Machines for if the Agent Smiths destroy all the humans, they will also destroy the Machines who need the humans as a source of energy. It is this fact that enables Neo to negotiate with the Machines and end the war against the humans. It is only Neo that can destroy the Agent Smiths because he created them by leaving part of himself in them…he destroys them by allowing the machines to funnel energy through him as a weapon. This process is successful but also ends in his death. Neo sacrifices himself to save the human race. At the end, the Machines transport away the body of Neo towards the source of all energy, perhaps to be transformed and reincarnated one more time.

Neo's victory is not a triumph over the Machines. The Machines still dominate, and the Matrix still exists. The Matrix is not destroyed in the climax scene. All that occurs is that the pending annihilation of the humans in Zion is stopped. A few humans survive the onslaught of the Machines.

In the resolution scene of the movie, three characters are shown within the Matrix: the Architect, the Oracle, and the little girl. The Architect and the Oracle are the duals of each other and are both needed to maintain the Matrix. The Architect does agree to allow any human to become free of the Matrix and go to Zion if they so choose. But, he does not agree to free all the humans, for to do so would remove the source of energy needed by the Machines to survive. The Machines and Humans will accept a symbiotic relationship in which they will need each other in order to exist. But there is a new addition: the little girl. She represents a human who can live in the Matrix without purpose. She never had a purpose besides being an object of love for her parents. In the new Matrix design, humans will be able to experience the world of the Matrix without being enslaved to serve the Machines. This is the new dawn that has been brought forth by Neo through his sacrifice.

In my opinion, *Matrix Revolutions* failed to become a megahit movie because the audiences were disappointed in the conclusion. In the first *Matrix* movie they were lead to believe that it was Neo's primary objective to free all mankind from the enslavement of the Matrix. He does not do this. At the end of the trilogy, the Matrix continues to exist, and the Machines continue to dominate. But worst than that, both the protagonist and the love interest die. Trinity allows herself to die because she believes that she can no longer be of service to Neo. She saved his life in the first movie and he saved her life in the second movie. For him to retrieve her from the dead again would be redundant. She also knows that Neo does not expect to survive the final battle with the Machines. Neo will not be coming back for her. Trinity dies. Neo also dies in the climax scene, because in order for the Machines to destroy all the Agent Smiths, they must destroy their essence, which is also the essence of Neo, since he gave birth to the Free Agent Smiths. Neo's death is necessary in order for the Machines to survive. In the climax scene, the audience experiences the death of the protagonist and love interest; the two characters for whom they had the most empathy and with whom they shared the adventures of the trilogy. This left them with an emotionally unsatisfying experience. Many people did go to see *Matrix Revolutions*, but would not return a second time, and it is the repeat audience that is necessary to make a film a megahit movie.

THE PASSION OF THE CHRIST

In the spring of 2004, *The Passion of the Christ,* produced and directed by Mel Gibson, became a megahit movie, grossing over $370 million.

To analyze or criticize the story of Christ would be to engage in a 2000 year old debate that has been carried on by theologians and historians and would be missing the point in explaining why this movie was so successful.

This movie became a megahit because it appealed to an audience of millions of Christians who wanted to see the story about the trial, persecution, crucifixion, and resurrection of Jesus Christ. It had a great pre-existing market for the story. This same audience will also watch it every year during the Christian Easter celebrations. Many people will also buy the DVD version to view at home or with their community.

HARRY POTTER and THE SORCERER'S STONE

The Opening Image: An owl is on Privet Drive. An old magician walks down the street. He sees a cat. The magician holds a device in his hand. When he points it at a lamp, it pulls the street lamp's light into it. The cat transforms into the witch, McGonagall. Hagrid rides a motorcycle across the sky and lands on the street in front of the house. He delivers the baby to Prof. Dumbledore, who believes that it is best for the child to grow up away from the world of magic until he is ready. The child, Harry Potter, has a scar on his forehead. The child is in jeopardy and must be protected from danger.

Ten years later Harry sleeps in a room under the staircase. He is bullied by his cousin, Dudley, who stomps on the stairs in order to make dirt and dust fall onto Harry. Dudley is a spoiled little boy who receives 36 presents for his birthday. Dudley is angry because last year he received 37. His father promises to buy him two more gifts on the way to the zoo. Harry is threatened by his uncle Vernon, who tells Harry that he does not want any funny tricks at the zoo.

They go to the reptilian house in the zoo. Dudley torments a snake. Harry uses magic to remove the glass and Dudley falls into the snake pit. Harry talks to the snake then helps him escape. Dudley is locked inside the snake's cage. The snake says thank you to Harry then slithers away. Uncle Vernon is very upset with Harry.

An owl flies by and drops a letter addressed to Harry Potter. Uncle Vernon takes it and will not let Harry read the letter. The owl delivers another letter, but Uncle Vernon rips it up. Owls gather outside the house. Harry's evil guardians burn all of the letters delivered by the owls. Uncle Vernon is happy because today is Sunday, and there is no post on Sunday. Suddenly, letters fly into the room from the fireplace and fill up the room. Harry fights with his uncle.

The family takes Harry away to a lighthouse, hoping that the owls will not find them there. It is Harry's 11th birthday. The door is smashed in by Hagrid. He brings a birthday cake for Harry. It is a gift from Hogwarts. "Harry is a wizard," says Hagrid. His aunt and uncle have been lying to him for years. They do not want Harry to go to a school for wizards. Hagrid uses magic to give Dudley a pig's tail then takes Harry away. This is the inciting event.

In London, Hagrid takes Harry along a street in order to buy school supplies. They enter a pub. The bartender announces that Harry Potter is in the pub. They all seem to know who Harry is, but he does not understand this. Hagrid taps on a brick, and a wall opens up. They walk into a street filled with magical shops. Harry admires the Nimbus 2000 Flying Broomstick. Hagrid takes Harry to Greengotts Bank which is run by Goblins. They go into Harry's vault. It is filled with gold coins left to him by his parents. They next go to vault 713 where Hagrid takes away a bundled wrapped in cloth. This is Hogwarts' business. This creates a mystery: the audience wants to know what Hagrid takes from vault 713.

Harry needs a wand, so he goes to a special wand store. The first tested wand is destructive, as is the second. The third wand is perfect. Wind blows through Harry's hair. This is a phoenix wand. The brother to this wand gave Harry the scar on his forehead. The storekeeper says that he expects great things from Harry. 'He that must not be named did great things…terrible things, but great things." Hagrid gives Harry a White Owl as a birthday gift. Voldemort followed the dark side. He killed Harry's mother and father, and gave Harry the scar. But Harry survived that night. "You are the boy that lived!" says Hagrid.

Harry has to take a train to Hogwarts. The ticket indicates platform 9 ¾. Harry can only find platforms 9 and 10. Mrs. Molly Weasley and her sons come up the platform pushing carts filled with luggage. Ron pushes the cart into the brick wall and goes right through it. Harry follows his example. On the other side of the wall he sees the Hogwarts train on platform 9 ¾.

The red-haired boy, Ron Weasley, shares a compartment with Harry. Harry buys candy from the cart. Both he and Ron eat all the candy they want. They are joined by Hermione Granger. Ron tries to do a magic trick which does not work. Hermione uses her magic wand to fix Harry's broken glasses. They finally arrive at the train station, where they are met by Hagrid. He gathers all the first year students around him. They ride on a boat across the waters to Hogwarts.

They are met by Ms. McGonagall. Welcome to Hogwarts! The school which gets the most points will win the house cup. They are all gathered in a massive dining hall. Candles float in the air above them. The new students are told that the dark forest is forbidden to all. The fourth quarter of the Hogwarts Castle is also forbidden. The students then must wear the sorting hat to be sent to the different houses. Hermoine is sorted to Gryffindor. Draco Malfoy goes to Slytherin. Ronald Weasley goes to

Gryffindor. Harry Potter prays not to go to Slytherin. The Hat sorts him to Gryffindor. The feast begins.

Professor Severus Snape leads some students through the hallway. A ghost floats though the dinner table: Nearly Headless Nick. The students climb the staircase. They are told to be careful because the staircases like to change. They walk past portraits hanging on the wall. The eyes follow them as they walk up the stairs. They must speak a password to the woman in the portrait who guards the entrance to the Gryffindor common room.

Harry, with his owl by his side, looks out his window.

In the classroom, Prof. Snape discusses potions which can be used to bewitch the mind and snare the senses. Prof. Snape asks Harry several questons, but he does not know the answers. Hermione does, and constantly raises her hand, but she is ignored by Snape. Draco snickers.

Harry Potter is writing something at the dinner table. Neville receives a crystal ball which glows red when he is to remember something. But he forgets what he is to remember. Mail is delivered by an owl. It is a newspaper with an article that Gringotts Bank has been broken into, and that someone tried to break into vault 713. This was the vault from which Hagrid had removed an object.

The students are out on the quad for a flying broomstick lesson. Nevell flies into the top of the tower and falls to the ground. He drops his crystal ball. Draco picks it up and mocks Nevell. Harry argues with him. Draco throws the crystal ball into the air and Harry flies on his broomstick to catch the ball. Ms. McGonagall sees this. Harry is then chosen to be a "seeker" in the game of Quidditch. He learns that his father, James Potter, was also a seeker. The three students are walking up the staircase when it changes direction and leads them to the third floor, which is forbidden. A cat follows them. They run into a room where they find a three-headed dog. The dog scares them, and they all run. The three-headed dog was standing on a doorway that leads into a secret chamber.

Harry is taught the rules of the Quidditch Game. The objective is to catch the golden snitch before the other team and your team wins.

The students practice levitating a feather.

It is the night of the Halloween Party. A Troll gets into Hogwarts. The students are sent to their houses while the teachers go down to confront the Troll. Hermione is in the girl's bathroom, and she doesn't know about the Troll. Harry and Ron run to rescue her. The Troll tries to get Hermione, but Harry and Ron save her. Ms. McGonagall punishes Hermione but gives points to Harry and Ron for bravery.

It is the day of the Quidditch Game. Prof. Snape wishes Harry the best of luck against Slytherin. An owl delivers a gift to Harry. It is a Nimbus 2000 broomstick, a gift from Ms. McGonagall. The game begins. Gryffindor is dressed in red and yellow, Slytherin in green and gray. Harry's broomstick goes wild and out of control. It appears that Prof. Snape is concentrating on casting a spell. Prof. Snape's cape catches fire. Harry regains control of his broomstick and catches the golden snitch. Gryffindor wins.

Christmas Holiday! All the students go home, except for Harry and Ron. They play chess. Harry wakes up on Christmas morning, and there is a present under his tree. It belonged to Harry's father: an invisible cloak. "Use it well" is written on the note. Harry goes into the library late at night, hiding under the invisible cloak. Quirrell and Snape meet in the hallway. They argue. Snape threatens Quirrell.

Harry breaks a lamp. The old guard finds it but cannot find Harry. Harry finds the magic mirror, looks into it, and sees his deceased mother and father. Harry then takes Ron to the mirror. Ron does not see what Harry sees. Ron sees himself as the captain of the Quidditch team.

Prof. Dumbledore explains the Mirror of Erised to Harry. It shows us the deepest desire of our hearts. It doesn't do well to dwell on dreams and to forget to live. Harry sits with the white owl by his side. He lets the white owl fly away into the sky.

Nicholas Flammel discovered the Sorcerer's Stone, the elixir of life, the dream of the alchemists.

Hagrid finds a dragon's egg which hatches and gives birth to Norbert. Draco Malfoy sees the dragon and tells Prof. McGonagall. They each get detention and lose 50 points for Gryffindor for being out at night. Hagrid takes them into the dark forest. They see the silver blood of a unicorn on the ground. Malvoy, Potter, and Fang go into the forest together. There they see a hooded figure drinking the blood of a dead unicorn. The hooded creature comes after Harry. But a Centaur runs into the clearing and fights the hooded figure. The Centaur saves the life of Harry Potter. He reveals that it was Voldemort who killed the unicorn.

Dumbledore will try to protect Harry. The scar on Harry's head is burning. It is a warning. Fluffy is the name of the three-headed dog. Play music to Fluffy and he will fall asleep, says Hagrid. Prof. Snape questions the three Gryffindor students: Harry, Ron, and Hermione. Neville tries to stop the three from going out, but Hermione knocks him out. The three go into the room guarded by the three-headed dog. The dog is sleeping. They move the dog's paw away from the trap door. The dog suddenly wakes up. The three students jump down into twines which entangle them. Hermione yells that they just should relax, and the twines will release them and let them slip through. Ron cannot relax. Hermione magically produces sunlight, the twines retract, and Ron falls to safety.

They enter another room which has a locked door. A broomstick floats in the air, waiting for Harry to take it. Keys with wings fly through the air. Harry uses his broomstick to find the key to the door, but the other keys attack. Harry grabs the key and gives it to Hermione. She opens the door. Harry flies through the door and slams it shut. Keys stick into the door.

They enter a new room with chessmen on the floor. They must play a game of wizard's chess to pass across the board. Ron sacrifices himself so that Harry can continue forward and get the sorcerer's stone. Hermione stays with Ron as Harry continues alone.

Harry enters the room alone. In the mirror, he sees Prof. Quirrell, who wants the stone. Harry looks into the mirror, and sees the stone in his pocket. Harry takes the stone out of his pocket. Quirrell takes the cloth off from his head and reveals that he has another face on the back of his head, that of Voldemort, a parasite who must live on another. Harry tries to run away. Flames surround Harry. Quirrell starts to choke Harry in order to get the stone. Harry's hands touching Quirrell causes him to crumble into dust. Harry keeps the Sorcerer's stone. The ghost spirit of the evil Voldemort runs through Harry, but Harry holds onto the stone.

Harry wakes up in the school hospital with Prof. Dumbledore by his side. Ron and Hermione are okay. Nicolas Flamel has decided to die so that the stone can be destroyed. "He who finds it, but does not use it, will get it." Voldemort can still return. There are ways, says Dumbledorf. It was Harry's mother's love that destroyed Quirrell.

Resolution Scene

It is the end of the school term, and everyone is sitting in the dining hall. Prof. Dumbledorf announces the points that each college has earned:

312 for Gryffindor
352 for Huffenpuff
426 for Ravenclaw
472 for Slytherin

But Hermione gets 50 more points, Ronald gets 50 more points, Harry gets 60 points, and Neville, who tried to stop them, gets 10 points for 170+312=482. Gryffindor (482) beats Slytherin (472) for the House Cup. The students cheer for Gryffindor and flags change to gryffindor colors

Harry is at the train station. He says goodbye to Hagrid. Harry gets a magic book which shows him as a baby with his mother and father. Hagrid waves goodbye as the train leaves the station.

THE END

COMMENTARY

Why do you think the movie was so popular? The movie captured the imagination of the young children. Harry is an "every kid" who becomes extraordinary; an ordinary character thrown into an extraordinary world. Harry is the young nerd who turns into a powerful wizard. How did the screenwriter get the audience to care about Harry? What happens to him in the first few scenes? He's an orphan with those awful muggle guardians. His home situation made him sympathetic. He's emotionally abused. He is hated by his aunt, uncle, and cousin. He is forced to live under the stairs. The first few minutes are all focused on creating empathy for Harry.

This is a standard Hollywood story design to get the audience to care about the protagonist. Study each of the situations Harry is in: he is an orphan placed on the doorstep of his aunt and uncle; he is forced to live under the stairs; he is abused by his guardians; they try to keep him from getting his mail; try to keep him in isolation. Creating audience empathy for the protagonist has to take place in the first few minutes of the story. Once the audience cares about the protagonist, you can then further develop the plot.

What is the inciting event? On his 11th birthday, he finds out he's a wizard! On his 11th birthday, he receives a visitor, Hagrid, who takes him away to Hogwarts. His world is changed by this event! This again is the classic story structure found in popular movies. He is told that he is a wizard, that he is special. Then, the writer creates mystery because she does not reveal all the facts about Harry at this time. This keeps the audience involved.

What is the unique object that both the Protagonist and the Antagonist desire? The Sorcerer's Stone! What is interesting about this movie is that it is a mystery about who Harry Potter is and what was in vault 713. The first two acts are really about the coming of age of Harry and the growth of his powers.

For most of the story, the focus is on winning the House Cup: getting the most points during the school year. There is also the Quidditch contest between the two houses: Gryffindor and Slytherin. It is only in the last act that the writer introduces the stone as the primary objective of the story. Harry and his friends want to know what Fluffy is guarding, and they discover that it is the Sorcerer's Stone. The stone is needed to focus the conflict and bring the story to a climax.

The story has lots of false leads. Most people thought Snape was the villain then found out it was Quirrell. Ultimately, the villain is Voldemort who lives in Prof. Quirrell's body, but for most of the story, we think that it is Snape. False leads are used to confuse the audience and to keep them engrossed in the story. This is a way to create plot twists and make the story unpredictable.

Harry has to face Voldemort without his friends. That is also common to most popular movies. Ultimately, the protagonist has to defeat the antagonist by himself in the climax scene. Most of the subplots show the characters developing skills they will use later on in the story. These subplots also bring out the virtues and vices of each character, especially in comparison to of Harry Potter to Draco Malfoy. The virtues and vices were created by the contrast with the House of Slytherin and Gryffindor. Especially in their behavior during the Quidditch game.

The mirror was quite interesting. They set it up so the audience understands it reveals the deepest desire of the person that looks into it. Then the mirror is used in the climax scene between Harry and Quirrell-Voldemort. Every object established in the first and second acts had a payoff in act three.

I think that this movie was such a blockbuster because of the magic, more than the story itself. They took the audience into a world that is extraordinary and not part of everyday experience. Shifting staircases, great special effects, and the magical scenes provided this in the Harry Potter movie.

The climax was filled with surprises and many twists. The audience was expecting Prof. Snape to be the villain who wanted to get the stone. The first surprise is that it was Prof. Quirrrell. The second surprise was that Voldemort was part of Quirrell. Then, the stone was in Harry's pocket. Then, Harry turned the flesh of Quirrell into dust. Then, the spirit of Voldemort flies away. Every good climax scene should have several twists in it. This keeps the story unpredictable.

The resolution scenes are also filled with surprises. In the ceremony for the awarding of the house cup, the audience is lead to believe that Slytherin has won. The audience is disappointed because they wanted Gryffindor to win. But then new points are awarded, and Gryffindor does win. We all celebrate with them. This is an example of the classic Hollywood story structure of giving the audience what they want (Gryffindor to win) but in an unexpected way. It is also more emotionally effective because the initial disappointment then becomes a greater joy!

What is the final happy ending? Harry receives the animated photograph of his parents with him as a baby. Even though the parents are long dead, the audience experiences this "reunion" as the last image of the movie and Harry is happy. It is like in the movie *Titanic* when Rose and Jack are reunited under the clock on the staircase of the Titanic, even though Jack has long been dead.

What is Harry's primary objective in the first part of the movie? Harry is not a very active character in the first part of the movie. Things just seem to happen to him. He gets letters. He finds himself the center of attention when he goes to the school of magic. But he does not have a driving goal until the third act when he desires to stop Prof. Snape from stealing the Sorcerer's Stone. But that is very late in the story.

I think that the audience's interest is maintained by all the magic that they see on the screen and not so much because of the character of Harry Potter. The mystery of his notoriety compels the viewer to find out more. Of course, his deepest desire (as revealed by the mirror) is to be reunited with his parents which happens with the animated photo at the end of the movie. This story is essentially the mystery of who Harry really is. Why should the stone all of a sudden just be in his pocket? In other stories, the protagonist has to struggle to obtain the unique object. In this movie, all he has to do is just be there. I found this part of the story design to be very weak. It appears that the audience doesn't care about these plot point problems as long as the characters they care about triumph in the end. This is another story that became a megahit movie because it is filled with magic and humor.

HARRY POTTER and THE PRISONER OF AZKABAN

There were three sequels to megahit movies in the summer of 2004, but only two of them became megahits: *Shrek 2* and *Spider-Man 2*. *Harry Potter and the Prisoner of Azkaban* did not make it. It came very close, but only reached $249 million, while *Shrek 2* made $438 million and *Spider-Man 2* made $372 million. Why did the Harry Potter make so much less than the other two? How did it lose another potential $200 million? In my opinion, *Harry Potter and the Prisoner of Azkaban* failed because of the structure of the third act and the climax scene. Even though it had a great built-in audience, it broke the standard paradigm of a megahit movie.

The classic megahit structure has a climax scene in which the protagonist fights the antagonist for control of the unique object and the love interest. *Spider-Man 2* fits this pattern. Spider-Man fights Doc Ock to shut down the nuclear fusion reaction that will kill MJ and destroy NYC. *Shrek 2* also fits this pattern. Shrek fights Prince Charming and the Fairy God Mother to save the Kingdom and to get back Princess Fiona. This structure is effective because it brings the audience to a heightened emotional peak during the climax scene.

Harry Potter and the Prisoner of Azkaban does not use this structure. It does not drive the audience to an emotional peak. In this movie, there are a series of climaxes and a series of antagonists, and the scenes are replayed twice with the use of Hermione's time travel device.

The third act of *Harry Potter and the Prisoner of Azkaban* becomes a series of puzzles that the audience has to resolve in order to understand what takes place in the story. It becomes an intellectual experience, rather than an emotional experience, for the audience. That's why, in my opinion, people are not going back to see it again. Once the puzzle is solved there is no need to figure it out a second time. Repeat viewing by an audience is essential for a film to become a megahit movie. This movie had a tremendous built in audience due to the popularity of the novels and the first two Harry Potter films. It has great production values, a lot of magical gimmicks, and neat objects, but in the end, it is not an emotionally satisfying experience.

The problem is that there is no one major climax! No emotional peak! There are a series of minor climaxes that all lead to other problems and confrontations. It has a flawed dramatic design. What was the most dramatic moment of *Harry Potter and the Prisoner of Azkaban*? In *Shrek 2*, it was when Shrek stops Prince Charming from kissing his wife Fiona. In *Spider-Man 2*, it is when he saves MJ from being destroyed by the fusion reaction, and she realizes that Peter is Spider-Man.

There is no one most powerful moment in *Harry Potter and the Prisoner of Azkaban.* No one big climax scene. The audience wants that climax scene. They have paid money and sat in the theater for two hours to see it. Give it to them, and they will come back for more! They expect it. This is good dramatic structure. Don't make your endings an intellectual puzzle. This is not what the mass audience wants. They want to see the protagonist destroy a villain that they have come to hate while saving the life of the love interest. This is the essential structure needed to design a story that can become megahit movie.

THE LORD OF THE RINGS TRILOGY

U.S. Domestic Box-Office
FELLOWSHIP OF THE RINGS $313
THE TWO TOWERS $340
RETURN OF THE KING $377

FELLOWSHIP OF THE RING

Unique Object: The One Ring which will Rule them All.

Protagonist: Frodo Baggins. His primary objective is to destroy the Ring in the Fires of Mordor to save Middle-Earth from destruction.

Antagonist: Sauron. His primary objective is to conquer Middle-Earth. Possession of the One Ring will enable him to do this.

Protagonist Supporters of Frodo
Sam, the Hobbit
Gandalf, the White Wizard
Aragorn, the heir of Isildur
Legolas, the Elf
Gimli, the Dwarf
Lord Elrond of the Elves
Arwen, the love interest for Aragorn
Peregrine Took (Pippin), the Hobbit
Meriadoc Brandybuck (Merry), the Hobbit
Ents, Tree-Folks

Antagonist Supporters of Sauron
Gollum (Sméagol)
Orcs
Uruk-hai Warriors
Ringwraiths, who patrol the skies with the Fell Beasts
Saruman, the Evil Wizard defeated in the Two Towers by the Ents

The Prologue: Opening Scene
The Story of the One Ring of Power

Introduction of the Antagonist: Lord Sauron

Voice of Elf, Queen Galadriel
"The World has changed. Much that once was is now lost."
"It began with the forging of the rings"
>3 to the Elves
>7 to the Dwarves
>9 to men who desire power most

They were deceived. Sauron created a master ring to rule all the others.

Men and Elves fought for the freedom of Middle-Earth. But Sauron, with the power of the ring, could not be undone. Isildur took up his father's sword and cut the ring off Sauron's finger. The ring passed to Isildur, who was ambushed and killed by other men. The ring was lost in a river bed for 2,500 years. History became legend which became myth.

The ring was found by Smeagol (Gollum). It consumed him but gave him unnatural long life. He lived for 500 years. Shadow rose in the east. The ring's time has now come. But Gollum lost the Ring, and it was found by a Hobbit, Bilbo Baggins of the Shire.

TITLE: FELLOWSHIP OF THE RING

60 years later.

Introduction of the Protagonist: Frodo

Frodo is reading a book under a tree. He hears a singing voice: the Wizard, Gandalf the Grey, rides in a cart. They stare at each other, then embrace.
Images of the Shire: the Hobbit Community during a celebration.
Happy Birthday Bilbo Baggins banner hangs over the town center.
Gandalf is known as a "Disturber of the Peace." Children love Gandalf. They run up to his cart. As he rides away he explodes fireworks. This is an idyllic Shire.

Gandalf visits Bilbo Baggins. He goes inside the Hobbits house. Bilbo gets him some tea. Gandalf looks at a map of Middle-Earth. Bilbo wants to see mountains, find peace and quiet, and finish his book. Bilbo feels old. He means to leave the Shire and not return.

Bilbo and Gandalf sit on the hillside and blow smoke rings into the night air. Bilbo blows a circle, and Gandalf blows a smoke boat which sails through the circle.

The Shire celebrates. Frodo tells Sam to ask Rosie to dance. Merry and Pippin steal fireworks. They set off a Dragon Firework which flies high in the sky, then zooms down into the party. Gandalf grabs Merry and Pippin and reprimands them. They get to wash the dishes.

Bilbo makes a speech. It is his 111 birthday. Bilbo puts his hand into his pocket and feels the ring. Gandalf sees him do this. Frodo watches Bilbo. Suddenly, Bilbo becomes invisible.

Gandalf confronts Bilbo in his house and tells him not to treat magic lightly. Gandalf wants Bilbo to leave the ring with Frodo, but Bilbo does not want to give it up. Bilbo is angry. "It is mine, my precious. You want it for yourself!"
"I am only trying to help you," answers Gandalf. "Let it go. The ring must go to Frodo. The ring is still in your pocket."
Bilbo drops it onto the floor and then says about his book: "He lived happily ever after, to the end of his days." Bilbo leaves.

The Ring is on the floor.

Gandalf tries to pick it up, but in a flash, he sees the Eye of Sauron.

Frodo enters and picks up the Ring. Gandalf has him place it in an envelop. Gandalf has to leave. "Questions need to be answered. Keep the ring a secret."

Dark Tower. Mount Doom. Green Castle with Ringwraiths.

Gandalf rides to Minas Tirith and reads old manuscripts which tell the story of the RING.

Ringwraiths search for Baggins.

Frodo is in the empty house. Gandalf runs in and throws the envelope with the ring into the fire. "What do you see?" Frodo sees Elfish markings. The Language of Mordor. "One Ring to Rule them All." Forged by Lord Sauron in Mount Doom.

Sauron's body was destroyed, but his spirit endured. His life force is bound to the RING. Sauron's spirit seeks the ring. The Ring and the Dark Lord are ONE!

Gollum knew that Bilbo had the ring. He was tortured and gave the name of Baggins of the Shire to his tormentors.

Frodo tries to give the Ring to Gandalf, but Gandalf refuses. They cannot keep the Ring in the Shire for it will bring destruction. Samwise Gamgee is listening to the conversation by the window. Gandalf pulls him into the room. His mission now is to help Frodo destroy the ring!
"Never put the Ring on! Agents of the Dark Lord Sauron will sense it's power. The Ring wants to be found!"

They agree to meet at Bree. Gandalf sets off to consult the head of his order, Saruman, while Sam and Frodo embark for Bree.

Frodo and Sam journey forth through the fields while the Ringwraiths search for Baggins.

Gandalf rides to Isengard. He talks with Saruman, who tells him that the Spirit of Sauron is strong, but cannot yet take shape in a body. It is a great Eye in a Flame.

Saruman looks into his crystal ball, the palantiri. Gandalf advises against this since all have not yet been found and someone else may be watching. It is a communications network.

They will kill the one who carries the ring: Frodo.
"Against the power of Mordor, there will be no victory," says Saruman.

Gandalf realizes that Saruman has gone to the Dark Side and has betrayed him. He fights with him, but Saruman is too strong, and takes away Gandalf's staff. With the two staffs, he tosses Gandalf up into the air to the top of the tower.

Sam and Frodo walk through a cornfield, where they meet Merry and Pippin, who are being chased by a farmer for stealing his vegetables. They all run then fall down the side of a hill. Frodo senses something, and tells the others to get off the road. They hide under tree roots as a Ringwraith appears. He looks down, but does not see them. Frodo almost puts the Ring on his finger, but Sam stops him.

They run through the forest chased by the Ringwraiths. They come to the ferry and start across the river. Frodo jumps onto the moving ferry. The Ringwraiths stop by the edge of the river then race 20 miles downstream where they can cross.

It is raining. The Hobbits knock on the gate of Bree. They tell the guard they want to go to the Prancing Pony. In the pub, they ask the bartender if he has seen Gandalf. He has not seen him in six months.

The Hobbits sit at a table and drink pints. A hooded man sitting in the corner has been watching Frodo. They ask a waiter who he is. He is the Ranger, Strider. Frodo then hears Merry at the bar tell people his companion's name is Baggins. Frodo runs to the bar to stop him but trips and falls. The Ring flies into the air then lands on Frodo's finger. Frodo becomes invisible.

Ringwraiths scream for they hear the voice of the embodied Ring on Frodo's finger.

Frodo sees the Eye of Sauron.

Ranger Strider drags Frodo away from the bar.

Ringwraiths break down the gates to Bree.

The Hobbits are seen sleeping in beds.

The Ringwraiths enter a bedroom, stand over the beds with their swords drawn, and stab the bodies. They remove the sheets to show pillows. The Hobbits have moved and are spending the night with Ranger Strider. The Nazgul are controlled by Sauron and they will never stop searching for you," says Strider.

Rivendell. The home of the Elf King, Elrond.

Saruman speaks into the crystal ball to Sauron. "The power of Isengard is at your command." "Build an army worthy of Mordor," answers Sauron. Saruman talks to an Orc. "We have work to do!" The Orcs cut down trees from the nearby forest. Gandalf is alone on the top of the tower. It rains on Gandalf.

The Hobbits and Strider travel across the countryside toward Rivendell. They spend the night at an old Great Watch Tower. Frodo goes to sleep while Strider searches the countryside. Frodo awakes to find that the other Hobbits have lit a fire to cook food. Frodo yells at them, but it is too late. The Ringwraiths have seen the fire and are now approaching the tower from below. The Hobbits grab their swords to defend themselves. The Hobbits fight the Nazgul. Frodo puts on the Ring to become invisible, but the Nazgul see him, and he sees them. The leader of the Nazgul, the Witch-King, stabs Frodo in the shoulder. Strider returns and fights off the Nazgul using flame and sword, but Frodo has been stabbed by a Mordor sword and has been poisoned by evil. Strider carries Frodo away.

Isengard builds an army of Orcs and Uruk-hai (a blend of Orcs and Goblins).

A moth flies by Gandalf on the top of the tower (precursor of eagles).

Sam looks for a plant to ease the wounds of Frodo. Arwen, the Elf, finds Aragorn. She wants to help Frodo. She places him on her horse and rides through the countryside. The Ringwraiths chase her. She rides to the river and challenges the Nazgul to cross. When they start, she calls upon the River Gods, who take the shape of White Horses as a raging river floods over the Nazgul. Arwen prays over the body of Frodo.

Frodo awakes in a bed in Rivendell. Gandalf watches over him.

Frodo asks why Gandalf did not meet them at the Prancing Pony in Bree. He tells Frodo of his fight with Saruman and how he was freed by an eagle from the top of the tower.

Sam joins Frodo in Rivendell, along with Merry and Pippin. They meet Bilbo, who shows him his book: "There and Back Again." Sam wants to return to the Shire and leave the Ring at Rivendell. That had been their mission. Now it is over. Frodo agrees.

Gandalf and Elrond discuss the Ring. Frodo is resistant to its powers. Elrond says that the Ring cannot stay in Rivendell. The Elves are not strong enough. Elrond tells the story of the weakness of men. He tried to get the last King of Gondor, Isildur, to throw the ring into the lava river of Mount Doom, but he was too weak.

Gandalf: "There is one who can reclaim the throne of Gondor." He is thinking of Aragorn (the RangerStrider).
Elrond: "He has abandoned that path and chosen exile!"

Arwen and Aragorn are lovers at Rivendell. Arwen pledges her love for him, and chooses a mortal life.

Gathering of the Fellowship. Frodo places the Ring on the stump in the center of the council. Boromir argues that the Ring should be given to Gondor to fight the Orcs. "You cannot use the Ring, it will destroy you. It must be destroyed!" says Gandalf.

Gimli, the Dwarf, tries to destroy the Ring with his axe but only shatters the blade of the axe.

The Ring must be cast back into Mount Doom from where it was forged. They all argue about the Ring, and who should have it.
Frodo says "I will take it to Mordor!"

The Fellowship of the Ring agree. Frodo will carry the Ring.

Bilbo gives Frodo his sword and armor. He then grabs for the ring, but stops, and says he is sorry.

The Fellowship sets out on their journey to Mordor. They climb along a mountain range. Boromir teaches the Hobbits how to fight with swords. They hide from a flock of birds who are spies for Saruman. They decide to take the road through the mountains instead of through the Mines of Moria which Gandalf fears.

They climb across ice-covered mountain trails. Frodo drops the Ring on his chain. Boromir picks it up, desires to keep it, but gives it back to Frodo.

The birds return to the caverns of Saruman.

Gandalf treks deep in the snow. Saruman tries to bring the mountain down upon the Fellowship. Snow and rocks fall upon them. They argue about the path. Gandalf says "Let the Ring Bearer decide." Frodo chooses the path through the Mines of Moria. Gandalf is afraid.

Moonlight. They approach the gates to the Mines of Moria. There is a riddle over the top of the gate. Gandalf cannot find the magical words which will open the gate. Pippin throws rocks into the lake water in front of the gate. Aragorn tells him to stop. "Do not disturb the waters." Frodo reads the riddle and asks the Elf word for "Friend." The gate opens. The Mine is a tomb, littered with dead bodies of Dwarfs.

The Lake Monster appears and grabs Frodo with his tentacles. The Fellowship fights the octopus-like monster. They run back into the mines as the rocks above the gate collapse.

Gandalf fears a monster that lives in the depths of the mountain. Gandalf leads. Frodo sees a naked creature in the darkness. It is Gollum. Gollum has been following them for days.

They enter the Great Hall of the Dwarves.
Gimli mourns the death of the King of the Dwarves.

Pippin accidentally knocks a skeleton into the well. It makes a great amount of noise as it falls to the bottom. Suddenly, drum beats and shrieks are heard from the cavern below. The Fellowship bars the door. The Orcs attack with a Cave Troll among them.

Frodo is stabbed by the Cave Troll but is saved by the body armor given to him by Bilbo.

The Fellowship runs through the Great Hall but they are surrounded by the Orcs and Goblins. Suddenly, a great red glow appears at the end of the hallway, and the creatures scatter. It is the demon Balrog. Gandalf tells them all to run. They run toward the stone bridge, part of which is missing. They have to jump across the gap. They finally all get across as Balrog approaches. Gandalf blocks his path and yells: "You shall not pass!" The rock bridge collapses, and Balrog falls into the depths. But his fiery whip catches Gandalf by the leg and drags him off the edge. Gandalf clings to the ledge, but finally lets go and falls into the depths. Frodo screams in anguish.

The Fellowship gets outside the cave. They rest, but Aragorn wants them to continue because the mountains will soon be filled with Orcs. They all get up and go forward. Aragorn leads them into the Forest of the Great Sorceress. They are captured by a band of Elves. "You are in the Realm of the Lady of the Wood. You cannot go back!" In a field of White Light appears the Elf Queen, Galadriel.

"Frodo, you bring great danger here," says Galadriel.

The Fellowship rests. Boromir and Aragorn talk of Gondor and bond in friendship. Aragorn is the Reluctant King.

Galadriel asks Frodo to look into the mirror and tell her what he sees. Frodo sees the Shire in flames, and the Hobbits enslaved by the Orcs. "This will come to pass if you fail; he will try to take the Ring," says Galadriel.

Frodo offers the Ring to Galadriel, but she refuses. If she takes it, she will become the Queen that they will all love, and they will despair. They will lose control of their own lives and no longer be free. She refuses the Ring. Frodo is the ring bearer. He must do the task.

Orcs were once Elves who were tortured. Saruman is creating new warriors: Uruk-hai made from the earth. They are sent out to get Frodo and to kill all the others.

Galadriel gives Frodo a phial of light.

The Fellowship floats down the river in canoes as they are hunted by the Uruk-Hai warriors. They sail past the giant statues of Kings.

Legolas feels the threat growing near. He tells Aragorn. Frodo goes off by himself. Boromir, who is gathering wood, sees him. Boromir tries to persuade Frodo to give him the RING, then he tries to take it from Frodo. Frodo puts it on and becomes invisible. Frodo sees the Eye of Sauron. Boromir begs for forgiveness.

Aragorn finds Frodo, but unlike Boromir, Aragorn pledges to help Frodo destroy the Ring.

Aragorn is attacked by the Uruk-Hai. A big fight ensues. Merry and Pippin are chased. Boromir tries to defend them, but is killed. Three arrows are shot into him. Pippin and Merry are captured and carried away. A Uruk-Hai stands over the dying Boromir and is about to kill him when Aragorn attacks. They fight, and Aragorn cuts off his head.

Aragorn comforts Boromir as he dies and pledges that "the world of our people is not yet over." "I would have followed you my brother, my Captain, my King," says the dying Boromir.

Frodo stands on the shore of the river holding the Ring. He departs in a canoe. Sam runs to the river edge. He wants to go with Frodo, but Frodo refuses. Sam jumps into the river but cannot swim. He begins to drown. Frodo leaps into the water and saves him. Frodo pulls Sam into the boat.

The Fellowship splits up. Aragorn, Gimli, and Legolas decide to rescue Pippin and Merry.

Frodo and Sam look toward Mordor. "Sam, I am glad that you are with me," says Frodo.

THE END of PART I

LORD OF THE RINGS II -- THE TWO TOWERS

Opening Scene: Snow Cap Mountains. Aerial views.

Gandalf fights Balrog.
Frodo watches Gandalf fall into the abyss.
Gandalf slashes Balrog with his sword.
Gandalf and Balrog fall into the lake at the bottom of the abyss.
Frodo awakes from his nightmare dream.

Sam and Frodo walk toward Mordor.
They are lost – The eye of Sauron – The Ring.

Elfin Bread. They eat some then walk. They smell something. Gollum. They are not alone. Sam and Frodo sleep. Gollum crawls on the rocks above them. He wants his precious. Gollum fights Frodo and Sam for the Ring. They subdue Gollum and tie a leash around his neck.

Frodo pities Gollum. Gollum swears that he will serve his new master, Frodo. Sam does not believe Gollum. Frodo tells Gollum to lead them to the Black Gates of Mordor.

Orcs carry Pippin and Merry. Orcs smell human flesh. They quicken their pace. Aragorn, Gimli, and Legolas are searching for the Hobbits. The Orcs are taking them to Isengard.

Saruman pledges his allegiance to Sauron, then he incites the hill people to attack the villages of Rohan. He believes that Rohan is ready to fall.

King Theoden's son has been wounded by Orcs. The Poisoned King sits on his throne, controlled by Grima Wormtongue. Eomer, nephew of the King, is banished from the court by Wormtongue, who lusts for Eowyn. Orcs stop for a breather. They chop down trees. They are hungry for meat, and some want to eat the Hobbits. If not the whole body, then perhaps the legs. They are attacked by Eomer and the Rohan soldiers, and are all killed. The Hobbits escape into the Fangorn Forest.

Aragon meets up with Eomer and asks him about the Hobbits, then they search among the burning Orcs. Aragorn traces the tracks of the Hobbits into the Forest.

Merry and Pippin escape into the forest, but they are followed by an Orc who wants to kill them. They climb up a tree. Treebeard steps on the Orc. He is an Ent. "Nobody cares for the trees anymore."

Gollum leads Sam and Frodo into a bog swamp. Sam sees dead faces in the swamp water. Frodo looks down then falls into the water. Dead spirits try to grab him. Gollum pulls Frodo out of the swamp. "Don't follow the lights."

Frodo rubs the Ring at night, as Gollum talks about his "precious." Sméagol, of the River People, was not much different from the Hobbits a long time ago. Shrieks of the Black Riders. Frodo, Sam, and Gollum hide in the swamps as Night Riders fly above them on Fell Beasts.

Aragorn, Gimli and Legolas enter the Forest looking for the Hobbits. They are confronted by the White Wizard, who quickly disarms all three. They discover that the White Wizard is Gandalf.

Gandalf had defeated Balgor then went to heaven. They sent him back to Middle-Earth because his work was not completed. Before he was Gandalf the Grey, now he is Gandalf the White. He whistles for his white horse, ShadowFax.

Treebeard with the two Hobbits walks through the forest.

Gollum leads Frodo and Sam to the Black Gates of Mordor. From a mountain top, they watch the Warriors march into Mordor. Sam falls down a hill. Two enemy soldiers see the rockslide and search the hill. Frodo runs down and covers Sam and himself with his Elf cloak. The enemy soldiers cannot see them.

Gollum stops Frodo and Sam from going in through the Black Gates. He tells them that there is another way into Mordor. Frodo trusts Sméagol, Sam does not.

Gandalf, Aragon, Gimli, and Legolas ride to Edoras.

Gima Wormtongue comforts Eowyn over the death of the King's son. She rejects his advances. She goes outside the building and stands by the White Horse Flag. Celtic Woodwork. The flag falls from the post and lands at the feet of Aragorn as he rides into Edoras. Guards disarm the Fellowship, but Gandalf keeps his staff. He confronts Wormtongue, and with his staff, pushes the spirit of Saruman out of King Théoden. The King recovers his strength and health then takes his sword in his hands. He throws Wormtongue down the stairs, and banishes him from Edoras.

King Théoden buries his son, and cries. "No parent should have to bury their child."

A horse rides up carrying the children from the Rohan village that was overrun by the mountain people.

King Théoden does not want to go to war and decides to go instead to Helms Deep, the Rohan stronghold in the mountains. Gandalf leaves to recall the Rohan soldiers, and he tells Aragorn that Helms Deep must hold. "Look to the East for my coming on the 5th day at Dawn!"

Eowyn sword plays with Aragorn. She is falling in love with him.

King Théoden leads his people from the village.
Wormtongue betrays them by telling his plans to Saruman.
Saruman plans to attack Rohan with his DogBeasts.

Frodo, Sam and Gollum journey. Frodo wants to help Gollum: "I want to believe that he can come back." Sam believes that "the Ring is taking hold of Frodo!" They sleep. Gollum talks to Sméagol. "Liar, thief, Murderer," says Gollum. Sméagol tells Gollum to leave. The Master will take care of Sméagol now!"

Sméagol catches two rabbits, and wants to eat them raw. Sam cooks them. Frodo hears birds calling. He goes into the forest and sees an army with elephants marching by. Soldiers from Gondor attack this army. They capture Frodo, Sam, and Gollum.

Eowyn falls in love with Aragorn, but Aragorn loves Arwen. He dreams of her. They kiss in his memory. Elrond argues with Aragorn. "Let Arwen take the ship to the West. She is immortal and you are mortal."

Rohan villagers travel to Helms Deep. Legolas senses something is wrong. They are attacked by the DogBeasts. They fight and finally defeat the Orcs with the DogBeasts, but Aragorn is pulled over the ledge and falls into the river below. Everyone thinks that he is dead.

Wormtongue and Saruman stand on a balcony and watch the army of 10,000 warriors that will attack Helms Deep. They march to war.

Treebeard, Merry, and Pippin watch troops as they march toward Helms Deep.

Aragorn floats down the river. He dreams of Arwen. He is found by his horse and gets back on the horse. They slowly ride toward Helms Deep.

Elrond and Arwen argue. Aragorn will die, but Arwen will not. She will grieve forever.

Warriors from Isengard have been released.
Frodo believes that the quest will claim his life.
Faramir questions Frodo.
Elves: "Do we leave Middle Earth to its Fate? Do we let them stand alone?"

Faramir questions Frodo and Sam. Boromir was Faramir's brother. Gollum is swimming in the sacred pool, unaware that he is surrounded by Faramir's men. Frodo pleads for his life. He goes down to the pool and persuades Gollum to come out. Gollum is then captured.

Sam tells Frodo to put on the Ring and become invisible so that he can escape. Frodo says no! Faramir wants the Ring of Power to save Gondor.

Aragorn rides to Helms Deep. He has survived. Legolas gives Aragorn back the Elf charm he dropped that was given to him by Arwen. Saruman has an army of 10,000 against the 300 Rohan defenders of Helms Deep.

Treebeard, Merry, and Pippin meet with the other Ents in the middle of the forest to discuss what to do.

Aragorn commits to the battle and will fight with the defenders of Rohan.

King Théoden: "How did it come to this?"

Aragorn: "There is always hope."

Army of Elf Archers come to Helms Deep. "Elves will be proud to fight alongside Men once more!"

Treebeard: "We have agreed that you are not Orcs," he says to the Hobbits.

The attack of Helms Deep begins in the rain. Explosions create a breach in the wall. A battering ram smashes against the front gate.

Ents to Hobbits: "This is not our War!"
Hobbits: "But you are part of this world!"
Ents: "Go home!"

Elves are killed in the battle of Helms Deep, including their leader.

Rohan retreats to its last stronghold.

Treebeard carries the Hobbits to the South, past Isengard.

Faramir will not let Frodo go. He wants to take the Ring to Gondor.

Treebeard sees his tree friends dead in the forest in front of Isengard. Treebeard declares war against Saruman. The Ents attack Isengard.

The Ring is driving Frodo mad. The Fell-Beasts carrying Ringwraiths attack the city.

Aragorn advises King Théoden to ride out and meet them. One last glorious charge for the people of Rohan. "The sun is rising," says Gimli. They mount their horses and charge out of the room when the Orc/Uruk-Hai army break through the door. They charge down the stone walkway, killing Orcs as they go. They look to the East, and see Gandalf with the Rising Sun at his back.

The Ents attack Isengard. They pull down the dam, and waters flood throughout the plain and flood Isengard, destroying the caverns that Saruman built.

Frodo is possessed. He walks to the tower and confronts a flying Fell-Beast that carries the Witch-King! Frodo holds out the Ring to the Fell-Beast. Frodo starts to put it on his finger, but Sam pulls him down off the wall. Frodo pulls his sword out and threatens to kill Sam. Frodo then drops his sword and says, "I can't do this Sam." Frodo almost gives up. "There is some good in this world worth fighting for," says Sam. Faramir lets Frodo go.

Gandalf, after the victory at Helms Deep, says "The battle of Helms Deep is over. The battle for Middle-Earth is about to begin!"

"Samwise the Brave," says Frodo, as they walk toward Mordor.

Sméagol-Gollum, argues with himself. "Kill them both, then we take the precious and be the Master. Kill Him! No, let her do it! Then we take it when they are dead. Follow me!" Gollum leads Sam and Frodo towards Mount Doom.

THE END OF PART TWO

LORD OF THE RINGS III - RETURN OF THE KING

Opening Scene: Introduction of the Antagonist
Gollum's Story: Déagol and Sméagol are fishing. A fish pulls Déagol into the water. Déagol finds the Ring. Sméagol wants it. It is his birthday. They fight. He chokes him and kills Deagol to get the Ring. "Precious." Sméagol goes into the mountains. He goes crazy. He eats raw fish and transforms into Gollum. He forgets his name. "Mine…Precious."

Introduction of the Protagonist
Sam and Frodo are asleep. Frodo looks at the Ring on the chain around his neck. Gollum wakes up. He wants to go. Mount Doom is behind them. Sam says that Frodo must eat. Sam says he is not hungry. There is not much left of the food. They must be careful or they will run out. They need food to get back home to the Shire. Gollum leads them toward Mordor.

Aragorn, Gandalf, and the others ride through the forest.

Pippin and Merry are celebrating the victory of the Ents over Isengard. Treebeard has taken control after the flooding of Isengard, and Saruman is locked in the tower. Gimli wants to kill him, but Gandalf says no, Saruman has no more power. Pippin finds the crystal ball in the water. Gandalf takes it from him. They ride to Edoras. King Théoden celebrates with a toast to the dead heroes of the battle of Helms Deep. Eowyn drinks a toast with Aragorn. She is deeply in love with him. King Théoden is happy for Eowyn. Pippin and Merry dance on the table. Aragorn and Gandalf talk. "No news of Frodo? What does your heart tell you?" "Frodo is still alive," says Gandalf.

Gollum argues with himself. "Lead them to her, upstairs, the tunnel, when they go in, no one comes out. She is always hungry, needs to feed. Sam hears Gollum's plans to get the Ring. Sam beats up Gollum, but Frodo stops him. Gollum wants to turn Frodo against Sam. Frodo needs Gollum as a guide. Frodo needs Sam for help.

Night. Aragorn and Legolas sense trouble. "Something stirs in the East. The Eye of the enemy is moving."

Pippin takes the crystal ball, palantiri, from Gandalf while he sleeps. The Eye of Sauron sees Pippin and takes possession of him. Gandalf awakes and throws a blanket over the palantiri. Gandalf questions Pippin. He saw a white tree in a burning city of stone. Sauron wants to attack Minas

Tirith. He wants to destroy men before a new King can take the throne. Gandalf wants Théoden to fight with Gondor, but Theoden refuses since Gondor did not help Rohan. Gandalf must take Pippin with him because the Eye-of-Sauron now thinks that Pippin is the Ring-bearer. Gandalf and Pippin ride to Minas Tirith. Merry stays behind.

Minas Tirith, The White City, is the seat of the Kingdom of Humans in Middle-Earth.
There is a sickly tree in the courtyard. It will become healthy when the King returns.

Elves with Arwen travel through the forest on the way to ships which will take them to the West. Arwen has a vision of a child running to an aged Aragorn. The child stares at Arwen. She returns to Elrond and asks him about her child.
Elrond: "There is nothing for you here, only death."
Arwen: "You saw my son."
Elrond: Nothing is certain."
Arwen: "Somethings are certain! It is time. Renew the blade that was broken. Reforge the sword of the King!"

Arwen's hands are getting cold. Sauron's evil is spreading and is killing the life force of the elves. Arwen refuses to leave. Two Elves reforge the sword.

Shadowfax, carrying Gandalf and Pippin, rides to Minas Tirith, the White City of Kings. They arrive at the courtyard of the tree and enter the court of the Steward, Denethor. He wants to know how his son, Boromir, died. Pippin tells him it was defending the Hobbits. Pippin offers himself as a servant to Denethor. Gandalf wants the Steward to light the beacons and call for help from Rohan. Denethor refuses because he knows that Aragorn is at Rohan, and he will not give him Minas Tirith. Denethor wants to be King!

Pippin is now in the service of Denethor. Gandalf talks about the impending battle. They see Mount Doom in the distance. The Witch-King that no man can kill will lead the Nazgul. Minas Morgul is his lair. A city covered by green light.

Gollum, Frodo, and Sam are near Minas Morgul, by the rock stairway which will lead them to Mordor. Frodo, in a trance, walks towards the gates of Minas Morgul. A white light gushes forth from the tower into the dark night sky. It is a beacon that the troops of the Witch-King are on the move. Gandalf watches.

The Witch-King rides a flying Fell-Beast from the castle over the marching troops.

Gollum, Sam, and Frodo climb up the rock staircase.

Gandalf tells Pippin to light the beacon on the tower.

Orcs in boats ride into Osgiliath and attack. Faramir and his soldiers fight the Orcs, but they are defeated.

Pippin lights the fire. Other beacons are lit across the mountains. Aragorn sees the beacon and runs to King Théoden. He agrees to help Gondor. He orders the Rohan army to assemble and to meet at Dunharrow. Eowyn says to Aragorn: "The men have found their Captain. They will follow him into battle...to death."

Faramir orders a retreat from Osgiliath. "The age of Men is over. The time of Orcs has come!" says the Orc leader. The Fell-Beasts attack the retreating soldiers of Gondor. Gandalf rides out to help them and with his staff produces a white light that chases away the Fell-Beasts. Faramir sees Pippin, then tells Gandalf that he saw Frodo and Sam.

Gollum, Frodo, and Sam climb the stairs of Cirith Ungol. Gollum lusts for the Ring, and reaches out for it, but instead, grabs Frodo's hand to help him up the steps. Sam argues with Gollum. Gollum and Frodo both share the experience of handling the ring, and it's power which Sam does not. Therefore, Frodo has some sympathy for Gollum. Gollum plans to poison the mind of Frodo against Sam. Gollum tells Frodo that soon Sam will ask to take the Ring from Frodo.

The Witch-King prepares for battle.

The White Wizard prepares for battle.

Pippin pledges fealty to Denethor, who wants his son Faramir to recapture Osgiliath. He shames Faramir by saying that Boromir would not have let the city fall. This is a suicide mission.

Sam and Frodo are asleep. Gollum takes the last bread from Sam's sack, spreads the crumbs over him, then throws the bread down the mountain. Sam wakens Frodo then realizes that the bread is gone. He blames Gollum, who points out the crumbs on Sam. Sam hits Gollum, then offers to carry the Ring, "share the load." "See, he wants it for himself," says Gollum. Frodo sends Sam away.

Faramir and his soldiers ride through the city on their way to the suicide mission. The people watch them go and throw flowers along their path. Gandalf tries to stop him, but Faramir has an allegiance to Gondor.

Denethor asks Pippin to sing him a song as Faramir and his soldiers ride to their deaths. Blood red juice from the small tomatoes he is eating spills from the mouth of Denethor.

Rohan army only gathers 6,000 spears, which is half of what Théoden hoped for. Aragorn explains that they must ride in the morning. Horses are nervous in the shadow of the mountain. None who venture there ever returns. The Mountain is evil. Aragorn stares into the passage. Eowyn dresses Merry in armor. The Rohan soldiers laugh and say Merry is too small to fight. Eowyn says Merry has a right to fight for those he loves.

Aragorn dreams of Arwen, who wishes she could see him one last time.

A cloaked figure rides up the mountain of the camp of Rohan. Aragorn is summoned to the tent of King Théoden, where Elrond reveals himself, and gives ANDURIL, the sword of flame, to Aragorn. Elrond tells Aragorn that he needs more men, and he should get the men of the mountains, who will answer to the sword of the King of Gondor. Aragorn takes the sword.

Aragon heads toward the mountain. Eowyn confronts him, but Aragorn tells her he does not love her. Gimli and Legolas join Aragorn. King Théoden tells Eowyn that she will rule if he falls in battle.

Aragorn goes into the Dwimorberg Mountain to confront the King of the Dead. Aragorn, Gimli, and Legolas approach the cave of the dead where lives a cursed army, who once swore allegiance to the last King of Gondor, but betrayed him in his time of need. The horses run away from the opening of the cave, Aragorn enters.

Rohan soldiers ride off to battle. Merry wants to join them, but King Théoden tells him to stay. Eowyn picks Merry up and they ride together.

The army of Sauron approaches Minas Tirith.

Aragorn in the cave confronts the dead king and his cursed army. "Fight for me, and I will hold your oaths fulfilled."

The Battle of Pelennor Fields begins.

A horse returns the body of Faramir to Minas Tirith. The mad Steward Denethor believes Faramir is dead and grieves for the end of his line. The attack begins. Denethor tells the soldiers to run for their lives. Gandalf beats him with his staff and tells the soldiers to hold their positions and fight!

Fell Beasts with the Nazgul enter the battle and fly into the city wreaking havoc. Pippin kills an Orc. The battle rages throughout the streets of Minas Tirith.

Gollum leads Frodo to the cave of the spider, Shelob. "This is the only way to Mordor," says Gollum. Gollum abandons Frodo in the spider cave. Frodo calls out for Sam.

Sam slips down the rock stairway. He finds the bread and knows that Gollum has betrayed him and Frodo. He runs back up the stairs.

Frodo uses the luminous glass phial, the gift of the Elf Queen, Galadriel. He sees the spider and runs for his life. He is caught in a spider web but cuts himself out. Frodo gets out of the cave, but then is attacked by Gollum. They struggle. Gollum blames the precious. Frodo lets him go, and explains that he has "to destroy the Ring for both our sakes." Gollum attacks him again. Gollum is thrown down the mountain side. Frodo collapses then has a vision of Galadriel, the Elf Queen. "If you do not find a way, no one else will," she tells Frodo.

Battle scenes. The Flaming Wolf-Head Battering Ram slams into the gates of Minas Tirith.

Denethor places Faramir on a pyre. He intends a burning death for them both. Pippin tries to stop him, saying that Faramir is still alive.

Frodo walks up a rocky path toward the burning tower of Mordor. He is stalked then attacked by Shelob. In the struggle, she stabs him with her stinger and then wraps him up in her webbing.

Sam comes onto the scene and fights Shelob for Frodo. He stabs her, and Shelob retreats. Sam thinks that Frodo is dead. The sword turns blue indicating that an Orc is near. Sam hides. An Orc and Uruk-hai find Frodo. He is still alive because this is how Shelob likes to feed on her flesh. They take the body of Frodo to a Mordor tower.

Pippin tries to save Faramir. Denethor throws Pippin out of the hall. He runs searching for Gandalf.

The Rohan army approaches the battlefield.

Pippin finds Gandalf, together they return. Gandalf tries to stop the burning. He knocks down Denethor as Pippin pulls Faramir off the burning funeral pyre. A burning Denethor runs down the hallway and off the edge of the 7th level of Minas Tirith. He falls to his death onto the battle field below.

A line of Mumak (elephant-like creatures) attack the Rohan army. The Rohans charge into the Mumak. The Army of the Haradrim attack.

Sauron's army has broken into Minas Tirith and are making their way up the levels. Gandalf and Pippin sit and talk about death being just another change into another world. This gives Pippin hope.

The Witch-King and his Fell-Beast attack King Théoden. They knock Théoden and his horse to the ground. The horse falls on Théoden. The Witch-King and the Fell-Beast come in for the kill, but thety are confronted by Eowyn dressed in Rohan armor. She cuts off the head of the Fell-Beast and engages in hand-to-hand combat with the Witch-King, who has both sword and malice.

The ships land at Osgiliath. Aragon, Gimli and Legolas disembark and confront the Orc army. The Green Army of the Dead pour out from the ship and swarm over Sauron's army.

The Witch-King has defeated Eowyn. He tells her that it is hopeless because no man can kill him. Eowyn removes her helmet, shows that she is a woman, says "I am no man," and then stabs the Witch-King with her sword in his face. He crumbles and dies!

The Green Army of the Dead swarm onto the battlefield.

Legolas climbs up the body of a Mumak and kills it.

Eowyn tries to save King Théoden, but his body is broken, and he dies in her arms.
Aragorn and his army triumph. Gandalf is on the battle field. Aragorn keeps his promise and frees the Army of the Dead. They vanish.

Pippin finds Merry and nurses him.

Frodo is bound in the Watchtower of Mordor. An Orc and Uruk-hai fight. Sam makes his way back to Frodo. He fights with three Orcs on the stairway. An Orc is about to stick Frodo, and Sam stabs him instead. Frodo thinks that the Ring is lost, but Sam had taken it from him when he thought Frodo was dead, wrapped in the Spider web. Sam shows Frodo the Ring. Frodo wants it back, saying that the Ring is his burden. Sam gives him the Ring.

Sam and Frodo, disguised as Orcs, make their way across the fields of Mordor toward Mount Doom.

In Minas Tirith, Gandalf and Aragorn talk about the fate of Frodo and the Ring. 10,000 Orcs stand between Frodo and Mount Doom. Aragorn wants to create a diversion to help Frodo. He wants to march to the Black Gates of Mordor to distract the Eye of Sauron.

The army of Mordor march toward the Black Gate. Sam and Frodo march toward Mount Doom. Frodo drinks the last of the water.
"I do not think there will be a return journey," says Sam.
Aragorn's army is at the Black Gates of Mordor.
The Eye of Sauron shines on Frodo.
The Black gates open. The Eye of Sauron shines toward the gate.

Sam and Frodo move and climb up Mount Doom.
Sauron's Army surrounds Aragorn's Army. This is their moment of desperation.

Both Sam and Frodo are out of strength. Sam carries Frodo.

The Eye of Sauron calls out to Aragorn and tells him to stop. Aragorn charges into battle for Frodo!

Gollum jumps on top of Sam, who is carrying Frodo. They fight, and Sam slashes Gollum with his sword. Frodo continues up the mountain.

Fell-Beasts swarm into the battle against the Army of Aragorn. A moth appears in front of Gandalf, then the Eagles appear. Eagles fight the Fell Beasts.

Frodo stands on the ledge over looking the lava rivers of Mount Doom. He holds the Ring in his hand, but he will not let it drop. Sam pleads with him to throw down the Ring, but Frodo refuses and says "It is mine!"

Frodo then puts the Ring on his finger.

Gollum hits Sam with a rock and knocks him to the ground. Gollum sees the feet marks of the invisible Frodo and jumps on him and fights for the ring. They struggle. Gollum bites the Ring finger off of Frodo, and gets the Rings for himself. Gollum dances with glee at the edge of the ledge. Frodo jumps Gollum and they fight, then together fall off the ledge. Gollum falls into the lava river below with the Ring. The Ring drops into the lava.

A Troll has his foot on the chest of Aragorn and is about to kill him.

The Ring dissolves in the lava river.

Barad-dur, the tower holding the Eye-of-Sauron collapses.
The Eye explodes, sending a shock wave across the battle field.

The Troll runs away as does the Army of Sauron.
The ground opens up and swallows Orcs and Uruk-hai soldiers.

The Army of Aragorn cheer, but then watch in gloom as Mount Doom explodes. They believe that Frodo and Sam have been killed.

Frodo and Sam make their way to a large rock in the middle of the lava river. They speak of the Shire and express their friendship as the river of lava surrounds them. Sam talks of Rosie being the Hobbit he would have married. They wait for their end, falling asleep on the rock.

Three Eagles appear in the sky. Gandalf rides on one of them which picks up Frodo. A second eagle picks up Sam. They fly to safety.

RESOLUTION SCENES

Frodo awakes in bed. White-brown light fills the room. Gandalf watches over him. Pippin and Merry enter. They laugh and play with Frodo in the bed. Gimli enters, then Legolas and Aragorn. Sam stands by the doorway. A special look of deep understanding passes between Frodo and Sam.

Minas Tirith, the 7th level. Turquoise colors dominate. Blue-greens and silver. Silver crown of Gondor. Gandalf crowns him. "Now comes Days of the King." Aragon is crowned the King of Gondor. He sings an elfish song. White flowers flow down on him. He greets Legolas and the other Elves. He sees Arwen. He kisses her. Man and Elf will marry and unite. The four Hobbits appear and are honored by the people of Gondor. "You bow to no one," says Aragorn.

The Fourth age of the Middle-Earth has begun.

The Hobbits return to the Shire, 13 months from the day they left. They celebrate at a pub. Sam sees Rosie, the barmaid. Sam marries Rosie.

Frodo writes the book: Lord of the Rings, but he is not happy. Frodo cannot go back to the old life of the Shire after the adventures that he has had. Four years to the day he completes his book.

Gandalf the White drives a cart that holds old Bilbo Baggins, who is to be taken to the mystical Elfin harbor known as Grey Havens. Bilbo asks for one last look of his old Ring, but Frodo says that he has lost it.

Elfin Harbor. Queen of the Elves says that the time has come for the dominion of Man.

A ship with Lord Elrond takes Bilbo to a new journey, along with Gandalf and Frodo. Frodo says goodbye to Sam, Pippin, and Merry. It sails away into the yellow sunset as the three remaining Hobbits watch.

Sam returns to his wife, two little children and house in the Shire. They enter the house and close the yellow door behind them.

THE END OF PART III

COMMENTARIES ON *THE LORD OF THE RING* TRILOGY

There are many common story structures that are found in these movies. These are standard Hollywood story structures, yet, they still worked to make these movies megahits.

Most of these popular movies have a unique object that both the antagonist and the protagonist desire to possess. It is obvious in these movies that this is the ONE RING. The antagonist group (Lord Sauron and Wizard Saruman) want it because of the ultimate power it will give them, while Frodo and the Fellowship want to destroy the Ring. Yet the Ring can make the bearer also desire the power it has. The unique object forces the conflict to be a life and death struggle: only one side can possess it. The Ring is used to expose very deep character traits in each character. It shows us how the different characters react to the power the Ring possesses. This device enables the writer to create different character motivations based on how a character reacts to the Ring.

The Ring gave Bilbo long life. It caused Boromir to threaten Frodo, and even Bilbo almost became violent when he tried to repossess it. Sméagol (Gollum) killed his friend Déagol for the Ring then its power drove him insane. Humans don't even have to touch it to feel compelled to own it, because the humans are the weakest creatures in Middle-Earth. It even transforms Frodo by the end of the movie. Frodo cannot destroy the Ring and desires to keep it for himself.

The antagonist side wants the Ring because it will give them the power to control others. Frodo and the Fellowship want to destroy this power and remain free. This is a very common theme found in many megahit movies and the Unique Object in these movies helps the writers to develop this theme. In *Star Wars*, it was the plans to the Death Star that would allow the Rebels or the Empire to control the most powerful weapon in the universe. In *MIB*, it was the "Galaxy around Orion's Belt," and it was the Ark of the Covenant in *Raiders of the Lost Ark*.

The first plot twist in *The Lord of the Ring* occurs when Gandalf goes to his master Saruman for advice about what to do with the Ring. The surprise twist is that Saruman has gone to the dark side and is in league with the evil spirit, Sauron. Betrayal is always an effective plot twist. Surprise plot twists create tension and excitement in the audience, especially, if there is a betrayal of trust. When the audience sees a wise wizard like Gandalf betrayed, they wonder who will be the next character to betray the protagonist. The betrayal of Gandalf raises the emotional stakes in the audience, since a character for whom they have empathy has been placed in grave danger. Jeopardy and danger are absolutely necessary to make a story exciting. The black Ringwraiths come after Frodo because of the unique object he has in his possession. The Ring forces Frodo to leave his home, the Shire, so that it will not be destroyed.

Themes are statements about the values that characters must exhibit in order to achieve their objectives. Some values will lead to success, others to failure and death. *The Lord of the Ring* movies are epic stories that follow the Hero's Journey structure, but not all megahit movies do this. In these popular movies, the villain is always much more powerful than the hero in the beginning, and this is obvious with Frodo versus Sauron. But in the beginning of the movie, the audience believes that Frodo has the powerful Gandalf as his mentor. Once Gandalf seems to be easily defeated, then the situation for Frodo appears even more desperate.

The Lord of the Ring has the classic inciting event as the catalyst for the story. Bilbo Baggins leaves the Ring for Frodo. At first, Gandalf does not realize that this is the "ONE RING," so he has Frodo place it in an envelope while he goes to Minas Tirith to read the ancient documents. Gandalf returns and throws the envelope into the fire. He then has Frodo look for the inscription which he finds written on the Ring. Once Gandalf realizes the evil in this Ring, he knows that it cannot stay in the Shire. He then has Frodo and Sam carry the Ring away. They plan to meet him in Bree. Frodo's life will never again be the same. His world will forever change because of this inciting event.

This story structure starts with a vulnerable character (Frodo) then making his vulnerability even worse with the loss of Gandalf. This increases the audience's emotional involvement in the story. The dramatic objective of the protagonist is NOT to find and keep "the Holy Grail," but to destroy an object that is the most powerful weapon in the universe before it destroys all life. He becomes the reluctant hero. His primary objective is to transport the Ring to its destruction which is the opposite of most quest movies. For the audience, the main question in this story is will Frodo destroy the Ring before it destroys him.

Frodo has a character arc. Once he is stabbed by the Witch-King, he will never be the same. That is why he cannot stay in the Shire after the journey is done. And carrying the Ring changes him, for the Ring has the spirit of Sauron within it. Frodo does not become the happy hobbit at the end of the movie that he was in the beginning. *The Lord of the Ring* is about what an obsession for power will do to a mind. Even the queen of the elves, Galadriel, was almost seduced by the power of the Ring. Yet, it is also the story of how Frodo and Sam must survive under the constant threat of betrayal by Gollum. They need Gollum to show them how to get to the mountain, but Sam does not trust him.

The Fellowship of the Ring ends with the apparent death of a major character that the audience has come to love, Gandalf. This is a bad way to end a movie you hope to become a mass market success. But, Gandalf does comes back to life in the second movie. Spielberg uses this often in many of his movies. In E.T., he makes everyone thinks ET dies then brings him back to life. In *Raiders*, he makes the audience believe that Marion dies then brings her back again. This structure has a powerful affect on the audience. They grieve when a character they love dies but then becomes overjoyed when this character is brought back to life. This is one of the structures used in popular movies to give the audience an "emotional roller-coaster" experience. You have to design the story so that it will be an emotionally satisfying experience for the audience.

But killing a protagonist and not bringing them back to life will result in box-office disaster. An example of this can be found in *League of Extraordinary Gentlemen* in which the hero, Allan Quatermain, dies at the end of the movie. It was a box-office failure with a U.S. Domestic Gross of only $66 million.

Self-sacrifice for the common good is the dominant theme of this movie. Sam is willing to sacrifice himself to help Frodo get to Mount Doom and destroy the Ring. Aragorn is willing to sacrifice himself to fight the army of Mordor and distract the Eye-of-Sauron so that Frodo will have a chance to destroy the Ring. The Elves made a great sacrifice to join the humans in the Battle of Helm's Deep because Elves are immortal unless killed. Many gave up their immortality in that battle. If they had gone away to the West, they would have lived forever!

Some people think that Sam is the real hero of *Return of the King*. He definitely had a pivotal role. We saw his strengths, weaknesses, and his sensitivity. And the movie does end with Sam back in the Shire. But the obligatory scene, the climax battle, is between Frodo and Gollum. So, from a structural point of view, Frodo is the protagonist and Sam is the most important protagonist-supporter in the story. Aragorn also played the important role of creating a diversion for the Eye of Sauron.
It is common to open a movie with the antagonist. This shows the audience what and who will be the main problem in the movie. *Return of the King* opens with the Gollum story. It shows how the Ring was found by Deagol and how Sméagol murders Deagol to take possession of the Ring. It also shows the power the Ring has on a character. The Ring transforms Sméagol into Gollum. It drives him mad. He becomes obsessed with the Ring, "his precious." So Gollum is definitely the primary villain of this movie, although Sauron is the prime villain of the Trilogy, as Saruman was the principal villain in *The TwoTowers*.

The climax fight scene in *Return of the King* is the fight between Frodo and Gollum for possession of the Ring. Gollum triumphs, gets the Ring, but falls to his death. The lava river dissolves the Ring, and this destroys Sauron. But the fight is not directly between Frodo and Sauron but with Gollum, one of the minions he controls through the Ring.

Another thing to realize is that Frodo does not directly kill Gollum. Gollum accidentally falls off the cliff during his struggle with Frodo. This is another common feature found in many popular movies. This event absolves the protagonist of guilt and lets the audience continue to feel good about him. It is also important to realize that Frodo does not triumph over the Ring, but that the Ring triumphs over him.

Frodo refuses to drop the Ring into the lava river, even as Sam begs him to do this. Frodo fights for the Ring, even after Gollum has chewed off his finger. This is the structure of the climax scene. Frodo does not fight Gollum to destroy the Ring, but to get it for himself. His last moment is not heroic: his intention is not to save the people of Middle-Earth, but to possess the Ring.

There are many Resolution scenes in this movie. *Return of the King* was the ending of the Trilogy: over 9 hours of film experience. The Director, Peter Jackson, wanted to make sure that the audience knew what happened to all the major characters that they had gotten involved with during all three movies. He did not want to leave any loose ends.

When the Ring dissolves, the Eye-of-Sauron explodes, and the tower collapses. This is the end of the Great Villain of the Trilogy. The Army of Mordor either gets swallowed up in the earth or runs away. At the same time, the army of Gondor watches Mount Doom explode, and they grieve because they think that Frodo and Sam are dead. Sam and Frodo escape to a rock in the middle of the lava river. They dream of the Shire. Sam says he would have married Rosie if he had the chance. The screen goes black then Gandalf and the three eagles appear and save Frodo and Sam. In the next scene, we are back to Minas Tirith. Frodo is in bed with a bandaged finger, joined by Pippin, Merry, Gandalf, Gimli, Legolas, Aragorn, and Sam. The survivors of the Fellowship reunite. This scene has the structure as the *Wizard of Oz* movie. There Dorothy awakes in her bed and is surrounded by her loved ones after her ordeal in Oz.

Next, Aragorn is crowned King of Gondor by Gandalf, and he is reunited with his true love, Arwen. Man and Elf will wed. The four Hobbits are honored by the people of Gondor. That could have ended the movie.

But then the Director decided to show the Hobbits returning to the Shire. They have drinks at the bar, and Sam goes up to Rosie. In the next scene, Sam marries Rosie. This is the resolution of Sam's dream but not quite the final resolution of the movie. Frodo has to write his book which takes four years to complete. But Frodo can no longer stay in the Shire after his adventures with the Ring on the journey to Mordor. He has seen too much and lived too much to be happy in the peaceful Shire.

Gandalf, the White Wizard, rides up with Bilbo in a horse drawn covered wagon. Everyone in the audience wanted to know what finally happened to Bilbo Baggins. We learn that he gets to sail away with the Elves to the land in the West as do Gandalf and Frodo. The Elf Queen, Galadriel, says that it is the end of the old world and now the time of Man. All the magic and wizards must go away. They all sail into the yellow sunset! A classic Hollywood Happy Ending!

But there is a second yellow sunset in this movie! Sam goes back to the Shire, to his little cottage where he is met by his wife and two little children. They go into the sunset of his HOME as they walk through the yellow circular front door of their cottage. The round yellow door closes after them. This is Sam's sunset ending; the last image of the movie.

The Resolution Scenes of megahit movies are very important. The characters take their time saying goodbye to other characters with whom they shared their journey. There are lots of hugs and tears. Study the closing scenes of the *Wizard of Oz* when Dorothy leaves Oz, or the movie ET when ET flies back home in his space ship. These scenes give the audience a chance to share in the emotional release expressed by the characters, for the audience was also part of this long journey.

Frodo does have a character arc in *Return of the King*. Frodo is caught between Sam and Sméagol (Gollum). Frodo has sympathy for Sméagol because he knows that Sméagol has also carried and worn the Ring. This is an experience that they do not share with Sam. Frodo wants to help Sméagol because he wants to hope that "Sméagol can come back" from the power of the Ring, so Frodo can believe that he also can come back, because the Ring is now possessing him. The real personal conflict in this movie is between Sam and Gollum and centers on the question of who will eventually win the trust of Frodo. We even have the empathy scene for Sméagol (Gollum) when he struggles with himself, and Sméagol finally banishes Gollum from his being because he believes that Master (Frodo) will take care of him. Frodo does not call Sméagol "Gollum," because he has pity for him. Sam hates Gollum and calls him by that name.

Gollum sets up Sam with the crumbs of bread and gets Frodo to send Sam away so that he can lead Frodo to his death in the cave of the spider Shelob. Sam represents ultimate loyalty and friendship...that is his true value. He has no desire for the Ring. He only takes it when he thinks that Frodo is dead so that he can complete the mission! But he gives it back to Frodo when Frodo asks for it. Sam resists the need for power! But so did Frodo in the beginning. The Ring will wear down anyone! Even Gandalf respects its power and refuses to take it when it is offered to him by Frodo in the first movie. Because of Sam, the mission is accomplished, and not because of the will of Frodo. But Sam is still a supporting character. Frodo is the true Ring-Bearer. The mission also would not have been completed without the efforts of Aragorn and the Fellowship, who attack the Black Gates of Mordor to create a diversion for Frodo to distract the Eye of Sauron.

The ONE RING TO RULE THEM ALL represents control over others! The loss of freedom! Some of the characters need and want this control, others do not! It is Man who is weakest of all the creatures of Middle-Earth and desires possession of the Ring! Sauron wants it, as do Saruman, Boromir, Faramir, Denethor, and Sméagol (Gollum). But Gandalf and the Elves do not desire this Ring. The Ring contains the spirit of Sauron, and it is through the Ring that he controls others. Even Frodo ultimately falls under its control and will not destroy it when the time comes!

For Middle-Earth to be free, it must be destroyed. If the Ring gets back into Sauron's possession, he will even control the world of the Elves. That is why Arwen becomes sick as the power of Sauron grows. The most interesting case is the Elf Queen, Galadriel. She says that if she takes the Ring, then all creatures will love her and despair! They will love her so completely that they will lose their freedom. Not taking the Ring from Frodo is her gift to them. How is she able to resist the Ring? Galadriel does not want to have power over the others. Even though Frodo offers it to her, she does not take it. The same thing happens with Gandalf in the Shire. They both know the corrupting influence of the Ring. It will take the most innocent and make them lust for power. This is shown in the scene between Bilbo and Frodo in Rivendell, when Bilbo asks for the Ring back. For a moment, Bilbo becomes a monster with vicious teeth when Frodo denies him the Ring! Because the corrupting spirit of Sauron is in the Ring, no one who carries it will remain free. It, therefore, had to be destroyed!

The RETURN OF THE KING won the Producers Guild of America (PGA) Award for Best Picture of the Year in 2004.

The RETURN OF THE KING won the Directors Guild of America (DGA) Award for Best Picture of the Year in 2004.

The RETURN OF THE KING won the Academy Award for Best Picture of the Year in 2004.

Screenwriting & Movie Magazines

Recommended Screenwriting Books

**The Megahit Movies
Hollywood Story Design Workshop™**

**The Megahit Movies Website
(www.TheMegahitMovies.com)**

SCREENWRITING & MOVIE MAGAZINES

The Independent
www.AIVF.org

Creative Screenwriting
www.CreativeScreenwriting.com

Fade In
www.FadeInOnline.com

Film Comment
www.Filmlinc.com

IndieWire
www.indiewire.com

The Hollywood Reporter
www.HollywoodReporter.com

Premiere
www.PremiereMag.com

MovieMaker
www.MovieMaker.com

ScreenTalk
www.ScreenTalk.biz

ScreenWriter
www.ScreenWriterMag.com

ScriptWriter
www.ScriptWriterMagazine.com

Scr(i)pt Magazine
www.ScriptMag.com

Written By
www.WGA.org

Daily Variety
www.Variety.com

RECOMMENDED SCREENWRITING BOOKS

Hollywood Story Structure

Field, Syd. *Screenplay: The Foundations of Screenwriting.* New York: Dell Publishing, 1982.

Hauge, Michael. *Writing Screenplays That Sell.* New York: McGraw Hill, 1988.

Seger, Linda. *Making a Good Script Great.* New York: Dodd, Mead and Company, 1994.

McKee, Robert. *Story.* New York: Harper Collins, 1997.

Character Development

Egri, Lagos. *The Art of Dramatic Writing.* New York: Touchstone Books, 1960.

Hood, Ann. *Creating Character Emotions.* Cincinnati: Story Press, 1998.

Seger, Linda. *Creating Unforgettable Characters.* New York: Henry Holt, 1990.

The Theory of Emotions and the Psychology of the Audience

Calhoun, Cheshire and Robert Solomon. *What is an Emotion?* New York: Oxford University Press, 1984.

Lazarus, Richard S. *Emotion and Adaptation.* Oxford: Oxford University Press, 1991.

Maslow, Abraham. *Toward a Psychology of Being.* New York: John Wiley & Sons, 1998.

Ortony, Andrew and Clore and Collins. *The Cognitive Structure of Emotions.* Cambridge: Cambridge University Press, 1988.

The Theory and Techniques of Humor

Carter, Judy. *Standup Comedy: The Book.* New York: Dell Publishing, 1989.

Goldstein, Jeffrey and Paul McPhee. *The Psychology of Humor.* New York: Academic Press, 1972.

Helitzer, Melvin. *Comedy Techniques for Writers and Performers.* Ohio: Lawhead Press, 1984.

Monro, D.H. *Argument of Laughter.* Indiana: University of Notre Dame Press, 1963.

Morreal, John. *Taking Laughter Seriously.* Albany: State University of New York, 1983.

Perret, Gene. *Comedy Writing Workbook.* New York: Sterling Publishing, 1990.

Perret, Gene. *How To Write and Sell Your Sense of Humor.* Cincinnati: Writer's Digest Books, 1986.

Vorhaus, John. *The Comic Toolbox.* Los Angeles:Silman-James Press, 1994.

The Practical Business of Writing and Selling Screenplays

Abreu, Carlos de and Howard Jay Smith. *Opening the Doors to Hollywood : How to Sell Your Idea, Story, Screenplay, Manuscript.* New York: Three Rivers Press, 1995.

Aronson, Linda. *Screenwriting Updated.*Los Angeles: Silman-James Press, 2000.

Atchity, Kenneth and Wong, Chi-Li. *Writing Treatments That Sell.* New York: Henry Holt and Company, 1997.

Breimer, Stephen. *Clause by Clause: The Screenwriters Legal Guide.* New York: Dell Publishing, 1995.

Cole, Hillis R. and Judith M. Haag. *Complete Guide to Standard Script Format.* Los Angeles: CMC, 1980.

Chiarella, Tom. *Writing Dialogue.* Cincinnati: Story Press, 1998.

Dancyger, Ken and Jeff Rush. *Alternative Scriptwriting: Successfully Breaking the Rules.* Boston: Focal Press, 2002.

Epstein, Alex. *Crafty Screenwriting: Writing Movies that Get Made.*Henry Holt & Company, 2002.

Field, Syd. *Selling a Screenplay.* New York: Dell Publishing, 1982.

Frensham, Ray. *Teach Yourself Screenwriting.* McGraw Hill, 2003.

Goldman,William. *Adventures in the Screen Trade.* New York: Warner Books, 1983.

Goldman,William. *Which Lie Did I Tell?* New York: Pantheon Books, 2000.

Hollywood Creative Directory. *Producers.* Hollywood: IFILM Publishing, 2001.

Hunter, Lew. *Screenwriting 434*. New York: Perigee Books, 1993.

Joseph, Erik. *How To Enter Screenplay Contests and Win!* Los Angeles: Lone Eagle, 1997.

Kosberg, Robert. *How To Sell Your Idea to Hollywood*. New York: Harper Collins, 1991.

Lucey, Paul. *Story Sense*. New York: McGraw Hill, 1996.

Press, Skip. *Writers Guide to Hollywood Producers, Directors and Screenwriting Agents.* Prima Publishing, 1999.

Seger, Linda. *Advanced Screenwriting: Raising Your Script to the Academy Award Level*. Los Angeles: Silman-James Press, 2003.

Seger, Linda. *Making a Good Writer Great: A Creativity Workbook for Screenwriters*. Los Angeles: Silman-James Press, 1999.

Stuart, Linda. *Getting Your Script Through The Hollywood Maze*. Los Angeles: Acrobat Books, 1993.

Taylor, Thom. *The Big Deal*. New York: William Morrow and Company, 1999.

Vale, Eugene. *The Technique of Screen and Television Writing*. New York: Simon & Schuster, 1982.

Walter, Richard. *Screenwriting: The Art, Craft and Business of Film and Television Writing*. New York: NAL, 1988.

Walter, Richard. *The Whole Picture: Strategies for Screenwriting Success in the New Hollywood.* New York: A Plume Book, 1997.

Walter, Richard. *Escape From Film School: A Novel*. New York: St. Martins Griffin, 2000.

Whitcomb, Cynthia. *Selling Your Screenplay.* The Writer Books, 2002.

Whitcomb, Cynthia. *Writing Your Screenplay*. The Writer Books, 2002.

THE MEGAHIT MOVIES
HOLLYWOOD STORY DESIGN WORKSHOP™
(Twelve Session Workshop)

Class 1 : **Introduction**
The Fundamental Question, Popular Movies, Story Design, and the Story Conceptual Framework

Assignment: Write a climax scene that includes a Protagonist, Antagonist, Love Interest, and the Unique Object.

Class 2 : **Characters**
WIZARD OF OZ scene-by-scene analysis
Protagonist, Antagonist, Love Interest, Audience Empathy, and the Psychology of the Audience

Assignment: Write an audience empathy scene for the Protagonist and Love Interest. Write and enmity scene for the antagonist. The audience should hate and fear the antagonist, while having sympathy for the protagonist and the love interest.

Class 3 : **Characters**
WIZARD OF OZ scene-by-scene analysis
Motivation, Objectives, Decisions, Relationships, Codes of Behavior, Transformations, Personalities, Supporting Characters, and Crowds

Assignment: Write a description for the protagonist supporter, who should be humorous and likeable, and the antagonist supporter, who should be very mean and hateful. Then, cast the three primary characters (Protagonist, Antagonist, and Love Interest) with currently bankable Hollywood Actors. Write a paragraph description of each actor in the role they have been cast.

Class 4 : **Objectives**
RAIDERS OF THE LOST ARK scene-by-scene analysis
Primary Objectives, Concrete Objects, Abstract Values, Subgoals and Plot Twists, and Strategies.

Assignment: Write three (3) subgoals that the protagonist must obtain in order to achieve his primary objective. Then, have him finally achieve his objective in an unexpected way. These will be the plot twists of your story.

THE MEGAHIT MOVIES
HOLLYWOOD STORY DESIGN WORKSHOP™
(Twelve Session Workshop)

Class 5 : **Conflicts**
RAIDERS OF THE LOST ARK scene-by-scene analysis
Obstacles, Jeopardy, Self-Conflicts, Enemies, Relatives, Friends, Lovers, Physical Objects, Natural World, and Supernatural World

Assignment: Write ten (10) obstacles that the protagonist must overcome in order to obtain his primary objective. Include at least one from each of the above types of obstacles.

Class 6 : **Plots**
BATMAN scene-by-scene analysis
Plot and Story, Events and Actions, Inciting Event, Subplots, Plot Arena, Plot Twists, Plot-Story Climax, and Plot Organization.

Assignment: Design a Prelude, Act 1, Act 2, Act 3 and Resolution structure for your story using the essential features described in the PLOT ORGANIZATION chapter. Write a one page structural description of your story.

Class 7 : **Story**
BATMAN scene-by-scene analysis
Human Values, Instrumental Values, Fundamental Values, Story Design

Assignment: Write a plot outline of your story that contains forty (40) major obstacles, one for each scene. Arrange the plot outline scenes within the Prelude, Act 1, Act 2, Act 3, and Resolution Structure. Write a one sentence statement of the "High Concept" for your story.

Class 8 : **Scenes**
E.T. scene-by-scene analysis
Scenes, Scene Actions, Point of Attack, Crisis, Confrontation, Climax, Resolution, A Standard Scene Example, Exposition Scenes, Transition Scenes, Opening Scenes, Protagonist Introduction, Antagonist Introduction, Climax Scenes, Resolution Scenes, and Summary of Essential Scene Elements

Assignment: Create an index card for each scene (40 in total). Include the major Obstacle, Crisis, Confrontation, Climax, and Resolution for each scene.

THE MEGAHIT MOVIES
HOLLYWOOD STORY DESIGN WORKSHOP™
(Twelve Session Workshop)

Class 9 : **Emotions**
E.T. scene-by-scene analysis
Story and Emotion, Theories of Emotion, Cognitive Theory, FActors Effecing the Intensity of Emotions, Reactions to Events, Reactions to Actions, and Reactions to Objects

Assignment: Write a character having an emotional reaction to an event, an emotional reaction to an action, and an emotional reaction to an object.

Class 10 : **Humor**
GHOSTBUSTERS scene-by-scene analysis
Theories of Humor, Humor and Emotion, Categories of Humor, Humorous Constructs, Humorous Situations, and Humorous Characters

Assignment: Create one humorous construct, one humorous situation and one humorous bit of character behavior for your story.

Class 11 : **Sequences**
GHOSTBUSTERS scene-by-scene analysis
Entertaining the Audience, Cinematic-Visual Material, Mythic Structures, High Concept, Excitement, Surprise, Setup and Payoff, Suspense, The Chase, Timelocks, Props, Exposition, and Dialogue

Assignment: Create a chase and timelock sequence for the climax scene in Act 3 of your story. Write the synopsis of your story and prepare a 5 minute pitch for the class.

Class 12 : **The Screenwriting Business**
Megahit Movie Themes, Pitching Stories, Writing A Query Letter, Writing a Synopsis, Screenplay Format, and Selling Screenplays

Assignment: Begin the first draft screenplay of your story based on the plot outline.

INDEX

A

abandonment 225
abstract value 125, 130
actions 20, 172, 173, 180, 183, 252, 255, 325
acts 187
antagonist
    18, 95, 104, 110, 117, 134, 148, 166, 180, 198, 201, 206, 213, 233, 236, 241, 304, 317, 322, 332, 335
antagonist introduction 20
antagonist supporter 18, 117
Aristotle 31, 104, 109, 151, 171, 183, 197, 237, 245, 282, 283, 284, 315

B

betrayal 233

C

characters
    104, 109, 113, 132, 139, 141, 151, 154, 163, 166, 173, 178, 180, 183, 213, 216, 222, 225, 229, 241, 247, 253, 255, 258, 280, 305, 314, 316, 325, 332, 490
chase 316, 317
choices 95, 206, 213
cinematic experience 171, 187
clichés 277, 293
climax scene 5, 7, 175, 184, 236, 237
climax scenes 20
codes of behavior 6, 18, 104, 172, 178, 206
cognitive theory 7, 245
community 96, 157, 166, 237
community ideals 7, 197, 200, 201
concrete objects 125, 128, 130, 201, 322
conflict
    19, 105, 130, 139, 141, 148, 154, 160, 163, 178, 180, 222, 236, 237, 241, 270, 310, 332
confrontation 20
cowardliness 299
crisis 20
crowds 118

D

decisions 18, 95, 130, 174
dialects 294
dialogue 20, 213, 258

double entendre 289
dual scripts 295

E

emotional reactions 20
emotionally satisfying experience for the audience 20
emotions 237, 245, 251, 252, 253, 255, 257, 263, 269, 316, 325, 490
empathy 5, 18, 114, 157, 184, 216, 225, 229, 246, 270, 309, 332
enemies 19, 148, 335
enmity 5, 18, 225, 233, 246, 332
entertain the audience 20
entertainment 309
establishing scenes 219
events 20, 130, 171, 173, 175, 180, 183, 187, 206, 252, 325
exaggeration 291, 299, 300
excitement 19, 141, 160, 184, 314, 325
exposition 134, 325
exposition scenes 20

F

fear 109, 245
final scene 237
friends 19, 154, 335

G

genres 17

H

hero 104, 139, 187, 331
high concepts 17
home 175, 200, 333, 338
humor 118, 144, 258, 263, 265, 274, 277, 309, 325, 490
humorous categories 287
humorous characters 21, 275, 285, 297
humorous constructs 275
humorous dialogue 21
humorous situations 21, 275, 296

I

inappropriateness 144, 265, 271, 287, 298, 299, 300
inciting event 175
incompetence 276, 301
incongruity 265, 270, 271, 272, 275, 287
irony 287

J

jeopardy 19, 31, 141, 160, 241, 309, 316, 317

L

laughter 263, 265, 276, 280, 303, 325
logic violations 289, 290
loglines 17
love interest 18
lovers 19, 157

M

malapropisms 293
misdirection 288
misinterpretation 289, 304
mispronunciations 293
misspellings 293
modal jokes 295
montages 222
motivation 18
mystery 316
myth 331

N

natural world 19
needs 91, 130
Nicomachean Ethics 197
nonsense 293

O

objects 252, 257
obligatory scene 236
obstacles
    19, 31, 113, 134, 139, 141, 145, 160, 163, 187, 206, 241, 315, 316, 317, 320
opening scenes 20
outlines 189

P

personal objectives 18
personalities 113
physical objects 19, 160
physical traits 113
pity 109, 245
plans 134, 183, 315, 325
plot 19, 178, 180, 187
plot arena 180

plot climax 206, 236
plot outline 19
plot twists 19, 132, 183, 214
Poetics 31, 104, 109, 151, 171, 183, 245, 315
point-of-attack 20
popular 32, 33, 166, 265, 310, 331, 332
practical jokes 303
prelude 19, 187
premise 201
pretense 280, 297
primary objective
    19, 87, 91, 96, 109, 125, 128, 130, 132, 172, 175, 178, 183, 187, 206, 213, 236, 333
props 322
protagonist
    18, 31, 95, 104, 109, 117, 134, 140, 145, 148, 151, 157, 160, 175, 180, 198, 201, 206, 213, 225, 229, 236, 237, 241, 317, 320, 322, 332, 335
protagonist introduction, 20
protagonist supporter 18, 117
psychology of humor 271
psychology of the audience 18, 32

R

relationships 109, 139, 151, 154, 172, 310, 325
relatives 19
relief theory 269, 272, 296
resolution scenes 20
reversal 109, 183
ruby slippers 367
rule of three 288

S

scene climax 213, 217, 218, 241
scene confrontation 213, 217, 218, 241
scene crisis 213, 217, 218, 241
scene point-of-attack 217, 218
scene resolution 188, 213, 217, 218, 241
self-conflicts 19, 95, 139, 145
setting of the story 180
setup and payoff 184
showing 247
story 19, 175, 180, 201, 213, 222, 225, 258, 310, 316, 325, 331, 490
story climax 178, 206, 236
story construction 139
story design 493
story objective 125
strategies 134, 183
Structures of Fantasy 9

subgoals 19, 87, 96, 125, 132, 172, 178, 183, 213, 222, 315
subplots 178
superiority theories 267, 272
supernatural 166, 335
supernatural world 19
supporting characters 18, 85, 117
surprise 132, 183, 225, 250, 267, 315, 325
suspense 20, 316, 320
synopsis 189

T

telling 247
terror 166, 335
theme 21, 201, 332
three-act structure 187
ticking clocks 20
transformations 18, 109, 213
transition scenes 20, 222
treatments 189

U

understatement 291, 299
unique object 18
unpredictability 19, 132, 134, 183, 325

V

values 109, 130, 154, 172, 178, 180, 197, 198, 200, 206, 213, 255, 332
vices 197, 199, 241, 282
virtues 197, 198, 241, 282

W

WGA 5, 9

Richard Michaels Stefanik
THE MEGAHIT MOVIES
www.TheMegahitMovies.com

* TITANIC *
STAR WARS * SHREK 2 * E.T.
THE PHANTOM MENACE * SHREK * SPIDER-MAN
LORD OF THE RINGS: RETURN OF THE KING
SPIDER-MAN 2 * THE PASSION OF THE CHRIST
JURASSIC PARK *THE TWO TOWERS
FINDING NEMO * FORREST GUMP * LION KING
HARRY POTTER: THE SORCERER'S STONE
LORD OF THE RINGS: FELLOWSHIP OF THE RING
STAR WARS: ATTACK OF THE CLONES * STAR WARS:
RETURN OF JEDI * INDEPENDENCE DAY * THE SIXTH
SENSE * STAR WARS: EMPIRE STRIKES BACK * PIRATES
OF THE CARIBBEAN * HOME ALONE * THE MATRIX
RELOADED* SHREK * HARRY POTTER: CHAMBER OF
SECRETS* MEET THE FOCKERS * THE INCREDIBLES *
THE GRINCH * JAWS * MONSTERS, INC.
BATMAN * MEN IN BLACK

This website analyzes the Megahit Movies, those films which have generated more than $250 million in North American Box Office receipts. It presents principles of story development that can be used to develop popular movies by providing an analysis of cinematic techniques. The site is designed for writers, directors and producers who want to create commercially successful films. The fundamentals of dramatic structure, the human emotions, and the creation of humorous characters and situations are explained, with example from the most popular Hollywood movies ever produced.

Richard Michaels Stefanik
www.TheMegahitMovies.com
rms@TheMegahitMovies.com

www.ingramcontent.com/pod-product-compliance
Lightning Source LLC
Chambersburg PA
CBHW071958150426
43194CB00008B/912